Studies in Epistemology and Cognitive Theory
General Editor: *Paul K. Moser, Loyola University of Chicago*

BELIEF AND KNOWLEDGE

BELIEF AND KNOWLEDGE
Mapping the Cognitive Landscape

KENNETH M. SAYRE

ROWMAN & LITTLEFIELD PUBLISHERS, INC.
Lanham • Boulder • New York • Oxford

ROWMAN & LITTLEFIELD PUBLISHERS, INC.

Published in the United States of America
by Rowman & Littlefield Publishers, Inc.
4720 Boston Way, Lanham, Maryland 20706

12 Hid's Copse Road
Cummor Hill, Oxford OX2 9JJ, England

British Library Cataloguing in Publication Information Available

Library of Congress Cataloging-in-Publication Data

Sayre, Kenneth M., 1928-
  Belief and knowledge : mapping the cognitive landscape / Kenneth M. Sayre.
     p.   cm.
  Includes bibliographical references and index.
  ISBN 0-8476-8472-5 (cloth : alk. paper). — ISBN 0-8476-8473-3 (pbk. : alk.
paper)

  1. Knowledge, Theory of.   2. Belief and doubt.
  BD215.S28 1997
  121'.6—dc21   97-14921
                                                              CIP

ISBN 0-8476-8472-5 (cloth : alk. paper)
ISBN 0-8476-8473-3 (pbk. : alk. paper)

Printed in the United States of America

⊗ ™ The paper used in this publication meets the minimum requirements of American
   National Standard for Information Sciences—Permanence of Paper for Printed Library Materials, ANSI Z39.48–1984.

CONTENTS

PREFACE

Every decade or so, in most branches of philosophy, a new wave of recruits takes its place on the frontiers of research and helps mark out the way to be followed by the next generation. The trail is blazed at each turn to point the way forward, leaving divergent ways behind to disappear in the underbrush. Under the leadership of scouts with a good sense of direction, the line of research along a given branch may be expected to flourish. But if the trailblazers lose their bearings and take a series of wrong turns, then research along that way is likely to founder. The trail they blazed, in effect, will have reached a dead end.

The conceptual explorations documented in this book began in the 1970s, with my growing conviction that cutting-edge initiatives in cognitive science—which at that time was my major research commitment—had veered in a seriously wrong direction. In retrospect, the mistake appears almost unavoidable, given the reliance of pioneering research in the field upon technological metaphors for how the brain operates (e.g., La Mettrie's "watchworks" in the eighteenth century, Babbage's "analytical engine" in the nineteenth century, Rosenblatt's "perceptrons" and Ashby's "homeostats" in the mid-twentieth century). The innovation I am describing as a "wrong turn," of course, is the now prevalent view of the mind as a biological computer, with its attendant conception of cognitive attitudes as relations between the brain and its internal propositional states. While the computational view of the mind continues to draw recruits, the ranks of its critics are swelling more quickly; and it seems a good bet that computationalism (as we know it) will reach a dead end before cognitive science finds its bearings in the twenty-first century.

Another branch of cognitive studies that seems to have taken a wrong turn somewhere in the not too distant past is the theory of knowledge. The mistake here is not so straightforward as adopting a problematic model of cognitive operations, as with computationalism above, but is more a matter of failing to react critically to a problematic assumption

xi

that became more deeply embedded as the cutting edge pressed forward. The assumption is that knowledge is a form of belief—namely, true belief backed up by appropriate justification. Under the sanction of this assumption, a major portion of research in epistemology today is aimed at an explication of appropriate justification (in the manner of foundationalism, reliabilism, coherentism, internalism, externalism, etc.), with the common expectation that when this issue is settled, the problem of the nature of knowledge will be settled along with it. If knowledge is not a form of belief, however, then the question of how beliefs are appropriately justified has no direct relevance to the nature of knowledge, which means that cutting-edge research in epistemology proper (the study of knowledge) has lost its bearings. Arguments aimed at showing that this indeed has happened constitute a major strand of the discussion that follows.

While this book is critical of key aspects of current research programs in both cognitive science and epistemology, however, its main purpose is not to subject either program to detailed criticism. The primary purpose of the book is to undertake a descriptive analysis of a representative sampling of cognitive attitudes, focused in particular upon the attitudes of believing and knowing. One finding that emerges in the initial stage of analysis is that only a limited subset of those attitudes (e.g., believing) takes propositional objects. There are others whose objects are states of affairs—in some cases (e.g., knowing) states of affairs that are actual, in others (e.g., hoping and fearing) states of affairs with indeterminate status. It is in this regard, to be sure, that concern with the misdirections of cutting-edge cognitive science and epistemology intersects with pursuit of the book's primary purpose. Within the context of computationalism, on the one hand, cognitive attitudes in general are conceived as relations to neuronal states with propositional characteristics. Within the going paradigms of epistemology, on the other, knowledge and belief are both thought to take propositional objects, which sets up the view that their main difference is a matter of knowledge (but not belief) requiring truth and appropriate justification. The misdirection in either case traces back to the same origin: the notion that all cognitive attitudes (belief and knowledge included) are propositional in character.

Corresponding to these respective wrong turns abetted by the erroneous notion that all cognitive attitudes take propositional objects, there must be some "right turns" which trailblazers in these fields might have taken instead, in which belief and knowledge are distinguished with respect to their objects. Whereas computationalism seems to have been on the wrong path from its beginning, there are moments in the development of recent epistemology when glimpses of the "right way" appeared to individual philosophers. Notable instances are H. H. Price ("Some Considerations about Belief," 1934–1935) and Zeno Vendler (chapter 5 of *Res Cogitans,* 1972). But the insights thus afforded were not developed systematically, leaving extensive territories of the affected landscape as yet unexplored. Another way of describing the main purpose of this book is in terms of a mapping of some of these territories. The book undertakes to chart in detail those portions of the cognitive landscape marked off by belief and knowledge and their respective objects.

While leaving room for brief side trips now and then into neighboring territories, this aim dictates the following sequence of topics. After a preliminary survey in chapter 1 of cognitive attitudes generally, the discussion turns in chapter 2 to belief specifically and to the correlative states of doubt and certainty. Since belief is paradigmatic of attitudes with propositional objects, chapter 3 considers what propositions must be like to serve in this role and to pass on their truth-values to the attitudes concerned. The essential features of a proposition are taken (following Wittgenstein) to be that (a) it represents a specific state of affairs to which (b) it ascribes a determinate status (being the case or not being the case). Chapter 4 takes up the issues of truth and falsity in turn, with special attention to the circumstances that render a proposition true—that is, to its truth-conditions. A general definition of truth is proposed, according to which a proposition is true just when the status it ascribes to a state of affairs is the status enjoyed by the latter in the actual world.

The discussion turns in chapter 5 to the conditions of knowledge and to its relation to justified true belief. Consideration is given to the relation between knowledge and certainty and to the threefold distinction among *having* access to how things stand in the world (i.e., knowing), *gaining* access of that sort originally (e.g., perceiving), and *retaining* access once it is gained (e.g., remembering). The next two chapters are given over to states of affairs in their characteristic role as objects of knowledge. Chapter 6 lays out a conception of states of affairs that makes them isomorphic with symbolic representations sanctioned for such use as part of public language. In developing this conception, two conditions are laid down for representation generally: (1) that a symbol must be capable of directing a subject's attention beyond the symbol itself to what it represents, and (2) that the relation between a symbol and what it represents does not require that the latter ever actually exists.

Chapter 7 develops a conception of being (and not being) the case that applies to both empirical and nonempirical (e.g., mathematical and logical) states of affairs. In combination with the previous definition of propositional truth, this yields an analysis of the truth of counterfactual statements and a correlative analysis of dispositional properties.

The final three chapters address a variety of topics of enduring interest in cognitive studies, building upon the findings of the preceding chapters. Chapter 8 shows how the notion of representation "in the brain" typical of current computationalism runs afoul of requirement (1) of chapter 6 and goes on to develop a way of thinking about internal representation that meets this requirement without loss of scientific plausibility. Chapter 9 takes up the topic of intentionality and shows how this conception of internal representations can be extended, in accord with requirement (2) of chapter 6, to yield an account of the intentional character of cognitive attitudes generally. As a notable by-product, this account provides an explication of intensionality (with an "s") showing how referential opacity is a consequence of a manner of reference that relies upon the intentionality (with a "t") of a cognitive attitude in identifying the object to which reference is made.

Chapter 10, finally, takes up the vexing question of whether knowledge can be extended by rational inference. Its conclusion (contrary to prevailing forms of realism) is that, while inference can isolate circumstances in which previously unknown states of affairs become accessible, it is incapable (for reasons of intentionality) of generating new knowledge itself. Belief may transcend the bounds of cognitive accessibility, but knowledge — as a mode of access — is incapable of following.

Given the way this exploration diverges from the prevailing paradigms in epistemology, it should not be surprising that justification does not figure in the synopsis of topics above. While a search for evidence might sometimes lead to knowledge of the states of affairs concerned, this topic does not loom large in the present perspective. A consequence is that little is said about the issues of foundationalism, reliabilism, internalism, and so forth, that dominate current discussion in cutting-edge epistemology. Apart from its wide-ranging concern with topics of representation, this study similarly has little to contribute to ongoing debates in cognitive science. While I have addressed various issues on this front in other contexts recently, the present study provides no occasion to pursue these matters further.

As these considerations make clear, indeed, the book would be a poor choice for any class or seminar aimed at introducing students to prevailing research paradigms in either of these disciplines. The book was written instead for scholars (advanced or neophyte) who are interested in cognitive attitudes generally and who are dissatisfied with what "mainline" literature has to say on such matters. In one way of putting it, the book lays out a new approach to such cognitive attitudes as belief and knowledge—an approach that in time might develop a cutting-edge of its own. But the present study is only a preliminary exploration at best; and there are many facets of the landscape left to be mapped before the territory at large becomes terra cognita.

Inasmuch as this talk of exploration and the like obviously tends toward metaphor itself, I feel obliged to say what I can in more direct terms about the method actually followed in the present study. One way of describing the method that some readers might find informative is to align it with the technique of conceptual analysis—a method typical of analytic philosophy before the days of numbered propositions and counterexamples. Whatever concepts amount to exactly, they tend to be interconnected in well-structured networks. And the task of analyzing these structures and making them perspicuous is one philosophers always have been ready to call their own.

Since the only public (and hence reliable) way of getting at concepts is to pay close attention to the ways they enter our speech, another way of identifying the approach of this study would be to liken it to the techniques of so-called ordinary language philosophy. Although obvious difficulties arise when well-trained people find different nuances in the same locutions, the way people commonly talk in certain well-structured situations can tell us a great deal about the conceptual structures that make communication possible. At one critical point in the argument of chapter 1, for example, I rely upon the "ear" of the critical reader to recognize that when we talk about discovering that the gate is shut, we are not referring to the discovery of a proposition. What we discover instead in such circumstances is a state of affairs (that of the gate's being shut). While I take this to be an objective fact regarding the concept of discovery—that is, regarding how the term "discover" is standardly used—there is no way of persuading a reader that this is the case when the reader cannot "hear" the oddness in the expression "N discovered a proposition" when used to describe what N discovered in coming upon the gate.

Whatever else an exploration of a conceptual landscape amounts to, at any rate, it includes a careful examination of facts like these that delineate the conceptual structures one is attempting to analyze. This observation makes appropriate yet another description of the method followed below—a method akin to what Austin once called "linguistic phenomenology" (J. L. Austin, "A Plea for Excuses"). To paraphrase what Austin said in characterizing the method, when we examine what exactly we would say in certain specific situations, we are not looking merely at the *words* (or meanings, or concepts) involved. We are using a heightened awareness of the words involved to sharpen our perception of the *phenomena* themselves. In that way, to look carefully at the words we use is to look carefully at the underlying facts as well. The fact that attitudes like discerning cannot be evaluated in terms of truth-value, for example, is made evident with the observation that corresponding terms like "discerning" cannot be qualified by either "true" or "false." In this way at least, the explorations reported below employ the techniques of linguistic phenomenology. The phenomena studied, to repeat, are prominent features of the cognitive landscape dominated by the concepts of belief and knowledge. And the technique followed in these explorations, by and large, is one of drawing attention to prominent features of these phenomena by attending carefully to how we would describe them under carefully defined circumstances.

This aspect of the method is worth bearing in mind as the reader prepares to follow the arguments laid out below. Although the subject matter at times gets rather technical (particularly in chapters 4 and 9), the mode of argument itself is (almost) always informal. This means that the conclusions to be established are not (critically speaking) *proved,* but rather are presented as what one will *notice* when one looks at the facts in the way the argument indicates. The form of argument, in other words, is not "this is true and this is true, therefore *that* is true as well," but rather "when you see this and this, *that* should also be apparent." The exploration in this way becomes a joint venture; and what a partner in the exploration (the "second person" to whom the argument is addressed) comes to know as a result is something that person comes to know firsthand.

Preliminary work on the manuscript began about twelve years ago while I held the rank of Visiting Fellow at Merton College in Oxford. My thanks go out to the Warden and Fellows of the College for electing me to that much appreciated position. The first complete draft of the book was prepared while I had a reduced teaching load during the spring term of 1990. I am grateful to the responsible administrators at the University of Notre Dame for making that time available. Substantial help along the way came from Thomas Blackburn, David Burrell, Richard Foley, Richard Fumerton, Steven Horst, John Lucas, Christopher Menzel, William Tolhurst, and (close to home) my son, Christopher, and wife, Patricia. I thank them all personally for their encouragement, without which this exploration could not have persisted.

The guideposts are set. Let us prepare to embark.

I

BELIEF AND ITS CONCEPTUAL ENVIRONMENT

Chapter 1

A SURFACE MAP
OF COGNITIVE ATTITUDES

1. The Orthodox Doctrine of Propositional Attitudes

Toward the end of his discussion of knowledge in the *Theaetetus,* Plato introduces the hypothesis that knowledge is identical with true belief (or judgment: *doxa*) accompanied by *logos.* Taking *logos* in the common sense of "ground" or "reason," we find here the locus classicus of the view that knowledge can be generated from true belief by the addition of supporting reasons. Contemporary epistemology, for the most part, has followed suit. Adopting as their point of departure this standard conception of knowledge as justified true belief, most epistemologists in twentieth-century analytic philosophy have understood their primary task to be that of elucidating the character of the justification capable of converting true belief into knowledge. The problem of justification provides the connecting link between the phenomenalism that prevailed during the early decades of the twentieth century and the various forms of reliabilism and coherentism that have dominated epistemology more recently.

The only major challenge to this standard conception of knowledge (within the analytic tradition at least) has come in the form of the so-called Gettier problem,[1] which questions whether justification by itself can be sufficient to generate knowledge out of true belief. But this challenge is premised upon a basic assumption that it shares with the standard conception of knowledge: the assumption that knowledge is true belief with something else added. For only if knowledge had true belief among its components would it be interesting to question whether justification suffices as the remaining constituent.

The conception of knowledge as a kind of true belief trades upon an even more basic assumption that both knowledge and belief are atti-

3

tudes toward propositional objects. Put in somewhat different terms, the standard conception is that a subject N knows a proposition p just in case (i) N believes that p, (ii) p is true, and (iii) N's true belief is augmented by other factors—such as a coherent body of supporting evidence or production by reliable belief-formation procedures—that are capable of converting belief into knowledge. If such a view is correct, then the only major difference between knowing p and believing p truly is the presence of this additional component. And if the only major difference between knowing p and merely believing p truly is the presence of this additional component, then the object of knowledge—what N knows in knowing p—is identical with the object of belief. In either case, according to the prevalent view, the object is the proposition p. When N's cognitive attitude changes to knowing p from merely believing p truly, the only difference in N's attitude before and after is the presence of this additional component. The propositional object of the attitude remains unchanged.

A more general version of the assumption that both knowledge and belief take propositional objects has found its way into contemporary cognitive science. For research guided by the computational theory of mind in particular, the basic idea[2] is that the brain operates as a computing device that accomplishes its major cognitive tasks as the cumulative upshot of many subtasks and that the intentional (i.e., the mental) features of these tasks are to be understood in terms of a mapping with the physical states involved in the brain's computations. Cognitive attitudes like fear and belief, according to this view, are relations between the organism and certain of its brain states that play the role of representations. To call these brain states "representations," for the cognitive theorist, is to say that they function as propositions, characterized by truth-value, reference, and intentional content. Under their computational description these brain states possess physical properties making them capable of causal interaction with other states of the organism, while under their propositional description they are endowed with semantic properties that account for the organism's cognitive activities.

Among cognitive attitudes explicitly identified as propositional, it is common to find believing, fearing, and wanting.[3] One prominent author adds forgetting, understanding, and predicting,[4] while reporting, commanding, and being aware are explicitly cited by another.[5] Turning from cognitive theory to epistemology, we hear of realizing, thinking, and judging as propositional attitudes, as well as, of course, believing and knowing.[6] Although our primary concern in the present study is with knowing and believing specifically, the dominant view in cognitive studies generally seems to be that all cognitive attitudes are propositional in character—that is, that cognitive attitudes across the board take propositional objects. This view is sufficiently prominent to merit an identifying label. Let us refer to it as "the orthodox doctrine of propositional attitudes" (ODOPA).

In the case of knowing and believing specifically, as already noted, ODOPA provides that the attitude of believing that p might give way to the attitude of knowing that p, without change in propositional object. If ODOPA should happen to be wrong in this regard, however, as argued below, then the prevalent view of knowledge as augmented true belief would be in trouble, regardless of particular accounts of how this augmentation is accomplished. Further discussion of this view of knowledge and its untenable predicament will be reserved for a later chapter. The purpose of the present chapter is to survey the domain of cognitive attitudes generally and to map certain varieties of cognitive attitudes that are structured quite differently from what ODOPA describes.

In its most general form, ODOPA is the doctrine that cognitive states consist of three independent components— (i) a cognitive attitude (A) relating (ii) a subject (N) to (iii) a propositional object (p)— and that each component in a particular case can be replaced by another of its kind without affecting the character of the other two components.[7] The three-part structure in question can be seen in the following sentences:

(1) Beatrice knows that snow is white (e.g., when observing a fresh snowfall).
(2) Camille believes that the sun is shining (e.g., at the beach).
(3) Deirdre hopes that the gate is shut (e.g., to the garden where her children are playing).

Each sentence attributes to a cognitive subject (Beatrice, Camille, Deirdre) an attitude (knowing, believing, hoping) toward a propositional object (that snow is white, that the sun is shining, that the gate is shut). The purported independence of component (ii) can be illustrated by replacing "Beatrice" in sentence (1) with either "Camille" or "Deirdre," which leaves the remainder of sentence (1) apparently unchanged in meaning. Camille and Deirdre, that is to say, might also know that snow is white, entertaining the same attitude (knowing) toward the same object (that snow is white) as does Beatrice according to (1). The presumed independence of component (iii) can be illustrated similarly by replacing "that the sun is shining" in sentence (2) with other propositional expressions. Camille might also believe that snow is white or that the gate is shut to the garden where the children are playing. The alleged independence of component (i), finally, can be illustrated by replacing "hopes" in sentence (3) with "knows" or "believes." The central tenet of ODOPA is that a subject might hold many and sundry different attitudes toward a given proposition. For instance, Deirdre might know or believe, as well as hope, that the gate is shut at the entrance of the garden.

Now it seems relatively unproblematic that, given a particular cognitive attitude toward a suitable object, the same attitude toward this object might be held by different subjects. B, C, and D all might know that snow is white, as might any number of other cognitive subjects. And it seems likewise unproblematic that a given subject might hold the same attitude toward a variety of suitable objects. C might believe not only that the sun is shining, or that snow is white, or that the gate is shut, but any number of other propositions as well. What is seriously problematic about ODOPA is the remaining tenet that cognitive subjects can hold an unrestricted variety of attitudes toward identical objects and that the objects of these attitudes are always propositional in character. To be sure, D might hope that the gate is shut, might believe that the gate is shut, and (upon checking) might even come to know that the gate is shut. But it does not follow from this—despite repetition of the phrase "that the gate is shut"—that what D hopes is the same as what she believes, or that either what she hopes or what she believes is the same as what she comes to know, and so forth. More specifically, it does not follow that her attitude in each case is directed toward a propositional object.

To see why none of this follows, it may be helpful to reconstruct an argument of the sort that presumably would be used in support of ODOPA and then to show where this argument goes wrong. I speak of "reconstructing" an argument for ODOPA, rather than examining arguments actually offered by its proponents, because I am not aware of any attempts among either epistemologists or cognitive theorists to defend this central doctrine explicitly. The usual procedure in this quarter is just to take the doctrine for granted, perhaps because the reasons for accepting it seem entirely straightforward. As far as I can make out, these reasons are bound up with a point of terminology. Just as in sentences (1), (2), and (3) the verbs "knows," "believes," and "hopes" are all followed by expressions of the form "that such-and-such," so any verb expressing a cognitive attitude might be followed by a sentential clause beginning with "that." It might be urged, indeed, that the identifying mark of a cognitive verb is the ability to take such a clause as its grammatical object.[8] But a sentential clause beginning with "that," the argument continues, is a standard grammatical expression for a proposition. Thus any verb of cognitive attitude takes a propositional expression for its grammatical object, and the proposition this expression represents is the cognitive object of the attitude in question.

The argument, in brief, is (a) that cognitive verbs invariably take sentential clauses beginning with "that" as their grammatical objects, (b) that clauses of this form invariably express propositions, and hence (c) that cognitive attitudes invariably take propositional objects. The final step of the argument would be something to the effect that, since all cognitive attitudes take objects of the same sort, a subject N might shift from one attitude to another without changing the object of the attitudes in question.

There are several respects in which this argument is open to criticism and, indeed, several things about it that one or another theorist might want to change depending upon his or her views regarding the relation between surface grammar and the structure of cognitive attitudes. But there is one premise upon which the argument depends for its very cogency, which most epistemologists and cognitive theorists appear to accept as self-evident. It is in connection with this key premise, I shall attempt to show, that the argument above is flawed beyond retrieval. This is the premise that sentential clauses beginning with "that" invariably are expressions of propositions.

The project for the remainder of this chapter, as already noted, is to map out an overview of cognitive attitudes generally and, in the process, to note respects in which ODOPA is erroneous. By way of anticipation, the main problem with ODOPA will turn out to be the appearance of certain important classes of cognitive attitude that do not take propositional objects, but that are directed toward states of affairs (SOAs) instead.[9] Inasmuch as the verbs reporting these nonconforming attitudes all take "that" clauses as their grammatical objects, a marshaling of various cases in point will serve to show that clauses beginning with "that" are not always propositional. Let us make a start on the larger project by taking a critical look at the premise that all "that" clauses are propositional, part of which will involve locating nonconforming cases.

2.   Why "That" Clauses Are Not Invariably Propositional

It seems to be a standard philosophic propensity (not confined to epistemologists and cognitive theorists) to look upon a sentential clause beginning with "that" as a ready locution for expressing propositions. If someone (a student, perhaps) were to ask for examples of propositions, we might find ourselves responding in some manner like, "There is the proposition that snow is white, the proposition that the sun is shining, the proposition that the gate is shut, and so forth." In this response, the "and so forth" would be intended as a gesture toward yet other sentential expressions, each beginning with the telltale "that."

This way of thinking about propositions amounts to treating the format "that __" as an operator applying to sentential locutions (e.g., "snow is white," "the sun is shining") to produce locutions of another sort that have propositional status ("that snow is white," "that the sun is shining"). Thinking this way, we then tend to parse the phrase "the proposition that snow is white" in the manner of "the proposition, namely, that snow is white," where the last four words express the proposition in question. This enables us to say things like "that snow is white is true," intending thereby to attribute truth to the proposition that snow is white.

To put it another way, we think of "that" as a kind of holder or binder by which the identity of a proposition is held inviolate as we shift it from one to another context—or as a kind of handle by which it can be moved intact from one attitudinal relation to another.[10] Relying upon this device, we consider ourselves enabled, for example, to say in sequence, "Camille believes that the sun is shining," "Camille has good evidence that the sun is shining," "That the sun is shining is a true proposition," hence "Camille knows that the sun is shining." Here we deftly move the proposition (allegedly, that the sun is shining) from contexts attributing belief and evidence to contexts attributing truth and finally knowledge.

But this treatment of "that" clauses can be seriously misleading. In point of fact, as we shall see, prefacing "that" to a sentential locution is neither necessary nor sufficient to make that locution an expression of a proposition. It follows from this that the appearance of the term in a report of a subject's cognitive attitude (as in "Beatrice knows that snow is white") has no immediate bearing, one way or the other, on whether that attitude is directed toward a propositional object.

Consider the matter of necessity first. Assume that Camille has adopted an attitude of belief toward the proposition that the sun is shining. In reporting that attitude, it is entirely natural to say "Camille believes that the sun is shining." But it is no less natural, and no less adequate for the purpose, to say simply "Camille believes the sun is shining" (eliminating the "that"). The presence of "that" in our report is wholly superfluous. According to the advice of the *Oxford English Dic-*

tionary, use of "that" in such contexts is a matter of style, its being preferred after such verbs as "conceive" and "agree," but often omitted after verbs such as "believe" and "think."[11] (This is not an argument from the authority of usage, but simply an observation that we regularly refer to propositions without relying upon "that" as a conjunctive operator.) In brief, prefixing "that" to a sentential locution is not necessary for that locution to be used as a propositional expression.

To show it is not sufficient requires more extensive argument. To get the argument under way, we may observe that when an attitude is taken toward a propositional object, it makes good sense to say so explicitly. If Camille believes that the sun is shining, for instance, and if what she believes is the proposition that the sun is shining, then to say of Camille that she believes a proposition is both intelligible and in point of fact true. Similarly, if N denies what C believes, and if what C believes is a proposition, then it both makes sense and in fact is true to say that N denies a proposition. Given that both believing and denying are propositional attitudes, what one believes and denies are propositions. And there is nothing amiss in stating this directly.

But now consider the case in which the sky is still sunny, but N predicts that it soon will turn cloudy. Let N remark explicitly, "I predict that the sky will soon turn cloudy." If the part of N's remark beginning with "that" indicates a proposition, it should be both intelligible and true to say that N predicts a proposition. Despite its surface similarity to talk of predicting storms (disaster, etc.), however, talk of predicting propositions is plainly unintelligible. Storms (disasters, etc.) are eventualities that might come to pass, and it makes sense to talk of predicting such occurrences. But a proposition is not an eventuality. To be sure, it makes sense to talk of eventualities that involve propositions in one way or another. There is the eventuality of the proposition that the sky will turn cloudy turning out to be a true proposition. But N's actual prediction is (merely) that the sky will turn cloudy, which says nothing (although it *implies* something) about a proposition's being true. Since N's prediction is that the sky will turn cloudy, and since N does not predict a proposition, the phrase "that the sky will soon turn cloudy" in N's prediction does not express a proposition. Here is one case in which "that" followed by a sentential expression does not function as a propositional locution.

For another case, suppose that C responds by saying she hopes that the sky stays clear. C says this in so many words, using the expression "that the sky stays clear." But that expression used as such cannot express a proposition, since propositions are not things one might intelligibly be said to hope. C might hope that the proposition that the sky stays clear turns out to be a true proposition. But this would be to hope that an eventuality turns out to be the case, rather than to hope a proposition itself. Talk of hoping propositions (merely and simply) is no more sensible than talk of predictions with propositions as objects. The "that" clause in C's response accordingly is not propositional. Other cognitive verbs typically followed by sentential "that" locutions that cannot intelligibly be said to pick out propositions include "anticipate," "guess," "wish," and "judge." While one might anticipate that a proposition will be proven false, for example, there is no sense in which one might anticipate the proposition itself. And so on for the other cases.

The foregoing cases are all counterexamples to the key premise in the argument for ODOPA offered in the section above—namely, the thesis that sentential clauses beginning with "that" invariably function as propositional expressions. While these are all cases of cognitive verbs typically followed by "that" clauses of the relevant sort, the cognitive attitudes to which they correspond cannot intelligibly be said to take propositions as objects. There is another class of counterexamples consisting of cognitive attitudes that might conceivably take propositions as objects, but are such that when interpreted as taking propositional objects yield senses sharply deviant from their plainly intended uses. The argument now shifts from a point of intelligibility to a point of what is normally meant in using such verbs.

Imagine that C leaves for the beach fully confident that the sun is shining, but once she gets there discovers that the sky is overcast. This is the state of affairs (SOA) that N has predicted, and what C discovers is the presence of this very SOA. In discovering this, she also discovers that N's prediction was accurate, inasmuch as that prediction is confirmed by the presence of this SOA. What C discovers, in this case, is not a proposition. Although there are circumstances in which one might be said to discover a proposition—for example, N discovers the proposition "snow is white" written as part of a syllogism in an old manuscript—C's current circumstances are not of this sort. Under the present circumstances what C discovers is an aspect of the local weather conditions—the SOA itself of the sky's being overcast.

For another example, imagine that Deirdre has been watching her children through a window in the study of her house and that she suddenly notices that the garden gate is open. What she notices is the SOA of the gate's being open, not a proposition to the effect that this is the case. While it is not inconceivable that on occasion one might notice a proposition, as when N notices the proposition that completes the syllogism, what D notices through the window is not a proposition about the gate, but the SOA itself of the gate's being open. It follows that the expression "that the gate is open," reporting what D has noticed, is not an expression of a proposition. Other verbs falling into this class are "find," "discern," "perceive," and "ascertain." While one conceivably might find certain propositions in a list of disputed theses, for example, when D checks further and finds that the children are still in the garden, what she finds in this case is not a proposition. And so on for the other verbs in question. Although verbs in this class all take "that" clauses that on odd occasions might admit a propositional reading, the intended reading for the most part would not be propositional. What we have with verbs of this sort is yet another set of counterinstances to the thesis that sentential clauses beginning with "that" invariably function as propositional expressions.

Inasmuch as this thesis about the exclusively propositional use of "that" clauses of this sort serves as a key premise in the argument for ODOPA offered above, the argument itself must be rejected. It is of course true that collapse of one of its supporting arguments does not necessarily constitute a refutation of ODOPA itself. What we should be prepared to see at this point, however, is that the various cases discussed in the paragraphs immediately above are enough in themselves to show ODOPA mistaken. Here is why. According to ODOPA, the sentence "Camille believes that the sun is shining" should be parsed in this fashion: "Camille—believes—that the sun is shining." In this parsing, "Camille" could be replaced by the name of another person, "believes" could be replaced by another cognitive verb, and "that the sun is shining" could be replaced by another sentential "that" expression (allegedly expressing a proposition), each replacement leaving the remaining components unchanged. But we have seen counterexamples that show, in the case of some cognitive verbs at least, that interchange of the verbs concerned can result in a distinct change in sense on the part of the "that" clause following.

While the expression "that the sun is shining" in "Camille believes that the sun is shining," for example, identifies the proposition that Camille believes, if "believes" in that sentence were replaced by "notices" then the expression in question could no longer be properly understood as identifying a propositional object. In the expression "Camille notices that the sun is shining," what "that the sun is shining" identifies is not a proposition, but the SOA instead that Camille has come to notice. Without any change in the wording of this expression (i.e., "that the sun is shining"), interchange of the terms "believes" and "notices" effects a change in its reference to cognitive objects. In "Camille believes that the sun is shining," the expression in question refers to a proposition; but in "Camille notices that the sun is shining" the typographically identical expression refers to an SOA instead. Conversely, while "that the gate is open" in "Deirdre discovers that the gate is open" identifies an SOA that Deirdre discovers, if "discovers" in this sentence were replaced by "asserts," then the expression in question comes to identify a proposition—the proposition that the gate is open, which Deirdre is said to assert. Again without any change in the wording of the expression "that the gate is open," interchange of the cognitive verbs "discovers" and "asserts" produces a change in the apparent referent of that expression. Countercases of this sort could be multiplied indefinitely. And what these countercases show is that the pivotal tenet of ODOPA, to the effect that terms for cognitive attitudes can be freely interchanged without change in reference of the expressions identifying their corresponding objects, is patently wrong and must be rejected.

What makes this erroneous tenet of ODOPA more or less plausible initially is its parsing of cognitive-attitude statements according to the form: N (the subject)—A's (the cognitive attitude)—that so-and-so (the object of the attitude). This parsing, accordingly, should be viewed with suspicion. In this regard, it is interesting to consider various alternatives to this parsing that have been suggested by recent philosophers. A. N. Prior, for instance, has argued that "thinks that," in the sentence "N thinks that there will be a nuclear war," is an operator (sometimes called a "relator") joining a name on its left side with a sentence on its right.[12] In effect, "N thinks that __" functions like a one-term sentential connective (compare "it is false that __"), while ". . . thinks that there will be a nuclear war" functions like a one-place predicate (compare ". . . is red"). Since this "dual-function" analysis is supposed to apply to attitudinal reports generally, it yields parsings such as "Camille—believes that—the sun is shining" and "Camille—notices that—the sun is shining."[13]

Another alternative is provided by Donald Davidson, along with his analysis of indirect discourse based on the notion of "samesaying."[14] According to this analysis, "Galileo said that the earth moves" is understood as roughly equivalent to "Galileo said (in his language, what I as samesayer say, in my language, in saying) the earth moves." More directly, suppressing reference to the samesaying relation, the sentence is to be understood as "The earth moves—Galileo said that." An equivalent parsing, identical in effect with that suggested by Prior, would be "Galileo—said that—the earth moves."

Davidson's approach is supported by an explicit appeal to the *Oxford English Dictionary*, which traces this use of "that" as a conjunction back to an earlier use as a demonstrative pronoun. In effect, the term "that" *points out*, in its respective contexts, *what* Galileo said, *what* Camille believes, *what* Beatrice knows, *what* Deirdre hopes, and so on. And it does so without prejudging the character (propositional or otherwise) of the object to which it points. This is the right way, it seems to me, of construing the role of "that" in such contexts. We may thank Davidson for drawing attention to this demonstrative conjunction, without wanting to extend his notion of the samesaying relation to "samebelieving," "sameknowing," "samehoping," et cetera.

The demonstrative function served by "that" in these various sentences could be served by other symbolic devices as well. One ready substitute is the versatile colon, in its common use of drawing attention to the expression or reference following it. Rendered accordingly, Prior's sentence would be written "N thinks: there will be a nuclear war," and Davidson's sentence would be written "Galileo said: the earth moves." In like fashion, we could rewrite sentences (1)–(3) from the first section as:

(1′) Beatrice knows: snow is white.
(2′) Camille believes: the sun is shining.
(3′) Deirdre hopes: the gate is shut.

And in each case, we could do so without begging any questions about the character of the object toward which the cognitive attitude is directed.

Given that the "that" clause typically following a cognitive attitude verb cannot be relied upon to indicate the character of the corresponding object, the question arises of how the object can be determined in a given case. While the "that" clause following "believes" may be trusted to pick out a propositional object, and while the same grammatical construction following "discovers" or "notices" reliably indicates an SOA as cognitive object instead, there are many cases in which the object indicated is less than obvious on an intuitive basis. What we need at this point is a set of working criteria by which the objects of cognitive attitudes for the most part can be identified.[15] This need sets the task of the following two sections.

3. Distinguishing Propositional Attitudes from Attitudes of Cognitive Access

The method to be employed through the remainder of the present chapter requires beginning with a small group of cognitive attitudes that quite clearly are attitudes toward propositions and with a second group of attitudes that no less clearly take SOAs as their proper objects. We then will formulate a set of features shared by all of the former but conspicuously absent in each of the latter. These features will provide criteria by which the two groups can be distinguished and by which additional members of both groups can be identified. By way of caveat, however, it bears restating that no effort will be made to produce criteria that apply unambiguously in all conceivable cases.[16] The present concern is to provide criteria that yield firm results over an ample range of common cognitive attitudes. It is enough if our criteria produce unambiguous results in application to attitudes of standard cognitive interest.

Believing and denying, along with asserting, have already been identified as attitudes we take toward propositional objects. Let us refer to them as "attitudes of propositional stance" (for short, "attitudes of stance"). One typical feature of such attitudes is that they are characterized in terms of truth and falsehood. If the proposition that the sun is shining is a true proposition, and if Camille believes that the sun is shining, then Camille sustains a true belief. She believes truly in this case that the sun is shining. To believe a false proposition, on the other hand, is to sustain a false belief, the upshot of which is that one believes falsely.

One similarly might assert, either truly or falsely, that storm clouds are gathering and it soon will rain. To assert this is to assert a proposition, the truth or falsity of which determines the truth-value of the assertion. And in denying the proposition that it soon will rain, one's stance of denial is true or false depending upon the truth-value of the proposition. So it is generally with attitudes of propositional stance. The truth-value of an affirmation, an attestation, or a declaration depends upon the truth-value in turn of its propositional object.

But things are otherwise with attitudes like discovering, finding, and noticing, which might be labeled "attitudes of cognitive access" (for short, "attitudes of access"). If Deirdre professes to have noticed that the gate is open, whereas in fact this is not the case, it is not intelligible to say that Deirdre noticed falsely or that in some sense her noticing was done incorrectly. What should be said instead is that D has failed to notice, since one can only notice what in fact is the case. D's error is not a matter of incorrect noticing, but a matter of mistaken profession. Neither can she be said, conversely, to have noticed truly or correctly, if what she professed to notice is in fact the case. There is no such thing as a true or false noticing. For noticing is not an attitude toward a propositional object and, hence, not an attitude to be characterized in terms of truth-values.

Similarly, when C arrives at the beach and finds that the sun is shining, what she finds is not a proposition, but an actual SOA. And since SOAs do not admit evaluation in terms of correctness or incorrectness, it is unintelligible to describe her finding as either true or false. She indeed might claim to have found an SOA that (contrary to her claim) is not the case, but this results in a false claim only and not in a finding that in fact is false.

The same goes for other attitudes toward actual SOAs, such as ascertaining, discerning, perceiving, and recognizing. An SOA either is or is not the case.[17] And if an SOA is not the case, it is not available to be recognized, or perceived, or discerned. To be sure, one might recognize the SOA of the sun's not shining, which is the case if in fact the sun is not shining. But this clearly is not a case of "false recognition," as if one purported to recognize what is not the case. The sun's being occluded might be an actual SOA every bit as much as its being fully exposed. And to recognize its being occluded, when this in fact is the case, is no more to entertain an attitude toward a nonactual SOA than recognizing the SOA of a cookie-jar's being empty is entertaining an attitude toward a missing cookie. In each case, what one recognizes is an actual SOA. It should be noted in passing that we sometimes speak of "true discernment," as when commending someone's ability for discriminating judgment. But this is not to say that discernment is an attitude admitting truth-values. What we are speaking of in such cases is not something done truly, but something done with a certain degree of keenness. The opposite here is not "false discernment," but a mode of awareness that is deficient in sensitivity.

What these paradigm instances show, in summary, is that it is intelligible to qualify verbs of propositional stance (forms of "believe," "assert," "deny," etc.) in terms of truth-value, whereas verbs of cognitive access (forms of "notice," "find," "discern," etc.) do not admit qualification in terms of truth and falsehood, or in terms generally of a distinction between correctness and incorrectness.[18] This provides our first criterion for distinguishing attitudes toward propositional objects from attitudes toward actual SOAs.

Criterion I: Believing, affirming, and other attitudes of propositional stance, but not discovering, noticing, or other attitudes of cognitive access, can be intelligibly assessed in terms of correctness and incorrectness. It is intelligible to talk of "true" or "false" belief, for instance, but not of "right" or "wrong" discovery.

"Noticing," "discovering," and "recognizing" are typical of what sometimes are referred to as "achievement verbs," in that they serve expressly to designate accomplishment or success on the part of the subjects concerned. Achievement verbs such as these convey evaluations of cognitive activities. Criterion I points out that, given success in these activities already accomplished, the attitudes typifying such accomplishments cannot be further evaluated in terms of truth and falsehood. Inasmuch as one can notice only what is there to be noticed, there is no such thing as a "substandard noticing" (discovering, finding, etc.), in the manner that a belief can be substandard in being directed toward a "substandard"—that is, a false—proposition.

Another criterion has to do with the kinds of questions we typically ask in querying what people say about their cognitive attitudes. Suppose that Camille says she believes that the sun is shining, in circumstances that make this belief somehow puzzling or problematic. We might then probe this belief (taking her report to be sincere) by asking, "*Why* do you believe that the sun is shining?" Similarly, we often ask, "*Why* do you assert. . . ?" or "*Why* do you deny. . . ?" in questioning the soundness of what a person asserts or denies. But we seldom ask, "*How* do you believe. . . ?" or "*How* do you assert. . . ?" in raising questions about such cognitive attitudes. (Seldom is not never. "How could you believe *that*?" is a somewhat outraged way of asking for reasons, of asking what possibly could make you think *that* belief is rationally respectable. Nonetheless, the question "How do you believe that the sun is shining?" would require elucidation to become intelligible.)

By contrast, we commonly ask "How did you notice. . . ?" or "How did you discover. . . ?" or "How did you recognize. . . ?" in probing the claim of another person to have gained some such form of cognitive access. Thus we might ask Deirdre how she could have found that the gate is open, if we had reason to think that she had not been near the garden recently. But we seldom hear questions like "Why did you notice. . . ?" or "Why did you recognize. . . ?" raised as challenges to someone's claim to have noticed or recognized. (Again, seldom is not never. One might ask, "Why did you recognize so-and-so but not such-and-such?" when the two SOAs are so closely associated that recognizing the latter usually goes hand in hand with recognizing the former, but when only the former was recognized.)

This distinction between asking "Why?" and asking "How?" has been thoroughly explored by J. L. Austin.[19] A brief look at its background will help shape a second criterion for distinguishing between attitudes of stance and of access.

Consider the relevance of asking "Why?" with respect to the stances people take toward propositional objects. People generally (not always, of course) enter discourse with other people under a shared presumption of rationality. We expect one another to adopt beliefs, to make assertions, and generally to arrive at various cognitive stances on the basis of reasons that are mutually intelligible. Suspecting a lapse, we ask for a disclosure of reasons by asking *why* another has adopted the attitude in question. In querying another person's belief or assertion, we query whether, under the relevant circumstances, it is proper to make that particular assertion or to entertain that particular belief. So it is with other attitudes toward propositional objects. Should N declare (propose, conclude, etc.) that rain is imminent, and we (in view of a cloudless sky) ask why N has taken that stand on the matter, we question the reason behind N's declaration (proposal, conclusion), perhaps suggesting that it should be reexamined.

Beliefs, assertions, conclusions, convictions—all can suffer defect for lack of reasons. But not so with findings, perceivings, or noticings. If N purports to perceive that the sky is cloudy, it would be extraordinary to question the reasons for that perception. It would be similarly out of order to ask *why* N noticed (discerned, recognized, etc.) the rumbling of thunder, as if it might somehow be *inappropriate* for N to have noticed.

Now consider the relevance of "How?" to attitudes of cognitive access. In order for N to notice (recognize, discern, etc.) a certain SOA, not only must N be capable of noticing such things generally, but N also must be properly situated to notice this SOA on this particular occasion. For N to notice that the sky is cloudy, for example, N not only must be awake and have reasonably good eyesight, but N also must currently be in view of the sky. If N's claim to notice that the sky is cloudy seems surprising or dubious, we can test its propriety by questioning N's current capacities for noticing. And if it turns out that N is visually incapacitated or was not in a position to notice on this occasion, then we conclude that N in fact was not capable of noticing. The upshot is not that N has fallen victim to a case of "substandard noticing" (akin to a case of false believing), but rather that N simply has not noticed the thing in question.

To take a stand with regard to a given proposition, on the other hand—to affirm, or to assert, or merely to believe it—requires no capacities beyond those we attribute to cognitive subjects generally and no special circumstances beyond cognizance of the proposition concerned. The doubts we have about another person's propositional attitudes are seldom such as to be resolved by probing the person's *capacity* to reach them, apart from the reasons brought to bear in a particular case. Hence we seldom challenge another person's propositional attitudes by raising questions about how they are reached. (Seldom, once again, is short of never. "How did you arrive at that belief?" is roughly equivalent to "Why do you believe that?" but with emphasis upon a person's capacity to evaluate the evidence, rather than upon capacities exercised in arriving at the belief itself.)

Criterion II: We typically ask "Why?" but not "How?" in probing attitudes of propositional stance such as believing, denying, and asserting; and we typically ask "How?" but not "Why?" in probing attitudes of cognitive access such as finding, noticing, and ascertaining.

Criterion I treats the intelligibility of assigning dimensions of correctness to certain cognitive attitudes, while criterion II treats the manner in which such attitudes are criticized. While the immediate purpose in formulating these criteria has been to distinguish between attitudes of stance and attitudes of access, we shall find them useful in making other such distinctions as well. Let us turn next to a class of attitudes typified by hoping and fearing.

4.   Attitudes of Anticipation and Assessment

As means for distinguishing between attitudes of stance and of access, the two criteria give the same result. In this application, strictly speaking, the set of two is redundant. But the criteria as a set have other applications. For there are other verbs of cognitive attitude that respond to them in tandem unlike either "believe" or "notice." In effect, there are other cognitive attitudes than those of propositional stance and cognitive access.

Consider the verbs "hope" and "fear," for example, along with "anticipate," "wish," "desire," and "dread." If D reports a hope that it soon will rain, and we think this is uncharacteristic under prevailing circumstances, we might intelligibly ask *why* she hopes this, but we generally would not ask *how* she is competent to do so.[20] Thus the attitude of hope draws "Why?" in response to criterion II. The same result would follow if "hope" in these sentences were replaced by any of the other verbs at the beginning of this paragraph. So these verbs resemble "believe" and other verbs of propositional stance in their response to criterion II.

Yet hope and fear are not attitudes toward propositional objects. When Deirdre hopes that the sun will be shining upon her arrival at the beach, the object of her hope is not a proposition. The object of her hope, rather, is a certain SOA. Unlike the case with discovery and other attitudes of access, however, the object of hope is not an actual SOA that the subject encounters. The object of D's hope is an SOA that currently lacks determinate status in her estimation, one that at the moment, as far as she knows, neither is nor is not the case determinately.[21] Her hope is directed toward the SOA of the sun's shining at the beach in the proximate future. And the sense of her hope is that this SOA might prove to be the case when that time arrives. Similarly, if Deirdre fears that it soon will rain instead, her fear is directed, not toward a proposition, but toward an SOA she thinks might soon eventuate. (One might also say that, in a sense, she fears that a certain proposition—that it will be raining when she gets to the beach—might turn out to be true. What she fears, once again, is not the proposition, but the SOA of its turning out to be true.)

Since hopes and fears are not attitudes toward propositions, and hence not attitudes toward objects with truth-values, hopes and fears themselves are neither correct nor incorrect. One's hopes may be realized, or one's fears prove groundless, but one does not thereby "hope truly" or "falsely fear." (One might be said to "truly hope" when one hopes wholeheartedly, devoutly, or without reservations; but here "truly" means genuinely, not the opposite of "falsely." Likewise, a "false hope" would be a hope that one holds vainly—for reasons involving wishful thinking or self-deception, perhaps—but not thereby a hope directed toward a false proposition.) Similar remarks hold for "wish," "desire," and so forth, which along with "hope" and "fear," call for "no" in response to criterion I.

In short, these verbs respond to criterion II like terms of propositional stance, while they respond to criterion I like terms of cognitive access. Hence the attitudes to which these verbs refer are attitudes neither toward propositional objects nor toward SOAs that expressly are the case. They are attitudes toward SOAs that have no determinate status—no status, at any rate, that is known to the subject.[22] One does not hope for an SOA one knows to be actual, nor fear an SOA one knows not to be the case. The difference between these attitudes and attitudes of cognitive access is that the objects of the latter (from the subject's viewpoint) have a determinate status, while the objects' status in the former case is expressly unsettled.

Inasmuch as hopes and fears concern the eventuality of such SOAs, we may use the term "eventuality" to refer to the objects of these attitudes. And inasmuch as these attitudes typically are directed toward future eventualities, we may refer to them generally as "attitudes of projection." The characteristic mark of verbs reporting these attitudes, relative to the criterion above, is that they respond "no" to the first criterion and "why?" to the second.

Among attitudes that characteristically take nonpropositional objects, we thus far have distinguished attitudes of access (like discovery), whose objects are always actual SOAs, and attitudes of anticipation (like hoping) that are directed toward eventualities—that is, toward SOAs the subject treats as having indeterminate status. There is another group of cognitive attitudes that take SOAs as objects, but SOAs the subject treats (perhaps incorrectly) as having a particular status. While this status might remain uncertain given the normal course of events, the subject makes a commitment regarding the status that applies as part of adopting one of the attitudes in question. As far as their respective objects are concerned, these attitudes differ from attitudes of anticipation in taking objects that are treated, not as eventualities, but as contingencies that in fact have one or the other determinate status, while they differ from attitudes of access in admitting as objects not only actual SOAs, but also SOAs that are not the case.

Paradigmatic of this further group is the attitude of prediction. For an illustration, we may return to N's prediction that the sky overhead will soon turn cloudy. What N predicts here is that the SOA of the sky's being cloudy will soon turn out to be the case. N might equivalently have predicted that the sky's remaining sunny will soon turn out not to be the case. Either way, N predicts that a certain SOA will turn out to have one or another determinate status. For another example, consider the estimation that in two hours the air will be too chilly for swimming. What one estimates here is that within a span of two hours a given SOA will turn out to be the case. Alternatively, one might estimate that within that time span the current temperate conditions will no longer prevail. What makes these SOAs suitable objects for the attitudes in question is that they are conceived by the subject to have one or another specific status, a matter on which the subject takes a stand in adopting the attitude.

Other common members of this group are expressed by the verbs "calculate," "figure," "forecast," and "foretell." Insofar as these attitudes generally involve reaching a considered verdict on the status of a relevant SOA, they may be referred to collectively as "attitudes of assessment." Let us consider how they fare with respect to our two criteria.

With regard to the first criterion, the question is whether attitudes of the type in question admit evaluation in terms like "true" and "false"— that is, in terms of correctness and incorrectness. The response for these attitudes is clearly affirmative. Predictions are often evaluated in terms of truth and falsehood explicitly, and the same may be said for estimations and judgments. In the case of forecasts, "accurate" and "inaccurate" are common terms of evaluation, while we are prone to speak of "correct" and "incorrect" calculations. Although a variety of terms are available to make the distinction, assessment generally is something done rightly and wrongly. A correct (sound, true)[23] prediction, of course, is one that assigns the same status to a given SOA that the SOA itself turns out to occupy. Similar accounts are available for other attitudes of assessment.

Such attitudes accordingly resemble attitudes of stance in admitting characterization with respect to correctness. What marks the distinction between these two types of attitude is their response to criterion II above. While no particular technique or skill is involved in arriving at a belief or in affirming or denying a proposition, assessment generally involves some procedure or another, or at least is accomplished through some sort of deliberation. When N makes the prediction that the sky will turn cloudy, N (if serious) will take note of such factors as wind direction and the appearance of the sky above the horizon. And when he estimates that in two hours it will be too cold for swimming, he does so (if serious) on the basis of similar factors. It is because of the involvement in assessment of some sort of deliberation that we typically question such attitudes by asking "How?" but seldom "Why?"

The case is clearer with assessments involving standard procedures. Suppose that N consults the instruments of the boat he is sailing and calculates that the wind is blowing east-northeast. Camille takes note of the instrument readings and sees reason to question N's calculation. A natural thing to say in posing the question is, "How did you arrive at that calculation?" or simply "How did you calculate that?" If she were to say, "Why did you calculate that?" instead, the sense would be to ask why a calculation was needed, rather than to question the calculation at hand. To query the result of a calculation, as distinct from why it was ventured, calls for the question "How?" instead.

In like manner, to challenge the results of a numerical tally it would be appropriate to ask "How?" rather than "Why?" To ask, "Why did you figure the total?"—say, in questioning a bill—would call for an explanation of why the tally was called for, whereas if one wished to question the result itself, "How did you figure that?" or "How did you arrive at that figure?" would be the appropriate query. The response to the second criterion of such attitudes thus typically is "How?" instead of "Why?" Despite the surface similarity to attitudes like believing and affirming, this is enough to warrant separating attitudes of assessment into a class by themselves.

5. Four Types of Cognitive Attitude Schematically Characterized

Criterion I might be phrased in the form of a question, "Does the attitude at issue admit assessment in terms of correctness and incorrectness?" with "Yes" and "No" as alternate responses. Criterion II, in turn, might be applied as the question "When N's attitude for some reason is considered problematic, which query is more appropriate in probing that attitude?" taking "Why?" and "How?" as available answers.

The major differences among the four classes of cognitive attitudes we have been discussing in the previous sections are summarized with regard to these criteria in table 1.1, along with the various types of objects the subject addresses in adopting these attitudes. Since only attitudes of stance are addressed toward propositional objects, only these are properly described as "propositional attitudes." The remaining three groups comprise attitudes addressed toward SOAs, whether actual with attitudes of cognitive access, expressly indeterminate with attitudes of anticipation, or specifically actual or nonactual with attitudes of assessment. Of the four groups of cognitive attitude we have isolated thus far, to repeat, only attitudes of stance typically take propositional objects. Insofar as the orthodox view of such matters (ODOPA) characterizes cognitive attitudes across the board as attitudes toward propositions, this view is faulty at its very foundation.

It may prove helpful to augment the chart above with short lists of cognitive attitudes typically falling under the groupings already identified. Attitudes of propositional *stance* include, among many others, affirming, asserting, attesting, believing, conceding, contending, declaring, denying, disbelieving, maintaining, presuming, stating, suspecting, supposing, testifying, and (simply) thinking.

Table 1.1. Types of Cognitive Attitudes with Criteria and Objects

Attitudes of	Criterion		Objects of Attitudes
	I	II	
Stance	Yes	Why?	Propositions
Access	No	How?	Actual SOAs
Projection	No	Why?	Eventualities
Assessment	Yes	How?	Contingencies

Notable attitudes of cognitive *access,* in turn, are ascertaining, discerning, discovering, finding, knowing, learning (in the sense of becoming apprised of), noticing, perceiving, realizing, and recognizing.

Attitudes of *projection* include, to name a few, desiring, dreading, fearing, hoping, preferring, suspecting, and wishing.

Among the more restricted group of attitudes having to do with *assessment* are anticipating, calculating, computing, estimating, figuring, forecasting, foreseeing, foretelling, judging, and predicting.

While this classification seems "natural" (i.e., not unduly artificial) and will prove useful for the purposes of the investigation to come, we should acknowledge that there are other ways in which cognitive attitudes might be divided. One alternative would be to distinguish attitudes that typically are engaged in speech acts from those typically enacted through nonverbal activity.[24] Included among the former would be most of those listed above under attitudes of stance (with several exceptions including believing and thinking), with perhaps a few (foretelling, predicting) from subsequent groupings. Given that speech is a common medium for most cognitive activity involving propositions, the fact that a vast majority of attitudes other than those of stance typically do not involve speech acts is a further sign that these other attitudes are not propositional.

Another alternative of possible interest would be to classify attitudes with regard to their involvement in deliberation. While most of the attitudes listed above are such that normally they are initiated as a deliberate act of the subject, there are nonetheless several into which one might fall inadvertently. Among the latter are such attitudes as assuming and discovering, along with most of those we have classified as attitudes of projection. The fact that this latter class stands by itself in generally excluding attitudes entered into only through deliberation is a further indication that attitudes of projection constitute a "natural" grouping.

Yet another distinction that might prove pertinent for some purposes is that between attitudes engaged within the confines of particular episodes and those that might be entertained for indefinite durations. Among attitudes confined to single episodes would be typical cases of discovering, finding, and learning. Typical of attitudes that might be engaged over indefinite periods, on the other hand, are believing, knowing, and realizing, along with most of those listed under the category of projection. Falling in between, however, is a sizable class of attitudes that we entertain on an episodic basis but nonetheless might entertain on repeated occasions. Included in this middle group are noticing, perceiving, and recognizing, along with a majority of attitudes engaging speech acts.

Developing other classifications of this sort, however, would be extraneous to the present project. The most useful classification for the investigation to follow is that distinguishing cognitive attitudes according to their objects. Our most important result in this regard so far is that only attitudes of stance take propositions as their proper objects, while attitudes of the remaining sorts take SOAs qualified with varying status assignments.

Unless more is said about what being the proper object of an attitude amounts to, however, this result could be seriously misleading. To illustrate a potential problem, assume that C not only believes that the sky will be sunny, but also hopes that this will be the case. C believes that the sky will be sunny, which is to believe the proposition that the sky will be sunny. C also hopes that the sky will be sunny, which is to hope for the eventuality of the sky's being sunny. Since propositions and eventualities are different kinds of objects, her hope and her belief might appear to be about different things. It thus might appear that one cannot hope the same thing that one believes, which seems patently contrary to the facts of the matter. We assumed that C both hopes and believes that the sky will be sunny, and there is nothing about that assumption to make us think of it as self-contradictory.

What we need to realize in order to see beyond apparent anomalies of this sort is that the *object* of a given cognitive attitude need not be the same as what the attitude is *about*. Consider the analogy of writing a letter—on a typewriter, say, to make the case simple. What N writes in typing a letter are the characters appearing on the printed sheet that is removed from the typewriter when the letter is done. The object of N's activity is a piece of paper marked with characters to form an intelligible message. But that object is not what N was writing about. What N was writing about is the content of the letter—that same thing that the letter itself is about. Perhaps N might have chosen to convey that content by speaking on the telephone instead. In that case, what N would speak—the object of his speech act—would be a series of sounds with the same intelligible content. The object of his speaking would be clearly different from the object of his writing, but the content of the two activities would be the same.

Although writing letters and speaking on the telephone are cognitive activities more complex than the simple attitudes we have been discussing, the distinction between object and content carries over to cognitive attitudes as well. The object of C's belief is the proposition that the sky will be sunny. The content of her belief, on the other hand, is what the belief is about. And obviously C's belief is not about a proposition. In like fashion, the content of C's hope is what her hope is about, and there is nothing to prevent C's hope from being about the same thing as her corresponding belief. Despite the difference between their respective *objects,* C's belief and her hope have the same cognitive content, which is to say that they are *about* the same thing.

This distinction between cognitive content and the object of cognitive attitudes will occupy us at length in chapter 9, along with various issues of intentionality. What remains for the present chapter is to fit the main results of the present project into a general overview and to mention various other projects that have not been attempted.

6.   Cognitive Attitudes Defined

The observant reader will note that although we have identified a number of individual cognitive attitudes and have sorted these into four distinguishable kinds, no definition has been given of cognitive attitudes as a general class. One purpose to be served by such definition, presumably, would be to distinguish cognitive attitudes from modes of cognitive involvement that are not attitudinal (e.g., states of contemplation or mental alertness) on the one hand and from attitudes of a noncognitive sort (e.g., attitudes of aggression or compliance) on the other. In terms of our metaphor of exploration, we should expect at least to be able to trace the boundaries of the domain occupied by cognitive attitudes on the conceptual map. Another purpose that might be served by such a definition would be to indicate the extent of this domain, thus providing some sense of how much of the interior remains to be mapped. What has been accomplished thus far is a fairly detailed delineation of four distinct subdomains, with no reason to think that these are exhaustive.

If the goals of the present inquiry called for a comprehensive map of this sort, the question would have to be faced of how precise a set of border markers it would be reasonable to expect. For those of us with a penchant for laying things out in terms of necessary and sufficient conditions, there might arise a temptation to assume the role of surveyors "officially commissioned" to make vague borders precise, which would invite disputes with others whose "intuitions" suggest the boundaries should be drawn differently. But our present purposes do not require precisely marked boundaries. While we will return in later chapters to pursue these results further, it is enough for present purposes to bear in mind that knowledge and belief have been located within different domains—those occupied by attitudes of access and by attitudes of stance, respectively—and that, as such, they take different kinds of objects.

Disclaimers regarding precision aside, there are a few features that seem to characterize cognitive attitudes generally that can be relied on to make their location on our conceptual map more conspicuous. Let us consider first what it is that marks them off as attitudes and then what it is that makes them cognitive. Attitudes generally may be divided into physical postures ("the rock was suspended in a precarious attitude") and modes of address adopted by a subject toward one thing or another (including the subject itself: "N projected an attitude of self-importance"). The thing toward which an attitude is addressed may be called its "object," and it is in this respect that cognitive attitudes have objects like propositions and SOAs. Not all attitudes of this sort are cognitive ("the dog displayed an attitude of aggression toward the intruder"); but among those that are, a general mark of their attitudinal character is that they are signified by a transitive verb in some relevant form. Thus for example we have "believing that so-and-so," and similar constructions, where the phrase beginning with "that" signifies the object of the attitude in question.[25]

What makes cognitive attitudes cognitive, on the other hand, is their intentional character. What this means is not that they are entered into deliberately and on purpose (as noted above, some are while some are not), but rather that they have the character of being *about* something or another. The class of cognitive phenomena generally, of course, is much broader than of cognitive attitudes specifically. In addition, there are cognitive states like being aware of something,[26] cognitive disciplines like scrutinizing something, and cognitive dispositions like valuing something, to name but a few. Like other phenomena of this general sort, however, cognitive attitudes have a directional structure, which is to say that they are oriented toward some content or another.

If we label the content toward which a cognitive activity is directed its 'intentional object',[27] then cognitive attitudes can be given the following succinct definition. Cognitive attitudes are intentional postures in which a subject takes up relationship simultaneously with an object determined by its mode of address and with an object determined by its intentional content. As we have seen already in the case of belief, these objects do not have to be identical. If C believes that the sun is shining, the object addressed by virtue of her posture of belief is the proposition that the sun is shining, while the intentional object of that belief is what the proposition is about—the content comprising the relevant state of the weather. In other cases, however, the two objects might be identical, as when the object of N's prediction that the sky will turn cloudy is the very same thing as what that prediction is about. The contrast between these two cases should become more easily apparent when we return to the topic of intentionality below.

With this definition finally at hand, we can easily see that the four-fold classification of cognitive attitudes developed above falls considerably short of being comprehensive. Consider the attitude of fancying that such-and-such is the case, as Ophelia fancied, in extreme distraction, that her garments would bear her up in the weeping brook (William Shakespeare, *Hamlet,* 4.7). In being under this misapprehension, Ophelia clearly was engaged in a cognitive attitude because her fancy was directed toward an intentional object. Ophelia's problem, of course, was that the content of her fancy was wholly illusory, being an SOA that pointedly was not the case. Our problem, in turn, is that none of the four types of attitude previously distinguished includes attitudes whose objects are SOAs that pointedly are nonactual. Other attitudes like fancying in this respect are misconceiving and hallucinating, which as a group might be labeled "attitudes of misapprehension." Another common attitude that falls outside our four categories is that of misjudging. What constitutes a misjudgment, by definition, is a judgment whose content is in some way mistaken. Since judgments themselves are attitudes of assessment, and since attitudes of assessment engage as objects SOAs that determinately either are or are not the case, the object of a misjudgment is an SOA that has exactly the opposite status from that of its intentional object. Such attitudes also fall outside the fourfold classification above.

Although it would be interesting in itself to attempt a more comprehensive classification, this again would be extraneous to our present purposes. Without dwelling further on the general topic of cognitive attitudes themselves, it is time to begin our systematic examination of the particular attitudes to which this study is dedicated. We begin in the next chapter with a careful look at the attitude of belief.

Notes

1. From Edmund Gettier, "Is Justified True Belief Knowledge?" *Analysis* 23 (1963): 121–123. Another serious challenge was raised by Zeno Vendler in chapter 5 of his *Res Cogitans: An Essay in Rational Psychology* (Ithaca, N.Y.: Cornell University Press, 1972), 90, 99, 112, 118. Vendler's challenge is based on observations similar to those pursued below, to the effect that knowledge and belief take different objects. It is regrettable that this challenge has not had a major impact on the course of recent epistemology.

2. For a standard statement of this basic idea (the term itself is Fodor's), see Jerry Fodor, *Representations: Philosophical Essays on the Foundations of Cognitive Science* (Brighton, Sussex: Harvester Press, 1981), 240. A similar statement may be found in John Haugeland, *Mind Design* (Cambridge, Mass.: MIT Press, 1981), 24.

3. See, for instance, Zenon W. Pylyshyn, *Computation and Cognition: Toward a Foundation for Cognitive Science* (Cambridge, Mass.: MIT Press, 1986), 65.

4. Fodor, *Representations,* 108.

5. D. C. Dennett, *Content and Consciousness* (New York: Humanities Press, 1969), 82–83, 118.

6. Fred I. Dretske, *Knowledge and the Flow of Information* (Cambridge, Mass.: MIT Press, 1981), 154. Dretske follows the usual practice of using the expressions "cognitive attitude" (e.g., in his index) and "cognitive state" (e.g., 154) interchangeably. This practice will be maintained in the present study, except in particular contexts where an explicitly noted distinction between attitude and state seems useful for a specific purpose.

7. A clear statement of the view may be found in Ernest Sosa's "Propositions and Indexical Attitudes," in *On Believing: Epistemological and Semiotic Approaches,* H. Parret, ed. (Berlin: Walter de Gruyter, 1983), 316–332. In Sosa's words, when "S A's (e.g., believes or knows) that-p, S is a subject of consciousness, that-p is a proposition, and A'ing is a propositional attitude such as belief or knowledge" (316).

8. I think that this would be incorrect. The verb "forget" normally takes a "that" clause as its grammatical object; but forgetting is not a cognitive attitude because it lacks intentionality (when one forgets that the door is locked, one's attention is not directed toward the door being locked). Forgetting, rather, is the absence of a relevant cognitive attitude. More will be said later about intentionality as a feature of cognition generally.

9. Not everyone recognizes a distinction between propositions and states of affairs, and among those who do, there are many divergent views about the respective natures of such entities. While detailed discussion of these matters must wait for subsequent chapters, enough is said in the following section to illustrate the distinction in the present context.

10. B. Russell holds a similar view in *The Philosophy of Logical Atomism,* David Pears, ed. (La Salle, Ill.: Open Court, 1985), 43–45; first published in 1913.

11. *Oxford English Dictionary,* Compact ed., 1971.

12. A. N. Prior, *Objects of Thought,* P. T. Geach and A. J. P. Kenny, eds. (Oxford: Clarendon Press, 1971), 17–19.

13. This analysis is part of Prior's project to show that propositions are logical constructs—that is, that talk of propositions can be eliminated from a logically perspicuous language. The parsing this view dictates can be retained without subscribing to this treatment of propositions.

14. Donald Davidson, "On Saying That," *Synthese* 19 (1968–1969): 130–146.

15. The qualification "for the most part" reflects my lack of confidence that any criteria of this sort could be totally reliable. What we can reasonably expect is a set of criteria that will provide unambiguous results in most interesting cases—that is, "for the most part"—but that leave other cases more or less uncertain. This marginal ambiguity is not a problem for the present study, inasmuch as the cases we will be dealing with fall in secure middle ground.

16. See the previous note. In particular, I am not committed to the probably hopeless task of providing criteria that are impervious to artificially contrived counterexamples. Distinctions among cognitive attitudes are not neat enough to be caught by unyielding "if and only ifs."

17. Reasons for restricting SOAs to these two conditions are considered in chapter 7.

18. The reader may note that the discussion proceeds sometimes with reference to cognitive attitudes as such (believing, asserting, etc.) and sometimes with reference to terms employed in referring to such attitudes (forms of "believe," "assert," etc.). The rationale for this procedure should be evident in the observation that there is no better way of ascertaining that a given attitude (e.g., discerning) can (or cannot) be said intelligibly to be either true or false than to note that terms referring to that attitude (e.g., "discerning") can (or cannot) be qualified intelligibly in terms of truth and falsehood (the expression "false discerning," e.g., is not intelligible). To avail oneself of this procedure

does not require a general theory (such as Austin may have had, but I do not) about the role of "linguistic analysis" in philosophic investigations. The reader with misgivings in this regard should bear in mind that the concern of this study is not with an analysis of linguistic usage, whatever that might amount to, but with an analysis of cognitive attitudes as such. When the latter can be advanced in clear and unproblematic ways by taking note of what we typically *say* about such attitudes, one should have no compunction in taking advantage of this procedure.

19. J. L. Austin, "Other Minds," in *Philosophical Papers,* J. O. Urmson and G. J. Warnock, eds. (Oxford: Clarendon Press, 1961). See also Vendler, *Res Cogitans,* 116–117.

20. Of course, one might ask, "How do you hope (fear, wish, anticipate) this?" in the fashion of "How do I love you? Let me count the ways," where the manner of, not the capacity for, hope (fear, etc.) is being queried. Criterion II treats "How?" as a call for an account, not for a listing of ways.

21. For reasons examined in chapter 7, all SOAs should be thought of as having one of two possible statuses—being the case or not being the case. The sense in which this SOA lacks determinate status in D's estimation is that she has no idea *which* status it occupies in the actual world.

22. The lack of determinate status in the relevant subject's estimation may stem from the fact that the SOA is described in the future tense, leaving its actual status yet to be determined. It also might stem from circumstances like the following. Suppose that Deirdre has entered a contest, which is now over, but the winner of which has yet to be announced. In hoping she has won the contest, Deirdre adopts an attitude toward an SOA the status of which already has been determined, but which remains indeterminate in her attitude toward it. The characterization of the object of such an attitude as indeterminate is epistemological in bearing, leaving its ontological status an open issue.

23. Use of the terms "true" and "false" specifically in connection with predictions and estimations in particular may be due to the fact that we tend to report these cognitive activities in the form of propositions (e.g., the proposition "it soon will rain" itself might express a prediction), which are the primary bearers of truth-values. This should not be taken as an indication that the objects of predictions and estimations themselves are propositional.

24. A clear example of an attitude typically engaged through speech activity is that of affirming. In affirming that the sky is cloudy, N adopts a cognitive attitude—that of affirming—toward the proposition in question; and the way this is accomplished is by some speech act or another, such as saying explicitly, "I affirm that the sky is cloudy," or simply saying, "the sky is cloudy" in an affirmative manner. The attitude of affirming in this case, that is to say, is engaged by undertaking the speech act involved. But there are other ways of engaging the attitude of affirming that do not involve speech acts, as when N considers the state of the sky and comes to the point of affirming privately— to himself, as it were—that indeed it is cloudy. What this example should show is that the cognitive attitude of affirming is not the same as the speech act with

which it is often associated. It should be noted that the above list of attitudes of propositional stance does not include speech acts as such, although some of the attitudes listed are typically engaged through speech activity.

25. While examples have been drawn thus far from cognitive attitudes taking objects typically reported in "that" clauses of this familiar sort, it should be recalled that there are other grammatical devices by which such objects might be reported—as, for example, in "C believes the sun to be shining" and "N fears what N anticipates."

26. The term "aware" is not a verb (transitive or otherwise). While *being* aware is a cognitive state, awareness itself is not an attitude. For a comparable case, see the discussion of the term "certain" in section 3 of chapter 2.

27. Use of this expression as a synonym for 'cognitive content' is explained further in chapter 9. Use of single quotes here (and henceforth) to single out specific technical terms for mention follows standard philosophic convention and is in accord with the *Chicago Manual of Style* (Chicago: University of Chicago Press, 1993), 14th ed., 213.

Chapter 2

BELIEF, DOUBT, AND CERTAINTY

1. Belief as an Attitude of Propositional Assent

Attitudes of propositional stance were defined in chapter 1 as cognitive attitudes addressed toward propositional objects. The identifying marks of such attitudes in this particular context are (1) that they are qualified in terms of correctness and incorrectness and (2) that they typically are queried by asking "Why?" but seldom "How?" It has been taken as unproblematic from the start that belief is an attitude of this sort. Indeed, instances of belief figured among the small group of paradigms from which these identifying features were drawn initially.

In the case of these attitudes specifically, being correct amounts to being true, while incorrectness is a matter of being false. When someone exhibits belief that appears to be false, and we take it upon ourselves to press the matter, we call the belief into question by asking *why* the person holds it, suggesting that the reasons for holding it are somehow faulty. In doing so, we assume that rational agents have a stake in avoiding false beliefs generally. If someone shows a tendency in the opposite direction, this is usually interpreted as a sign of cognitive disorder.

A belief is true, of course, if it is addressed toward a true proposition. But why is this so? What is it about the relation between a belief and a proposition that qualifies the belief for a particular truth-value? And how is the truth-value of a given proposition "transposed" into a feature of an associated belief? While a full answer to these questions requires a more detailed conception of the nature of propositions and of propositional truth than will be available before the discussion of the next two chapters, a preliminary view of these complex issues will help us get the discussion under way.

The point of labeling cognitive attitudes such as belief "attitudes of propositional stance" is that in adopting such an attitude one takes a stand on the correctness of the proposition concerned. But what is it for a proposition to be correct? What does a proposition "do" that might be done incorrectly and that when done correctly makes the proposition true? As a bare minimum, a proposition provides a representation of how things might stand in the world at large. Put in the terminology of the previous chapter, a proposition represents a state of affairs. There are, of course, many views among philosophers about the relation between propositions and SOAs, and many views as well about how propositions represent. These matters will come under detailed discussion in later chapters. Whatever view of propositions and of propositional representation one is inclined to adopt, however, a bare minimum for making sense of propositional truth is that propositions somehow serve as representations. A proposition represents how things might stand in the world, in one or another of its various aspects.

Merely to represent how things *might* stand in the world, however, is not enough to qualify a proposition for a truth-value. To be either true or false, a proposition also must say something about how things *actually* stand. Although the world might be such that Camille's beach is sunny, the world also might be such that it is cloudy instead. In order for the proposition that C's beach is sunny to be either true or false, it must do more than provide a representation of that SOA. It must in addition provide an indication of whether that SOA is or is not the case. To qualify as a bearer of truth-value, that is to say, a proposition must both represent an intelligible SOA and ascribe a determinate status to what it represents. If the status it ascribes is the same as that occupied by the SOA in the actual world, then the proposition represents the world correctly; and as a consequence of representing the world correctly, the proposition is true. If the proposition ascribes a status other than that occupied by the concerned SOA in the actual world, on the other hand, its representation of the world is incorrect, and the proposition accordingly is false. In brief, a proposition represents some SOA as having a particular status, and it thereby represents (purportedly) how things actually stand in the world. If the world is such as the proposition represents it as being, then the proposition represents the world correctly. Otherwise its representation is incorrect. It is on the correctness of a proposition in its representational role that one takes a stand in adopting an attitude of propositional stance.

Now, there are several stances that one might adopt toward the correctness of a proposition in its representational role. One such stance, typified by the cognitive attitude of denial, rejects the propositional representation toward which it is directed as incorrect. If the proposition in question provides a representation that is in fact incorrect, then the denial is true, while if the representation in fact is correct, the denial is false in turn. Another stance of this general sort is typified by the attitudes of declaring and testifying. To declare that the sky is sunny, for example, is to take an affirmative stand on the matter in some rhetorically significant fashion, and one's declaration is true or false depending upon the truth-value of what one declares. Among propositional stances generally, however, perhaps the most numerous subgroup consists of those involving one or another mode of simple acceptance. These we might call "attitudes of propositional assent," typical members of which are affirming, supposing, and believing itself.

Returning now to the case of believing specifically, we see that what qualifies a given belief for truth-value is the relation of assent it incorporates regarding the correctness of its corresponding propositional representation.[1] If C believes that the beach is sunny, then the effect of that belief is to accept as correct some propositional representation of the beach's being sunny. If the beach in fact is sunny, then the representation of this being the case as a matter of fact is correct, and C's assent to this effect is correct in turn. To put it in terms of truth-values, C's belief that the beach is sunny is true just in case it constitutes assent to a proposition that the beach is sunny and this proposition in fact is true. In general, a belief is true just in case it constitutes assent to a true proposition, whereas a false belief is one assenting to a proposition that is false.

Further discussion of truth and falsehood in matters relating to propositions must be reserved for subsequent chapters. Nevertheless, we already have at least the beginnings of a workable definition of belief as a cognitive attitude of propositional stance. A belief is a stance incorporating assent (right or wrong) to its associated proposition as a correct representation of how things stand in the world. The reason this does not amount to a complete definition of belief is that there are other cognitive attitudes that meet basically the same description. Affirming and supposing are examples that have already been noted; others are thinking, presuming, and declaring. In order to distinguish belief from near neighbors like these, we will have to rely on features beyond those of propositional assent.[2]

One consideration that promises to help distinguish belief from attitudes such as affirming and declaring is that these latter are episodic, while belief can be sustained over an extended period. What I mean by calling a certain attitude "episodic" is that it typically is adopted within the confines of a particular occasion or episode, so that when its occasion is over it no longer remains current. In order for there to be a point in declaring that the sky is sunny, for example, there must be something about the circumstances in which the declaration is made to render a stand of this rhetorically distinctive sort appropriate—perhaps some uncertainty about the weather that the declaration is intended to settle. Once the occasion for taking a stand of this sort is past, however, we would normally resist saying that the person involved maintains an attitude of declaration. There are other cognitive attitudes, however, that we tend to think of as remaining current on an extended basis, often well past the occasions upon which they might have been adopted initially. Belief, of course, is a salient case in point, along with thinking, supposing, and presuming. Although C's belief that the beach was sunny on a given afternoon might have originated when she first arrived on the scene, she might continue to believe this for many days afterward. While beliefs, that is to say, might be adopted on particular occasions, they also may persist when their immediate occasion is past. Beliefs for this reason might be described as "protracted," in a sense suggesting a propensity to remain current over extended periods of time. This feature of beliefs is examined in the following section, along with the sense in which beliefs typically are dispositional.[3]

Another feature of belief that is notably absent in some of its near neighbors is that beliefs can be held with varying levels of confidence. Given N's belief that the sky is cloudy, for instance, this belief may be held firmly or with a high degree of confidence. Alternatively, N might believe, but not be certain, that the sky is cloudy, or he may be merely inclined to the opinion that this is so. On the other hand, if someone were to suppose or to presume that such-and-such is the case, we normally would not qualify the stance in question in terms of higher or lower levels of confidence. If N supposes that C is speaking sincerely in saying she hopes that the sky is sunny, it would seem odd to qualify N's supposition as either very firm or somewhat uncertain; and to speak of firm or tentative presumptions seems equally odd. The reason may be that supposing and presuming (unlike more deliberate forms of taking for granted, like assuming) are attitudes commonly adopted on a casual basis, without much concern for the consequences of being mistaken and hence without incentive to weigh the evidence in a manner producing certainty or uncertainty. The topic of degrees of confidence will be examined in section 3 below, along with other topics bearing on certainty.

Another interesting feature of belief lies in its relation to its opposite, disbelief, which is like the relation between affirming and denying. What is distinctive about this relation, of course, is that its members take opposing truth-values when directed toward the same propositional object. If it is true to affirm that the sky is cloudy, then it is false to deny the same proposition, whereas if the affirmation is false, then the denial is true. Similarly, whether one's belief that so-and-so is true or false, one's disbelief to the same effect takes the opposite truth-value. What makes this relation unusual is that it holds between members both of which are propositional attitudes in their own right, and belief and disbelief appear to be the only other such attitudes sharing this relation with affirming and denying.[4] With other propositional attitudes, however, the only way to set up a logical opposition of this sort appears to be through negation of their propositional objects: the thought that p, for instance, is true if and only if the thought that not-p is false. But this is quite different from a logical opposition between cognitive attitudes themselves, when these attitudes are taken toward the same proposition. Further discussion of such matters will be appropriate in section 4, which is concerned primarily with an examination of doubt.

The final section of the chapter considers various forms of belief that are not propositional, including *believing in* persons and institutions and what we shall call "believing sources" of information.

2.   Beliefs as Dispositions

In his early book *Perception and the Physical World,* D. M. Armstrong favors what he describes as a "dispositional analysis of belief." As he puts it (using 'p' as a variable covering propositions):

> If A believes p at time T, this does not imply that there is any physical event occurring in A at time T. All that is implied is that *in some circumstances* A will act or speak in a certain way, or think certain thoughts.[5]

In the same place, he makes a point of allowing that "the *acquiring* of a belief may itself be an event"—indeed, that it might be a conscious event. There is no difficulty, he says, "in being conscious of acquiring a belief, even if we give a dispositional analysis of the nature of belief."[6]

Now, there are some forms of belief for which a dispositional analysis seems obviously correct. Suppose someone's confidence in the *New*

York Times is so unreserved as to warrant our saying that he or she believes everything printed in that particular newspaper. What we mean in saying this is not that the person in question enters into an attitude of belief with respect to every proposition appearing in the paper, day after day and week after week. What we mean is that this person has a tendency to accept news reports encountered in that paper as basically accurate, regardless of how thoroughly the paper is read on any given day. Such a tendency is clearly dispositional, which makes it typical of the belief we reside in information sources.

The case for a dispositional analysis of propositional belief, on the other hand, is not so straightforward. Suppose that Camille checks the weather section of the morning paper and finds a forecast predicting sunny weather that day at the seashore. The forecast takes the form of a printed proposition; and insofar as C accepts the forecast at face value, she enters into an attitude of belief toward the proposition concerned. C's attitude with regard to the proposition in this instance is not one merely of tending to accept it, or of being disposed to think or act in certain ways in appropriate circumstances. Her attitude is one of outright acceptance, and one she enters into on a specific occasion. C's belief on this occasion is episodic, with no implications for its persistence over an extended period. Such beliefs, accordingly, are not dispositional. And insofar as beliefs like this are typical of propositional beliefs generally, the indication is that beliefs consisting of attitudes toward propositions do not yield routinely to a dispositional analysis.

But it is not yet clear to what extent this result conflicts with Armstrong's account. For Armstrong allowed that the acquiring of a belief might be an event—that is, that the onset of belief might be episodic. All that needs be done to accommodate our analysis thus far to Armstrong's account, it might seem, is to identify propositional beliefs that occur episodically (like that of C above) with beliefs in his sense at their point of acquisition, then to proceed with a dispositional analysis of beliefs that have already been acquired.

While this tactic is not entirely without promise, however, it is not at all clear how it would work in detail. One problem is that entertaining a belief, for Armstrong (in the text cited above), is primarily a matter of having a certain disposition, and there is no requirement that the onset of the disposition—while episodic—constitutes an episode of *belief* in itself. By way of analogy, consider the case of a heating element in an electric stove. The element has a disposition to glow when current is passed through it, and it acquired this disposition at the moment of manufacture. But the element did not glow at the moment the disposition was acquired, since there was no current passing through it at that particular moment. In like fashion, if we think of belief as primarily dispositional, this in itself is no reason to think of the disposition concerned as active at the point of acquisition. Yet when C adopts an attitude of assent toward the proposition that the afternoon will be sunny, this is something she does actively—that is, in her role as a cognitive agent. This is one reason we should resist identifying propositional belief of the sort under consideration with the onset of dispositions in Armstrong's sense.

Another problem is that Armstrong's analysis provides no insight whatsoever into how a belief relates to its propositional object. Although it is reasonably clear that he considers belief to be propositional in some sense or another (when A believes p at time T, the p that A believes presumably is a proposition), his analysis of what A's belief amounts to is conducted entirely in terms of A's disposition to think or speak in certain ways in appropriate circumstances. Whatever its merits, a shortcoming of Armstrong's account is that it pays too little attention to the role of propositions in these enduring dispositions.[7]

Armstrong's approach seems clearly right-headed in calling for a dispositional analysis of beliefs that endure over extended periods of time. But a different tactic is needed to bring out the structure of what it is that endures. The tactic adopted in the following discussion is to take belief as basically episodic by nature and then to develop an account of how the propositional attitude that it constitutes can persist over time on a dispositional basis. In what sense might a propositional attitude persist? And in what sense might its persistence be dispositional in character?[8]

The thought of a relationship persisting in dispositional form beyond its inception is not peculiar to propositional attitudes. Once a university adopts a policy of affirmative action toward a particular minority group, for another example, the attitude dictated by that policy remains in effect even when its admissions office is closed for the holidays. In like fashion, there is nothing inherently problematic about attitudes toward propositions persisting dispositionally, even during periods when there is no occasion for the disposition to be exercised. There nonetheless is a question to be faced about what this persistence might amount to in the case of such attitudes. Affirmative action involves an attitude toward a particular group of people, a group that retains its identity through the periods in which the policy is not exercised. Insofar as affirmative action is an attitude toward this identifiable group of people, there is no difficulty in thinking of the attitude as persisting in the absence of relevant activity. But in what sense might propositions be thought to retain their identity when not serving as objects of active cognitive attitudes?

To give the problem focus, we may return to C's belief that the beach will be sunny, which begins as an assent to some particular proposition comprising the forecast printed in the daily newspaper. When she arrives at the beach, the belief continues on a reinforced basis, but it now takes the form of a robust acceptance of a proposition taking the form of a representation of some sort in C's central nervous system. Then when the day is over, and C reflects on the day's experiences, she continues to believe that the beach had been sunny. And at this latter stage, the belief may have yet another object—a proposition, as it were, with a different "tense inflection," albeit still a representation in her central nervous system. In what sense might we say that her belief persists, when it is addressed in sequence toward these seemingly different propositional objects?

In order to make sense of C's cognitive circumstances, we need an account of mental representation and, in particular, an account of propositions as states of the central nervous system. The topic of representations is discussed at length in chapter 6, while that of mental representations specifically is reserved for chapter 8. What we need more immediately, however, is an account of propositions that explains how they can retain identity, despite being instantiated in different physical forms. This account is the concern of chapter 3, and it involves the application to propositions themselves of the type/token distinction familiar to most readers in connection with sentences of a natural language. For the moment, we must remain content to accept the distinction provisionally and to think of the several objects of C's belief as her day progresses as different instances pertaining to the same propositional type—that is, as different propositional occurrences representing the sky as being sunny during the time she spent at the beach.

Given that we can make tolerably good sense of what it means for a propositional attitude to persist, there is the further problem of making clear the manner in which this persistence is dispositional. In the account we have been considering, Armstrong seems to suggest that attitudes like belief are dispositions to think or speak in certain ways. But this cannot be entirely right. If believing is a different conceptual attitude from thinking, as our considerations in section 1 above have indicated, then it seems dubious to conceive of belief as a disposition to think in any particular way at all. And the same may be said of the suggestion making belief a matter of speaking, inasmuch as belief is distinct from the various speech acts (affirming, asserting, attesting, etc.) implicated in our list of propositional attitudes.

A more promising suggestion is found in a later work by Armstrong titled *The Nature of Mind*. This suggestion is introduced as an answer to the following query:

> Consider two persons, A and B, unconscious at the same time, where it is true of A that he believes that p, but false of B. Must there not be a difference between A and B at that time to contribute this difference in belief-state? What else in the world could act as a truth-maker (the ground in the world) for the different conditional statements that are true of A and B?[9]

Armstrong's response rests on an analogy between an unconscious person and a programmed computer that is not actually operating. The computer has certain items of information loaded into its operating systems, but this information has no effect while the computer remains inoperational. The belief of an unconscious person, in like fashion, is "*causally quiescent,*" where this means "not producing any *mental effect*" in the person involved.[10] Although the account is introduced to help explain what might be called "unconscious belief," Armstrong goes on to observe that belief "may remain causally quiescent in this sense even when the mind is operational"[11] — for instance, when the belief has no bearing on what the person is doing currently.

In this later account, Armstrong in effect shifts the focus of his analysis from the dispositional features of belief to the mental states that underlie these features. But the account nonetheless remains dispositional. Instead of dwelling upon what the believer is inclined to say and think, which confuses belief with attitudes of saying and thinking, his attention is now directed to the causal influence of belief within the cognitive affairs of the conscious organism. This is a step in the right direction, inasmuch as the causal aspects of belief must be rendered intelligible by any account of this sort with a chance of succeeding. But the fact remains that a belief is not identical with its causal influences, which for all we know might be shared with other mental activities. And this suggests that a dispositional analysis in terms of causal features exclusively will miss the essential features of belief specifically.

What an analysis stressing the causal consequences of belief is likely to miss is the distinctive character of the cognitive attitude that produces those consequences. In order to identify the causal features that pertain to belief specifically, as seemingly required for the completion of Armstrong's line of analysis, we would have to locate those aspects of its causal presence that are due specifically to its character as an attitude of propositional assent. Locating those features would involve empirical inquiry and is probably beyond reach by current neurophysiology. But it is not important for our own purposes that those features be identified. The point we need to note for present purposes is merely that, whatever those features might turn out to be, they are the causal features that mark the presence of sustained belief. Given that sustained belief is a disposition to *reactivate* the causal influence exercised by that particular attitude at its initial occurrence, and given that those influences flow from the distinctive character of belief as an attitude of propositional assent, it follows that the disposition involved in sustained belief is a tendency to *renew* the assent by which the belief in question was first constituted.[12]

By way of illustration, we may return to Camille's belief that the sky will be sunny during her afternoon at the beach. C's belief in the first instance involved assent to a proposition appearing in the newspaper's forecast of the afternoon's weather. This initial belief was episodic, occupying just the time required for reading the forecast. But C continued to believe that proposition as the day unfolded and as she reflected on her experience after the day had ended. This continuing belief was not episodic, since C in the interim was preoccupied with many other matters. Her continued belief, rather, was dispositional, in that she remained ready to reiterate the acceptance that marked her belief in its initial occurrence. If the state of the weather during this period were to come into question, she would have been ready to repeat without further ado the propositional assent by which her belief was initially constituted. The sense in which sustained belief is dispositional is that it involves a readiness to reinstitute, in some such fashion, the cognitive stance that characterized the belief concerned in its initial episodic form.

Belief thus remains an attitude of propositional assent, whether episodic at its inception or dispositional as it continues. But this is a feature belief shares with certain other propositional attitudes, including notably both thinking and supposing. We turn next to another distinctive feature that constitutes a difference between supposing and believing.

3.   Certainty as a Quality of Propositional Assent

There is a tendency evident in twentieth-century philosophy to think of certainty as a specific type of cognitive attitude. H. A. Pritchard, for example, maintained in his *Knowledge and Perception* that being certain of something is the same as knowing it.[13] And A. J. Ayer at one point asserted that knowing p is rightfully being sure that p is true.[14] A somewhat different tack was taken by R. M. Chisholm when he defined certainty in terms of knowing (rather than vice versa). According to Chisholm's definition, the expression "S is certain that h is true" means (i) S knows that h is true and (ii) there is no proposition more worthy of S's belief than h.[15] Thus one way of saying "I am certain," he goes on to note, is to say "I know" with emphasis.[16] The effect of this definition is to equate being certain of h with knowing h, when the latter is a result of believing h for indefeasible reasons.

Whether knowing is conceived as a matter of being certain, or being certain conceived as a matter of knowing, in either case there is an assumption that being certain is a cognitive attitude. But there are reasons for being suspicious of that assumption. One is that the term "certain" is an adjective with no verbal (verb-form) equivalent. To see why this is relevant, consider a few paradigms from our lists of cognitive attitudes (chapter 1, section 5)—the attitudes, say, of believing, knowing, and fearing. Believing is an attitude of propositional stance, belief is the state of being in that attitude,[17] and to believe is the way we enter that state. Likewise, knowing is an attitude of cognitive access, knowledge is the state of being in that attitude, and to know is how that state is entered. Again, fearing is an attitude of anticipation, fear is the state of being in that attitude, and to fear is what we do by way of entering that state. In each case, we have a way of speaking both about the attitude in question (e.g., believing) and about what it takes to enter that attitude (e.g., to believe). And in each case that way of speaking involves transitive verbal constructions (e.g., the gerund "believing," the infinitive "to believe"). The reason is that adopting a cognitive attitude is something one does, while engaging the attitude subsequently is a result of that doing. In the case of being certain, on the other hand, whatever that state might amount to (something we have yet to consider), there is no transitive verb for entering or remaining in that state ("to certain" is not a verb in English and "certaining" is not a recognizable gerund). The closest approximation is the phrase "being certain" itself, which is a gerundive form of "to be" with "certain" as a modifier. Being certain, in short, is not something we *do,* but something we *are* for reasons that often require no particular activity on our part.

Since being in a cognitive attitude is always a result of something we do (believe, know, fear, etc.), this in itself is enough to indicate that being certain is not itself a cognitive attitude. The point is secured by looking at a few straighforward reasons why being certain does not fall within any of the categories of cognitive attitudes distinguished in chapter 1. A general characteristic of attitudes of access is that a contradiction results from placing a verb designating a given such attitude in the blank of "N that so-and-so, but so-and-so may not be the case." Thus "N discovers (finds, knows, etc.) that X is the case, but X in fact may not be the case" is a sentence speaking at cross-purposes with itself, inasmuch as the object of any attitude of cognitive access is always an SOA that is the case. Since there is no contradiction in "N is certain that X is the case, but X in fact may not be the case," on the other hand, being certain (if it were an attitude at all) could not be an attitude of cognitive access.

But neither can certainty be an attitude toward a propositional object. An invariable mark of such attitudes (criterion in chapter 1) is that they are qualified in terms of correctness and incorrectness—typically in terms of truth and falsehood specifically. But application of truth-valued qualifiers of this sort to terms of certainty ("being certain," "being positive," etc.) typically fails even to make sense. Although indeed we might sensibly speak of someone's "being truly certain," for example, what this expression means has nothing to do with truth-value but is the approximate equivalent of "being genuinely certain," or "being certain without reservation." Its opposite, moreover, is something like "not really being certain"; whereas the expression "being falsely certain" lacks meaning entirely. This response to criterion I also prevents certainty from being an attitude of assessment. And the suggestion that it might be an attitude of projection lacks even initial credibility.

But if being certain is not a cognitive attitude of one of these sorts, what is it? The answer seems obvious once we consider the question carefully. Being certain is a matter of having reached a certain *level of confidence* in maintaining a propositional attitude of either assent or dissent. Let us consider a few examples to see how this works.

Among the attitudes of propositional assent identified above are affirming, assuming, agreeing, and maintaining, as well as the attitude of believing itself. Such attitudes might be held with varying degrees of confidence. Deirdre, for example, might be more or less confident in her belief that the children are still in the garden. At the highest level of confidence, we might say that she is certain (or positive, or completely sure); at lower levels she is less sure, shading off into being doubtful. She might be fully confident—that is, certain—after seeing the children actually playing there, but less confident, even doubtful, after a long period of inattention.

Among attitudes of dissent, in turn, are denying and disbelieving. If Duncan (the children's father) disbelieves what Deirdre says about the children's being in the garden, or if he comes to the point of flatly denying it, he may do so with varying degrees of conviction. If he has heard no noise from that direction within the last twenty minutes, he might tend to disbelieve that they are still in the garden; whereas if he himself has just checked and found the garden empty, he may deny with full certainty what Deirdre believes.

Certainty, in brief, is a *quality* of propositional stance, along with confidence, assurance, surety, and so forth. These qualities characterize the firmness of such attitudes as believing and disbelieving, along with other attitudes we maintain toward propositional objects. While certainty itself is not an attitude of propositional stance, it nonetheless is a feature of one or another such attitude: being certain of p is a quality of some cognitive attitude that a person adopts toward proposition p. It is to believe (assert, affirm, etc.) that proposition with a high degree of confidence, but it is not itself a mode of propositional stance. In this respect, being certain is analogous to being swift, in that being swift is a *quality* of motion (walking, running, swimming, etc.) but not itself a form of motion in which one might engage independently.

4. Doubt and Being Indubitable

To someone who finds paradox in the claim that certainty is not a cognitive attitude, the plight of doubt in this regard may be even more unsettling. There is a strain of modern epistemology, beginning with Descartes, that has been given over to the search for an indubitable basis for knowledge. And if the foundations of knowledge are to be beyond doubt, then doubt itself would seem to be an attitude of some cognitive significance. But what kind of cognitive attitude should we take it to be? It seems natural, on the one hand, to think of doubt as the opposite of belief; and belief is an attitude toward a propositional object. Does this make doubt itself a propositional attitude? If knowledge is to be founded on what is indubitable, on the other hand, then the absence of doubt would seem to be an attitude of cognitive access — that is, an attitude toward actual SOAs. And how could doubt be an attitude toward propositions if its absence constitutes an attitude toward SOAs?

The relation between knowledge and indubitability is complicated by the fact that the term "doubt" and its cognates are commonly used in quite distinct senses, which often are not distinguished in epistemological discussions. For one, there is the sense (a) generally opposed to the cognitive attitude of belief. Used in this general sense, "doubt" can serve either as a verb or as a noun. In its verbal use, it functions in contrast with "believe"—as in "N doubts (rather than believes) that so-and-so." In its use as a noun, it functions in contrast with "belief" instead, as when we say N was in a state of doubt (rather than of belief). The other sense (b) is one in which doubt stands in opposition to certainty, rather than to belief. Used in this sense, "doubt" normally functions as a noun exclusively, as in "N's posture overall was one of doubt (instead of certainty)." Purporting to use the term as a verb in *this* sense would be as unintelligible as the use of "certains" in "N certains that so-and-so." Let us look more carefully at this contrast between doubt(b) and certainty, before returning to the contrast between doubt(a) and belief.

As part of the discussion of certainty in the preceding section, such selected attitudes of propositional stance as affirming, agreeing, and believing were grouped together under the heading "attitudes of assent," and the point was made that assent can be attained at various levels of confidence. When N assents to a proposition at the highest level of confidence, we say N is certain or entirely confident; N's manner of assent is one of certainty. But assent also might be given in a manner falling short of full confidence. If Deirdre has not checked on the children lately, she may still believe they are in the garden but no longer be certain. And if she pauses to listen for their voices but does not hear them, she may begin to feel doubtful regarding their whereabouts. At some point, she may become sufficiently uncertain to step outside for a look in the garden. If the point arrives at which her confidence has eroded completely, her posture of assent will have dissolved into doubt(b). Doubt(b) and certainty are separated by a series of intermediate stages, which comprise something like a sliding scale of firmness in one's propositional assent. Certainty stands as the limit in the direction of increasing confidence, while unqualified doubt(b) marks the limit in the other direction.[18]

The relation seen here between doubt(b) and certainty is similar to the relation between being empty and being full, or more exactly (since "doubt" and "certainty" are nouns, not adjectives), to that between emptiness and repletion. Just as a container becomes more empty as it becomes less full, so a subject's cognitive attitude toward a given proposition becomes more doubtful (sense [b]) as it becomes less certain. And just as increasing fullness terminates in a container's repletion, so increasing confidence on the part of the subject terminates in a state of certainty. As emptiness, moreover, is the complete absence of contents, so doubt(b) is the evacuation of confident assent. The important thing to note, in this regard, is that doubt(b) (unqualified doubt, as distinct from a tinge of doubtfulness) is more than just the absence of certainty. It is the absence of confidence at any level whatever.

Since the confidence we have been considering in this context is a quality of our assent to propositions, the absence of confidence means an absence of propositional assent. But the mere absence of any attitude of propositional assent cannot itself be conceived as another attitude toward the proposition in question. Doubt in sense (b) is no more a propositional attitude than emptiness is another content that might be held by a container. This ties in with the fact, noted previously, that there is no verbal form of the term "doubt" when used in this sense. To be in doubt(b) is to be in a state marked by lack of confidence; and this is not something one *does,* but something that befalls one. So being in doubt, in the sense opposed to being certain, is not an attitude one adopts toward some proposition or another. It is rather the lack of a propositional attitude carrying even a modicum of confidence.[19]

For a predicative use of the term "doubt," we must turn to sense (a) of the term in which doubt is an active state opposed to belief. Let us return for a closer look at the nature of this particular opposition.

One thing to notice immediately in this regard is that the relation between doubt(a) and belief is importantly unlike that between denial and affirmation. When N denies that SOA X is the case, as noted in section 1 above, this denial has the opposite truth-value from an affirmation of the proposition that X is the case. It follows that denying a particular proposition always has the same truth-value as affirming its negative counterpart. The denial that the sun is shining, for instance, is true under exactly the same circumstances as the assertion that the sun is not shining; and when one is false, the other is likewise.

One sign that doubt and belief are not related in this manner is that someone might doubt(a) that p without being in a position at the same time to believe that not-p. We normally would expect someone denying p to be prepared to affirm not-p and, of course, vice versa. But there is middle ground between doubting p and believing its negation. For example, one might doubt(a) that Dole would make a good president, but not really believe that he would *not* do so either; one just might not know what to think, one way or the other. Another sign is that doubt(a) is not equivalent to disbelieving, which as we have seen (in section 1) *is* related to believing as denying is related to affirming. To doubt(a) is to withhold assent on a matter, but withholding assent does not amount to disbelieving. To disbelieve is to take a definite stand on a matter, and one may withhold assent while taking no stand whatever.

The clearest sign that doubting and believing are not related in the manner of denying and affirming, however, is that doubt(a) does not admit characterization in terms of truth-values. A belief takes on the same truth-value as its propositional object. Thus Deirdre believes truly that the children are in the garden just when she believes a proposition to this effect that in fact is true. But the expressions "doubting truly" and "false doubt" have no clear meaning that pertains to truth-values. Truly doubting, at best, is a matter of doubting sincerely, while the notion of "false doubt(a)" seems simply to lack intelligibility. This is not to deny that there is a relation between believing and doubting that precludes a given person's doubting and believing the same things under the same circumstances. The point of the comparison with denying and affirming is just that the manner in which believing and doubting are mutually exclusive is not one to be characterized in terms of truth-values.[20]

If the opposition between doubting and believing is not properly characterized in terms of truth-value, then how should we understand it? When it is correct to believe, it is a mistake to doubt(a); and when it is correct to doubt(a), it is a mistake to believe. This much seems unproblematic. Correctness of belief is basically a matter of believing the right propositions—propositions that in fact are true; while mistaken belief is a matter of believing false propositions. But correctness and error in doubting are importantly different. The basis of the difference is that while doubt(a) indeed is *concerned* with propositions, strictly speaking it is not a propositional attitude. It is an attitude *toward attitudes* we take toward propositions, rather than an attitude toward propositions themselves. In what sense is this so?

Belief and doubt(a), as just noted, are mutually exclusive, in that when either is in order, the other is inappropriate. But belief is not alone in relating to doubt(a) in this manner. If it is correct to doubt(a), then it is likewise incorrect to *affirm;* and if correct to affirm, then incorrect to doubt in turn. Similarly, the appropriateness of doubt(a) renders *assertion* inappropriate, whereas if assertion is in order, then doubt(a) is incorrect.[21] Such is the case as well with most of the other attitudes we have been treating as attitudes of propositional assent.

But if this relation holds between doubt(a) and individual attitudes of propositional assent, it holds between doubt(a) and such attitudes taken generally. In brief, if it is correct to doubt(a) that such-and-such is the case, it is incorrect to assent to that proposition in any matter whatever; and if it is correct to assent in any manner to a given proposition, then it is incorrect to doubt(a) the proposition in question. The relation between doubt(a) and belief is merely a specific instance of the relation between doubt(a) and propositional assent generally. To adopt an attitude of doubt(a) with respect to proposition p is actively to decline taking a stand toward p involving any form of assent. Doubt in this respect is an attitude toward a *set* of propositional attitudes, rather than an attitude primarily toward propositions themselves.[22]

While doubt(a), to be sure, is an attitude one takes *with respect to* propositions, strictly speaking it is not a propositional attitude itself. Accordingly, while it makes perfectly good sense to speak of doubting a given proposition p, the stance in question should be understood as opposed to attitudes of assent toward p generally, rather than as opposed to p itself. This presumably is the reason doubt(a) is not qualified in terms of truth and falsehood. Inasmuch as doubt(a) is not an attitude toward a proposition, it lacks an object with a truth-value that it might reflect in turn.[23]

There are other "second-order" attitudes of this sort that we commonly take toward propositional attitudes either severally or in groups and that, accordingly, are neither true nor false themselves. In *repudiating* the belief that the earth is flat, for instance, one repudiates (refuses to admit) an attitude toward the concerned proposition. But one does not repudiate the proposition itself (as if it were vying for admission), which is why one repudiates neither truly nor falsely. When one *rejects* a certain supposition or assertion, similarly, one is taking a stance toward a propositional attitude; but since the object of one's stance is not a proposition, one's rejection is neither true nor false. Again, one might take a stand against any form of propositional assent whatever, as in *disavowing* the very thought that personal freedom should be restricted. Disavowing, rejecting, and repudiating, accordingly, are "second-order" attitudes, similar in this respect to the attitudes of doubting.

Let us summarize the results of this section. When "doubt" is understood in the sense opposed to "certainty," it refers in general to a lack of confidence. To be in a state of doubt, in this sense, is not to have adopted an attitude toward a proposition. Indeed, it is not to have *adopted* an attitude toward anything at all; for being in doubt in this sense is not something one does, but rather a state one reaches or just happens to fall into. To doubt in the sense opposed to belief, on the other hand, is actively to decline adopting an attitude of propositional assent. Doubt in this latter sense, accordingly, is a cognitive attitude, but one taken toward *other* cognitive attitudes,[24] rather than toward a propositional object. One effect of doubting in either sense, we might note, is the absence in the subject of any attitude of propositional assent. But only in the latter sense—that opposed to believing, in which "doubt" functions as a verb—is this absence the result of a cognitive act (an act of doubting) undertaken by the subject.

5. Belief in Other Than Propositional Form

There are various senses of the term "belief" in which belief is an attitude—indeed, an attitude of cognitive significance—but not an attitude toward a propositional object. Although this is not the place to look at these other senses in detail, our account of propositional belief might helpfully be brought to a close by considering how it differs from belief in these other senses.

Believing Sources. Suppose that Duncan has been looking for a reliable newspaper and finally settles on the *New York Times*. Duncan finds the *Times* a credible source of information, and in cases of conflict with other sources he usually ends up believing the *Times*. Now, to believe the *Times* in this sense is not to believe a particular proposition or any set of particular propositions. There may be many propositions on its pages of which Duncan remains unaware, and there may be a few he notes now and then that he tends to disbelieve. To believe the *Times,* rather, is to consider that publication generally trustworthy—to trust it by and large as a source of information. Similarly, Duncan might believe Deirdre as a source of information about the children, as the children might believe their father when he explains the dangers of leaving the garden. To believe a publication or a person as a source of information is not itself to enter an attitude toward one or another proposition. It is to trust that source as being generally reliable. Insofar as the information it provides comes in propositional form (which it need not), we might say that believing a source is tantamount to being disposed to accept as generally credible the propositions it brings to one's attention.

When Duncan believes the *Times* as a source of information, we might note, his belief is neither true nor false. Depending upon its record for accurate reportage, he may believe the *Times* wisely, imprudently, naively, and so on. But he never believes it truly or falsely. This is the case even when its information is communicated in propositional form (as distinct from pictorial form, or the form of graphs or diagrams, for example). What he believes is a source from which true or false propositions emanate; but the source itself is not a representation of how things stand in the world, and in itself it does not possess truth-values.[25] So while belief (in the primary sense) as an attitude of propositional stance takes its truth-value from its propositional objects, belief in sources is not an attitude toward a true or false object and, hence, is not characterized itself in terms of truth-values.

Believing In (Type 1). Another variety of nonpropositional belief is indicated by the expression "believing in." Suppose that Duncan professes to believe in capitalism. What we would understand this to mean, among other things, is that he endorses the goals of the capitalist system, is sympathetic with its economic policies, and generally approves of its methods and practices. A person similarly might believe in constitutional democracy, in liberal education, or in the environmental movement. Although someone who believes in capitalism (or the environmental movement, etc.) will tend to trust the *Wall Street Journal* (or *Sierra* magazine, etc.) as a source of information, belief in an institution or cause is more than a matter of believing sources. The trust involved extends to its priorities and values, and to the policies it maintains on public issues. As is the case with belief we repose in sources of information, however, believing in causes or institutions is not something we do either truly or falsely. Duncan's belief in capitalism might be enlightened or benighted, selfishly motivated or altruistic, but it is not an attitude to be evaluated in terms of truth-values.

In the disposition of one's trust in institutions like the capitalist system, or in causes like the environmental movement, the *existence* of these institutions or causes themselves typically is not a point at issue. Although a person who thought that no such institution in fact exists normally would not claim to believe in capitalism, someone who does *not* believe in capitalism may be no less disposed to admit its existence than someone who does. In other words, to believe or not to believe in a given institution is not to take a stand on its existence. The existence of the thing is taken for granted. What is at issue is whether one should join forces with it.

Believing In (Type 2). There is another use of the expression "believing in," however, that makes the existence of the thing in which one believes the central point of the believing. To believe in ghosts, for instance, is roughly equivalent to believing the proposition that ghosts exist. If Deirdre and Duncan agree in their conception of what ghosts are supposed to be, but disagree in their beliefs about the existence of such entities, then a natural way to express their disagreement would be to say that one believes in ghosts while the other does not. To say under such circumstances that Duncan believes in ghosts would not be a report on his trust in one or another institution; it would be a report, rather, on his acceptance of the proposition that ghosts exist. To *believe in* disputed entities like ghosts (or flying saucers, or intelligent beings on other planets), in other words, is a state of mind that often tends toward *propositional* belief. Such belief accordingly might be characterized in terms of truth-values, as when someone says that Duncan's belief in ghosts is most probably false.

Believing In (Mixed Type). On the one hand are "believings in" (e.g., believing in capitalism) that focus the subject's trust in a cause or institution. On the other are "believings in" (e.g., believing in ghosts) that tend to shade into propositional attitudes (e.g., believing the proposition that ghosts exist). If all "believings in" of this latter sort could be unambiguously resolved into propositional attitudes, there would be little point in retaining them as a distinct type of believing. As becomes apparent upon reflection, however, there is a range of interesting cases that fall somewhere between believing in institutions and straightforward belief of a propositional nature. What appears to be typical of these cases is that the question of existence tends to be bound up with the subject's trust in some particular practice or institution.

Consider, as a relatively unproblematic example, the matter of believing in Santa Claus. Most of us grow up with the story of this colorful person who brings holiday gifts to deserving children, and many of us in our early years probably believe that he actually exists. By the time we have reached responsible adulthood, however, we are firmly convinced that the whole story is fictional. Yet it is not uncommon to hear responsible adults—newspaper columnists, for example—unabashedly professing belief in Santa's existence. What we usually find in reading further, of course, is that Santa Claus is being treated as a symbol for the spirit of generosity (or suchlike) that prevails during the holidays at the end of the year. Whereas belief in Santa Claus on the part of kindergarten children (like belief in ghosts) is often equivalent to belief that this person exists, an adult expressing belief in these terms is likely to be thinking of the customs and practices that the person of Santa has come to symbolize. Santa Claus does "exist" for these adult expositors, to be sure, but what counts as his existence is inextricably bound up with the institutions of goodwill and gift giving that they want to encourage during the holiday season. Other symbolic figures in which people express similar belief are Cinderella, Peter Pan, and Smokey Bear. Belief in figures of this sort, while more than a matter merely of supporting the public attitudes or institutions with which they are bound up, seems to contain a larger "portion," as it were, of belief *in* the attitudes or institutions involved than of propositional belief *that* these figures exist.

Another kind of intermediate case in which believing in institutions is intermingled with propositional belief is the belief in God fostered by the institutions involved. Let us again take Duncan for our example, assuming him to be a faithful member of the Church of Scotland who sincerely professes to believe in God. In assuming that Duncan believes in God, we assume he believes the proposition that God exists. At the very least, we would consider it extraordinary (although not inconceivable)[26] for him not to acknowledge the existence of what he believes in. But Duncan's belief that God exists remains closely bound up with his belief in God generally, which in turn is bound up with the religious teaching of the particular church to which he belongs. For the God Duncan believes in is the God of the Church of Scotland, not a god of the (ancient) Roman pantheon or the God of Islam. And to the extent that his belief has a propositional object, the content of the proposition that he believes reflects the doctrine of the Church of Scotland on God's nature and existence.

Along with Duncan's belief in God, that is to say, goes his belief in the Church of Scotland. And this institution provides the conception of divine existence that gives focus to his belief that God exists. Duncan's belief in God is thus an amalgam of his belief in the Church of Scotland (more specifically, in the teachings of that institution) and of his assent to a proposition affirming the existence of God (more specifically, of the Supreme Being worshiped within that community).

In the case of responsible persons who believe in Santa Claus, we tend to exempt these beliefs from evaluation in terms of truth-values, whereas in the case of persons who responsibly believe in God, we tend to think of these beliefs as either true or false. What accounts for the difference? While belief in Santa Claus typically includes elements of belief in institutions and of propositional belief alike, as already noted, belief of the former sort tends to dominate. Since belief in institutions is not characterized in terms of truth-values, neither is a hybrid belief comprising belief in institutions primarily. In thinking about the significance of religious belief, on the other hand, we tend to give precedence to its propositional content, notably to beliefs ascribing existence to the divinities involved. Since propositional belief is characterized in terms of truth and falsehood, so too typically is belief in God. Inasmuch as such belief contains an admixture of belief in institutions, however, the contribution of the institutions involved should not be overlooked in assessing its truth-value. Duncan's belief in God is true just in case the God identified by the teachings of the Church of Scotland in fact exists; otherwise, that belief is false.

Notes

1. As pointed out in Paul Moser's *Knowledge and Evidence* (Cambridge: Cambridge University Press, 1989), 15, the assent involved in belief might be either conscious or unconscious. Assent would likely be unconscious in the case of beliefs sustained over time, or in the case of dispositional beliefs generally (for which, see section 2 below).

2. The analytic procedure followed here is closely akin to Plato's method of collection and division (illustrated most perspicuously in the *Sophist*), the two stages of which concern the identification of necessary and sufficient conditions, respectively. A necessary condition for being an attitude of belief, I am suggesting, is that the attitude in question incorporate propositional assent as explained above. But this is not sufficient for being such an attitude, inasmuch as attitudes other than belief incorporate propositional assent as well. From this point to the end of the section, the analysis is directed toward the identification of features that distinguish belief from other attitudes of propositional assent. Whether or not this "division" is fully successful, the procedure will at least help specify the manner of belief to be contrasted with knowledge in chapter 5.

3. The distinction here between episodic and protracted attitudes overlaps Gilbert Ryle's distinction in *The Concept of Mind* (New York: Barnes & Noble, 1949) between occurrences and dispositions. The overlap is not exact, however, inasmuch as not all protracted attitudes are dispositional. An example is presuming, which is an attitude one occupies more or less continuously, rather than a (dispositional) liability "to be in a particular state" when a particular condition is realized (see Ryle's definition, p. 43).

4. A possible exception is the attitude of asserting, which in certain contexts is equivalent to affirming and hence itself is related in this way to denying.

5. D. M. Armstrong, *Perception and the Physical World* (London: Routledge & Kegan Paul, 1961), 121, author's emphasis.

6. *Perception and the Physical World*, 122, author's emphasis.

7. To Armstong's credit, it may be noted that in his later work of the 1960s he professes to "have been unable to work out an account of the nature of belief in the concrete detail that would be desirable" (*A Materialist Theory of the Mind*

[London: Routledge & Kegan Paul, 1968], 339). Among the details in question, presumably, are those pertaining to the propositional character of belief.

8. To readers familiar with Stephen Stich's heroic *From Folk Psychology to Cognitive Science: The Case Against Belief* (Cambridge, Mass.: MIT Press, 1983), the present account in some respects may appear passé. While there will be occasion to draw upon some of Stich's insights as the discussion progresses, to keep the record straight I should say that at this point I am concerned neither to explicate the "theory" implicit in "folk psychology" (I do not think there is any such theory) nor to take sides on the various conceptions of belief found in contemporary cognitive science (which I find generally unconvincing). The data on which the present account relies come primarily from the observations about the nature of belief developed above in section 1, concerning the accuracy of which the critical reader already will have developed at least a provisional opinion. Technical issues in cognitive science will come to the fore in chapters 8 and 9.

9. D. M. Armstrong, *The Nature of Mind and Other Essays* (Ithaca, N.Y.: Cornell University Press, 1981), 56–57.

10. *The Nature of Mind,* 57, author's emphasis.

11. *The Nature of Mind,* 57–58.

12. Moser considers a belief to be "dispositional in the sense that if one is in a belief state with respect to the proposition, P, then one will assent to P in any circumstances where one sincerely and understandingly answers the question whether it is the case that P" (*Knowledge and Evidence,* 16). The characterization of dispositional belief above differs from Moser's primarily in not limiting the circumstances of renewed assent to responses to questions about the truth-status of the propositions involved.

13. H. A. Pritchard, *Knowledge and Perception* (Oxford: Clarendon Press, 1950), 96.

14. A. J. Ayer, *The Problem of Knowledge* (London: Macmillan, 1956), 34.

15. R. M. Chisholm, *Perceiving: A Philosophical Study* (Ithaca, N.Y.: Cornell University Press, 1957), 19.

16. *Perceiving,* 21.

17. While there appears to be a ready distinction between a cognitive attitude and the state of being in that attitude, there is no intention here to mark that distinction by exclusive use of gerundive (e.g., "believing") and nominal (e.g., "belief") expressions. The expressions "attitude of belief" and "attitude of believing" seem equally felicitous, as do "state of belief" and "state of believing." See note 6, chapter 1, in this regard.

18. Doubt is typically qualified as slight, moderate, strong, and so on. Unqualified doubt may be thought of as a complete lack of confidence.

19. Needless to say, one does not come to be in a state of doubt(b) regarding a proposition *merely* by failing to adopt an attitude of assent toward it. If so, one would be in doubt regarding propositions one never happens to con-

sider. Being in doubt(b) is a state one occupies with regard to propositions that are candidates for assent, which means propositions under consideration for acceptance or rejection.

20. Doubting so-and-so might be correct under certain circumstances and incorrect under others. Thus doubting meets criterion I (in chapter 1), namely, that the attitude in question admit assessment in terms of correctness and incorrectness. The crucial point is that doubting does not meet this criterion *in the manner* of believing and of propositional attitudes generally. A mark of propositional attitudes as a class is that they all take on truth-values in one way or another reflecting the truth-values of the propositions toward which they are addressed. It follows that attitudes that do not take truth-values are not attitudes addressed toward propositions. More will be said on this topic in the text below.

21. We should note that the converse does not always hold. Its being incorrect to doubt(a) does not make assertion appropriate (there are many things it is incorrect to doubt—e.g., that one knows one's own name—that it would be odd to assert save in certain specific circumstances), and the inappropriateness of assertion is not enough to make doubt(a) appropriate (for similar reasons). The same may be said for the other attitudes currently under discussion. While the appropriateness of doubt(a) makes any one of them inappropriate and vice versa, none of them is related to doubt(a) in such a fashion that the inappropriateness of doubt(a) makes *it* appropriate, or vice versa.

22. A point made in the previous note is that no individual attitude of propositional assent is related to doubt in such a fashion that the inappropriateness of doubt makes it appropriate, or vice versa. What *is* related to doubt(a) in this fashion is the *class* of attitudes of assent taken as disjunctive alternatives. Since in doubting one declines to adopt an attitude of assent toward the proposition in question, if it is inappropriate to doubt(a) (inappropriate thus to decline), then it is appropriate to adopt some attitude within that general class; and if it is inappropriate to adopt any attitude within that class, it is appropriate to doubt(a).

23. A propositional attitude reflects the truth-value of its propositional object, as already noted, in the manner that believing a true proposition is true, disbelieving a true proposition is false, and so forth.

24. Attitudes *toward* cognitive attitudes constitute yet another class of cognitive attitude beyond those examined in chapter 1. Attitudes of this further sort are characterized by the same responses to the two criteria as are attitudes of projection. The difference between them, of course, is that attitudes of projection take eventualities as objects, while these further attitudes are directed toward other cognitive attitudes themselves.

25. If a purported source of information (like a checkout-stand tabloid) is characteristically unreliable, we might call it "false" in the sense of not being genuinely what it purports to be. But not being itself a representation of how things stand in the world, the source itself cannot be false in the sense pertaining to propositions.

26. Santayana, we are told, believed in God, but withheld assent to the proposition that God exists. See D. C. Williams, "Of Essence and Existence and Santayana," in *Animal Faith and Spiritual Life,* John Lachs, ed. (New York: Appleton-Century-Crofts, 1967). An analogous case might be believing in pure democracy as a form of government, while conceding that no pure democracy has ever existed.

Chapter 3

PROPOSITIONS

1. The "Queerness" of Propositions as Artifacts of Logical Theory

When not speaking in the more or less technical idioms of philosophy, there is little we say by use of the term "proposition" that could not be said with terms like "statement" or "proposal" instead. Presumably it was this nontechnical employment of "proposition" that Wittgenstein had in mind when he had one voice in the *Philosophical Investigations* say "A proposition is the most ordinary thing in the world."[1] And undoubtedly it was the philosopher's use that prompted the other voice's response: "A proposition—that's something very queer!" Wittgenstein was speaking in his own voice, however, when he went on to remark, "And the latter is unable simply to look and see how propositions really work."

My intent in this chapter is to follow Wittgenstein's lead and to articulate a view of propositions that responds to the way they "work" in nontechnical cognitive contexts. The primary requirements to be met by this view are (1) that it provide a credible account of how propositions might stand as objects of cognitive attitudes like asserting and believing, and (2) that it make clear how propositions are capable of bearing truth-values. Before setting about this project, however, it may be helpful—as a cautionary measure—to review some of the theoretical pressures that lead to the development of "queer" technical conceptions of propositions like those Wittgenstein was talking about.

At the end of the section quoted above, Wittgenstein remarks that "a misunderstanding of the logic of language . . . makes it look to us as if a proposition *did* something queer,"[2] and goes on to muse, in the following section, that, "[h]ere we have in germ the subliming of our whole account of logic."[3] As this observation suggests, the technical conception of what propositions "do" is by and large an artifact of logical theory. It all began with the theory of demonstration in Aristotle's *Organon,* where a proposition (*protasis*) is defined as an affirmation or negation that is either true or false,[4] and an account of inference is given according to which true conclusions can be secured by correct inference from true premises. Although Aristotle's canons of inference have been expanded, and in several respects superseded, by the work of logicians during the intervening centuries, most logical theorists today remain content with the concept of the proposition as a bearer of truth-values. Some, for various reasons, prefer statements[5] in this role, and some hold the line at sentences instead.[6] But as far as rules of inference go, the effect is essentially the same. There is nothing queer, at any rate, about propositions admitting truth-values, and the requirement that they should be able to do so intelligibly has been adopted as a guideline for the present undertaking.

The point at which propositions begin to appear "queer" from the vantage point of the *Philosophical Investigations,* presumably, is when they no longer are conceived merely as *vehicles* of inference, but become entities in their own right *about which* the logician can make inferences as well. For a simple example, it seems innocuous enough to infer *from* the fact (1) that one can validly deduce the conclusion (C) "Socrates is mortal" from the premises (A) "All men are mortal" and (B) "Socrates is a man" *to* the consequence (2) that propositions (A) and (B) together *entail* proposition (C). But the inference from (1) to (2) is far from trivial. Deduction is something *we* do with the help of propositions; but entailing is something propositions do—seemingly all by themselves. Propositions now begin to appear as if they *do* something rather puzzling—something that seemingly requires logical theory to make intelligible.

The degree of queerness is advanced a notch or two with the theorist's attempt to explain *how* propositions are able to entail other propositions.[7] For (A) and (B) to entail (C) is for it to be the case that, if (A) and (B) are true, then necessarily (C) is true as well. For (A) and (B) to be true is for the world to be such that all men are mortal *and* that Socrates is a man, and for (C) to be true, in turn, is for the world to be such that Socrates is mortal. For propositions (A) and (B) to entail proposition (C), accordingly, is for the world to be such that, if (a) all men are mortal and (b), Socrates is a man, then necessarily (c) Socrates is mortal. But (a), (b), and (c) look like states of affairs— things that might be the case in the actual world. So now entailment among propositions apparently begins to involve certain relationships among SOAs as well. Corresponding to the entailment relating (A) and (B) with (C), that is to say, there seems to be another relation connecting (a) and (b) with (c)—a relation that involves some sort of necessity. If SOAs (a) and (b) are the case, then as a consequence SOA (c) *necessarily* is also the case. And, like it or not, there is something "queer" about this relation of necessary consequentiality. It is something above and beyond the (nonmodal) relation of cause to effect by which events are related in the physical order. It is a relation that seems to hold in a *meta*physical order—an order to which one gains access not by observation, but by philosophical theory.

The natural extension of this line of theoretical extrapolation is the notion that there are aspects of the world that elude ordinary perceptual observation but that might be discovered through the powers of logical inference. Although sometimes observation might catch up with inference (the suspect confesses, as it were, after being found out by the detective), in other cases the discovery is the work of inference alone. The proposition somehow has become a "mirror" of its own sector of reality—a reflective device that can be manipulated, in combination with other "mirrors" in its general vicinity, to produce an image that shows features of the world we could not have known otherwise. The proposition by this point has become a special kind of entity (abstract, eternal, possessing a "life of its own"), with distinct properties (notably, its logical connections) that reveal how things stand in the actual world. At the limit, we find talk about propositions in possible worlds, which by their truth-values fix the identity of the worlds paired with them.[8]

By this time, the proposition has become a very queer entity indeed. Here, in spectral outline, is an elusive body of theory that grows out of the "germ" in which "the subliming of our whole account of logic" is at first contained. The "germ," as Wittgenstein goes on to elaborate, is the "tendency to assume a pure intermediary between the propositional *signs* and the facts."[9] By 'propositional signs', Wittgenstein means individual (token) sentences like "Socrates is a man" and "Socrates is mortal," while the associated facts are SOAs like Socrates actually being a man, and so forth. Propositional signs of this sort are the symbolic expressions that serve as vehicles for inferences *we* make from premises to conclusions, while the facts in question are the SOAs responsible for the truth-values that attach to these expressions. The "pure intermediary" inserted between the two by logical theory, on the other hand, is the abstract propositional entity with "a life of its own," which we—through "a misunderstanding of the logic of language"—come to think of as having those extraordinary powers of extending the probes of rational inference into realms beyond the reach of the keenest observation. The kind of queerness that goes along with this conception of the "pure propositional intermediary," one may agree with Wittgenstein, is something better to be avoided by any plausible account of how propositions figure in our day-by-day cognitive affairs. This is a further requirement for the account developed below.

2. The Misconception of Propositions as Interlinguistic Meanings

So much by way of a brief survey of certain dangers inherent in trying to reach a coherent conception of propositions through the contrivances of logical theory. There is another source of queerness we should look at, however, before undertaking a positive account of propositions that avoids these dangers. This has to do with the putative relation between propositions and meanings.[10]

One way of bringing out this putative relation is the following. Consider the printed words "snow is white." These words constitute an instance of a common English sentence form that is understood (according to the view under discussion) as an expression of the proposition that snow is white. A second instance of that sentence form, which is typographically identical to the one indicated by quotation marks above, occurs as the last three words of the immediately preceding sentence. In the first case, the words are surrounded by quotes to indicate that the sentence-instance they comprise is being mentioned only and is not being used as part of any broader linguistic act. In the second case, by contrast (according to this view), the sentence-instance is not itself being mentioned, but instead is being used as a linguistic expression of the proposition in question. The conventional parlance for distinguishing instances like these from the sentence forms they instantiate is to refer to the instances as sentence- "tokens" and to what they instantiate as sentence- "types." Other tokens of the same English sentence-type (that instantiated by the word sequence "snow is white") include other type-written, handwritten, and spoken instances of those particular English words in that particular order.

When a sentence-token is being mentioned, as in the first instance above, whatever meaning it might have is beside the point. Strictly speaking, it carries no meaning at all, inasmuch as the meanings of linguistic expressions are engaged only when the expressions are being used. When a sentence-token actually is being used, however, it carries the same meaning as any other token of the same sentence-type would carry if used in the same context. Moreover (the view continues), there are likely to be other sentence-types whose tokens might carry identically the same meaning in the same context of use. For example, both "snow is white" and "white is the color of snow" betoken sentence-types whose instances are commonly used to express the proposition that snow is white. In light of the fact that tokens of these different sentence-types can be used to convey the same meanings, it is considered useful to have a comprehensive term under which the sentence-types can be grouped indifferently. One term that commonly serves this purpose is "statement." The sentence-types betokened respectively by "snow is white" and "white is the color of snow," it is said accordingly, both are types of the same English statement: the English statement to the effect that snow is white.

The final step in this ascent toward generality comes with the observation that there are statements in other languages—for example, those betokened by "*der Schnee ist weiss*" and "*le neige est blanche*"—that carry the same meaning as the English statement that snow is white. This shared meaning then is identified as a proposition. Another way of making the same point, for those who advocate this approach to propositions, is to say that the tokens "snow is white," "*der Schnee ist weiss*," and "*le neige est blanche*," all express the same proposition: the proposition that snow is white. The proposition, in short, is invoked as the basis of meaning-equivalence among sentence-tokens from different languages, secured through the mediation of sentence-types and statements in order of increasing generality. Conceived in this fashion, propositions are reached as the result of several stages of abstraction. There is the abstraction, first, from different tokens to the same sentence-type, next the abstraction from different sentence-types to the same general statement, and finally the abstraction from different statements to the same propositional meaning.[11]

One of the more straightforward objections raised against this approach to propositions by way of progressive abstraction is that it amounts to defining the obscure (propositions) in terms of the no less obscure (meanings).[12] A more telling objection to similar effect, for present purposes, is that the existence of propositions seems far more secure than the existence of abstract entities identifiable as meanings shared by locutions in diverse natural languages. Suppose that Beatrice is instructing a group of kindergarten children in the use of color terms and finds occasion to assert that snow is white. Given that an assertion comprises an attitude of propositional stance, what B asserts on that occasion is a proposition; and her assertion is accomplished by articulating a vocal equivalent of the words "snow is white" under appropriate locutionary circumstances. Whatever account one might choose to give of how exactly B's words relate to the proposition in question, here is a clear-cut case of a speech act engaging a proposition. Propositions thus conceived most surely exist, no less certainly than the language in which assertions are formulated. If we start thinking of propositions as interlinguistic meanings, however, their very existence becomes problematic. Quite apart from theoretical problems regarding the association of other persons' verbal reports with the stimulus events that occasioned them,[13] there is the brute fact common among practicing translators that some word sequences convey meanings that resist accurate expression in alternative languages.[14] At the very least, we ought to resist any theoretical gloss that would require propositions to be expressible in more than one language. Not only might there be propositions that resist translation between languages; it is even conceivable that at some stage in the development of mass media all cognitive agents come to speak the same language. In either case, we would have propositions that cannot be identified with meanings in fact shared by different natural languages. The clear lesson, in view of such possibilities, is that propositions should not be thought of as interlinguistic meanings.

The only unproblematic feature of propositions encountered thus far in the discussion is that propositions are capable of sustaining truth-values. There is nothing about this feature in itself that carries with it an ability to "mirror" aspects of the world that are beyond observation, and nothing about this feature, in turn, that becomes more intelligible with the notion of propositions as abstract meanings. The queerness that attaches to propositions as a result of theoretical attributions like these can be avoided, as will appear in due course, without compromising the capacity of propositions to be characterized in terms of truth and falsehood. We consider in the next section what is required for propositions to admit truth-values.

3.   Propositions as Bearers of Truth-Value

In the *Tractatus,* Wittgenstein gives two distinct descriptions of the "general form of a proposition" (in Nos. 4.5 and 6), which characterize propositions in quite different ways. The characterization of No. 6 shows, in a single formalism,[15] how all compound propositions can be got from elementary propositions by successive applications of a single binary operator. Inasmuch as elementary propositions themselves are covered by the symbolism of 6 as a limiting case, this formal characterization gives the "general form of a proposition"—any proposition—in its *logical relation* to other propositions. But 6 says nothing about the form propositions must exhibit to *be* propositions in the first place. This latter is the business of the informal characterization at 4.5, which gives as the "general form of a proposition," *es verhält sich so und so*. In effect, this characterization identifies two components that must be present in any genuine proposition. One component (expressed *"so und so"*—"such-and-such"—in Wittgenstein's formulation) represents an SOA, while the other (expressed *"es verhält sich"*—"it is the case that") ascribes a status to what is represented. The first component identifies an SOA, and the second says whether or not that SOA is the case.

Now quite apart from the technical merits of treating propositions in the manner of the *Tractatus,* it seems natural to ask why Wittgenstein characterized propositions as comprising these two distinct components. This question is particularly relevant in view of the fact that there is a very common (informal) conception of propositions—one might even label it the "standard" conception—according to which the general form of a proposition is more like 'x is F', where 'x' stands for some object or another and 'F' stands for some property being attributed to that object. Examples of propositions in this standard form are provided by locutions (in appropriate contexts of use) like "snow is white," "grass is green," "the cat is on the mat," and so forth. What is notable about these locutions in comparison with 4.5 of the *Tractatus,* however, is that they do not exhibit the two distinct components called for by Wittgenstein's characterization. At least they do not exhibit these two components as explicitly distinct. In "snow is white," for example, the SOA in question is snow's being white, and the status apparently ascribed to that SOA is that of being so or being the case. But while (i) representing an SOA and (ii) ascribing status to the SOA represented obviously are functions of quite different sorts, the components accomplishing these functions are not distinguished in the three-word locution "snow is white." The best to be made of it, apparently, is that the middle term ("is") does double duty, in one respect serving as part of the predicate ("is white") and in another serving to indicate being the case ("*is* [white]"). Does this mean that the locution "snow is white" is not a genuine proposition, according to the norm provided by the *Tractatus*? Is there a conflict between the general form characterized at 4.5 and the standard form exemplified by "snow is white"?

Despite having labeled this the "standard" propositional form, I confess to having no idea where to find it spelled out in the kind of detail that would be required for answering these questions. But the general drift presumably would go as follows. The locution "snow is white," because of its affirmative (i.e., positive) copula, expresses the proposition that it *is* the case that snow is white, whereas if the copula were negative, as in "snow is not white," a proposition to the opposite effect would be expressed, saying that it is *not* the case that snow is white. With regard to the copula "is" doing double duty, as it were, one can think of the mere *absence* of a negative adverb in the predicate as establishing the affirmative cast of the proposition overall. Construed in this manner, the standard form seems to correlate tolerably well with the format of *Tractatus* 4.5, to the extent at least that any appearance of conflict dissipates.

But there are problems with the standard form when construed in this manner. One is that a locution like "snow is white" might commonly be used in such a fashion as not to express a proposition at all. Consider the case in which a grade-school pupil is assigned 100 inscriptions of "snow is white" as part of a penmanship exercise, or that in which an English teacher writes "snow is white" on the board merely as an illustration of a grammatical sentence. In neither case would the inscription be employed as an expression of a proposition. One does not employ such a locution as a propositional expression just as a matter of course if one does not choose to do so, and these seem to be clear cases in which the choice to do so is missing. Another case in point arises with the propositional expression "it is the case that snow is white" itself, in which the business of status-ascription is clearly handled by the first four terms of the expression and, hence (since the expression seems not to be redundant), appears to have nothing to do with the use of the last three terms themselves. The lesson to be learned from such cases is that a locution like "snow is white" does not *automatically* say that the SOA it normally represents (snow's being white) is the case. Whether it says this or not depends upon context of use (including conversational circumstances, user's intentions, etc.). And it would be preferable to have a propositional notation at hand that would allow a proposition to be identified on the basis of its internal structure alone, something the standard form obviously does not provide.

A more serious problem for this common view of propositions is that adverbs such as "not" commonly serve in different roles that are not always distinguishable in terms of syntax. A given occurrence of "not," in addition to (i) ascribing negative status to an SOA ("snow is not white" parsed as "it is not the case that snow is white"), might have the effect of (ii) indicating a "negative SOA" to which positive status is being ascribed ("snow is not white" parsed as "it is the case that snow is not white"), of (iii) negating a proposition that is positive itself ("snow is not white" parsed as not-p, when p is "it is the case that snow is white"), and even of (iv) expressing an attitude of denial ("snow is not white," uttered by a particular person, by way of saying, "I deny that it is the case that snow is white"). Although these various uses obviously are closely connected, the *speech act* (iv) of denying a proposition is not the same as the *logical operation* (iii) of negating one, and neither is it the same as *ascribing status* (positive, as with [ii], or negative, as with [i]) to an SOA. The reason the status-ascripting role of (ii) and (i) *must* be different from the roles of denying and of negating, in (iv) and (iii) respectively, is that these latter two roles involve operations on fully formed propositions, but that a status-ascription is required to constitute a proposition in the first place. The roles of "not" in (i) and (ii), in other words, contribute to the formulation of the propositions in question, while its roles in (iii) and (iv) apply to propositions that have already been formulated. Another reason for dissatisfaction with the standard form of propositions is that it lacks the flexibility to make the distinctions among these roles notationally apparent.

Why is a status-ascription required for the formulation of a full-fledged proposition? For a proposition to be true or false, it must say something about how things stand in the world.[16] And for a proposition to say something about how things stand in the world, it must indicate (identify, isolate, pick out) a distinguishable SOA. One requirement a proposition obviously must meet in order to take on a truth-value, in other words, is that it succeed in representing an SOA. But why is it necessary for a proposition also to ascribe a *status* to the SOA it represents, in addition merely to succeed in representing it? To put the question another way, why is a representation of an SOA not enough by itself to constitute a well-formulated proposition?

An SOA might be represented by a drawing or a photograph, as well as by an expression like "snow's being white." Let us consider the question in connection with a pictorial representation.[17] Imagine Monet in the process of painting a grainstack, when it suddenly catches fire and burns to the ground. Undaunted, Monet finishes the painting and hangs it by a window in a house near where it was painted, as a representation of what once could be seen through the window. The picture represents the presence of a grainstack in a field not far from Giverny, but does nothing to ascribe a status to the SOA represented. It represents the SOA of a grainstack's being present, but remains silent on whether or not that SOA is the case. The picture as such is not falsified by the grainstack's burning, nor is it true as long as the stack of grain is present. No matter how things stand with the grainstack, the picture is neither true nor false. It lacks truth-value because it makes no claims about how things stand in the world.

To ascribe status to the circumstances depicted in the painting would require symbolism beyond that involved in the depiction of the circumstances themselves—for instance, a label reading *"comme ça,"* or "such is the case," or a star or asterisk with equivalent meaning. Recognizing the effect of such symbolism, moreover, we would have to acknowledge symbols to the opposite effect as well, such as a label reading "things are not as hereby pictured," or the notable absence of a star or asterisk. With the label *"comme ça"* affixed, the painting would represent as being the case the SOA of a grainstack's being present in this field near Giverny. Unorthodox as it may be in form, the picture-cum-label would constitute a proposition to the effect that a grainstack is present in that vicinity. The picture-cum-label would be true if the grainstack is actually present, and would be falsified in turn by the burning of the grainstack. But the picture by itself is nonpropositional, since it says nothing about the status of the SOA it represents.[18]

The reason a proposition must contain an ascription of status, in addition to a representation of an SOA, is that a representation, taken by itself, provides no indication of how things stand in the world. If a representation meets certain requirements of coherence and distinctness, it could in appropriate circumstances be viewed as a characterization of what *might* (but also *might not*) be the case.[19] But as long as a representation fails to provide an indication of how the world *is* (or *is not*), there is nothing about the world as it is that could make the representation either true or false. It follows from this that for a proposition to admit truth-values it must contain these two distinct components: (1) a representation of an SOA, and (2) an indication of the status that SOA occupies given the world as it is.[20]

4. A Regimented Notation for Propositions

The primary source of the difficulties with the standard conception of propositional form discussed in the section above is that it relies largely upon context for an indication of status. If a pupil is observed inscribing one after another instance of "snow is white" on a piece of notebook paper, it would normally be assumed that he or she is not engaged in multiple assertions of the proposition that snow is white. When a college lecturer illustrates a logical point with reference to the sentence "the cat is on the mat," those listening or watching would normally assume that no claim is being made about the relative positions of a particular cat and a particular mat. On the other hand, when the pupil addresses the words "I'm through now" to the teacher, or when the lecturer observes in so many words that a cat's being on a mat is not the same as a mat's being on a cat, we assume that the locution in question is intended by the pupil or the lecturer to be understood as a proposition about how things actually stand in the world. Leaving the status-ascribing aspect of the proposition implicit in this manner seems to work by and large in most conventional contexts.

As the difficulties discussed above indicate, however, in undertaking a reflective examination of the roles propositions play in human discourse, it is desirable to have a way of formulating propositions that makes the two components entirely explicit. One way of managing this is to employ notationally distinct expressions for each of the components. In place of the customary "snow is white" as an expression of the proposition that snow is white, for instance, we might write instead "it is the case that snow is white," intending the final three words of the sequence to serve only as a representation of an SOA and relying upon the first four words explicitly as an indication of the status being assigned that SOA. Another device that might be used for this purpose is that of italicizing (or otherwise emphasizing) terms used to ascribe status in standard propositional expressions. Thus one might write "snow *is* white," for example, if one's intention were to use this written locution as an expression of the proposition that snow is white. (One consequence would be that if a pupil wrote the locution 100 times with emphasis in place—underlining the "is" in each inscription—then we would be entitled to interpret the results as 100 assertions that snow is white.)

For reasons of generality, however, as well as general tidiness, it seems better to adopt a notational format that accommodates nonverbal as well as linguistic representations of SOAs and that allows flexibility in the devices by which status is ascribed to them. The format to be adopted for present purposes is that of a representation (. . .) followed by a status-ascription (__), placed within a matrix ([. . . /__]) to distinguish their respective functions. An illustration is [snow being white/is the case][21] which in appropriate circumstances might serve as an instance of the proposition that snow is white. Another illustration would be comprised by Monet's painting (perhaps miniaturized in reproduction) in the first blank and "*comme ça*" in the second.

It should go without saying that there is nothing sacrosanct about this particular notational format. There will be contexts, moreover, wherein we shall want to speak of propositions the components of which probably cannot be exhibited in spatial formats of any sort whatever. A case in point is that of propositional representations sustained in thought as objects of beliefs that never receive linguistic formulation. Even allowing that mental representations are neuronal structures of some sort or another in the upper reaches of the central nervous system, as many philosophers today maintain, there is no perspicuous way in which such structures could be exhibited as part of the notational device proposed above. (The topic of mental representation receives further discussion in chapter 8.)

For the present, it is enough to emphasize that what is required of a proposition is only that it contain both (1) a component representing an SOA and (2) a component ascribing status to the SOA represented, not that these components can be fit into one or another notational format. The advantage of the regimented format proposed above is only that it exhibits these components in a perspicuous manner. Before this advantage becomes fully available, however, the format will have to be extended to allow reference to propositions on a more general level. The first step in this direction is to establish a distinction between proposition-tokens and proposition-types.

5.   Proposition-Tokens and Proposition-Types

The requirement that a proposition both (1) represent an SOA and (2) ascribe status to the SOA represented provides further insight into why a proposition is not something to be arrived at by a series of abstractions from sentence-tokens to sentence-types to statements, and so on. Consider a particular token instance of a sentence representing the SOA of snow's being white. Either that token also contains a component ascribing status to the SOA in question or it does not. If the token contains a status-ascription, then it is already a proposition, and further abstraction adds nothing to its character as such. On the other hand, if the token does not contain a status-ascription, then the sentence-type abstracted from it will lack a status-ascription as well, and so will the statement abstracted from the sentence-type, and so forth. In this case, the highest-level abstraction—the meaning (if such there be) shared by statements in different languages—itself will lack a status-ascription and hence cannot qualify as a proposition. As far as the goal of clarifying the nature of propositions is concerned, we see once again that the path of abstraction from sentence-token to sentence-type, and so on, is nothing more than a dead end.

To reject the approach to propositions by way of the distinction between sentence-tokens and sentence-types, however, is not to reject the type/token distinction itself. Indeed, the distinction is one we shall need to retain in order to make sense of the fact that different people are often able to adopt attitudes toward one and the same proposition. Suppose that Beatrice asserts that snow is white by audibly articulating (vocal equivalents of) the words "it is the case that snow is white" and that Camille subsequently articulates words to the same effect. The actual words articulated by B incorporate both (1) a representation of an SOA (i.e., the last three terms of the sequence) and (2) an ascription of status to that SOA (i.e., the first four terms). Hence the words actually articulated by B constitute a proposition—the proposition she asserts in the speech act in question. The words actually articulated by C, in like fashion, constitute a proposition that she asserts in turn. But the words actually spoken by C are not identical (being spoken in a different voice by a different person) with the words actually spoken by B. So in one sense, B and C assert different propositions. Adopting the type/token distinction for application to propositions, we may say that the two persons articulate different token propositions. But there is another sense, clear enough in itself, in which the two persons both assert the same proposition—the proposition, namely, that snow is white. The proposition that B and C assert in common is the proposition-type of which their individual locutions are different instances. By the very act of asserting her respective proposition-token, each person also asserts a proposition-type.[22] It is with regard to the proposition considered as a type, in brief, that we can sensibly say that B and C both assert the proposition that snow is white.

The main task of the present section is to develop an intelligible and generally accessible account of the relation between a proposition-type and its token instances. Part of the account will be familiar to anyone acquainted with the distinction between sentence-types and their respective tokens. One important aspect of the distinction for our purposes is that, whereas a token proposition is in an unproblematic sense *concrete,* its corresponding type is invariably *abstract.*[23] A token proposition is concrete in the sense of being both individual and physical—a series of marks on paper, a sequence of vocally produced sounds, a pattern of neuronal activity in the cortex, or whatever. Speaking of a proposition-type as abstract, however, is far from unproblematic and engages a conversation about the nature of universals that goes back at least as far as Aristotle. To forestall distractions from this direction, it may be helpful to say that the sense of the present view of proposition-types as abstract is close to the sense in which philosophers of language have spoken of sentence-types as abstract all along. Proposition-types, that is to say, are merely classes of their token instances.

While classes are often considered to be among the least problematic of abstract entities,[24] however, the proposal to think of proposition-types as classes leaves a number of issues in need of discussion. Most crucial among these, perhaps, is the question of how such classes receive their identity. The identity of a class is fixed by the criteria by which its membership is identified. The identity of the class of sentence-tokens typographically identical to *"der Schnee ist weiss,"* for instance, is given by the unique typographical form of the sentences in question. In the case of proposition-types, however, straightforward lexico-syntactic criteria of this sort are not available. The reason is that a given proposition-type is to include among its membership all equivalent token propositions, regardless of their language, grammar, or mode of expression (vocal, written, printed, etc.). The proposition-type that snow is white, for example, includes among its members the English tokens "it is the case that snow is white" and [snow being white/is the case], as well as the German token *"Er ist der Fall dass Schnee weiss ist,"* and any number of other locutions in any language available. What do tokens as diverse as these have in common that identifies them as members of the same class of propositions?

Part of the answer is that they have the same logical quality (affirmative or negative) and are the same in level of structural complexity.[25] Given *sameness* of quality and structural level, however, for a given token proposition to be a member of the proposition-type that snow is white, it is both necessary and sufficient that it be rendered true under indentically the same circumstances as [snow being white/is the case] (alternatively, as [*dass Schnee weiss ist/ist der Fall*], etc.). To locate a given token proposition within this class, that is to say, it suffices to identify it as a proposition that is true in this set of circumstances.[26]

The proposition-type that snow is white, accordingly, has identity as the class all members of which are qualitatively and structurally similar and are true under the same conditions as a given (arbitrarily selected) token instance. In general, a proposition-type is a class of qualitatively and structurally similar token propositions that share identical truth-conditions. While further discussion is needed before this conception of truth-conditions as applied to token propositions can be made sufficiently precise,[27] the source of the identity of proposition-types is clearly indicated. The deciding factor in the identity of a proposition-type is the truth-conditions of its token instances.

There are other matters that require discussion before we can rest comfortably with the type/token distinction in application to propositions. Before returning to these matters, however, let us see how the notation provided in the section above might be extended to proposition-types.

6. The Notation Extended to Proposition-Types

Proposition-types are abstract entities, in contrast with their tokens which are always concrete. Inasmuch as abstract entities cannot be entered into physical spaces, this indicates that the regimented notational format introduced in section 4 above requires adjustment to accommodate proposition-types. The provisions of this format, we remember, call for a concrete representation of an SOA to be followed by a status-ascription, from which it is separated by a slash or stroke, and for the result to be inserted within a pair of brackets to distinguish the proposition from the surrounding text. As a reproduction of the illustration offered previously, [snow being white/is the case] is a token instance of the proposition-type that snow is white. The intention is that this entire expression, brackets included, be taken as one regimented instance (among many unregimented instances) of the type in question. The token proposition resulting is exhibited by being placed on the printed page.[28] How might this format be extended to permit the exhibition of proposition-types as well?

What we need is an expanded notation that applies to proposition-types unambiguously, in contrast to their token instances, and that clearly identifies the type in question. One step toward this end is to make available a notational device that enables us to symbolize collectively all representations of a given SOA. Among the countless symbolic expressions provided by language, there is a certain group the members of which serve unequivocally as representations of the SOA of snow's being white. Included in this group are "white's being the color of snow," "snow's being white," and the last three words of "it is the case that snow is white." Other members of this group might not be so easy to identify. And there is always the question to be faced of how one is to tell whether one or another symbolic expression represents a given SOA or not. Pending further discussion (in chapter 6) of the relationship between SOAs and their symbolic representations, however, it is enough for the moment to observe that the ultimate source of authority in these matters is the practice of competent users of the representations in question. If the community of competent users of a pair of expressions agree that the expressions are descriptively equivalent, then in fact they serve to represent the same SOA. Otherwise, either the expressions are not equivalent in this respect, or there are ambiguities to be worked through before they find a stable use in the community.

Taking for granted for the moment that we can refer intelligibly to the group of all representations, in whatever symbol-system, of the SOA that snow is white, let us now adopt a specific device for symbolizing the membership of this group collectively. The device is that simply of affixing an asterisk to any particular representation of the SOA in question.[29] One example is '*snow's being white', another, '*dass Schnee weiss ist'.[30]

The next step toward a notational format specifically adapted for the expression of proposition-types is to work this asterisk device into the regimented notational format previously applied to token propositions. The result is an expression consisting of a token proposition immediately preceded by an asterisk, intended to be understood as standing for the group of all token propositions comprising an equivalent representation of the SOA in question, and accompanied by an equivalent status-ascription.[31] An example is '*[snow being white/is the case]', to be understood as standing in for the group of all token propositions representing snow's being white as being the case. Another example, standing in for the same group of token propositions, is '*[dass Schnee weiss ist/ist der Fall]'. Both should be considered available as standardized names for the proposition-type that snow is white.

Just as '*snow being white' is not a name for "snow being white,"[32] so '*[snow being white/is the case]' is not a name for [snow being white/is the case]. To the contrary, it is a name for all token instances, taken collectively, of the proposition-type that snow is white, which is the same as being a name for that proposition-type itself.

It should also be noted that the formulation '*[snow being white/is the case]' is not itself a token instance of the proposition-type it represents. Indeed, that formulation itself is not a proposition at all, being rather a *symbol* for a proposition-type. Hence, unlike the token proposition [snow being white/is the case], the token notation '*[snow being white/is the case]' itself is incapable of bearing a truth-value.[33] Since formulations of the latter sort symbolize proposition-types, however, and since proposition-types have truth-values, it is correct to say that *[snow being white/is the case] (i.e., that proposition-type) is either true or false. The meaning of attributing truth and falsehood to token propositions and to proposition-types is discussed in the following chapter.

7. Use and Mention

Since we shall have occasion both to employ ("use") and to refer to ("mention") notations of both sorts above, conventions should be established to help indicate when they are being used and when merely mentioned. And since formulations like [snow being white/is the case] and '*[snow being white/is the case]' function quite differently on the printed page (the former but not the latter, for example, being either true or false), different conventions will be needed for the two sorts of propositional expression in question.

It is interesting to note, by way of preliminary, that proposition-types (as distinct from their notations) are not things of a kind that normally should be considered available for *use* at all. The way people use propositions is by asserting them, denying them, believing them, and the like. And when someone asserts or denies a proposition, there is always some token instance to serve as immediate object of the assertion or denial. One cannot assert that the sun is shining, for instance, by relying upon the proposition-type alone. Proposition-types by themselves, *apart* from their instances, are not accessible as objects of our propositional attitudes. To say this is not to say, of course, that there is no sense in which proposition-types can relate to attitudes like asserting and believing. If there were no sense in which M and N could assert the proposition-type that the sun is shining, then there would be no way in which they could both assert the same proposition, since under normal circumstances M and N would not both be in a position to assert identically the same token instance. The point, rather, is that any assertion (denial, affirmation, etc.) of a proposition-type comes *by way of* an assertion (denial, etc.) of a corresponding token proposition. The way M and N both assert the proposition that the sun is shining is for each to assert an appropriate token instance, the effect of which is for both to assert the same proposition-type. In a closely analogous fashion, the way in which both M and N might drive the same car is for each to drive a different instance of the same model type. It makes no more sense to speak of *using* a proposition-type, just by itself apart from its token instances, than it does to speak of driving the class of Model T Fords, taken apart from concrete instances of that type of automobile.

As far as *mentioning* a proposition-type is concerned, on the other hand, we already have a device for that purpose. The expression '*[snow being white/is the case]' (or an equivalent notation) has been introduced specifically as a symbol for, or name of, the proposition-type that snow is white. In order to refer to, or mention, that proposition-type, it is enough to employ that expression in some appropriate fashion. So the distinction between use and mention in connection with proposition-types has already been accommodated. Proposition-types, as such, are never "used," but may be mentioned by use of expressions like '*[snow being white/is the case]'. All that remains in this regard is the distinction between using and mentioning such expressions themselves. And for this particular purpose, the familiar device of single quotes suffices. When the name for a proposition-type occurs in a text without additional symbolism, the expression is being used to refer to the proposition-type in question. When it occurs in a text flanked on either side by single quotation marks, however, the entire configuration (including the quotes) is being used to mention the name itself.[34]

An entirely different set of provisions is needed for token propositions. Unlike proposition-types, the token instances of these types can be both used and mentioned. One typical use of token propositions in discourse at large is to serve as immediate objects of propositional attitudes. The understanding in this regard that will be observed in this study, however, is that token propositions in the regimented format developed above will never be used in this fashion. When the discussion calls for communicating an attitude toward a particular proposition (in effect, using the proposition as object of that attitude), that proposition will always be expressed in terms of unregimented locutions of natural language. When a regimented proposition-token appears in the text, accordingly, the understanding should be that the token has been entered there for purposes other than incorporation in the expression of a propositional attitude.

Turning now to the matter of mention, we find various devices already available for referring to token propositions. One is simply an explicit manner of phrasing. If I should say something like, "the first proposition in my copy of the *Tractatus* is poorly printed," I clearly would be referring to the token proposition with which the text of my particular copy begins, since only tokens (and never types) are ever printed in any manner whatever. Other devices for mentioning token propositions include arbitrarily assigned labels (letters, numbers, etc.). Yet another would be provided by an extension of the use of single quotation marks in the manner indicated above for mentioning the names of proposition-types. With the understanding that token propositions in regimented form will never be used in the actual expression of propositional attitudes, however, devices like that of single quotes become unnecessary. Whenever there is occasion to refer to a particular token proposition, in the context of the present discussion at least, this can be managed through the expedient simply of exhibiting that token in the physical text. When physically inserted in the actual text, the regimented proposition is enabled to "show itself" like any other depiction. There is no more need to put quotes around the token in order to make comments about it than there is to do the same with a painting or photograph.

For purposes of the present discussion, in summary, proposition-types will be referred to (mentioned) by use of specifically formulated expressions like '*[snow being white/is the case]*', while token propositions in regimented form will be allowed, as it were, to "show" themselves by their physical presence in the text. With regard to the employment (use) of type and token propositions, in turn, it is enough to observe, on the one hand, that proposition-types are simply not the sorts of things that can be used and, on the other, that any use of token propositions in this discussion will be limited to propositional expressions in unregimented form.

There is one more matter of symbolism to be discussed before leaving the topic of propositional notation. From time to time it will prove convenient to be able to talk about both proposition-types and token propositions in a more general fashion than made available by the formats of regimentation provided above. One way of generalizing these formats is the following. Let 'X' and 'Y' (and other tokens of capital letters from the end of the alphabet) serve as variables ranging over SOAs. This means they are to be replaced by token representations of

SOAs, like "snow being white" and "the gate being shut." Let token instances of "yes," in turn, stand in for positive status-ascriptions generally ("is the case," "*ist der Fall*," "*comme ça*," "is so," "obtains," etc.), and let "no" do the same for negative status-ascriptions ("is not the case," "does not obtain," etc.). The expression [X/yes] thus illustrates the form of affirmative token propositions generally, while that of negative token propositions is illustrated by [X/no].

A further degree of generalization can be achieved by adopting 's' as a variable for affirmative and negative status-ascriptions indifferently. The result is the general format for proposition tokens [X/s] consisting of two variables plus punctuation, in which 's' stands for a determinate status-ascription (being the case, not being the case) and 'X' is a variable replaceable by representations of SOAs. The corresponding form for names of proposition-types, in turn, is that of '*[X/s]'. As replacement of the variables in [X/s] by a representation of an SOA and a determinate status-ascription respectively yields a particular token proposition (e.g., [snow being white/yes]), so replacement of the variables in '*[X/s]' yields a particular name of a proposition-type (e.g., '*[snow being white/yes]').

A noteworthy consequence of adopting these notational conventions is that the result of substituting for the variables in:

*[X/s] is true if and only if X has the status s

not only is well formed, but also is such that the two occurrences of either variable ('X' or 's') admit replacement in just the same manner. The biconditional thus admits meaningful generalization by quantification. The importance of this will become apparent when we turn to the task of formulating a general definition of truth and falsehood in the following chapter.

8.   The Ontological Status of Proposition-Types

The proposal that proposition-types be conceived as classes of their corresponding tokens engages various disputed issues about the status of classes. While there is no reason to think that this proposal will contribute much toward their resolution, a brief discussion of how it stands on these issues will help flesh out the view of propositions in question.

One position on the status of classes is that "classes have their membership essentially," which means that a class cannot have "a different membership from what it does have."[35] Are the classes constituting proposition-types such that the identity of a specific type depends upon the particular token instances that happen to be included in it? In other words, does a proposition-type change identity with a change in membership?

Now, there are some classes, to be sure, whose very identity seems to depend upon their particular members. An example is the class of a given person's grandparents. The class of N's grandparents includes both sets of parents of N's father and mother—no more and no less than those four people. If a single person is replaced in (or removed from) this group, it no longer comprises the class of N's grandparents. And if other persons are added (say, N's parents), then the group comes to comprise another class instead (say, N's ancestors through two generations). But there clearly are other classes, which seem no less common, such that their membership might alter without change in class identity. A case in point is the class of N's descendants, which retains its identity generation after generation, as N's sons and daughters have sons and daughters, and so on indefinitely. The intent of the proposal that we think of proposition-types as classes of their token instances is that we should think of these types as classes of the latter sort exclusively. Surely the proposition-type that snow is white does not change identity each time someone issues a new token of that proposition.

Like the class of N's descendants, a proposition-type retains its identity as its membership becomes augmented by additional token instances. And like the class of N's descendants as well, the identity of such a type remains unchanged when all of its members pass out of existence. If each and every instance of Caesar's famous proposition that all Gaul is divided into three parts should lapse from currency—all printed tokens destroyed and none currently being spoken—the corresponding proposition-type retains identity from the truth-conditions of its currently lapsed membership. Proposition-types do not pop in and out of existence with the comings and goings of their particular tokens. Once the identity of a proposition-type has been established, it constitutes a class available for future membership.

A further question is whether a proposition-type might conceivably exist that has *never* been exemplified by concrete tokens. Do proposition-types, that is to say, have independent status, or does their being what they are depend upon their either having or *having had* individual instances?

The answer to this question comes in three stages. First is to endorse the principle that no two things are indistinguishable. According to one familiar version (Leibniz' principle of the "Identity of Indiscernibles"), if x and y are indistinguishable, then they are not two things but one thing only. If x and y are to count as two distinct entities, there must be some feature enabling them to be independently identified. Each must have its own identifying feature.

A corollary of this principle is that every *single* thing that exists must have an identifying feature. In each case, the identifying feature is the feature marking the thing in question for what it is and distinguishing it from other things of similar character. A condition of the conceivability of any putative entity thus is that it be distinct in identity from other things that exist. From this, it follows that nothing conceivably exists that lacks an identifying feature.

The second stage of the answer brings to bear the concluding observation of section 5 above, to the effect that the identity of a proposition-type is determined by the truth-conditions of its token instances. In the case of a putative proposition-type that has never been instantiated by a concrete token, there are no truth-conditions to establish its identity. The consequence is that a putative type totally lacking in concrete membership thereby lacks an identifying feature, from which it follows that the proposition-type in question cannot be conceived to exist.

One objection to the argument at this stage is to call into question the apparent assumption that the truth-conditions by which a proposition-type is identified depend upon the existence of a concrete token instance. If the identity of such a type might be established by the truth-conditions of tokens that once existed but are no longer current, as granted above, why could it not be established as well by the truth-conditions of tokens that do not exist but conceivably might exist in the future? What more is needed for type identity, that is to say, than a specification of the conditions under which its members *would* be true, regardless of whether or when these members exist?

The third and final stage of our argument in progress comes with a response to this objection. In general terms, the response is that there is no way of specifying the truth-conditions that identify a proposition-type without employing a token instance. To attribute truth-conditions to the proposition that snow is white, for example, one must engage a token of that very proposition, as in '*[snow is white/is the case] is true if and only if it is the case that snow is white'.

To see clearly the reason why this is so, we have only to put the point in terms of the device for referring to (mentioning) proposition-types provided in section 7 above. According to the provisions of this device, proposition-types are mentioned by use of an expression consisting of an asterisk prefixed to a token of the type in question. The expression '*[snow being white/yes]', for example, is a designation available for use in referring to the proposition-type that snow is white. While another token of this type would serve as well in this role, *some* such token must be at hand in order to achieve reference to that proposition-type. Thus it is that a token of a proposition-type must be available in order to attribute truth-conditions to the type in question.

This completes our argument to the effect that proposition-types depend for what they are upon the (present or past) existence of concrete instances. The main stages of this argument, by way of recapitulation, are to show (1) that for a thing to exist requires its having an identifying feature, (2) that the identifying feature of a given proposition-type is given by the truth-conditions of its token instances, and (3) that the truth-conditions of a given type cannot be established without the involvement of at least one such instance. The upshot is that proposition-types do not enjoy an independent status, but have existence only conditionally upon the sometime existence of their token instances.

One consequence of the present view of propositions, accordingly, is that they do not have the "eternal" status historically associated with Platonic Forms.[36] Another consequence is that one cannot intelligibly quantify over propositions that have never been instantiated.[37] While for some philosophers these consequences might count as detrimental, for others with more modest metaphysical agendas they might come as an indication of the basic sobriety of the present treatment of propositions.

Notes

1. L. Wittgenstein, *Philosophical Investigations,* G. E. M. Anscombe, trans. (New York: Macmillan, 1953), 93.
2. *Philosophical Investigations,* 93 (author's emphasis).
3. *Philosophical Investigations,* 94.
4. *Prior Analytics* 24a12ff.; *De Interpretatione* 18a28–29. Plato, interestingly enough, did not have a *theory* of logic, nor did he have a technical term corresponding to our "proposition." The term *logos* which "true" and "false" are said to qualify at *Sophist* 263B is better translated as "statement," or better yet, simply "saying."
5. For example, P. Strawson, *Introduction to Logical Theory* (London: Methuen, 1952).
6. For example, W. V. O. Quine, *Word and Object* (Cambridge, Mass.: MIT Press, 1960), for instance, sec. 40.

7. It should be understood, of course, that this exposition of increasing "degrees of queerness" is not intended to be historical and that different logical theorists might have different ideas than those sketched here about how these "queer" properties of propositions ought to be described and/or explained. The purpose of this exposition is only to provide some sense of what one might want to avoid in attempting to arrive at a conception of propositions in which "nothing out of the ordinary is involved" (Wittgenstein, *Philosophical Investigations,* 94).

8. By way of example, consider Plantinga's notion of a "book" as "a maximal set of propositions—one that is possible and that, for any proposition q, contains either q or its denial not-q." "A book, clearly enough," he continues, "is a superproposition; and a possible world is just some value of F for some book," where F is a function "from superpropositions to states of affairs." See A. Plantinga, "World and Essence," in *Universals and Particulars: Readings in Ontology,* M. Loux, ed. (Notre Dame, Ind.: University of Notre Dame Press, 1976), 356.

9. Wittgenstein, *Philosophical Investigations,* 94; author's emphasis. As any student of the *Tractatus* knows full well, Wittgenstein himself fell prey to this "germ" in working out the elaborate theory of propositions to which the bulk of that little volume is devoted. One sign of this is the general form of a proposition exhibited in No. 6 ($[\bar{p}, \bar{\xi}, N(\bar{\xi})]$). The initial term '$\bar{p}$' of this expression represents the set of all elementary propositions. The middle term, '$\bar{\xi}$' represents an arbitrarily selected constituent of a series of sets of propositions, beginning with $\bar{p}$, each constituent of which is constructed by application of the operator N to all members taken pairwise of the immediately preceding set. And the third term '$N(\bar{\xi})$' represents the application of that operator with respect to $\bar{\xi}$, N being the binary operator symbolized in '(FFFT) (p,q)' in 5.101 (more recently known as "Sheffer's dagger"). In referring to this expression as the "general form of a proposition," Wittgenstein goes on to say in 6.001, he means to say "just that every proposition is a result of successive applications to elementary propositions of the operation $N(\bar{\xi})$."

One problem with thinking of propositions in the manner indicated by 6, considerations of queerness aside, is that it makes all propositions dependent for their distinctive character upon elementary propositions and suggests that elementary propositions (despite 4.24) can never be expressed as part of any working symbol-system. The reason is that elementary propositions are composed of "simple signs" (3.201), which are names of the simple objects (2.02) comprising atomic states of affairs. Since these simple objects are not perceptible (2.0232), and since they cannot be individuated by language (being *presupposed* by meaningful language, according to the *Tractatus,* they cannot be linguistically described [4.121]), there is no way in which names picking them out individually could be introduced into a working language. The upshot is that all propositions are functions of entities that can be grasped by inference alone (by a line of reasoning sketched all too briefly in 2.021–2.0212), and can never be exhibited as part of any usable set of symbols. It is no wonder Wittgenstein had become distrustful of this conception of propositions by the time of the *Philosophical Investigations*.

The reader may note that, while it is customary to refer to the numbered passages of the *Tractatus* by number alone, where appropriate the abbreviation "No." might be added to the referring expression (following Wittgenstein's own use in *Philosophical Investigations*, 97).

10. Frege, for example, held that the sense, or meaning, of a sentence is the proposition (which he called a "thought") it expresses. For a translation of Frege's article elaborating this and related views about the sense and reference of sentences, see "The Thought: A Logical Inquiry," A. M. and Marcelle Quinton, trans., *Mind*, 65 (1956): 289–311. The view that propositions are meanings has been criticized by various philosophers, most forcefully, perhaps, by Quine (see, e.g., section 42 of *Word and Object*). The presentation of this view in the present text is not intended to be historical and does not include a survey either of the main advocates of the view or of the major criticisms raised against it. For a more complete exposition of this view, the reader may wish to refer to Susan Haack's *Philosophy of Logics* (Cambridge: Cambridge University Press, 1978), 75–78.

11. If one has misgivings about shared interlinguistic meanings of this sort—say for reasons having to do with indeterminacy of translation (see Quine, *Word and Object*, sec. 16)—then the existence of propositions (thus conceived) is called into question.

12. This complaint is raised by A. C. Grayling in *An Introduction to Philosophical Logic* (Brighton, Sussex: Harvester Press, 1982), 36–38.

13. For an early statement of problems associated with so-called indeterminancy of translation, see Quine's *Word and Object*, 72–79. A critical review of Quine's views in this regard is contained in Michael Dummet's "The Significance of Quine's Indeterminacy Thesis," in *Truth and Other Enigmas* (Cambridge, Mass.: Harvard University Press, 1978), 375–419.

14. Even such a commonplace locution as "snow is white" might encounter difficulty in this regard. The language of the Inuit peoples of the Arctic, for instance, contains over thirty words with different meanings roughly corresponding to the single word "snow" in English, leaving it up in the air how to translate what we as English-speakers have in mind in articulating the proposition that snow is white.

15. See the last paragraph of note 9 above.

16. My concern in this chapter and beyond is with propositions that are true or false on the basis of how things stand in the world, which excludes propositions (e.g., of the form "all A is A") that are true or false on the basis of form alone. For a discussion of so-called analytic propositions, see chapter 7.

17. In the *Tractatus*, as is well known, Wittgenstein considered all propositions to be "pictures" of reality (4.01), depicting SOAs by virtue of their shared "logical forms" (2.18). But the "pictures" Wittgenstein had in mind

seem not to have been pictures in the sense of drawings and photographs. They were, instead, "logical pictures" (2.181) capable of representing both "positive" and "negative facts" (2.06, 2.201), which is to say that they were pictures with what I am calling "status-ascriptions" already built in.

18. Things may appear otherwise when the picture is a photograph, under the assumption that only what is the case can be captured on photographic film. Consider a photograph of Franklin Roosevelt bundled up in a wheelchair. Should this count as a proposition that FDR was handicapped? Does the picture by itself possess a truth-value, true if he was crippled and false if he was not? But now think of a frame from a fictional movie, in which an actor playing President Roosevelt is portrayed in similar circumstances. As representations, the two pictures might be indistinguishable, containing no signs of their differing origins. Is the latter photograph a proposition, to the same effect as the first? Clearly not, for there is no reason on the face of it why we should not think of it as part of a photographic "nonhistory" of things that never happened in the lives of recently prominent Americans, along with pictures of George Bush shaking hands with Saddam Hussein and of Woody Allen standing next to Adolf Hitler. Indeed, in the absence of background information, there is no reason why we should not think this of the former photograph as well. The mere fact that an SOA is depicted on film, in short, is not by itself an indication that this SOA is the case. Photographs are no different from other pictures in not ascribing status to what they represent. The upshot is that photographs, like other pictures, do not by themselves constitute propositions.

19. Requirements to be met by a representation capable of identifying an SOA are discussed in chapter 6.

20. The status-ascription required as part of any well-formed proposition is not just another version of the vertical stroke (the so-called judgment stroke) in Frege's *Begriffsschrift*, which was intended to express an *assertion* of the judgment expressed by the system of symbols that follows it. Devices similar to Frege's were used by Russell and Whitehead in *Principia Mathematica*, and by C. I. Lewis in *An Analysis of Knowledge and Valuation*, as well as by others. But insofar as asserting a proposition is quite a different matter from assigning status to an SOA (something necessary for formulating a proposition in the first place), none of these devices corresponds to the second essential component of a proposition identified above.

21. For general notational convenience, the possessive form before the gerund (as in "snow's being white") will be dropped in this format.

22. This is not to say that the act of asserting a proposition-type is a different speech act from that of asserting the corresponding token. The sense, rather, is that one asserts the type *by* asserting the token, in much the manner in which one sings the "Star-Spangled Banner" by singing the notes actually voiced on the occasion of doing so.

23. A conception of propositions as by nature abstract goes hand in hand with the view that propositions are asserted by the utterance of sentence-tokens. See Grayling, *An Introduction to Philosophical Logic*, 25–26, for one

expression of this conception. It also is an obvious consequence of views that appeal to propositions to explain meaning-equivalence between sentences or statements in different languages—that is, as Fodor puts it, views that call upon propositions to "neutralize the lexico-syntactic differences between various ways of saying the same thing" (*Representations,* 201). While retaining the conception of proposition-types as abstract, the present view differs from these in giving individual propositional utterances the status of (token) propositions themselves, rather than that merely of speech acts (e.g., sentences) by which propositions are expressed.

24. Not all philosophers would agree. See, for example, the misgivings expressed in Quine's *Word and Object,* 266–270.

25. The affirmative proposition [snow not being white/is the case] and the negative proposition [snow being white/is not the case] have the same truth-conditions but should not be considered tokens of the same proposition-type. The same may be said for [snow being white/is the case] and the higher-level proposition that [snow being white/is the case] is true. The conception of different levels of proposition is developed in chapter 4.

26. Quine's indictment of propositions as lacking a clear principle of individuation is well known. (See, e.g., Quine's *Word and Object,* 206–209; and his *Ontological Relativity and Other Essays* [New York: Columbia University Press, 1969], 21–22.) While the conception of propositions impugned by Quine is quite different from that being developed here—and in fact is a conception criticized in section 2 above—the author of this indictment could not be expected to applaud a definition of proposition-type in terms of the truth-conditions of its token instances that has nothing specific to say about how these truth-conditions are to be identified. Without willfully taking issue with my former teacher, I admit that I do not share Quine's compunctions in this regard. The conception of the class of all persons in Boston who have violated a civil law makes adequately clear sense even though we are not able to say precisely (in a manner applying to all cases) how membership in that class is to be determined. And so, I submit, does the class of all token propositions true under a given set of truth-making circumstances. The nature of these circumstances is discussed below (chapters 4, 6, and 7).

A criticism of Quine's dealings with the issue of propositional identity may be found in Paul Moser's "Types, Tokens, and Propositions: Quine's Alternative to Propositions," *Philosophy and Phenomenological Research* 44, no. 3 (March 1984), 361–375.

27. The topic of truth-conditions generally is addressed in the following chapter. Special problems arise in connection with the propositions associated with analytic statements, which are sometimes conceived as being true unconditionally. Discussion of such propositions and their corresponding truth-conditions is reserved for chapter 7.

28. This is why the token in question does not require additional notational devices to indicate "mention" as distinct from "use." The use/mention distinction is discussed in section 7 below.

29. This device derives from Sellars's "dot quotes," but differs in that (i) it applies to representations of SOAs rather than to nouns, (ii) it precedes these representations rather than surrounding them (relying on context to indicate the other terminus), and (iii) it produces expressions for collections of representations rather than for their members individually. A clear discussion of Sellars's quotation technique can be found in Michael Loux's chapter "Ontology" in *The Synoptic Vision: Essays in the Philosophy of Wilfred Sellars,* C. F. Delaney, Michael Loux, Gary Gutting, and W. David Solomon, eds. (Notre Dame, Ind.: University of Notre Dame Press, 1977).

30. It should be noted that the asterisk does not function here in the manner of single quotes, to form a name of the expression to which it is affixed. The expression '*snow's being white' (i.e., the expression within those single quotes) is not a name for "snow's being white."

31. This notational device, in effect, results from extending the asterisk convention from representations of SOAs proper to entire propositions. An alternative notation, retaining application to SOAs proper, would locate the asterisk within the brackets—as in '[*snow being white/is the case]'. But this alternative seems intuitively inapt, inasmuch as classes of representations (as symbolized by '*snow being white'), strictly speaking, neither are nor are not the case.

32. See note 30 above.

33. The use of single quotes to mention the notation in question is crucial for the sense of this sentence. Conventions for the use and mention of such expressions are discussed immediately below.

34. This convention has been observed in the preceding discussion of expressions naming proposition-types.

35. Nicholas Wolterstorff, in his *On Universals* (Chicago: University of Chicago Press, 1970), maintains that of "every class it is true that it is impossible that it should have or should have had a different membership from that which it does in fact have" (177), a claim he summarizes by saying that "classes have their membership essentially" (178). Although there are some classes that fit this very restrictive definition, there are others that clearly do not, as exemplified in the discussion following.

36. It does not follow that the present view is "antirealist" with respect to propositions. Propositions, by this view, most assuredly have real existence, primarily as concrete tokens and derivatively as abstract types. Given this view, however, the only way to secure "eternal" status for propositions would be to stipulate that God (or some other supercognitive agent) employs a symbol-system in which features of the world and the status they occupy are represented in the form of "timeless" propositions. While this option remains available, not all philosophers would consider that preserving an eternal status for propositions is worth the cost.

37. For one philosophic project involving quantifying over such propositions, consider Robert Adams's notion of a "world-story" as a "maximal consistent set of propositions," which is a set comprising one of "every pair of mutually con-

tradictory propositions," such that it is possible for all its members to be true together (Robert M. Adams, "Theories of Actuality," *Nous* 8 (1974): 211–231; reprinted in *The Possible and the Actual,* Michael J. Loux, ed. [Ithaca, N.Y.: Cornell University Press, 1979], see 204). The intention behind the quantifier "every," presumably, is to bring into account not only propositions that at some time or another in the actual world's temporal passage have actually been formulated in token instances, but also indefinitely many other propositions that "might have been" so formulated but never were. The consequence above is that there are no such other propositions. Whether this result should be judged severe depends upon how happy one should be with "maximal consistent sets" limited in membership to propositions that at one time or another have actually been formulated in token form.

Chapter 4

TRUTH

1. An Aristotelian Definition of Truth

A basic requirement for any plausible account of propositions is that it should make clear what it is about propositions that enables them to serve as bearers of truth-values. It was in view of this requirement that propositions were characterized in the preceding chapter as comprising two distinct components: (i) a component picking out or representing an SOA and (ii) a component ascribing a specific status (being the case or not being the case) to the SOA represented. A proposition, accordingly, is not just a representation of an SOA, but more fully is a representation of an SOA *as* having a certain status.

The intuitive idea of truth that goes along with this characterization of propositions is that a proposition's being true amounts to nothing more nor less than its providing a correct indication of the status occupied by the SOA concerned. For example, the token proposition [snow being white/is the case] represents as being the case the SOA of snow's being white. If the world is such that this SOA in fact is the case, then the proposition provides a correct representation and, accordingly, is a true proposition. If the world is such that this SOA in fact is not the case, on the other hand, then the proposition is false.

This, in a nutshell, is what it means to call a proposition true and what it means in turn to call a proposition false. To say that a proposition is true is to say that the SOA it represents actually has the status it is represented as having.[1] And to say that the proposition is false is to say that the SOA fails to have the status indicated. The main task of the present chapter is to make these definitions precise and to render them in entirely general terms. Ancillary to this task will be that of showing how the present account relates to other conceptions of propositional truth, with particular attention to Alfred Tarski's semantic conception of truth

89

and the problem of self-referential paradox by which it was motivated, as well as to the so-called redundancy theory of truth championed by F. P. Ramsey and others. The chapter concludes with an attempt to relate the concept of truth as it attaches to propositions to other senses of truth that often figure in philosophic discussion.

Aristotle was basically right, I believe, in his dictum at *Metaphysics* 1011b26–27 (literally translated): to say of what is that it is not, or of what is not that it is, is false. If snow's being green is "what is not" (i.e., snow's being green is not the case), then and only then to say of snow's being green "that it is" (i.e., to say that snow's being green is the case) is false. For example, the token proposition [snow being green/is the case] is false just when snow's being green is not the case. Similarly, if snow's being white is "what is" (i.e., snow's being white is the case), then and only then to say of snow's being white "that it is not" (i.e., to say of snow's being white that it is not the case) is false. The token proposition [snow being white/is not the case], for example, is false just when snow's being white in fact is the case.

The dictum of *Metaphysics* 1011b26–27 continues: to say of what is that it is, and of what is not that it is not, is true. If snow's being white is "what is" (i.e., snow's being white is the case), then and only then to say of snow's being white "that it is" (i.e., to say that snow's being white is the case) is true. The token proposition [snow being white/is the case], for example, is true just when snow's being white in fact is the case. Likewise, if snow's being green is "what is not" (i.e., snow's being green is not the case), then and only then to say of snow's being green "that it is not" (i.e., to say that snow's being green is not the case) is true. For example, the token proposition [snow being green/is not the case] is true just when snow's being green in fact is not the case.

It is apparent from these definitions that [snow being white/is the case] is true just when [snow being white/is not the case] is false, and vice versa, and also that [snow being green/is not the case] is true just when [snow being green/is the case] is false, and vice versa. And so it is with other token propositions that are comparably opposed.

In general, we may say that for any SOA X and any token proposition of the form [X/yes] or [X/no]:

[X/yes] is true if and only if X is the case.
[X/no] is true if and only if X is not the case.
[X/yes] is false if and only if X is not the case.
[X/no] is false if and only if X is the case.

These four biconditionals exhibit the sense of Aristotle's dictum explicitly. With the help of the variable 's' for status-ascriptions generally, they can be combined into a single biconditional (with '*iff*' standing for "if and only if")—namely, for any token proposition [X/s]:

> [X/s] is true *iff* X has the status s, and is false otherwise.

This summary statement of Aristotle's dictum defines truth and falsehood for token propositions generally.

With the help of notational devices provided previously, a similar definition can be provided for proposition-types. Given the present conception of proposition-types as classes of token propositions, a separate definition is needed, inasmuch as a class of propositions itself is not a representation and hence does not provide a representation of an SOA as having a certain status that might be considered either correct or incorrect. The sense in which a proposition-type is true or false is akin to what Gregory Vlastos has called "Pauline predication."[2] In St. Paul's observation that charity is kind, Vlastos pointed out, the sense is not that the abstract property of charity is characterized by kindness, but rather that individual persons who are charitable are also kind. The proposition-type *[snow being white/yes] is true in a similar sense—that is, in the sense that each of its members is a true proposition.

The proposition-type *[snow being white/yes], accordingly, may be said to be true under just the circumstances specified in the biconditional:

> *[snow being white/yes] is true *iff* [snow being white/yes] is true.

This biconditional says that the proposition-type named by the expression to the left is true if and only if the token proposition to the right is true. Since we already have (from the definition of truth for token propositions) the following biconditional:

> [snow being white/yes] is true *iff* snow's being white is the case,

we now may gain by substitution:

> *[snow being white/yes] is true *iff* snow's being white is the case.

This latter biconditional defines truth in particular application to the proposition-type that snow is white. An exactly parallel definition could be provided for falsehood in this particular application.

This definition can be generalized in the obvious fashion. For any SOA X and any proposition-type *[X/s]:

*[X/s] is true *iff* X has the status s, and is false otherwise.

This biconditional provides a definition of truth and falsehood applying to proposition-types generally. Comparison with the generalized biconditional provided above for token propositions shows that a proposition-type is true under the same circumstances as its token instances, and likewise is false just when its token instances are false. This, of course, is the outcome that should have been anticipated.

Although these results are unremarkable in themselves, doing little more than spelling out details that were intuitively obvious already, it is noteworthy that these details can be specified without notational incoherence. The importance of our being able to do this may be better appreciated against the background of the difficulties encountered by Tarski in working out his well-known "semantic conception" of truth.

2.   Tarski's Goal of a Generalized "Semantic Conception" of Truth

Tarski's theory of truth[3] was motivated rhetorically by paradoxes that arise in what he called 'semantically closed' languages—that is, languages (like those of everyday discourse) with self-referential capacities. A simple form of self-referential paradox is exhibited by the following derivation:

(1) S is true *iff* p   ("Convention T")[4]
(2) p = S is false   (stipulated identity of p)
(3) S is true *iff* S is false   (paradox, by [1] and [2])

where 'S' is replaced by the name of a sentence and 'p' is replaced by the sentence itself. The source of paradox, obviously enough, is the identification of p as a sentence attributing falsehood to itself.

Tarski's theoretical motivation was to provide a definition of truth that, in his words, is "materially adequate and formally correct."[5] To be materially adequate, the theory was required to preserve the intuitions of "Convention T" as in (1) above (e.g., the intuition that "snow is white" is true *iff* snow is white). Among his requirements of formal correctness were that the structure of the language in which the definition is rendered be formally specifiable, that the definition rely on extensional (roughly, truth-functional) primitives only and, of course, that the definition forestall paradox of the sort in question.

Paradox is avoided, in Tarski's formal solution, by relegating 'true' and 'false' to a metalanguage (relative to the object-language in which a sentence p is formulated), thus preventing self-reference in the manner of (2) above. Extensionality is secured by defining 'true' in terms of a notion of satisfaction[6] tied to the predicate calculus. The definition then is extended, in a formally specifiable manner to the (presumably) infinitely many sentences of the language in question, by recursion based on a specified list of primitive sentences. Material adequacy, finally, is assured with the requirement that the theory entails as theorems, for each well-formed sentence of the object-language, biconditionals of the form of "Convention T" (e.g., " 'snow is white' is true *iff* snow is white," "'the sun is shining' is true *iff* the sun is shining," and so forth).

Tarski's theory thus provides a definition of truth in terms of the extensional relation of satisfaction and in terms of the semantic intuitions bound up with "Convention T." This definition, however, applies only within the formal language of the theory. Tarski despaired of finding a definition of truth that would apply to "semantically closed" natural languages without leaving them open to the threat of self-referential paradox. The account of truth developed in the present chapter, on the other hand, both applies to natural languages and has provisions by which such paradox is automatically avoided.

As part of the present goal of providing an account of the sort Tarski despaired of finding, it is important to note why "Convention T" itself cannot count as a definition of truth. The reason is that it contains free variables — 'p' for sentences and 'S' for their names. But could it not be converted into a general definition of truth by quantification over names and sentences? Suppose one were to invoke the common convention of forming names for expressions by placing single quotes around their token instances, and assign to sentential variables flanked by quotes the role of variables for sentence names, purporting to generalize "Convention T" in the following manner:

(T1) (p) ('p' is true *iff* p).

The difficulty with this, as Tarski saw, is that a variable letter flanked by single quotes is not the same variable as the letter itself, standing in as it does for sentence-names rather than for sentences like the latter. Hence the two variables cannot be governed by the same quantifier '(p)' (by any understanding of the quantifiers preserving extensionality). The schema (T1) requires yet another quantifier like '('p')' to make it a closed sentence, which would break the semantic connection between variables that "Convention T" requires. A specific sign that something is amiss with (T1), construed in light of this requirement, is that it admits contradictory instantiations. Replacing 'p' with "snow is green," for instance, yields '"p' is true *iff* snow is green', while replacing the same variable with "snow is not green" (which the universal quantifier authorizes) results in '"p' is true *iff* snow is not green'. Such considerations show (T1) unsuitable as a general definition of truth.

The final biconditional of section 1 provides an account of truth superficially similar to "Convention T," but one that can be generalized in a manner avoiding the difficulty of different language levels that opens (T1) to contradiction. With '(X)' functioning as a quantifier over SOAs generally, and with the understanding that 's' indicates the same status-ascription throughout, this biconditional can be generalized as follows:[7]

(T2) (X) (*[X/s] is true *iff* X has the status s, and is false otherwise).

The use of the variable 'X' in (T2) differs from that of 'p' in (T1) in the following key respects. First, as already specified, 'X' is to be replaced in all its occurrences by representations of SOAs, rather than by sentences as with 'p' in (T1). As a consequence, second, both occurrences of the relevant variable in (T2) are governed by the same quantifier '(X)', whereas only one variable of the two in (T1) is governed by '(p)'. Third, as noted at the end of the preceding chapter, substitution instances of '*[X/s]' are not names of substitution instances of '[X/s]' and, hence, are not on a meta-level with respect to the latter. Substitution instances of the former are names of proposition-types, while those of the latter are token propositions; and the names of proposition-types (incorporating asterisks) clearly do not apply to their token instances. Accordingly, as a fourth point of comparison, whereas flanking a variable 'p' with single quotes renders it inaccessible to quantification by '(p)' (in the manner, roughly, of the 'p' in "nap"), the notation '*[__/s]' receives variables in a manner leaving them open to quantification. The notation receives its variable in something like the manner in which a generic label for a storage container might receive an identifying mark. Imagine a generic label of the form "This box contains ___," in which the blank is to be filled with an actual sample of the things contained in the box (e.g., postage stamps or business cards). Inasmuch as the identifying mark on the label would be changed in exactly the same manner as the contents of the box (replacement by instances of another type of thing), a "quantifier" governing potential occupants of the container would govern potential occupants of the blank in the label as well.

The biconditional of (T2) provides an account of truth and falsehood for proposition-types (and by extension for token propositions) that is more intuitive than Tarski's definition in terms of satisfaction and that captures the truth-making relation no less exactly than (T1). A further advantage of (T2) for our purposes is that it applies to natural languages in which philosophy is usually conducted and is not restricted to the formal language of the technical logician. These advantages would be nullified, however, if (T2) could not be relied upon to forestall self-referential paradox of the sort that Tarski explicitly was trying to avoid. In the next section, we see how the present treatment of propositions precludes self-reference by making it unintelligible.

3.   Forestalling Paradox by Avoiding Self-Reference

Tractatus 3.332 contains the remark, "No proposition can make a statement about itself, because a propositional sign cannot be contained in itself (that is the whole of the 'theory of types')." This remark of Wittgenstein remains correct from the present point of view as well. What it says, in upshot, is that the *internal* hierarchy manifested in the structure of a fully analyzed proposition makes an *external* hierarchy like Russell's theory of types unnecessary for the avoidance of self-referential paradox. What is meant by speaking of a proposition's fully analyzed structure, and in what manner does that structure involve an internal hierarchy?

Consider first the distinction between compound and elementary propositions. Propositions are compound when they are constructed out of other propositions by application of logical operators.[8] An example is the logical negation of the proposition that the sun is shining, which is constructed out of the proposition that the sun is shining by application of the negation operator. Another example is the logical disjunction of the proposition that the sun is shining and the proposition that snow is white, constructed by application of the disjunction operator. The first example represents as being the case the SOA of its constituent proposition's being false. The second represents as being the case the SOA of at least one of its constituent's being true. Like all compound propositions, these are propositions *about* the propositions from which they are compounded.[9] Compound propositions thus are on a higher level (analogous to what Tarski called a "meta-level") than their component propositions.

Compound propositions may be constructed from other compound propositions (e.g., a conjunction of the negation and the disjunction above). But these latter themselves, at some level within their structure, must be compounded from propositions that are not compound in turn. Propositions that are not compounded from other propositions are what I shall refer to as "elementary propositions." By definition, a proposition is elementary just when it is not compound, and a proposition is compound just when it contains a representation of a proposition within its structure. An elementary proposition, accordingly, is one that does not contain a representation of a proposition. An example of an elementary proposition is [snow being white/yes]; while [[snow's being white/yes]/no] (the negation of the proposition that snow is white), by contrast, is a compound proposition.

Just as a compound proposition is constructed by application of logical operators to (ultimately) elementary propositions, so a compound proposition is analyzed by tracing backward, as it were, the individual steps of its construction. When a proposition is in fully analyzed form, each elementary proposition within its structure is individually exhibited, along with each connective applied in the course of composition. When a proposition has been rendered in fully analyzed form, accordingly, it will exhibit unambiguously the relations among its individual components that were established by the operations of its original construction.

If one step in the construction of a compound proposition, for example, was the negation of the elementary proposition that the sun is shining, and a subsequent step was the conjunction of the compound proposition that resulted from this negation with another compound proposition (as in the illustration of the second paragraph above), then the fully analyzed form will show explicitly the sequence in which these steps were taken. In showing this, however, the fully analyzed form will show as well that the elementary proposition that the sun is shining was incorporated by the operation of negation into a compound proposition and that this latter, in turn, was incorporated by conjunction into a compound proposition of yet a higher level. The fully analyzed form of the proposition, in short, will exhibit the compound formed by negation as being on one level higher than the proposition that was negated, and it will exhibit the compound formed by conjunction, in turn, as being on one level higher than the component formed by negation. The combined effect, in this case, will be to show that the compound formed by conjunction is two levels higher than the original proposition that the sun is shining.

These relations among levels occupied by a compound proposition's components resulting from sequential stages in its construction constitute what I have called the "internal hierarchy" of a compound proposition. The particular manner in which this hierarchy will be exhibited depends upon the notations adopted for the expression of compound propositions.[10]

The relevant lesson to be drawn from these considerations is that no proposition can contain a representation of itself. An elementary proposition, by definition, contains no representations of propositions within its structure, and therefore cannot contain a representation of itself. In a compound proposition, on the other hand, the propositions represented are always (by the rules governing logical compounding) on a lower level than the propositions representing them. And since (for the same reason) no genuine proposition can occupy two levels simultaneously, once again a proposition cannot represent itself.

If a proposition cannot represent itself, moreover, it cannot be about itself, inasmuch as a proposition is about just the circumstances to which it ascribes status. By the very nature of the operations involved in its construction, it follows that a genuine proposition is incapable of self-reference. And if a proposition is incapable of referring to itself, it is immune to the threat of self-referential paradox.

It was the threat of self-referential paradox, we recall from above, that motivated Tarski to distinguish metalanguage from object-language and that prevented his pursuing a general definition of truth applicable to expressions in the semantically closed languages of everyday discourse. But now this threat appears otiose. Self-referential paradox is nipped in the bud by showing why no coherent proposition may refer to itself. Recasting in regimented form the derivation of paradox shown at the beginning of section 2 shows exactly where incoherency arises. In the following version, line (2) of the earlier derivation is replaced by (i), which stipulates the identity of SOA X:

(i)   X = [X/yes] being false   (stipulation)
(ii) [X/yes] = [[X/yes] being false/yes]   ((i))
(iii) [[X/yes] being false/yes] *iff* not-[X/yes]   (T-F equivalence)
(iv) [X/yes] *iff* not-[X/yes]   (paradox, by (ii) and
                                                   (iii))

Here, (i) appears to yield, by substitution of identities in the schema '[___/yes] = [___/yes]', an equality (ii) in which a proposition purports to assign a truth-value to itself. In conjunction with the truth-functional equivalence (in (iii)) between a proposition negating a given proposition and a proposition representing the latter as being false, (ii) then appears to yield the paradox of (iv). But the apparent consequence of (iv) not only is paradoxical; strictly speaking, it is not a genuine consequence of anything at all. The reason is that although (iv) appears to be entailed by (ii) and (iii), (ii) is incapable of participating in intelligible entailments. The reason that (ii) is incapable of participating in intelligible entailments, in turn, is that (ii) itself is unintelligible. For (ii) purports to identify propositions on two different levels, and no genuine proposition (for reasons noted above) is capable of such bilocation.[11]

In brief, stipulation (i) robs [X/yes] of its propositional character. Since further moves toward (iv) depend upon propositional equivalence, the incipient paradox dissipates before it can be formulated.

Wittgenstein's remark at *Tractatus* 3.332 mentioned Russell's theory of types as being unnecessary, on the grounds that "[n]o proposition can make a statement about itself. . . ." The same may be said for a distinction like Tarski's between object-language and metalanguage. Not only is a general definition of truth available for natural language without threat of self-referential paradox[12], but, moreover, the onset of paradox can be avoided without dividing language up arbitrarily into different levels.[13]

4. Truth-Conditions

The question of what it *means* to call a proposition true is different from the question of what *makes* a proposition true. What it means for a proposition to be true, according to (T2), is for it to represent correctly how things stand in the world. For a given SOA X, a proposition representing X as being the case is true when and only when X in fact is the case, for then and only then does the proposition provide a correct representation. What makes a proposition true, on the other hand, is for the world actually to be such as the proposition represents it as being. What makes the proposition that snow is white true, for example, is the world's actually being such that snow is white. The source of truth of the proposition that snow is not green, in like fashion, is the world's actually being such that snow is not green. For any SOA X, the truth-source of the proposition that X is the case is the world's actually being such that X is the case; and the truth-source of the proposition that X is not the case is the world's actually being such that X is not the case. That is to say, while the *meaning* of truth has to do primarily with the correctness of a propositional representation, the *source* of truth has to do primarily with the way things stand in the world.

In the case of a given true proposition representing SOA X as having a certain status, the proposition derives its truth from the world's being such that X has the status it is represented as having. The circumstance of the world's being such is the source of the proposition's truth. Inasmuch as the proposition's truth is conditional upon X's having the status the proposition represents it as having, this circumstance could also be referred to as the *truth-condition* of the proposition. What makes a proposition true, in other words, is for the world to be such that its truth-condition is met, which is the same as for the world to present the circumstances that constitute its source of truth.

The truth-condition of a given proposition, we may now see, is precisely what the proposition represents. Consider the proposition that snow is white, consisting of (i) a representation of the SOA of snow's being white and (ii) an ascription to that SOA of the status of being the case. For present purposes, we may refer to these constituents as (i) the descriptive and (ii) the status-ascribing components, respectively. Now, what the proposition that snow is white represents is not just the SOA of snow's being white. This latter is represented by its descriptive component; and what a proposition in its entirety represents is not the same as what is represented by its descriptive component alone. What the proposition that snow is white represents as a whole is snow's being white—that SOA—*being the case*.

The circumstances of snow's being white *being the case* themselves constitute an SOA that the world might present. But this is not the same SOA as that merely of snow's being white. While the latter SOA is represented by the proposition's descriptive component alone, the former is represented by the proposition as a whole. Since the former—snow's being white being the case—is none other than the truth-condition of the proposition in question, its truth-condition, as noted above, is the same as what the proposition as a whole represents. What the proposition as a whole represents, in brief, is identical with its truth-condition.

What a proposition as a whole represents, however, is not affected by its truth-value, which is to say that a proposition represents the same thing whether true or false. Put another way, the truth-condition of a proposition remains the same, without regard to whether that truth-condition in fact is met. It follows that a proposition, while representing its

Table 4.1

Propositional Representations

Representation	SOA Represented
"snow being white" (substitution for 'X')	X
[X/yes]	X (i) being the case
[[X/yes] being true/yes]	X (i) being the case, (ii) being the case

truth-condition, cannot represent the further SOA of this truth-condition being met.

The truth-condition of the proposition that snow is white, we recall from above, is the SOA of snow's being white being the case — not just snow's being white itself, but snow's being white itself being the case. For this truth-condition to be met, in turn, is for the SOA of snow's being white being the case (the truth-condition itself) to be actually present, given the world as it is. Put somewhat differently, for the truth-condition of the proposition that snow is white to be met is for the world to be such that the SOA of snow's being white being the case (its truth-condition) *itself* is the case. This is why the proposition cannot represent its own truth-condition's being met: what the proposition represents is the SOA of snow's being white being the case, while the circumstance of its truth-condition's being met is the circumstance of that SOA's being the case in turn.

Here we encounter a nested series of SOAs that threatens to proliferate beyond perspicuous conception. There is the SOA of snow's being white, which is represented by the descriptive component of the proposition in question. There is the SOA of snow's being white (i) being the case, which is represented by the proposition that snow is white in its entirety. And there is the further SOA of this latter SOA — snow's being white (i) being the case — itself (ii) being the case, which amounts to the truth-condition of the proposition that snow is white actually being met and which, accordingly, is represented by the proposition that the proposition that snow is white is true. The initial members of this series of SOAs are displayed in table 4.1 along with the propositions (or propositional component) representing them.

Next in the series, if we find need to continue it, would be the SOA of snow's being white (i) being the case, (ii) being the case, (iii) being the case—that is, the SOA that amounts to the truth-condition being met of the proposition that the truth-condition of the proposition that snow is white is met—which already poses a challenge to conceptual clarity. In order to bring this nested series of SOAs under perspicuous management, it will be helpful to tie it in explicitly with the conception of the hierarchy of propositions introduced above.

5. The Rank-Ordering of Propositions and States of Affairs

A compound proposition, as defined in section 3 above, is one that incorporates another proposition within its structure. An example is the proposition [[snow being white/yes] being true/yes], which incorporates a token of the proposition that snow is white within its descriptive component (the component ending with the penultimate bracket). An elementary proposition, by contrast, is one that is not compound, and hence one that does not incorporate another proposition within its structure. An example is the token proposition incorporated within the structure of the compound proposition above—that is, the token of the proposition that snow is white. In the order of stages in which compound propositions are built up, as it were, the compound proposition above is on the second level with respect to the proposition that snow is white. Inasmuch as the latter is an elementary proposition, it contains no further propositions within its structure. For that reason, elementary propositions across the board may appropriately be referred to as *first-level* propositions.

A paradigmatic hierarchy of nested propositions may be constructed by recursive application of the truth-functional operation of iteration.[14] As negation of the elementary proposition that snow is white produces a second-level proposition to the effect that the proposition that snow is white is false, so iteration of that elementary proposition produces a second-level proposition (an instance of which appears in the paragraph above) to the effect that the proposition that snow is white is true. In general, for any elementary proposition [X/yes], the iteration of that proposition is a second-level proposition [[X/yes] being true/yes], the iteration of this latter is a third-level proposition [[[X/yes] being true/yes] being true/yes], and so on for fourth-, fifth-, and yet higher-level propositions. The level of a given proposition in this ascending series is indicated by the number of appearances of "yes" (for "is the case") in the fully analyzed proposition.[15]

For each member of this ascending series of propositions there is a corresponding SOA that it represents.[16] These SOAs themselves fall into a series ordered in accord with the propositions representing them. Corresponding to the first-level proposition [X/yes] is the SOA of X being the case. Although this SOA incorporates the SOA X itself as a component, there are obvious advantages in assigning rank-orderings to SOAs matching those of the propositions by which they are represented. Accordingly, we may wish to speak of X itself as a *zero-order* (or base-order) SOA, reserving the first-order ranking for the SOA represented by the first-level proposition [X/yes]—namely, for the SOA of X being the case (as in the second line of table 4.1). Represented by the second-level proposition [[X/yes] being true/yes], in turn, will be the second-order SOA of X being the case itself being the case (as in the third line of table 4.1); and so on for SOAs of yet higher orders. Given this stratagem of numbering, the rank-order of an SOA in this series is indicated by the number of appearances of the phrase "being the case" (or equivalent) in its fully explicit representation.[17]

This device for rank-ordering SOAs enables a succinct account of the relation between propositions and their truth-conditions. Just as the truth-condition of the first-level proposition that snow is white is the first-order SOA of snow's being white being the case, so in general the truth-condition of [X/yes] is the SOA of X being the case. By representing X as being the case, [X/yes] represents its truth-condition. But [X/yes], as previously noted, cannot represent the SOA of its truth-condition's being met. The SOA of its truth-condition's being met is the second-order SOA of X (i) being the case itself (ii) being the case. And for the representation of this second-order SOA, a second-level proposition is required— for instance, the proposition [[X/yes] being true/yes]. The truth-condition of this second-level proposition, in turn, is the second-order SOA of X (i) being the case itself (ii) being the case; and for this truth-condition to be met is for this second-order SOA (iii) to be the case. A representation of the truth-condition of the second-level proposition being met, accordingly, requires a third-level proposition like [[[X/yes] being true/yes] being true/yes], as in table 4.2. In similar fashion, the representation of the truth-conditions of a third-level proposition being met requires a fourth-level proposition, and so on for propositions of yet higher levels.[18]

Let us now look at the same relation from the perspective, not of truth-conditions, but of truth. When the proposition [X/yes] is true, the SOA of that proposition's being true obtains in the world—in other words, that SOA in fact is the case. There are several equivalent ways to describe what it is for that SOA to be the case. For it to be the case that the proposition [X/yes] is true is (a) for the world to be such that

Table 4.2

Truth-Conditions (T-C) and Representations (Rep.) Thereof

	First Level	Second Level
Proposition:	[X/yes]	[[X/yes] being T/yes]
T-C of Proposition:	X being the case	X (i) being the case, (ii) do
T-C met by:	X (i) being the case, (ii) do	X (i) being the case, (ii) do, (iii) do
Rep. of T-C being met:	[[X/yes] being T/yes]	[[[x/yes] being T/yes] being T/yes]

Note: Here, "do" = "ditto," and "T" = "True."

the truth-condition of [X/yes] is met. As indicated in table 4.2, the world's being such that the truth-condition of [X/yes] is met is represented by the second-level proposition [[X/yes] being true/yes]. Alternatively, for the SOA of [X/yes] being true to be the case is (b) for the world to be such as [X/yes] represents it as being, which is the same as (c) for what [X/yes] represents to be the case. But [X/yes] represents X as being the case; hence, for what [X/yes] represents to be the case is the same as (d) for X being the case to be the case. As indicated by table 4.2, however, the SOA of X being the case is represented by the first-level proposition [X/yes]. Hence, the circumstances of X (i) being the case itself (ii) being the case—the circumstances of (d)—are represented by the second-level proposition [[X/yes]/yes]. Given the equivalence of (a) and (d), moreover, and given that (a) is represented by the proposition [[X/yes] being true/yes], it follows that [[X/yes] being true/yes] and [[X/yes]/yes] represent the same SOA. The two, in effect, are equivalent second-order propositions.

Exactly parallel considerations show the equivalence of [[X/no] being true/yes] and [[X/no]/yes]. But if [[X/yes] being true/yes] is equivalent to [[X/yes]/yes], and [[X/no] being true/yes] is equivalent to [[X/no]/yes], then it appears that the expression "being true" can be eliminated from the two propositions in which it occurs without changing the signification of either proposition. A careful consideration of this result, one might expect, should throw light on the so-called redundancy theory of truth.

6.   The Redundancy Theory of Truth

Simply put, the redundancy theory of truth is the general claim that saying that a proposition is true means no more than simply stating the proposition and that saying that a proposition is false means no more than denying the proposition.[19] Saying, for example, "It is true that Caesar was murdered" means no more than simply saying that Caesar was murdered; and saying, "It is false that Caesar was murdered" means no more than simply saying that he was not murdered. But if so, then "true" and "false" can be dropped without loss of meaning. Whatever they add by way of style or emphasis, according to this theory, the terms "true" and "false" are semantically redundant.

According to the account of the section above, seemingly in similar fashion, the SOA of its being the case that [X/yes] is true can be represented either by [[X/yes] being true/yes] or by [[X/yes]/yes], which means that the latter two propositions are equivalent as representations. The two propositions [[X/no] being true/yes] and [[X/no]/yes] are equivalent in exactly the same fashion. One way of describing this equivalence, it might seem, is to say that the expression "being true" is redundant in [[X/yes(no)] being true/yes]. In order to see whether this result provides support for the redundancy theory of truth, however, we must recall the reason why the propositions in question are equivalent.

The proposition [[X/yes] being true/yes] represents the second-order SOA of the truth-condition of the proposition [X/yes] being met. For this truth-condition to be met is for it to be the case that X is the case. The same second-order SOA, accordingly, is also represented by the proposition [[X/yes]/yes]. It is because [[X/yes] being true/yes] and [[X/yes/yes] represent the same SOA that they are equivalent propositions; and it is because these two propositions are equivalent that the reference to truth appears able to be eliminated from the former without change in meaning. The reason the two propositions represent the same SOA in the first place, however, is that the SOA of the truth-condition of [X/yes] being met admits different characterizations. One characterization alludes explicitly to the truth of the proposition (e.g., "its being the case that [X/yes] is true"); another alludes to what this truth-condition's being met amounts to, without mentioning truth explicitly (e.g., "its being the case that X is the case"). The proposition [[X/yes] being true/yes] represents the SOA in question in terms of the former characterization, while the proposition [[X/yes]/yes] represents the same SOA in terms of the latter. Although it does not allude to truth explicitly, the proposition [[X/yes]/yes] is still a representation of the truth-condition of [X/yes] being met.

The right way to describe the difference in formulation between the equivalent propositions [[X/yes] being true/yes] and [[X/yes]/yes], accordingly, is not to say that reference to truth can be eliminated from the former. The right way to put the difference is to say that the former makes explicit what the latter leaves implicit. Both propositions represent the SOA of the truth-condition of [X/yes] being met. Despite the lack of any explicit reference to truth in its formulation, the latter proposition remains a representation of that SOA.

What the equivalence of [[X/yes] being true/yes] and [[X/yes]/yes] shows us, in brief, is not that mention of truth is redundant, but that there are more and less explicit ways of representing the truth-status of a proposition. The fact that truth-status can be referred to in different ways certainly does not add support to the claim of the redundancy theory that reference to truth (as, for example, by use of the expression "truth-status" above) generally can be eliminated without loss of meaning.

The orderly marshaling of propositions and their corresponding truth-conditions of section 5, to be sure, indicates several respects in which the redundancy theory of truth is erroneous. One problem has to do with the fact that the proposition "It is true that Caesar was murdered" and the proposition simply that Caesar was murdered are propositions on different levels. The former is a second-level proposition, representing the second-order SOA of its being the case that Caesar's being murdered is the case—an SOA equivalent to the SOA of the proposition that Caesar was murdered being a true proposition. The proposition that Caesar was murdered itself, however, is a first-level proposition, representing the first-order SOA of Caesar's being murdered being the case. Since they represent SOAs of different orders, the first-level proposition that Caesar was murdered cannot be equivalent in meaning to the second-level proposition that the former proposition is true. Inasmuch as elimination of reference to truth from the second-level proposition "It is true that Caesar was murdered" makes it over into the first-level proposition merely that Caesar was murdered, the two propositions cannot be equivalent in meaning as the redundancy theory claims.[20]

Another problem with the claim that "It is true that Caesar was murdered" is equivalent in meaning to the proposition merely that Caesar was murdered has to do with an asymmetry of truth-conditions. The truth-condition of the former is the SOA of the proposition that Caesar was murdered being a true proposition, while the truth-condition of the latter proposition that Caesar was murdered is the SOA of its being the case that Caesar was murdered. The asymmetry in question is that the SOA of its being the case that Caesar was murdered (the latter SOA) is the *reason why* the proposition saying Caesar was murdered is true (the former SOA), whereas the SOA of the proposition that Caesar was murdered being true (the former SOA) clearly is not the reason why it is the case that Caesar was murdered (the latter SOA). This is directly parallel to the asymmetry noticed by Aristotle in *Categories* 14b15–22, where he observed that the fact that a man exists is somehow the cause of the truth of the proposition that the man exists, while the truth of the proposition in no sense is the cause of the man's existence. In Aristotle's terms, the fact that Caesar was murdered (represented by the first-level proposition that Caesar was murdered) is the cause of the fact that the proposition saying as much is true (represented by the second-level proposition that the proposition saying this is true), whereas clearly the fact that the proposition is true is not the cause of the fact that Caesar was murdered. Given this asymmetry, we see again that "It is true that Caesar was murdered" has a different truth-condition from that of the proposition that Caesar was murdered, and hence cannot be equivalent in meaning to that proposition.

Similar difficulties affect the alleged equivalence in meaning between "It is false that Caesar was murdered" and the proposition that Caesar was not murdered. The truth-condition of the latter is the first-order SOA of its not being the case that Caesar was murdered, while that of the former is the second-order SOA of the proposition that Caesar was murdered being a false proposition. Since these two SOAs not only are on different levels, but also are asymmetrical in the manner indicated above, the proposition "It is false that Caesar was murdered" cannot be equivalent in meaning to the proposition that Caesar was not murdered. The basic flaw of the redundancy theory, in brief, is that it assimilates propositions on different levels, which are propositions with different truth-conditions and hence with different meanings.

7. Other Senses of Truth

There is an obvious relation among the referents of the noun "truth," of the adjective "true," and of the adverb "truly": truth is the upshot of something's being true, which in turn is the upshot of something done truly. Of these three terms, "truly" is the most concrete, referring as it does to a quality of particular acts (the truly aimed shot that goes straight to the target, the truly spoken words that tell things as they are). The term "truth," on the other hand, is the most abstract, possessing features that are independent of its particular instances (the truth that "sets one free" or that is "stranger than fiction"). Not only is the term "truth" the most abstract of the lot, but moreover it is a term that carries a variety of different senses. It seems fitting to end the chapter with some brief remarks contrasting several senses of the term that are of specific interest to epistemology, as well as to logic and ontology.

Sense (1): "truth" as the nominal form of the adjective "true." This seems to be the basic sense of the term as used in epistemology, and it is the sense of primary concern in the present chapter. The sense is that of truth as a property of propositions and, derivatively, as a property of propositional attitudes (beliefs, judgments, etc.). In this basic use (a) of the term, truth is the property of simply being true, in direct opposition to the property of falsehood. Familiar expressions in which this use of the term occurs are "truth-bearer" (applicable to whatever has the property of being true) and "truth-condition" (applicable to the circumstances that render something true).

An extended use (b) of "truth" in this regard (truth as a property) is to signify the status of being true or of being false indifferently. It is in this extended use of the term that being false is a "truth-value" along with being true. Other expressions in which the term is used in this extended sense are "truth-assessment," "truth-table," and "truth-status" itself.

Sense (2): truth as a proposition (or belief, or judgment, etc.) that has the status of being true. The generic meaning of "truth" in this sense is (a) that of one or another true proposition, as in "The truth you speak doth lack some gentleness" (Shakespeare, *The Tempest*). Another example, employing the plural of the term, is "We hold these truths to be self-evident." By extrapolation, a truth might also be a true assertion (an assertion of a true proposition), a true belief (a belief with a true proposition as object), and so forth.

A more relaxed use of the term in this general sense is (b) that of a group of true propositions expressly relevant to a given concern. An example is in "Do you swear to tell the truth, the whole truth, and nothing but the truth?" In swearing this, the witness swears to speak no falsehood in response to questions and to withhold no relevant information, as distinct from telling the jury all and only what is the case in the world generally.

Sense (3): truth as what obtains in the actual world. In this sense, the truth might be (a) one or more actual SOAs somehow relevant to a given concern, as in "He finally discovered the truth." What one finds, in discovering the truth, is not a group of true propositions (discovering is not a propositional attitude), but rather various particulars of how things stand in the world that are relevant to one's specific circumstances.

More generally, the truth also might be (b) what is the case at large—that is, SOAs that are actual without restriction to some particular set of interests. It is in this sense, presumably, that we sometimes say of scholarship that it is "dedicated to a search for the truth."

The distinction between senses (2) and (3) of the term "truth" is parallel to a similar distinction between two senses of "fact." A fact in one sense is the same as a true proposition (a truth in sense [2]). Telling "the facts of the case" is generally equivalent to telling "the truth of the matter," where what one tells in either event takes the form of a set of propositions that are both true and relevant to the case at hand. Another sense of the term "fact" is equivalent to that of "truth" in sense (3), in which a truth is an SOA that is actually the case. Here, "facing the facts" is tantamount to "facing the truth," neither of which is a matter of facing propositions. For future reference, these two senses of "fact" might be labeled "fact(p)" (for fact as a true proposition) and "fact(s)" (for fact as an actual SOA).[21]

Sense (4): truth as the source of truth in some other sense. When Tarski titled his theory "The Semantic Conception of Truth," what he had in mind, presumably, was not truth merely as a property of linguistic entities (sentences, propositions, or suchlike), but rather truth as a relation between such entities and the SOAs by which the former acquire that property. According to the standard conception of the correspondence theory of truth,[22] moreover, where truth is identified as a correspondence between (true) propositions and reality, correspondence is not being put forward as the property of being true itself (truth in sense [1]), nor as a number of propositions that happen to be true (sense [2]), nor as what is the case in the actual world (sense [3]). Correspondence, rather, is being identified as that relation between propositions and what is the case that is the source of truth in sense (1) and sense (2). In both of these theories, truth is being treated (a) as a relation conferring the status of being true. Truth here is the *source* of truth in senses (1) and (2) above.

In other contexts, truth might be conceived more broadly (b) as the source of truth in sense (3)—that is, as some mode of being responsible for what is the case in the world. This meaning seems less common in English than in certain other languages. The term *alētheia* ('truth') in classical Greek, for example, often calls for the translation "reality" as well; and the term *Wahrheit* in modern German commonly means reality as well as truth. In religious discourse, moreover, the term "truth" sometimes conveys the sense of the ground of being at large—of what is fully real and not dependent upon anything else for its reality. This is the sense, one may assume, implicated in the New Testament pronouncement "I am the way, the truth, and the life." When used in such contexts, the term is often capitalized.

The purpose of distinguishing these other senses from truth in sense (1a) is not to initiate an extension of the current analysis, but merely to forestall confusion that might result if one or another of these other senses were conflated with truth as a property of propositions.

Notes

1. In its general formulation, this definition is similar to what Paul Moser calls "the minimal correspondence definition" of truth (in Paul Moser, *Knowledge and Evidence* [Cambridge: Cambridge University Press, 1989], 26; see also J. L. Mackie, "Simple Truth," *Philosophical Quarterly* 20 [1970], 321–333). A possible advantage of the present formulation is that it is put in terms of propositions representing SOAs as having some particular status, a mode of representation admitting precise characterization (see chapters 6 and 7), while the formulation of Mackie and Moser is put in terms of the seemingly less precise notion of how things are "stated to be" by the truth-bearing proposition or statement.

2. Gregory Vlastos, "The Unity of Virtues in the *Protagoras*," *Review of Metaphysics* 25 (1972), 415–458.

3. See Alfred Tarski, "The Concept of Truth in Formalized Language," chap. 8 in *Logic, Semantics, Metamathematics,* J. H. Woodger, trans. (Oxford: Oxford University Press, 1956). Tarski's theory, it should be noted, deals with truth as a property of formulae or "sentences" in a formal language. The distinction between propositions and sentences in a natural language that figured in the discussion of chapter 2 above was not relevant to his theoretical purposes.

4. This expression is commonly used with reference to Tarski's biconditional (T): X is true if and only if P, where P is a sentence and X its name. An example is "the sentence 'snow is white' is true if and only if snow is white."

5. Tarski, "The Concept of Truth in Formalized Language," 152.

6. Examples of satisfaction are: (i) the two-place sentential function 'x taught y' being satisfied by all ordered sequences of object-pairs beginning with Socrates and Plato, or Quine and Davidson, among others, but by none beginning, for example, with Einstein and Aristotle, (ii) the one-place function 'x was Greek' being satisfied by all sequences beginning with Socrates or Plato, and so on, but none beginning, for example, with Einstein, while (iii) a sentence with no free variables (a "zero-place function") either is satisfied by all sequences whatever or is satisfied by none. A true sentence, then, is defined

as one satisfied by all sequences; and a false sentence, one satisfied by none.

7. The reader will note that (T2) generalizes over SOAs rather than propositions. The biconditional nonetheless covers all propositions, inasmuch as all propositions, by definition, represent SOAs. One way of reading (T2) that makes this evident is: Any SOA is such that any proposition representing it as leaving status s is true *iff* it has status s, and is false otherwise.

8. Included among what I here call "logical operators" are the sixteen operators of truth-functional logic (displayed, e.g., in *Tractatus* 5.101) and the modal operators of modal logic (attributing possibility, necessity, and consistency).

9. The conception of compound propositions as being propositions about their components is not new, being present in Russell's *An Inquiry into Meaning and Truth* (London: George Allen & Unwin, 1940); see 78, 259. It might be germane to note at this point that [grass being moist and green/yes], while it has a compound predicate, is not a compound proposition, unlike the proposition that both [grass being moist/yes] and [grass being green/yes] are true, which is compound in the relevant sense.

10. It is interesting to note that the fully analyzed form of a proposition cannot be expressed through use of variables, inasmuch as there is no special notation generally recognized in logic for variables confined to elementary propositions (*pace Tractatus* 4.24). This is evident in the case of the standard notation for propositional variables ('p', 'q', etc.), inasmuch as these variables may stand for propositions of any level of complexity. The variable in the token propositional form [X/yes], in similar fashion, might be replaced by a representation of an SOA involving another proposition (e.g., the SOA of the proposition that the sun is shining being true), in which case the notation [X/yes] stands for a compound proposition, or by a representation of an SOA with no proposition involved (e.g., the SOA of the sun's shining), in which case the notation stands for an elementary proposition.

11. The unintelligibility of (ii) is evident from another angle. According to the present understanding of propositions, a proposition represents an SOA as having one or another determinate status (being the case or not being the case). For a proposition to be true is for the SOA actually to have the status it is represented as having. If there is no SOA the determinate status of which would render it true (or false), the purported proposition does not represent an SOA and, hence, is not a genuine proposition at all. But such is the case with [X/yes] in (ii) above. This may be seen in the following considerations. Assume that [X/yes] is (or at least "starts out" as being) an elementary proposition, true when and only when X *is* the case. But (ii) then identifies it with a second-level proposition, true just when X *is not* the case. Further substitution in the schema '[____/yes] = [____/yes]' of the terms identified in (ii) equates it with a third-level proposition, congruent with the truth-conditions of [X/yes] initially (i.e., X being the case). Yet a further substitution yields a fourth-level proposition, congruent with those on the second level in turn (i.e., X not being the case).

Since the truth-conditions of the putative proposition reverse with each successive level, there is no determinate status of X that would render the inconstant proposition-like expression true. As a consequence, [X/yes] of (ii) is not a coherent proposition at all. Not being a coherent proposition, however, the [X/yes] of (ii) has no truth-value and is incapable of participating in truth-functional relations like the biconditional (iii) and (iv) both purport to be.

12. There are many notational devices by which propositions may be contorted into postures of alleged self-reference other than the direct means discussed here. Among the more familiar, perhaps, are those of employing other propositions to convey the self-reference indirectly (e.g., P saying Q is false and Q saying P is true) and those of propositions that cite themselves by physical location (e.g., "the proposition in this rectangle is false" inscribed within a rectangle). Regardless of format, however, self-reference involves a proposition making truth-claims about itself. But for a proposition to make claims of any sort about any proposition at all, it must be on a higher level than the proposition about which the claim is made. So for a proposition to make a truth-claim about itself, it would have to be on a higher level than itself, which is unintelligible.

An attempt might be made to avoid this stricture by devising a formulation in which self-reference is achieved by a nonpropositional locution that subsequently, as it were, is given a propositional role. In the formulation "this sentence is false or does not express a proposition," for example, the first two words might be taken to refer to the formulation itself, which (self-reference achieved) then is said to have one of two features—not expressing a proposition or being false. Since it purports to attribute that disjunction of features to itself, the formulation appears to express a proposition, which accordingly must be false. The incoherence of this maneuver may be seen by observing that if the locution in question achieves self-reference, then the formulation in which it occurs is not (by the present conception) a proposition and has no truth-value (thus invalidating the alleged disjunction of features), whereas if it does not achieve self-reference it cannot attribute a truth-value to itself. Either way, no paradox arises.

13. Although there are obvious parallels between the internal hierarchy of a compound proposition, as characterized above, and the relation between object and metalanguage applied to a formal language like Tarski's, there is as much difference between these layered structures as there is between the ascending levels of a particular high-rise apartment dwelling and the "system" of second floors of buildings nationwide. While the former is entirely commonplace, the latter seems to be an unnecessary abstraction. Similarly abstract and (for purposes of avoiding paradox) unnecessary is the notion of successive and "systematic" (languagewide) levels in the language of day-by-day discourse.

14. Iteration is the operator assigning truth to the proposition to which it is applied, in contrast with the operation of negation assigning falsehood. It is the

tenth of the sixteen truth-functional operators defined in Wittgenstein's *Tractatus* 5.101.

15. In general, the level of a fully analyzed proposition is indicated by the number of appearances of a status-ascription ("yes" or "no," "is the case," or "is not the case") within its longest nested sequence. The qualification is needed for compound propositions incorporating negative propositions within their structure and for propositions including more than one appearance of a status-ascription on the same level—as, for example, in the second-level proposition [[snow being white/yes] being true or [grass being green/yes] being true/yes]. For the concept of a fully analyzed proposition, see section 3 above.

16. As already noted, the descriptive component of the proposition [snow being white/yes] represents the SOA of snow's being white. The proposition as a whole represents that SOA as being the case, which is to represent the higher-order SOA of snow's being white being the case. A similar parallelism between levels of propositions and of SOAs may be found at work in Richard Fumerton's *Metaphysical and Epistemological Problems of Perception* (Lincoln: University of Nebraska Press, 1985), 58.

17. In general, the order of an SOA is indicated by the number of appearances of a gerundive like "being the case" or "not being the case" within the longest nested sequence of such gerundives in an explicit representation of that SOA.

18. An exactly parallel account can be given for negative propositions. Just as the truth-condition of the proposition that snow is not green is the SOA of snow's being green not being the case, so the truth-condition of any negative proposition [X/no] is the SOA of X not being the case—that is, the world's being such that X is not actual. The circumstance of the truth-condition of [X/no] being met is represented by the second-level proposition [[X/no] being true/yes]. Apart from the negative status-ascription in the proposition [X/no] with which the series begins, truth-conditions of higher-level negative propositions are handled in the same manner as are those of affirmative propositions above.

19. This notion of truth traces back to F. P. Ramsey's "Facts and Propositions," *Proceedings of the Aristotelian Society,* supplementary vol. 7 (1927); excerpted in *Truth,* George Pitcher, ed. (Englewood Cliffs, N.J.: Prentice-Hall, 1964).

20. One criterion of two propositions being the same in meaning is that they share the same truth-condition. But the truth-condition of the first-level [Caesar having been murdered/yes] is Caesar's having been murdered being the case, while that of the second-level [[Caesar's having been murdered] being true/yes] is Caesar's having been murdered (i) being the case, (ii) being the case. Although extensionally equivalent, and hence true (or false) simultaneously, the two propositions have truth-conditions that are not identical.

21. Given these two senses of "fact" (fact[p] as a true proposition and fact[s] as an actual SOA), the statement "It is a fact(p) that the sun is shining

iff it is a fact(s) that the sun is shining" is not a tautology. What it says, in effect, is that the proposition that the sun is shining is true *iff* it is the case that the sun is shining.

22. For the standard conception of the correspondence theory of truth, see *Truth,* Pitcher, ed., Introduction.

II
THE PRECINCTS OF KNOWLEDGE

Chapter 5

KNOWLEDGE AND ITS PRECONDITIONS

1. Knowledge as a Mode of Access

The primary thesis of this chapter is that knowledge is a mode of cognitive access and, as such, is fundamentally distinct from states of mind bearing on propositional objects. In particular, knowledge is distinct from attitudes of propositional stance, like belief, and from their characteristic features, like indubitability and certainty. A correlative thesis is that knowledge is gained through other modes of access, such as various forms of perception, and is retained through yet others of which memory is typical. These latter topics provide the subject matter of subsequent sections of the chapter. The purpose of the present section is to elaborate the considerations underlying the primary thesis that knowledge is a mode of cognitive access.

Attitudes of cognitive access have been distinguished from attitudes of propositional stance by two criteria laid out in chapter 1, phrased for convenience in interrogative terms. These criteria are: (1) Does the attitude at issue admit assessment in terms of correctness and incorrectness? ("No" for attitudes of access, "Yes" for attitudes of stance), and (2) When a subject's attitude for some reason comes under question, which query is more appropriate in probing that attitude? ("How?" for attitudes of access and "Why?" for those of stance). The source of these criteria, it may be recalled, was a series of generalizations based on paradigmatic instances of the various types of attitude in question, including attitudes not only of access and stance, but attitudes of projection and assessment as well. In this initial extraction of the characteristic features of attitudes of cognitive access, however, there was a deliberate avoidance of more than incidental mention of the attitude of knowing itself, with reliance instead upon paradigms like finding and noticing. The purpose of this tactic, it should now be evident, was to avoid begging the question in the crucial case of knowledge by simply *assuming* that knowing is an attitude of access. It is time now to apply these previously developed criteria to knowing specifically. The unambiguous result will be to show that knowing, no less clearly than finding and noticing, is an attitude taken toward actual SOAs—that is, is an attitude of cognitive access.

Criterion I. There is no intelligible sense in which one might be said to "know incorrectly" or to "know falsely." If Deirdre should profess to know that the gate is shut, whereas in fact the gate is open, then her profession in this regard is false. Professing is a typical attitude of propositional stance. And her profession is false in this case, not because she has something we might call "false knowledge," but simply because she fails to know. The reason she fails to know that the gate is open is that one cannot know an SOA that is not the case. One can know *that* a given SOA is not the case, of course, which is to know an actual SOA pertaining to the status of the (nonactual) SOA initially in question.[1] But to know that a nonactual SOA is not the case is not to know that SOA itself, for what is not actual cannot be known.

Nor can we intelligibly say of a person, conversely, that he or she "truly knows" a given SOA. This is not to say that the phrase "truly knows" never finds intelligible use. If N is said truly to know how to deal with adversity, for example, the sense of "truly" in question is that of "unmistakably" or "genuinely," not the sense opposed to "falsely." What N knows truly (i.e., genuinely) in this case is how to do something, which is quite different from knowing an SOA. Since SOAs (unlike propositions) are neither true nor false, the attitude of knowing (unlike that of believing, for instance) is not evaluated in terms of truth-values.

Criterion II. In querying purported attitudes of knowing, we typically ask "How?" but seldom "Why?" In order for Deirdre to know that the gate into the garden is shut, to continue the example, she must be generally capable of knowing (not be comatose, etc.), and she must be situated so as to be able to know this SOA in particular (not be asleep, or away at her office). Thus, if Deirdre claims to know that the gate is shut, and we have reason to question her claim, a suitable query would be, "*How* do you know that?" or "*How* are you in a position to know?" To ask "How?" is to question her abilities or the manner in which the thing (in this case, coming to know) was accomplished.

To query "*Why* do you know?" in such a circumstance, however, would be distinctly inappropriate. Asking "Why?" generally is a call for reasons; and one typically does not have reasons for being in a state of knowledge. One might have reasons, of course, for situating oneself so that knowing becomes possible. For example, Deirdre might leave the house to go check the gate, out of concern for her children. In this case, we could sensibly ask *why* she checked the gate, and her answer might be that she was concerned for the children's safety. But we could not sensibly ask, after the gate had been checked, *why* she knows that the gate is shut. To be sure, there may be reasons in a given case why knowledge is not possible. For instance, Deirdre might have been in another city. So it might make sense on a given occasion to explain why someone was *able* to arrive at a state of knowledge. But the circumstances that explain one's being in a position to know (Deirdre in fact was at home, in view of the gate) are not reasons "explaining" one's state of knowing itself. This is why the question "Why do you know?" is inappropriate in challenging a person's claim to know.

In isolation, these results are unremarkable. It is no novelty among philosophers that "false knowledge" is a deviant expression (criterion I), and the ears of most competent speakers of English are probably tuned as a matter of course to distinguish the familiar "How do you know?" from "Why do you know?"—its distinctly peculiar counterpart (criterion II).[2] Yet taken together, these results have fundamental consequences for our understanding of the nature of knowledge. What they show is that knowing belongs to the same class of cognitive attitude as finding and noticing. Knowing thus is a mode of access to the world as it is, which is to say that it is an attitude toward actual SOAs.

Given that knowledge clearly responds to these criteria in a manner marking it off as an attitude of cognitive access, and given that its response is directly opposed to that identifying attitudes of propositional stance, it follows that knowledge is not an attitude toward propositional objects. And this is a result that will strike many philosophers as counterintuitive. What is to be said, for example, about the seemingly commonplace observation that anyone who knows arithmetic knows the proposition that $2 + 2 = 4$? The answer comes with the realization that the fact that propositions themselves do not count among the objects of knowledge does not preclude our knowing SOAs in which propositions are involved. To know that $2 + 2 = 4$ is not to know a *proposition* to that effect. It is to know, instead, that $2 + 2 = 4$ is a true proposition. And to know this is tantamount, in turn, to knowing the *SOA* of this proposition's being true. If someone makes a point of "knowing the proposition that $2 + 2 = 4$," the point might be allowed as turning upon an elliptical rephrasing of "knowing that $2 + 2 = 4$ is a true proposition," which expresses knowledge of a mathematical SOA.

Consider the case also of a man who "knows a proposition when he sees one" or that of someone who "knows the first proposition in Aristotle's *Physics*." The person in the first case knows what a proposition *is*—knows enough to tell a proposition from, say, a pronominal clause. What this person knows, accordingly, is the SOA of a proposition's having certain defining characteristics. On this basis, he is able to distinguish a proposition from comparable expressions. What is at issue in the second case is a particular proposition's identity (the first proposition in the *Physics* is the proposition that knowledge is attained through acquaintance with causes). So what is known here is the SOA of this being the identity of that particular proposition. Cases of this sort could be multiplied indefinitely. What one knows in any such case, however, is not a proposition per se, in the sense of the proposition serving as an object of knowledge. What one knows is always an SOA, in these cases an SOA in which a proposition somehow figures.

These considerations show that, despite initial appearances, there is nothing counterintuitive about the result above locating knowledge squarely among attitudes of cognitive access. What we should be prepared to see next is that knowing occupies a unique position among attitudes of this sort. If one occupies any other such attitude toward a given SOA, it follows that one also knows the SOA in question.

To take an example, consider the relation between discovering and knowing. If one happens to discover a given SOA X, then perforce one also knows the same SOA. But no consequence follows in the opposite direction, in that one might know X without having discovered it. Suppose that Beatrice (a native of Botswana, let us say) first encounters snow on a trip to Canada and on that occasion discovers that snow is white. With this discovery she comes to know that SOA. Her discovery provides entry into the relevant state of knowing. But now change the story so that Beatrice has never left her native country and has learned the color of snow by a diligent study of her science textbooks. The fact that snow is white in this case is not something she discovers personally (discovers in the sense of perceiving it directly), but is a fact nonetheless of which she may claim knowledge. To discover perforce is to come to know, but there is no such consequence in the other direction between knowing and discovering.

Other entries appearing in our partial list of attitudes of cognitive access in chapter 1 include ascertaining, discerning, learning, noticing, and perceiving. In each of these cases, the attitude in question brings knowledge with it as a normal consequence. Each in this sense is a source of knowledge, a way of entering into a state of knowing. Inasmuch as knowledge has many sources, however, none of these serves as a necessary condition for its presence. Thus, while knowledge invariably accompanies each of these other modes of access, none is entailed particularly by the presence of knowledge in turn.[3]

Another attitude of access invariably accompanied by knowing, but in a rather different sense, is that of remembering (also recalling, recollecting, etc.). One remembers a given fact only if one has known that fact previously.[4] But once again there is no entailment in the other direction, inasmuch as one might know some SOA without having occasion to remember it. While the several other attitudes discussed in the paragraph above are ways of gaining knowledge, remembering in turn is a way of retaining it. These contrasting relations between knowing and its antecedents (e.g., discovering and discerning) on the one hand, and knowing and remembering on the other, are examined more fully in section 4 below.

2.   Knowledge, True Belief, and Justification

Knowledge is a key member of the class of cognitive attitudes that take actual SOAs as their objects, while belief is paradigmatic of attitudes we take toward propositions. A clear-cut consequence is that knowledge and belief are inherently distinct kinds of cognitive attitude. This result stands in direct opposition to the conception of knowledge that has remained standard through most of twentieth-century epistemology, identifying knowledge with (i) belief that (ii) is true and (iii) adequately justified.[5] Let us review the reasons for the opposition.

The standard conception incorporates a division of (i) beliefs into (ii) true and (ii') false, and a further division of true beliefs into (iii) justified and (iii') not justified. True beliefs are thus conceived (unproblematically) as a subclass of beliefs in general and as containing true beliefs that are justified as a further subclass. Appropriately justified true belief, that is to say, is a subdivision of beliefs in general. In thus identifying knowledge with true belief that is justified, the standard conception makes knowledge out to be a special kind of belief. But if knowledge and belief are inherently distinct, as the above section indicates, then belief cannot include knowledge as a special subclass.

Needless to say, there are other ways of showing that knowledge is not the same as justified true belief. The most direct way is to point out instances of justified true belief that can be seen upon reflection not to be instances of knowledge. This is the approach behind the so-called "Gettier problem,"[6] which has tested the mettle of a whole generation of aspiring epistemologists. Gettier takes for granted, in setting up the problem, that justified true belief is necessary for knowledge,[7] but then goes on to argue that it is not sufficient. His case consists of a series of counterexamples in which the subject entertains beliefs that are both true and justified, but can be seen intuitively not to constitute knowledge.

In one typical counterexample, there is a proposition P (to the effect that the successful applicant for a given job has ten coins in his pocket) (i) that is believed by subject S (Smith, who actually gets the job), (ii) that in fact is true (Smith indeed has ten coins in his pocket), and (iii) that is strongly supported by evidence in S's possession (the employer has told Smith that Jones will get the job, and Smith knows that Jones has ten coins in his pocket), but that S nonetheless appears not to know (because Smith believes P for inappropriate reasons). So it appears that something else is needed, beyond truth and justification, to convert S's belief into knowledge that P. The challenge to the aspiring epistemologist then becomes to locate the missing ingredient.

What such counterexamples purport to show is at least partially correct: justification is not sufficient to convert true belief into knowledge. But the manner in which Gettier purports to show this can be seriously misleading. In setting up the problem, as noted above, he assumes that "S's being justified in believing P is a necessary condition of S's knowing that P."[8] In terms of our division above of belief (factor [i]) into beliefs that are true (factor [ii]) and also justified (factor [iii]), this is to assume that justification is a necessary ingredient of knowledge. The challenge then becomes to find yet another ingredient (in effect, factor [iv]) that will distinguish knowledge from "nonknowledge" among true beliefs that are justified. But this is to locate the problem at the wrong node in the division. Properly conceived, the problem is not that some further feature is needed to isolate a subspecies of justified true belief that is equivalent to knowledge. The source of the problem is that knowledge is not equivalent to any form of belief, no matter how qualified in terms of specifying features.

In brief, the defect in the standard conception of knowledge is not merely that justification by itself is insufficient to make knowledge out of true belief (which indeed it is). The mistake made in equating knowledge with justified true belief, rather, is to assume that belief is an ingredient of knowledge in the first place—the assumption behind the search for the alleged *remaining* ingredients. Since knowledge is not an attitude toward a propositional object, nothing will convert a state of believing that a certain SOA is the case into a state of knowing the SOA in question. The "Gettier problem," as it stands, admits no solution, being in effect an invitation to chase a will-o'-the-wisp.

It is interesting to speculate why philosophers have so long remained content with the mistaken conception of knowledge that Gettier challenged. One guess is that the mistake may be bound up with the fact that knowledge and true belief often seem to occur together[9] and that they seem more likely to do so when the belief is well justified. If someone knows a given SOA, on the one hand, and has occasion to form a belief about that SOA's status, then the belief presumably would be both well justified and true. On the other hand, if someone believes that a certain SOA is the case and undertakes to find justification for that belief, the search for justification might lead to a direct cognitive encounter with the SOA in question, as a consequence of which the person would come to know that SOA. In one case, justified true belief would occur as a consequence of knowing. In the other, knowledge would follow in the train of the belief's becoming justified. While knowledge and belief remain distinct cognitive attitudes in either case, they are attitudes a subject typically might come to hold simultaneously.

If knowledge and justified true belief occur regularly enough in each other's presence, this would go a long way toward explaining the widespread acceptance among philosophers of the thesis that knowledge is tantamount to belief that is true and well justified. Moreover, if justified true belief and knowledge were *invariably* associated, this would actually vindicate an equivalence of sorts between the two types of mental phenomena. Granting, as it appears we must, that knowledge cannot be defined as justified true belief, and hence that there is no logical (or meaning) equivalence between them, it might still be the case that they are materially equivalent, in the sense of each being a condition for the occurrence of the other.[10] Let us look more carefully at what this might involve.

Suppose the circumstances of knowledge to be such that it is *always* accompanied by justified true belief, in such a fashion as to support the following material conditional:[11]

(MC1)   For every subject N and every SOA X, N knows X only if N has justified true belief that X is the case.

This supposition, in effect, makes justified true belief a material condition of knowledge, in the sense that knowledge is present only if justi-

fied true belief is present as well. Suppose further that justified true belief is always accompanied by knowledge, in the fashion indicated by
the second material conditional:

(MC2)   For every subject N and every SOA X, N has justified true belief that X is the case only if N knows X.

This further supposition makes knowledge a material condition of justified true belief, being in effect the supposition that justified true belief
is present only if knowledge is present also. The effect of (MC1) and
(MC2) taken together is that a given subject N knows a given SOA X
if and only if N also has justified true belief that X is the case, for every
N and for every X.

One interesting consequence that would follow if this pair of suppo-
sitions were true is that knowledge and justified true belief might be
causally dependent upon each other, despite knowledge and belief being different types of cognitive attitude. Thus one could admit the conclusion argued above that knowledge is not a form of belief and still
maintain a view rather like the standard conception of knowledge as
justified true belief. Instead of conceiving knowledge as a cognitive
state *identical* to justified true belief, that is to say, one could view
knowledge and justified true belief as causally interdependent. One
could even view them as being so intimately related (e.g., as joint effects of the same causal process) that the presence of one is both necessary and sufficient for the presence of the other in the same cognitive
subject. The relation between having knowledge and having justified
true belief on the part of cognitive subjects, accordingly, would be like
that between having a heart and having a liver on the part of mammals;
the presence of one would be a reliable indicator that the other is present also.

Another consequence of interest for epistemology would be the
preservation of justification as a primary factor in the process of achieving knowledge. Largely because of the presumed identity of knowledge
with appropriately justified belief, epistemologists have tended during
the last few decades to concentrate upon issues of justification. The
sense of the matter is that if adequate justification is enough to convert
true belief into knowledge, then an understanding of how justification
is accomplished would move us a considerable way toward understanding the achievement of knowledge.[12] If the argument above that
knowledge is not identical with justified true belief is successful, however, the importance of justification in the study of knowledge tends to

diminish significantly, since it can no longer be claimed that the process of achieving knowledge as such typically amounts to finding adequate justification for one's beliefs. But the epistemological importance of justification might be reinstated if the material conditionals above could be defended. Picking up on (MC1), one might take the position that justification is *necessary* for gaining knowledge, in the sense that N has knowledge of X only when N has a belief that X is the case which is both true and adequately justified. One could then argue that the process of accumulating justification, although not enough by itself to convert N's true belief into knowledge, nonetheless satisfies a condition that must be met before N can arrive at a state of knowledge.

A more direct tactic in this regard would be to appeal to (MC2), which could be taken as security for the claim that justified true belief is *sufficient* for the presence of knowledge. On this basis, one might argue that there are causal connections of some sort between the processes of accumulating evidence and the processes of gaining knowledge such that the latter is facilitated by pursuit of the former. The idea here, presumably, would be that N might be brought to a state of knowledge as a causal result of any process that added a sufficient degree of justification to N's true beliefs, inasmuch as justified true belief never occurs without knowledge following in its train. Either way, the conditionals (MC1) and (MC2) suggest a dependency between knowledge and justification that (like the standard conception of knowledge) makes pursuit of justification directly relevant to the pursuit of knowledge.

With consequences like these in the offing, it is a matter of some moment to determine whether (MC1) and (MC2) can be defended. And a moment's thought should be enough to convince one that (MC2), at least, is indefensible. What (MC2) says is that all cases of justified true belief are cases of knowledge as well. And the literature generated by the "Gettier problem" has identified many cases in which justified true belief is present and knowledge is missing. Given that readers of this literature generally seem to find counterexamples of this sort convincing, the supposition behind (MC2) is unlikely to find many supporters.[13]

The case against (MC1) is not so immediately apparent, but a variety of plausible counterexamples seem available here as well. A counterexample to (MC1) would be an instance in which someone knows a certain SOA but lacks justified true belief that this SOA is the case. What form might a counterexample of this sort take? It seems obvious enough, for one thing, that if a person knows a given SOA X, and concurrently entertains a belief that X is the case, then that belief will be true. (How could one know a given SOA and at the same time believe falsely that this SOA is the case?) Moreover, if someone knows SOA X, and at the same time believes that X is the case, then surely that belief will be fully justified. (What better justification could there be for believing that an SOA is the case than actually knowing that SOA?) So if we want to find instances of knowledge unaccompanied by justified true belief, we had best look for knowledge unaccompanied by belief of any sort.

One direction in which to look for instances of knowledge without belief is toward facts that are known by virtue of their sheer immediacy but that fall outside the range of circumstances the subject is prepared to accept as credible. Suppose that Deirdre has just won a much coveted prize in jurisprudence, which will open up a number of career opportunities she finds highly desirable. Although she knows for a fact that the prize is hers—having official notification in hand, and so on— she cannot believe her good luck when she dwells upon its consequences. Deirdre knows she has won the prize, but is not yet ready to really believe it (she keeps pinching herself, figuratively, to make sure she is not imagining it). Other examples of this general sort can be found in cases of extreme distress or anguish, as when a person knows that some terrible thing has happened but cannot accept that it really occurred. As in Deirdre's case of unbelievably good luck, when something dire like this happens, the subject's view of "what is possible" has to expand in unprecedented directions, as it were, before acceptance can catch up with what is already known.

Although cases like this tend at least to call (MC1) into question, there are counterexamples of a more commonplace sort that may seem more weighty as well. Suppose that Deirdre glances inadvertently out the window, happens to notice the children in the garden, and without any particular thoughts on the matter returns to the work laid out on her desk. She knows the children are in the garden; but does she believe it? Since the children were absent from her consideration through the whole transaction, it seems best to say that she has no beliefs about them at all, one way or another. Belief is an attitude toward a propositional object, and there is nothing in our description of Deirdre's situation that would require her entertaining propositions in the children's regard. She must somehow be aware of the children to have noticed them in the garden, needless to say; but being aware of an SOA does not require formulating a proposition about it of any sort whatever.[14] If Deirdre had been *asked* whether she had seen the children after looking out the window, then a proposition of some sort would be involved in her answer (attitudes such as stating and replying take propositional objects). But as matters stand, the case seems accurately described as one in which she knows the children are in the garden (having noticed them there) but has no propositional beliefs to that effect (having never assented to the relevant proposition).[15]

Now, if there were some *contradiction* in the conception of someone knowing a given SOA but entertaining no beliefs in its regard, then counterexamples like that above would have to be disallowed. And if knowledge were identical with a kind of belief (justified or otherwise), as epistemologists have so often assumed, then the conception of knowledge without belief would be no less contradictory than the conception of a square without four corners. But we have seen reason already to reject that assumption; and no other grounds are evident on which to maintain that knowledge without belief is contradictory. There is no reason, accordingly, to disallow the possibility of counterexamples like those of Deirdre above, further instances of which could be supplied at will.[16] Although the matter cannot be settled by a discussion as brief as this, it at least appears that (MC1) cannot be relied upon to hold as a true conditional.[17]

For purposes of showing justification *relevant* to the achievement of knowledge given the conclusions of the section above, however, it is not necessary that (MC1) hold true without exception. It would be enough if justification were seen to be a contributing factor to the achievement of knowledge in a number of cases that appear commonplace in that regard. And this is something that can be seen without difficulty. Let us return to Deirdre and her children for a typical example.

Suppose that Deirdre has been hard at work in her office, when presently her thoughts return to the children. She had taken them into the garden some time ago before going up to her office and had carefully locked the gate to ensure their safety. While she remains relatively sure that they are still in the garden, she has not heard their voices for several minutes and thinks it prudent to check on her belief that they are safely situated. First, she listens carefully from the window; upon still failing to hear them, she next goes downstairs and out into the garden. Although the gate is still shut, it is only after looking around several bushes that she finally finds them hiding in an old apple tree. Her belief that they are safe has been verified beyond question, for now she knows by direct experience that they are secure in the garden. The relevant sequence of events in this case is that Deirdre initially has a relatively firm belief that the children are safe, yet feels need for justification, subsequent to which she undertakes a process of inquiry that not only verifies her belief but also leads to positive knowledge of their safety. Here is a case in which the search for justification has produced knowledge as a causal consequence, a case commonplace enough to count as typical of a broad range of similar cases.

What cases like this show is that there are frequent occasions in which justification may play a role in the acquisition of knowledge. And this result in itself vindicates justification as a topic relevant to the main concerns of epistemology. What should be noted in this regard, however, is that there is nothing about such cases to suggest that justification is either necessary or sufficient for knowledge to occur. It is not necessary,[18] since we frequently gain access to actual SOAs without the evidential status of our beliefs being in any way relevant. Deirdre, for example, might have discovered the children hiding in the garden without any concern at all to check out her beliefs in the matter. And it is not sufficient, for reasons well known in connection with Gettier-style counterexamples. In Deirdre's case, the process of justification might have concluded with her hearing familiar childlike noises from the garden, which would leave her short of positive knowledge that the children were still there. Above all, we should note that there is nothing in such cases to reinstate the flawed view that knowledge is brought about merely by the addition of appropriate justification to true belief. Although there undoubtedly are many cases in which knowledge comes about as a result of some process of justification, the reason this is so is that such a process often leads one to a direct encounter with the SOA concerned, not that justification by itself is ever enough to convert true belief into knowledge.

3. Knowledge, Certainty, and Indubitability

If knowledge were true belief that is adequately justified, and if adequate justification in one's belief were signified by a state of certainty, then certainty would indicate the presence of knowledge. This would provide a rationale for the view once maintained by H. A. Pritchard, among others,[19] that being certain of something is the same as knowing it. As matters stand, however, both of the theses on which this rationale is premised are false. If the argument of the previous sections is cogent, then knowledge is not true belief that is adequately justified. And given the evident disparity between the evidence available for some beliefs and the degree of confidence with which they are sometimes held, it seems safe to presume that certainty is no sign that one's beliefs are adequately justified.

There are reasons of a more direct sort for rejecting the view that being certain is the same as knowing. According to the analysis developed in chapter 2, certainty is a level of assurance with which we maintain particular attitudes of propositional stance—the attitude of believing, notably, along with various others (e.g., affirming and maintaining). Given that belief itself is a propositional attitude, moreover, a belief that is certain remains a belief with a propositional object. But knowledge is a mode of access to the actual world and cannot be equivalent to a mental state directed toward propositions only. It follows that no matter how certain one may be in one's beliefs, being certain is not the same as knowing something about the world.

There is a related view in epistemology, backed by a long-standing tradition, that seeks to explicate knowledge in terms of indubitability. In one common interpretation of Descartes's enterprise, his goal was to found the edifice of knowledge generally on a common indubitable basis.[20] In more recent versions, like the phenomenalism of the early twentieth century,[21] the tendency is to analyze bits of knowledge piecemeal into reports of appearances that the subject finds indubitable. In either case, it is the indubitable character of its foundational layers that purportedly provides warranty for the rest of human knowledge.

One result of chapter 2 that bears upon this matter is that the term "doubt" in epistemology carries two quite distinct senses. There is the doubt that stands in contrast with the property of being certain, and there is the doubt that stands opposed to the attitude of belief. For something to be indubitable in the first sense would amount to a subject's always being confident in assenting to it. And as we have already seen in the above discussion of certainty, mere confidence provides no entry into the province of knowledge. If indubitability has a role to play in the grounding of knowledge, it must pertain to doubt in the sense opposed to belief. How might being indubitable in the manner of resisting disbelief endow what it characterizes with the status of knowledge?

Doubt in this latter sense, as explicated in chapter 2, is an active rejection of assent to a given proposition. Thus being indubitable in the corresponding sense would amount to some property that makes assent inevitable under relevant conditions.[22] When Descartes, upon reflection, found the "cogito" indubitable, the sense was that he found himself unable to withhold assent from the (Latin version of the) proposition "I think." While the fact that a person is unable to resist assent to a proposition might indicate something of interest about either the person or the proposition (or both), however, there is no immediately apparent reason why irresistible assent should result in a state of knowledge. Even under the by-now-disqualified assumption that knowledge is a form of belief, the fact that belief (or some comparable attitude of assent) in a certain case is inevitable would not assure that other conditions of knowledge were met. It would not assure, in particular, that the belief is true or that (despite being irresistible) it is adequately justified.

Backing away from these considerations for a moment, however, one might be excused for finding a certain prima facie plausibility in the claim that N knows whatever N finds indubitable. One fact that seems to count in its favor is that the circumstances of someone's knowing a given SOA seem generally to coincide with circumstances in which that person will be unable seriously to doubt that this SOA in fact is the case. For example, when Camille comes to know that the sun is shining by deliberately stepping outside to check, she comes to encounter the SOA of the sun's shining directly; and such a direct encounter with an SOA should normally be enough to produce conviction that the SOA is the case. Again, if Camille's situation antecedently were such that she found it indubitable that the sun was shining (for example, if she were lying on a sunny beach), then very likely she would know something about that SOA just by virtue of being so situated. In general, if N's situation is such that it is (for whatever reason) indubitable that a given SOA is the case, then very likely there is something about the SOA that N knows in that situation. Thus, when Descartes (according to the present interpretation) found, upon reflection, that he was unable to doubt that he thought, he was properly situated (insofar as he was actively thinking about the matter) to claim to know the premise (*cogito*) on which knowledge of his existence (*sum*) could be demonstrated.

But what constitutes knowledge in cases like this is the subject's being in the presence of the SOA known, not the indubitable character of the accompanying belief. What Descartes needed to establish his existence beyond reasonable denial was not a belief impervious to doubt, but a belief such that the very fact of believing it put the believer in the direct presence of what the belief was about. As another possible candidate, consider the belief expressed by "there is a belief I am currently entertaining." If subject N actually entertains a belief to that effect, then N is aware of the content of the belief in question, which means that N is directly aware of entertaining a certain belief. But N's entertaining a certain belief is an SOA; and for N to be directly aware of the SOA, it must be actual. The upshot is that N is directly aware of an SOA that is actual, which is tantamount to N's knowing that SOA. Thus, by believing that there is a belief that he is believing, Descartes could secure knowledge that he is believing, from which knowledge of his existence would follow as surely as from his original *cogito*.

What is important to see for our purposes is that this result follows without regard to whether the belief in question is indubitable. The reason it is important to see this is that it reinforces the conclusion reached on other grounds above that indubitability is not a factor productive of knowledge. Whether Descartes—or anyone else, including the twentieth-century phenomenalists—had reasonable hopes of reconstructing human knowledge on unshakable foundations is a further question beyond the concerns of this inquiry.[23] The point to be retained from the present discussion is that indubitability is not a source of unshakable knowledge. Even if propositions can be found that are impervious to doubt, no knowledge is forthcoming by taking note of this property.

4. Gaining, Having, and Retaining Access

A feature typifying attitudes of cognitive access as a class, we may recall, is that they are properly queried by asking "How?" (instead of "Why?").[24] If someone purports to know something that we find less than perspicuous, for instance, we might properly inquire, "How do you know that?" Or if someone notices something that escaped our ken, a proper question would be, "How did you (come to) notice that?" And so on for other attitudes like discerning and discovering, learning, perceiving, recognizing, and remembering. In posing questions of this sort, we might be challenging a person's claim to have achieved such an attitude, or we might merely be seeking information about how the attitude was reached. In either case, the query calls for an explanation of what was done to bring the achievement about, or perhaps an account of the circumstances in which the other person managed to achieve it.

There is an interesting asymmetry among different subclasses of the attitudes in question, however, with respect to explanations that are suitable in response to such queries. This asymmetry ties in with a similar disparity already noted in section 1 above. Whereas perceiving and noticing, we observed, are common sources of knowing, neither typically would be said to have stemmed from knowing in turn.[25] In general, knowing stands apart from these and similar attitudes of access in that the others result in knowledge, but not vice versa. And since identifying the source of something is a standard way of explaining how it came about, a corresponding disparity exists between explanations of how one knows and explanations of other such attitudes. In response to the query "How do you know?" for instance, one might properly respond that one had noticed or perceived the SOA in question. The reason such a response would be appropriate is that noticing and perceiving are common ways of coming to know. But if asked how one comes to perceive or notice a given SOA, it normally would not count as a proper answer to say merely that one knows it. The reason in this case, by opposite tack, is that neither perceiving nor noticing is a standard consequence of the attitude of knowing. The same asymmetry holds between knowing and most remaining attitudes of cognitive access;[26] while any of these others might figure properly in an explanation of how one knows, the presence of knowledge does not explain how the others are achieved.

Another respect in which knowing differs from the other cognitive attitudes, not unrelated to that above, has to do with the durations of the attitudes in question. Although knowledge resembles the other attitudes in having a definite time of beginning, once begun the state of knowing might continue indefinitely. Upon discovering that the sun is shining when first arriving at the beach, Camille comes to know that the sun is shining, and she might continue to know for a long period afterward that the sun was shining during that day at the beach. But the period during which her *discovery* was current scarcely begins before it is over. Although a moment or two might be required for her to scan the sky, and thereby to discover that it is virtually cloudless, it would be distinctly odd to say an hour or so later that she still is discovering that the sun is shining. Discovering and finding belong to that type of achievement that occurs momentarily and then slips into the past.[27] The same may be said for most attitudes of cognitive access, the main exceptions being the attitudes of knowing and remembering. We will return to remembering in the final paragraphs of this section. For the moment, the thing to note is that knowing is a cognitive posture one might occupy over an extended period, while the other attitudes are sharply limited in temporal extent.

How is this difference related to the asymmetry noted above, according to which the other attitudes serve as sources of knowledge but are not themselves results of knowledge in turn? Part of the answer appears in the following consideration. If knowing by itself were a cause of discovering and finding, or of other cognitive attitudes like perceiving and noticing, then the fact that we often maintain a state of knowing indefinitely would entail that these other attitudes likewise were of indefinite duration. But these other attitudes are of momentary duration at best, which means that knowing by itself does not bring about their occurrence. However, there is no restriction of this sort in the other direction. Upon perceiving or finding that such-and-such is the case, one perforce comes to know that SOA. And the fact that perception itself is an attitude of short duration is not germane to the length of the resulting state of knowledge. Similar remarks are in order for the other attitudes in question. Each remains capable of producing knowledge that might last indefinitely, despite being confined itself to a tenure that is only momentary.

The other part of the answer takes us back to the observation above that the "How?" question asked of these other attitudes generally cannot be answered with reference to a prior attitude of knowing. In response to the question "How do you know?" to say it again, we typically refer to other attitudes of cognitive access, pointing out that we previously have discovered, noticed, or perceived (etc.) the actual SOA we have come to know. In short, when responding to the "How?" question posed with respect to knowing, we typically cite some antecedent manner of cognitive access. But this mode of explanation is not reciprocal, in that these other forms of access cannot be accounted for by prior knowledge in turn. When the "How?" question arises regarding these other forms of access, what manner of explanation is normally available?

Suppose that Deirdre has just noticed that the children were still playing in the garden and has said as much to her husband, Duncan. And suppose that Duncan, not realizing that his wife had recently left her office, confronts her with the question of how she happened to notice that. Deirdre's response might well be that she had stepped outside and found herself in full view of where the children were playing. Or suppose that Duncan had perceived subsequently that the children were hiding. On being asked how he perceived them if in fact they were hiding, he responds by saying that he had crept up behind them and had observed them carefully without being detected. One form of response available to queries like this, accordingly, is to explain how one is situated in a manner conducive to cognitive access of the kind in question.[28]

There are other ways of responding as well. If Deirdre were chronically inattentive to other matters while engrossed in her law books, she might cite a momentary lapse in concentration by way of explaining how she happened to notice the children's whereabouts. Or if Duncan's eyesight were particularly bad, and the children a considerable distance off, he might mention using his binoculars when asked how he had perceived them.[29] The general conclusion to be drawn from such examples is that when the achievement of cognitive attitudes like finding, noticing, and perceiving is queried, it is relatively unusual to explain them with reference to other attitudes of cognitive access. Unlike the question of how one knows some thing or another, which is commonly answered with reference to one of these other modes of access, the "How?" question when asked of these other attitudes themselves does not typically elicit responses in terms of yet another cognitive attitude.

The cumulative upshot of these various dissimilarities between knowing and the other attitudes we have been discussing may be recapitulated in the following fashion. Although all are attitudes of cognitive access, and thus attitudes one adopts toward actual SOAs, there are substantial differences among them regarding manner of access involved. To perceive (discern, discover, notice, etc.) is a matter of initially *gaining* access — a matter, that is to say, of a given SOA being introduced into the presence of a cognitive subject. Attitudes of this initiating sort are of short duration and typically do not persist past their moment of achievement. To know a given SOA, on the other hand, is a matter of *having* access to some facet of the actual world. Although the access provided by knowing might be initiated through one of the more fleeting attitudes, once achieved it has potential for persisting indefinitely. Indeed, it has the potential for persisting long after the SOA that is its object has vacated the immediate presence of the knowing subject. Although Camille, for example, initially came to know that the sun was shining by taking notice of that fact when she arrived at the beach, she may continue to know for many days after that the sun was shining on that particular occasion.

How can a person continue to have access to an SOA that is no longer in that person's immediate presence?[30] If noticing and perceiving, for example, are modes of gaining cognitive access, and knowing a mode of having access once it is gained, what is involved in keeping that access current? In what manner, that is to say, might that access be retained? These questions introduce the topic of memory.

Memory constitutes one of the most vexing topics of epistemology, as any seasoned philosopher knows, and most of its complexities are beyond the reach of the present study. Our present concern is with memory (and similar attitudes like recalling and recollecting) as it serves in the preservation of knowledge, and that concern must be confined to a few points of particular relevance. The first is an extension of the prior observation (in section 1 above) that one can remember a given fact only if one has known that fact previously. Two requirements are built into this precondition. One is that memory is by nature veridical,[31] in that we remember only what was actually the case. Since knowledge is veridical in exactly the same sense, the conditionality of memory upon prior knowledge assures that this requirement will be met. The other requirement is that one can remember SOAs only of which one was previously aware, which is to say that remembering something cannot be the first time it has come to one's attention. Since knowing itself involves some manner of awareness, this requirement also is taken care of by the conditionality of memory on knowing.

The extension of this basic conditionality that concerns us presently is that remembering is not a way of entering a state of knowing. Unlike such attitudes as finding and noticing, which are modes of gaining access to the world as it is, remembering is a way of retaining access that has been gained by some other mode of entry. The temporal sequencing among such attitudes is thus invariable: *having* access (knowing) is always preceded by some means of *gaining* it (finding, noticing, etc.); and only access gained previously can be *retained* (by remembering, recalling, etc.).

A second point of immediate relevance is that remembering, like knowing, is a mode of access that does not require a physical copresence between subject and object. Although modes of gaining access, like discovering and perceiving, generally require some sort of spatiotemporal proximity between the subject and the occurrences that constitute the SOA in question, memory generally is not bound by requirements of proximity. For an SOA to be available as an object of memory, to be sure, that SOA must have been an aspect of the actual world at some point in time, but this typically will be a different time than when the SOA is remembered.[32]

A final point has to do with the kinds of explanation we typically find appropriate in response to "How?" questions posed with respect to memory. As with the various modes of gaining access discussed above, the achievement of remembering generally is not explained in terms of other cognitive attitudes or states. If someone asks Camille how she remembered that the sun was shining on a particular day long past, the query would not be satisfied by her saying that she had perceived that it was shining or that she knew it was shining a day or so afterward. Instead, she might mention some particular mnemonic resource ("Every weekend that spring had sunny weather") or some feature of the event that made it especially memorable ("It was my birthday and my first day at the beach for over a year"). A no less common type of response would be to cite some record one had kept of the circumstances in question ("I checked my diary," or "I have a news clipping concerning that outing").[33] It is by devices such as these that human knowledge remains in currency, a matter due for further discussion in chapter 10.

5. Knowledge of Sorts Other Than Cognitive

There are various senses of the term "know" other than that of cognitive access, with which latter we thus far have been concerned exclusively. Several of these other senses are worth discussing briefly, if only to help us see that taking them into account does not compromise the general thesis upon which most of the argument of this chapter is based—namely, the thesis that knowing is not a propositional attitude.

Among the (nonarchaic) senses of "know" in the scholarly dictionaries is that of "being acquainted with"[34] or "being familiar with." To know a person (well, vaguely, or incidentally) is in some manner to be (well, vaguely, or incidentally) acquainted with that person, and to know a city (thoroughly or casually) is to be (thoroughly or casually) familiar with its thoroughfares and public spaces. Other things known in this sense, beyond persons and places, include institutions (the stock market, the judicial system), works of art (Sophocles' *Antigone,* Beethoven's Ninth Symphony), and intellectual disciplines (physics, the calculus).

Now, it indeed is the case that we sometimes speak of knowing certain doctrines or principles (Heraclitus's dictum that everything is in motion, the Second Law of Thermodynamics), which might be loosely described as a matter of "knowing propositions." But there is no exception here to the general conclusion above that knowledge is not an attitude toward propositions. To know the Heraclitean dictum that everything is in motion is to be familiar with the proposition to that effect and to realize that the proposition has been attributed to Heraclitus. But familiarity of this sort is not a propositional attitude. Merely to have heard of (learned of, or otherwise become apprised of) a notable saying is not to address that saying as having a particular truth-value. Accordingly, it is not to address that saying in any role it might have as a proposition, in which its truth or falsity would be a matter of primary relevance. Put otherwise, it is not to address the saying in an attitude of propositional stance—belief, assertion, and so on—in such a manner that one's attitude itself takes on a truth-value. One might come to believe (or disbelieve) the proposition that everything is in motion, of course, in which case its truth-value would be relevant to the character of the belief. But the cognitive attitude one takes toward the saying in this case would be extraneous to the sense in which one might be said to know the Heraclitean dictum—the sense merely of being familiar with that particular saying. Merely to know a proposition in the sense of being familiar with it, in brief, is not to take a stance regarding the success of the proposition in its representational role. Hence, knowing in this sense is not a propositional attitude.

Another sense of "know" clearly distinct from any manner of cognitive access is that of "knowing how," which covers a wide variety of abilities and skills. The oriole knows how to build a nest, the spider knows how to spin a web, and the infant mammal knows how to suck milk. Capacities of this sort appear to be innate, having more to do with reflexes than with cognitively guided activity. Other types of ability, to be sure, require cognitive direction. Knowing how to use a slide rule, or how to do long division, involves skills achieved only with the help of a disciplined intellect. There are even skills that, if exercised auspiciously, might be instrumental in providing the subject access to the world as it is—that is, skills that might *support* a cognitive attitude like recognizing or knowing. When Deirdre walks through the gate into the garden, for example, her knowing how to identify the song of a spotted thrush (that ability) may lead directly to her coming to know (that cognitive attitude) that a thrush is singing in the bush around the corner. Regardless of its degree of cognitive involvement, however, the mere possession of a skill of this sort does not by itself constitute an attitude of cognitive access to the world as it is. Merely knowing how to identify (recognize, discern, etc.) an object as having a certain property, that is to say, never amounts to actually knowing (recognizing, discerning) a particular SOA consisting of the object's actually having that property. Knowing how to tell whether a politician is honest, for instance, is not equivalent to knowing that any given politician is honest. The reason, obviously enough, is that knowing how to identify or recognize an SOA, as distinct from actually recognizing or discerning the SOA in question, does not require that the SOA in fact be the case. The upshot is that knowledge *how,* like the knowledge of being familiar with persons and places, is not an attitude toward actual SOAs.

But neither is knowledge *how* an attitude toward a propositional object. Knowing how to identify the song of a thrush is an ability devoid of any involvement with propositions, as is knowing how to use a calculator or knowing how to swim. One might even know how to deal with propositions in some particular fashion, such as testing them for consistency or drawing out their consequences. But even skills like these do not constitute cognitive attitudes, and thus perforce are not attitudes toward propositional objects. As a consequence, knowing *how* is simply irrelevant to the general thesis that knowing is not a propositional attitude.

Notes

1. To know that a given SOA X is not the case is to know a second-order SOA concerning the status of the first-order SOA X. The rank-ordering of SOAs is explained in chapter 4.

2. This second criterion, as noted in chapter 1, is derived from J. L. Austin's well-known article "Other Minds," in *Philosophical Papers*, J. O. Urmson and G. J. Warnock, eds. (Oxford: Oxford University Press, 1961). One of Austin's main concerns in this article is to examine the nuances involved in our ordinary use of the expressions "*Why* do you believe?" and "*How* do you know?" and to consider why we seldom ask "*How* do you believe?" or "*Why* do you know?"

3. As far as I can tell, there is only one attitude of cognitive access listed in chapter 1 that both entails (in the sense of involves) the presence of knowledge and is entailed by it in turn. This is the attitude of realizing which, although not terminologically equivalent to knowing in all rhetorical contexts, nonetheless appears to be tantamount to knowing as a cognitive state.

4. As we saw in the previous chapter, section 7, there is a sense of the term "fact" (fact[s]) in which a fact is equivalent to an actual SOA. This is not to be confused with the other sense (fact[p]) in which a fact is a true proposition. The sense of remembering here under discussion, it should be noted, is distinct from what might be termed "seeming to remember," which of course is compatible with not actually remembering in the present ("vertical") sense. Seeming to remember is akin to fancying (see chapter 1, section 6) and, as such, cannot be identified in terms of the criteria above. It should be apparent, nonetheless, that seeming to remember is not an attitude of cognitive access.

5. With a few notable exceptions (see below), epistemologists writing in the twentieth century are near unanimity in defending views equating knowledge with true belief that is reinforced in some appropriate manner. Before Gettier's 1963 paper (see note 6 below), the standard view was that knowledge is justified true belief, for which see R. B. Braithwaite, "The Nature of Believing," *Proceedings of the Aristotelian Society* 33 (1932–1933), 129–146; A. J. Ayer, *The Problem of Knowledge* (London: Macmillan, 1956), 34; and R. M. Chisholm, *Perceiving: A Philosophical Study* (Ithaca, N.Y.: Cornell University Press, 1957), 16. After 1963, philosophers have been more guarded

in their views about what constitutes appropriate reinforcement, but most have maintained that some form of justification is adequate to convert true belief into knowledge. For cases in point, see Ernest Sosa, "The Raft and the Pyramid: Coherence versus Foundations in the Theory of Knowledge," in *Empirical Knowledge: Readings in Contemporary Epistemology*, Paul K. Moser, ed., 1st ed. (Lanham, Md.: Rowman & Littlefield, 1986); Alvin Goldman, "What Is Justified Belief?" *Empirical Knowledge*, Moser, ed.; John Pollock, *Contemporary Theories of Knowledge* (Lanham, Md.: Rowman & Littlefield, 1986), 9; and Robert Audi, *Belief, Justification, and Knowledge* (Belmont, Calif.: Wadsworth, 1988), 153. R.M. Chisholm, in *Theory of Knowledge*, 3rd ed. (Englewood Cliffs, N.J.: Prentice-Hall, 1989), 11, focuses on the property of being evident in place of justification as the reinforcing factor, but joins the consensus in identifying knowledge with true belief plus appropriate substantiation.

Among dissenting voices prior to 1963 are those of H. H. Price (see, e.g., "Some Considerations about Belief," *Proceedings of the Aristotelian Society* 35 [1934–1935], 229–252) and of H. A. Pritchard (*Knowledge and Perception* [Oxford: Clarendon Press, 1950]). More recent opponents of the view that knowledge is a kind of belief include Zeno Vendler (*Res Cogitans: An Essay in Rational Psychology* [Ithaca, N.Y.: Cornell University Press, 1972], chap. 5), and (with qualification) Keith Lehrer (see, e.g., "Belief, Acceptance, and Cognition," in *On Believing: Epistemological and Semiotic Approaches*, H. Parret, ed. [Berlin: Walter de Gruyter, 1983], 172–183), Paul Moser (*Knowledge and Evidence* [Cambridge: Cambridge University Press, 1989]), and Merrill Ring ("Knowledge: The Cessation of Belief," *American Philosophical Quarterly* 14, no. 1 [January 1977], 51–59). The relevant qualification in these latter cases is that the authors all conceive of knowledge as relating a cognitive subject to a proposition, which suggests that their dissent from the prevailing view is based on reasons that may themselves be problematic.

The earliest known version of the thesis that knowledge is equivalent to justified true belief is proposed (but not defended) in Plato's *Theaetetus*. Plato's own considered view (found in several texts, including the *Republic*, the *Sophist*, and the *Seventh Letter*) seems to have been that knowledge, in the strictest sense, is immediate awareness of reality, which for Plato amounted to direct awareness of Forms. A consequence of this view is that knowledge is a cognitive state that cannot be analyzed into more basic cognitive components (such as evidence and belief). The present approach agrees with Plato's in treating knowledge as cognitively basic, and hence not subject to the type of analysis with which most of the literature cited above is concerned.

6. From Edmund Gettier, "Is Justified True Belief Knowledge?" *Analysis* 23 (1963): 121–123.

7. "Is Justified True Belief Knowledge?" 121. Although Gettier does not say in so many words that justified true belief is necessary for knowledge, he does refer to "S's being justified in believing P" as "a necessary condition of

S's knowing that P" (second paragraph). Presumably, S's believing *truly* counts for him as a necessary condition as well.

8. Gettier, "Is Justified True Belief Knowledge?" 122.

9. In his book *Knowledge and Perception,* Pritchard anticipated the result above that belief cannot be converted into knowledge, on the basis of the claim that knowing and believing are opposed mental conditions (87). His discussion left it unclear whether in his opinion this opposition made them mutually exclusive, but he allowed at least "that believing is a stage we sometimes reach in the endeavor to attain knowledge" (62).

10. A biconditional of the form "p if and only if q" is a material equivalence just in case there is no logical entailment in either direction between p and q, but the relation between them nonetheless is such that p is true whenever q is true, and vice versa. For further elucidation of this terminology, see W. V. O. Quine's *Methods of Logic,* rev. ed. (New York: Henry Holt & Co., 1960).

11. Proposition p is materially conditional upon q just in case p is true only if q is true and there is no entailment making q consequent upon p.

12. For explanations along this line of the supposed importance of justfication as a central issue in epistemology, see Goldman, "What Is Justified Belief?" 171–192 (esp. 171); and Pollock, *Contemporary Theories of Knowledge,* 9.

13. The "Gettier problem" was criticized above for being premised on the assumption that knowledge is a kind of belief. This flaw in the problem as originally formulated does not disqualify "Gettier-style" counterinstances from showing that not all cases of justified true belief are cases of knowledge as well. It may be noted in passing that proffered solutions to the problem initially posed by Gettier tend to focus on the "accidental" character of the relation between the fact known (e.g., Smith's getting the job) and the evidence on which the associated belief is based (e.g., Jones' having the requisite number of coins in his pocket), and that as a consequence some philosophers have come to construe the problem as calling for an account that makes this relation "nonaccidental." A consequence of the falsehood of (MC2), to which the present approach is committed, is that no matter how intimate the relation between N's reasons for believeing that X is the case and N's knowing that X, the accrual of evidence by itself can never produce knowledge.

14. While representation of some sort is involved in every cognitive state, for reasons discussed in chapter 9, representations that take the form of propositions are required only with attitudes of stance.

15. A philosopher who operates comfortably with the notion of "unconscious beliefs" presumably would respond by suggesting that, although D in this case might not consciously assent to the proposition that the children are in the garden, she will maintain a belief to this effect in "unconscious" form. Now, whatever sense one might attach to "unconscious belief," it seems that at the very least one would have to think of such beliefs as dispositional. According to the account of dispositional belief given in chapter 2 (section 2), however, the disposition to believe a given proposition is just a tendency to re-

new the assent by which the belief in question was initially constituted. Given this sense of dispositional belief (which the reader, of course, may or may not consider adequate for his or her own purposes), if there is no initial assent—that is, if the subject has never adopted the relevant belief "consciously"—then there is no matter of the belief's continuing on a dispositional basis. So if D has never assented to the relevant proposition, there is no matter of her believing it "unconsciously." D's case remains one in which she knows the children are in the garden but has no beliefs in that regard.

16. Someone might attempt to mount an argument against the possibility of such counterexamples to the effect that it is inconceivable that anyone should ever be in a position to say (seriously, in an assertoric mode, etc.) "I know that . . . , but I don't believe it." Since saying this would involve both articulating the proposition in question and alluding to the possibility of entertaining it, it is indeed true that no plausible example of someone's knowing a given thing but not believing its propositional counterpart can be described in first-person terms. The examples discussed in the text, accordingly, are all formulated in the third person. And there is no anomaly of an "ordinary language" sort in saying, "He knows very well that . . . , but he can't (yet) believe it." To be sure, since if he *cannot* believe it, then perforce he *does* not, the basic intelligibility of such a saying provides additional evidence that it is conceivable (however rare) that someone might know a certain SOA but not believe any proposition in its regard.

17. Other arguments against the view that knowledge entails belief, and hence implicitly against (MC1), are put forward by Paul Moser (*Knowledge and Evidence,* 20–22), Keith Lehrer ("Belief, Acceptance, and Cognition," 172–183), and Wayne Davis ("Knowledge, Acceptance, and Belief," *Southern Journal of Philosophy* 26, [1988], 169–178). Moser's case rests on the distinction between what he calls "dispositional" and "nondispositional knowledge," the latter of which involves some manner of assent toward a proposition, falling short of belief, that relates a knower psychologically to the propositional object of knowledge. While Moser's argument seems plausible once its premises are granted, his conception of propositions as suitable objects of knowledge prevents relying upon this argument for purposes presently at hand.

18. This is contrary to the view of Goldman in "What Is Justified Belief?"171.

19. Pritchard, *Knowledge and Perception,* 96. As noted in chapter 2, a view close to this was also held by Ayer in *The Problem of Knowledge,* see p. 34.

20. Descartes's enterprise in his *Meditations on First Philosophy* is subject to various interpretations, some of which lay more stress on the indubitable character of the *cogito* than others. There is no intent here to defend the interpretation discussed above as fully accurate historically.

21. For a typical account, see A. J. Ayer's "Phenomenalism," *Proceedings of the Aristotelian Society* 47 (1946–1947), 163–196. For a related account that also traces knowledge back to indubitable foundations, see B. Russell's "The

Relation of Sense-Data to Physics," in *Mysticism and Logic* (London: George Allen & Unwin, 1910).

22. The qualification takes account of such provisos as that no proposition can command assent on the part of a subject who is not considering it.

23. Whether the project of foundationalism itself is defensible, quite apart from the forms it takes at various stages in its history, has been frequently debated in recent epistemological literature. An insightful recent discussion of this topic may be found in chapters 5 and 6 of Richard Fumerton's *Metaphysical and Epistemological Problems of Perception* (Lincoln: University of Nebraska Press, 1985).

24. See section 1 above; for more detail, see section 3 of chapter 1.

25. This is not to take a stand on the issue whether one in some sense must know a given thing in order to be able to perceive it, and so forth. The point is merely that perception produces knowledge in a way in which knowledge in turn cannot be said to produce perception. To *perceive* that so-and-so perforce is to *know* that so-and-so as well, but not vice versa.

26. A notable exception is the attitude of realizing, which seems to be on a par with knowing in this respect. For the apparent equivalence between knowing and realizing from the present perspective, see note 3 above. An exception of another sort is remembering (recalling, etc.), discussed later in the present section.

27. This difference between knowing, on the one hand, and discovering and finding, on the other, is reflected in the different tenses typically involved when these attitudes are being queried. While there are any number of commonplace circumstances in which the query "How do you know that so-and-so?" might appropriately be raised, the questions "How *do* you discover that so-and-so?" and "How *do* you find that so-and-so?" seem quite uncommon. What we would be much more likely to ask in querying a person's claim to have discovered (or found) something is "How *did* you discover (or find) so-and-so?" To be sure, a person normally would not claim merely "to discover" (present tense) something in the first place, which is probably why the question "How do you discover so-and-so?" (present tense) sounds so distinctly odd. Given the momentary character of discoveries and findings, by the time someone gets around to reporting such an achievement, the achievement itself is a thing of the past. The typical claim, accordingly, is to *have* discovered so-and-so; and the typical query, in turn, is "How *did* you discover that?"

28. See the penetrating discussion of such explanations in Austin's "Other Minds."

29. A distinctly different kind of answer might be elicited by the question of how one perceives (notices, recognizes, etc.) when the question is actually posed (rather than merely discussed) in a context of epistemology or of cognitive science. In such a setting, the answer might take the form of a technical theory of perception. An account germane to this issue is sketched in chapter 8, in connection with the topic of mental representation.

30. An even more perplexing question lurks in the background: given that

knowing is an attitude one comes to occupy toward an actual SOA, how can one continue to know an SOA that is no longer actual—as Camille continues to know for many days after that the sun was shining during her day at the beach? Part of the answer has to do with knowledge not being an attitude with spatiotemporal restrictions, so that knowing does not require the spatiotemporal copresence of subject and object. Another part has to do with the temporal indexing of SOAs. The latter topic is taken up in the following chapter; the former is discussed briefly in the text in this chapter.

31. As noted in chapter 1, memory properly speaking is neither true nor false, and to speak of memory as veridical is not to say otherwise. Put negatively, the point is that if someone purports to remember something that did not actually happen, then that person in fact did not remember. The penalty of thinking one remembers something that did not happen is not to "remember falsely" or "incorrectly," but not to remember at all. (The not uncommon proviso "If I remember correctly" should be taken to mean, not "If my memory is right," but something like "If things are as I seem to remember them.")

32. For N to remember a given SOA, that SOA must have been the case at some time prior to N's achievement of remembering it. The veridicality of memory (see note 31 above) requires the SOA remembered to have been the case at the relevant earlier time, not its being the case at the time it is remembered.

33. Written records of course employ propositions, which makes germane the observation that when written records serve as a prompt of memory, it is not the propositions that are remembered, but the SOAs they record. The content of a proposition might convey one's cognitive awareness back to events of the past without the proposition itself standing as an object of memory. Like all other modes of cognitive access, memory finds its objects among actual SOAs, not among propositions of any form by which such SOAs might be recorded.

34. The sense here is other than that associated with Russell's "knowledge by acquaintance," which he describes as a form of direct awareness achieved "without the intermediary of any kind of inference" (Bertrand Russell, *The Problems of Philosophy* [London: Oxford University Press, 1912], 46), and which obviously is a sense carrying cognitive significance. While there is precedent in Russell for recognizing immediate awareness as a source of knowledge, and for treating memory as a faculty by which that awareness can be retained, the present approach provides no support for his view that sense-data figure prominently among the objects of direct acquaintance (46–48).

Chapter 6

REPRESENTATIONS AND STATES OF AFFAIRS

1. The Ontological Neutrality of States of Affairs

In the discussion thus far we have relied upon a more or less intuitive conception of SOAs, illustrated by examples selected for their commonplace character. One example is the SOA of snow's being white, which is an actual feature of the world that B can know by engaging it in an attitude of cognitive access. Another is the SOA of the sun's shining at the beach, a representation of which as being the case constitutes a proposition toward which C might adopt an attitude of belief. Yet another is the SOA of the gate's being shut, which is a circumstance D hopes will turn out to be actual because of its consequences for the safety of her children.

The characterization of commonplace SOAs like these as features of the world that a subject might engage if actual, or as aspects of the world that might be represented in propositions, or as eventualities one might hope for when not actually present, nonetheless leaves questions unanswered about how less commonplace SOAs are to be conceived. Are SOAs to be counted among things in the world, in the manner of atoms and molecules and various other constituents? How do SOAs acquire distinct identities, and how are they to be distinguished from one another? A particularly difficult set of issues concerns the relation between SOAs and their representations. What enables a re*present*ation to "stand in" for the thing represented, in such a manner as to "present" an SOA that is not itself present? And to what extent does the *re*presentation of an SOA depend upon communal agreement about what is represented? These are only some of the issues that require clarification if our conception of SOAs is to be consolidated on more than an intuitive basis.

The need for clarification is compounded by the fact that a variety of

145

different conceptions of SOAs can be found in current literature.[1] Without taking on the gratuitous burden of examining all of these in detail, and without suggesting that any among them is without merit in its immediate context, the present chapter undertakes to provide a self-contained account of the nature of SOAs sufficiently well worked out to provide reliable support for our ongoing analysis of belief and knowledge. Let us begin with certain ways in which SOAs ought *not* be conceived.

What is the case at any given moment depends upon how things stand in the world at that particular time. And change in time brings change in how things stand in the world. To say this, however, is not to say that SOAs are events *in* time. Among events that have occurred in time is Socrates' death by taking hemlock. This event occurred during a certain day in the early fourth century B.C. As a result of the occurrence of this event, it is the case that Socrates died by taking hemlock. But the SOA of Socrates' having died by taking hemlock is not the same as the *event* of his death itself. The event of his death took place in the fourth century. It also took place within the precinct of Athens. But the SOA of Socrates' having died in that manner at that time and place is not itself localizable either temporally or spatially. It is the case that Socrates died under those particular circumstances. But this is no more the case *in* Athens than in Cairo or Corinth, and no more the case *at* that particular time than at any time thereafter.

SOAs, in brief, are not occurrences—they are not events that take place or happen in space and time. While an event's occurring or not occurring might constitute an SOA, the SOA itself is not something that occurs in turn. Socrates' death is an event that occurred, and this event's having occurred is an SOA. But the SOA is not a further occurrence of this event's occurrence. For an SOA is not an event and, accordingly, is not something that might be thought of as either occurring or not occurring.

An SOA, further, is not a process—not an activity or happening with a beginning or an end. The sun is in a process of gradually cooling, and may have been in this process for most of its existence. Accordingly, it is the case that the sun is gradually cooling. But the SOA of the sun's undergoing this process is not something itself that had a beginning. Neither is it something that happens gradually or that happens in the center of the solar system. The reason is that the SOA of the sun's gradually cooling is not a thing of the sort that happens at all. For the sun to cool gradually is for something to happen—namely, the process of the sun's gradually cooling. But the SOA of this happening is not yet another happening.

Nor is an SOA an object in possession of certain properties. At least, it is not a propertied object in the concrete world, like a rock that is hard or a molecule in solution.[2] An object as such is neither the case nor not the case, regardless of how it happens to be characterized. Yet if an object x (e.g., a rock) possesses a property F (e.g., hardness), then it is the case that x possesses F. And whatever is the case is an SOA. The SOA here is not x-cum-property-F, but rather x's *having* the property F—or what comes to the same thing, x's *being* F. We might think of it this way: whereas a certain object with a certain property (e.g., the hard rock) might be *part* of the actual world, that object-cum-property is not an *aspect* of the world as it is. What stands as an aspect of the world as it is, given the hard rock among its constituents, is the SOA of the rock's being hard. If property F is an actual feature of object x, then x's being F is an aspect of the actual world. The SOA itself is not a constituent of the world, but an aspect of the world as it happens to be constituted.

An SOA, once again, is not something that occurs; but the occurrence of something might be an SOA. An SOA is not a process; but the process of something's happening might be an SOA. An SOA, further, is not an object with certain properties; but an object's possessing certain properties might be an SOA. In general, an SOA is an aspect or feature of the world as it is, or as it might be should other circumstances prevail. In either regard, an SOA is *possible;* and if an SOA is an aspect of the world as it actually is, it counts as *actual* as well.

It follows from this characterization that the present conception of SOAs does not fit well with that of Wittgenstein's *Tractatus,* according to which the world is constituted by what is the case. Comparison with the *Tractatus* is warranted, if for no other reason, by the fact that this early work of Wittgenstein contains what probably stands as the most carefully worked out account of SOAs to the present day. While there are several respects in which the present treatment differs from that of the *Tractatus,* the most important difference concerns the ontological status of SOAs.

The role of states of affairs[3] in the world, according to the *Tractatus,* is pinned down in a few remarks at its very beginning: "The world is all that is the case" (1) and, "What is the case—a fact—is the existence of states of affairs" (2). The implication of (1) and (2) is drawn out explicitly in 2.04, where Wittgenstein says, "The totality of existing states of affairs is the world." In 2.06 he goes on to distinguish the existence from the nonexistence of states of affairs, referring to these as "positive facts" and "negative facts," respectively. Inasmuch as the "totality of existing states of affairs also determines which states of affairs do not exist" (2.05;

also 1.12), however, the world could also be specified by indicating all the states of affairs that do not exist. Whether specified positively or negatively, what the world is comprises just those states of affairs whose mode of being is that of *being the case* (in contrast with that of *not being the case*).[4]

Prominent among Wittgenstein's motivations for thinking of the world as being made up of states of affairs was the intention of working out an account of how the world can be meaningfully depicted in propositional language. The result, as any persistent student of the *Tractatus* comes to realize, is what amounts to a multileveled parallelism between language and reality. On the side of language, there are elementary propositions and all the other (compound) propositions that can be constructed from elementary propositions by the operations of truth-functional logic.[5] An elementary proposition consists of a configuration (as he puts it, "a nexus, a concatenation" [4.22]) of names, where the names in question are signs for his so-called simple objects (2.02). On the other side are atomic states of affairs (the positive and negative facts of 2.06) and their combinations, the occupation by which of their respective modes of being (their "existence and non-existence" [2.06]) comprises reality. An atomic state of affairs consists of a configuration of simple objects (2.0271) that "fit into one another like the links of a chain" (2.03). (The point of this simile is that, in the context of atomic states of affairs, "objects stand in a determinate relation to one another" [2.031]). Since the names of these objects occurring in elementary propositions stand in correspondingly determinate relations, there is an isomorphism in configuration between a given proposition and its corresponding state of affairs on this elementary level that enables the former to pick out the latter uniquely. Inasmuch as the atomic state of affairs it represents constitutes the meaning or sense (*Sinn*) of an elementary proposition (2.221), such a proposition has meaning just in case it picks out an atomic state of affairs in this unambiguous manner.

Complex states of affairs, moreover, are combined out of atomic states of affairs in a manner directly parallel to the combination of compound out of elementary propositions.[6] The meaning of a compound proposition, accordingly, is the combination of atomic states of affairs to which it corresponds in structure; and a compound proposition has meaning just in case it corresponds in this way to a unique combination of atomic states of affairs. The upshot is an account of language and reality according to which every meaningful proposition uniquely depicts a possible state of affairs and every possible state of affairs is uniquely depicted by a meaningful proposition.

This isomorphism between meaningful propositions and states of affairs is essential to the account of language in the *Tractatus,* and has much to recommend it on other grounds as well. There is something intuitively fitting about a principle calling for a distinct state of affairs to be represented by every meaningful proposition and for a distinct proposition to represent the status of every intelligible state of affairs. But the way in which Wittgenstein sought to guarantee this isomorphism carries with it a substantial ontological liability. Wittgenstein's tactic, in retrospect, was to give states of affairs determinate structure independent of how we come to speak of them, to locate a subset of these states of affairs (those that exist) in the world as its basic constituents, and then to account for the meaning of propositions in terms of a corresponding structure by which every meaningful proposition is paired with a unique state of affairs. By their very definition, propositions acquire both identity and meaning according to the structure they share with the basic constituents of reality. The difficulty with this tactic is that it yields a conception of propositions that is beholden to a particular conception of the nature of reality. If the world in fact is not constituted as Wittgenstein here conceived it—if the logical atomism of the *Tractatus,* that is to say, is an incorrect ontology—then the account of propositions that goes with it is also faulty.

The present account of propositions, on the other hand, is ontologically neutral. A proposition, as defined in chapter 3, is to be conceived as a representation of an SOA that ascribes to that SOA a determinate status. And a proposition is true just in case the SOA represented actually has the status it is represented as having. In this conception of propositions and propositional truth, nothing is presupposed about the nature of the world. Ontological neutrality is preserved with the understanding of SOAs as aspects or features that the world might present and that can be *re*presented by a variety of symbolic expressions. Whereas the particular aspects presented from time to time of course depend upon how the world happens to be constituted, SOAs themselves are not among its constituents. Our understanding of what it is to be an SOA, accordingly, is not affected by our conception of the basic makeup of the world.[7]

2.   The Respect in Which States of Affairs Lack Independent Identity

A second respect in which this view of SOAs differs from that of the *Tractatus* has to do with the requirement of determinate structure by which Wittgenstein sought to secure the complete isomorphism he needed between states of affairs and the propositions depicting them. By the time of the *Philosophical Investigations,* as most readers will be aware, Wittgenstein himself had seen that determinate sense is not needed for language to be meaningful and that the attempt to reduce discursive language to "logically pure" propositional components amounts to little more than the "pursuit of chimeras."[8] But someone might repudiate the ideals of logical atomism and still find motivation for viewing the world as exhibiting aspects or SOAs that are entirely determinate. There are other reasons than those of Wittgenstein, that is to say, that might recommend a view of the world as presenting features that are fixed in the very nature of things.

Consider someone who accepts a physicalist ontology and thinks of the world as a vast collection of basic particles which in various combinations comprise all there is. Reflecting that for any two or more of these particles there must be a determinate SOA of their being related in some specific manner, this person might then come to think of the world as receiving a determinate structure from the totality of such SOAs. The character of the world would be determined by these SOAs, which would be determined by the disposition of its basic particles in turn. Like its counterpart in the *Tractatus,* this hypothetical conception of a wholly "particulate" universe posits SOAs that are entirely determinate, standing ready to be depicted by an appropriately crafted language. Only in this case it would be the language of an adequate physical science, instead of the language of logical atomism. The upshot in either case is to view the world as naturally *pre*sorted into SOAs which language subsequently is crafted to symbolize. An explanation of how language can be adjusted to these presorted facts, in turn, provides a neat account of how language comes to mirror reality.

But this conception of predetermined SOAs is no less "chimerical" than its counterpart in the *Tractatus.* Consider the following thought experiment by way of conceptual antidote to the notion of a world *pre*-sorted into determinate SOAs. Imagine a world consisting of just two discrete objects (x and y), with just two spaces (a and b) each containing exactly one object, and just two times (1 and 2) for either object to occupy a space—that is, a world of two objects in a four-cell spacetime. Let 'O(a,1)' symbolize the occupant of space a at time 1, and so forth. There are four possible ways for objects to be arranged in this world. That of x = O(a,1) = O(b,2), for instance, might be schematized as follows:

	1	2
a	x	y
b	y	x

If x and y are thought of as the simplest of physical entities, instead of Wittgenstein's simple objects, and the matrix in which they are situated as physical space-time, instead of Wittgenstein's logical space, then this world is the simplest of physicalist counterparts to the world envisaged in the *Tractatus*. Since there are exactly four ways for x and y to be grouped together, this world might be thought to admit exactly four possible SOAs, only one of which is actual in a given version of the world.

Yet there are many different ways in which this world might be described, and hence many aspects that might be distinguished when we come to characterize it. Assume first (A) a language describing the world as a whole, without applying to the circumstances of its individual components. This language enables the following characterizations: (i) the world at any moment comprising exactly two objects, and (ii) its actual course consisting entirely in these two objects' standing in just one of four possible spatiotemporal relationships. Characterizations (i) and (ii) are representations of SOAs, where the SOAs in question are aspects of the world at large. Other characterizations follow when we add (B) a language of space-time occupancy, including: (iii) O(a,1) being identical to O(b,2) (the state of the world depicted by the diagram above); (iv) O(a,1) being different from O(b,2) (in a state other than depicted above); and (v) the occupants of a and b being different at any given time (which is the case in any of the four possible arrangements). Now add (C) a language allowing identification of the objects individually, which provides the further characterizations: (vi) x occupying a at both time 1 and time 2; (vii) x occupying b at both time 1 and time 2; and (viii) x at any time being cotemporal with y (which also is the case in any possible arrangement). Here we have eight different characterizations of the imaginary world, each representing an SOA that is distinct from the others. With (D) a language of interactions, yet more could be added: for example, (ix) y replacing x as occupant of a (also represented by the diagram above); (x) x replacing y as occupant of a; (xi) a change in place of x requiring the same of y; and (xii) a change in place of y requiring the same of x. More again might be added with yet other languages, such as (E) a language expressing spatiotemporal symmetry.

Despite the world of this thought experiment being one of the simplest imaginable, admitting only four different arrangements of its constituent objects, there are at least a dozen distinct features by which this world might be characterized. And each characterization picks out a distinct SOA. It is apparent that these SOAs reflect the nature of the world—in particular, its being constituted by exactly two spatiotemporal objects. But it is apparent also that the characters of these SOAs are not dictated by the nature of the world alone. These characters depend as well upon the descriptive resources of the various languages (here, the languages A through E) in which the SOAs come to be represented. For someone who did not know in advance what distinctions could be drawn within these languages, there would be no way of specifying these SOAs on a basis merely of knowing the world's basic constituency. These SOAs, in brief, are not *pre*determined. They have no identity independent from the way we come to represent them.

Let us apply the lessons of this thought experiment to some comparable circumstances of the actual world. Like the two-object world considered above, the world as we know it contains particular objects, undergoing specific processes that comprise distinct events. And our world undoubtedly was characterized by factors such as these long before symbol-systems of any sort appeared on the scene. Consider a child born to a distinct set of parents, with a distinct genetic makeup, distinct fingerprints, and the like, all properties independent of how they come to be symbolized. Or take Lake Superior for another example, the largest lake on the North American continent quite apart from the descriptions by which it has been known. Or, consider the trajectory of Venus, which had a determinate path of movement around the sun before there were humans present to make planetary observations. The child's birth is a specific biological event; but the SOA of the child's being born with a distinct set of features is not an event, biological or otherwise. The relative size of Lake Superior is a determinate geographical property; but the SOA of its being the largest lake on the continent is not the same as that object (Lake Superior) with that property (its relative size) inhering. And the movement of Venus around the sun is a particular physical process; but the SOA of Venus orbiting the sun in a particular pattern is not a process of any sort whatever.

An SOA, in brief, is not an object with properties, nor a process or event that occurs or transpires. When arguments to this effect were presented in the section above, the immediate purpose was to show that SOAs are not among the constituents of which the world is composed. Another purpose was to prepare the way for the present point: that the world is not *pre*sorted into SOAs with distinct identities. As was the case in our simple thought experiment, the SOAs that figure among the world's many aspects are not predetermined by the world's basic constituency, but depend as well upon the symbol-systems in which we undertake to describe it. What generates SOAs with discernible identity are the distinctions we employ in applying these descriptions. What the world itself contributes in turn are the distinguishable circumstances to which we find it feasible to apply the distinctions made available by these symbol-systems.

The point is not that SOAs are by origin "subjective." If the phenomena the subject encounters are themselves subjective (i.e., are phenomena to which the subject's presence makes a direct contribution), then to be sure the SOAs to which these phenomena contribute will be subjective in a derivative manner. A typical example of subjective phenomena is the hunger we encounter in the course of a day's business. If there were no conscious subjects to experience hunger, then hunger would not be a factor in the world for anyone to encounter. Other phenomena that presumably are subjective in a similar manner (although some philosophers would disagree) are the many colors and sounds and tastes and odors that we experience in response to our sensory surroundings. When such features come to participate in one or another SOA, the SOA itself is accordingly subjective.

But it is not because a given SOA happens to be subjective in this manner that its identity depends upon the way it is symbolized. Consider by way of contrast an SOA that is entirely objective (in the sense of involving no factors to which a subject makes an essential contribution)—say, the SOA of D's having a unique set of fingerprints. Given our current techniques for recording impressions of the lines on a person's fingertips and for comparing different sets of fingerprints in magnified detail, we can establish certain patterns of loops and whorls by which most persons can be uniquely identified. Assuming that D is a normal person in this regard, we can speak with confidence about there being a distinct SOA consisting of D's having a unique set of fingerprints. This SOA reflects our being able not only to analyze the prints in question, but also to deal with them symbolically (to establish authoritative records, to discuss them publicly, etc.) in a manner that has significance for the rest of society.

But now consider, by way of counterpoint, the case of King Tutankhamen—or any other person at the far end of antiquity—who lived at a time before fingerprints became socially consequential. Although we speak confidently, in retrospect, of the SOA of Tutankhamen's *having had* unique fingerprints, there was no SOA accessible to anyone of his time consisting of his (currently) having a unique set of fingerprints. Since there was no way of understanding what might have been *unique* about his fingerprints, there was no way of representing in any available symbol-system the SOA of his having fingerprints that were somehow unique. And inasmuch as there was no way of dealing with this SOA symbolically, the circumstance of his having unique fingerprints was not among the aspects the world might have presented to anyone living during his time. King Tutankhamen undoubtedly *had* a distinct set of fingerprints; the status of that fact (as we conceive it) is not in question. Nonetheless, there was no SOA within the ken of his contemporaries consisting of this person's (currently) *having* a distinct set of fingerprints. For similar reasons, there was no SOA available to early inhabitants of North America consisting of Lake Superior's being the continent's largest enclosed body of water. Lacking techniques to measure the dimensions in question, these people lacked the capacity to represent symbolically the circumstances we now recognize as comprising this fact.[9] The SOA of Lake Superior's being the largest lake on the continent, accordingly, would not be among the discernible aspects of the world these people inhabited. Nor, for similar reasons, would any SOA involving Venus's trajectory.

The manner in which an SOA takes its identity from the symbolic resources that provide for its representation, in short, is indifferent to whether the SOA involves objective or subjective features. In both cases, the identity attaching to an SOA—the characteristics by which we know it and discuss it with other people—reflects the resources of the symbol-systems that provide for its representation.

A basic tenet of Wittgenstein's *Tractatus* noted in the section above is that every meaningful proposition uniquely depicts a possible SOA and that every possible SOA, in turn, is depicted uniquely by a meaningful proposition. A roughly similar isomorphism is beginning to take shape in the present account, despite substantial differences in the way SOAs are conceived. The corresponding tenet toward which the present account is driving is that, in general, every SOA has a representation by which it is uniquely depicted and that every significant representation of the sort in question depicts a unique SOA. Before this account can be developed further, however, we need to look carefully at the manner of representation involved. These remarks set the agenda for the remainder of the present chapter.

3. Some General Requirements for Representation

One way for an SOA to gain the attention of subject S is for it to be present (in effect, to "present itself") within S's cognitive presence. Another is for it to be represented by a symbolic surrogate that S recognizes as standing in for that SOA. An SOA can be represented by an appropriate sign or symbol, in much the manner that a client's interests can be represented by a lawyer or advocate. The client's interests are made present to a court of law, for instance, by the lawyer serving as the client's proxy. Similarly, an SOA is made present to a cognitive subject by a sign or symbol standing in for the SOA itself. The topics to which we now turn concern the requirements that must be met by a symbolic surrogate in order to serve as a representation of an SOA. We begin with certain requirements for representation generally.[10]

In order to make something other than itself present to a subject's awareness, a representation must be present within that awareness itself. Just as a lawyer who never appeared in court could not represent a client's interests in that particular venue, so a symbol of which S is not aware could not represent another thing in S's awareness. This much seems obvious. What makes this requirement worth dwelling upon is the manner in which the representation must present itself. If a lawyer is to represent a client in a courtroom setting, the presence of the lawyer must serve to make the interests of the client present to the court (the judge, magistrate, etc.) as well. In a context of communication, similarly, if a symbol (or set of symbols) is to represent a certain SOA, the presence of the symbol must serve in turn to make that SOA present to the subjects involved. Whatever its context, it is crucial to the role of a representation that it direct attention, as it were, away from itself and toward the thing it represents.

Put somewhat differently, what this requirement amounts to is that a representation must function on two distinct levels. On one level, its function is to engage the attention of a subject in such a manner as to become an object of awareness itself. On the other level, it functions to point beyond itself, to direct the awareness of the subject to the thing it represents.

For a simple illustration, consider the term "mat" in the context, say, of "the cat's being on the mat." In order to represent some relevant mat to a given subject S, the term must engage S's awareness in such a fashion as to be distinguishable from similar symbols ("cat," for instance), but it also must direct S's attention to the mat in question. Sometimes the first function might predominate (as when S is checking how "mat" is spelled), and sometimes the second (when S is reading fluently without dwelling on the text).[11] The essential thing to note, in this regard, is that a representation is capable of directing a subject S's attention to the thing it represents only when present to S itself, but in such a manner as to present that other thing to S's awareness as well.

Let us put this down as the first general requirement of representation:

(GR1)   In order to serve as a representation, a symbol must both be present itself to a cognitive subject and also direct the attention of the subject beyond itself to the thing it comes to represent.

Inasmuch as almost any object of awareness might come to serve in a representational role in some context or another, this function of directing attention beyond itself cannot be due solely to a capacity of the symbol itself. Such a function, instead, must be an aspect of how we deal with the symbol and thus something learned when we learn its representational use. Further discussion of this function will be deferred to the sections below where we take up the question of how representations are learned.

A second general requirement comes into view with the observation that representations often function to direct attention not only to things that happen to be absent from the subject's immediate presence, but also to things that do not actually exist. "Pegasus" is an example any recent philosopher would recognize, along with the old standby "the present king of France." An example more germane to the present context is the expression "snow's being green," which represents an SOA not found (naturally) in the actual world. What is the nature of the relation between representation and object that allows a symbol to stand in for something that does not exist?

Let us begin with some disclaimers about what this relation is not. It is not like the relation between smoke and fire, which is a commonplace example of a causal relation. The causal relation between a particular fire and a particular column of smoke requires that both actually exist (at identical or closely proximate times) for the relation to hold between them. No smoke is produced by a nonexistent fire, and no actual fire produces smoke that never exists. A cause by nature is a thing that brings an effect into existence, just as the effect is the result of its cause's having existed.

The relation of an effect (e.g., smoke) to its cause (e.g., fire) is what might be called a *concrete* relation. A relation is concrete, in the sense intended, if its coming to hold between two or more terms depends upon all those terms existing at some time or another. The point of referring to a relation of this sort as concrete is to identify it as a relation that holds typically between two concretely existing entities.[12] A relation between term A and term B is concrete, by definition, just in case the existence of both A and B is required, within some appropriate time frame, for the relation to hold between them.

There are other cases of concrete relations that are not causal in character. One straightforward example is the relation of *being contained within* holding between a particular flower and a particular flowerpot. In order for the flower actually to be contained within the flowerpot, both entities must exist and (in this case) exist simultaneously. No nonexistent flower is ever contained in an actual flowerpot, and no nonexistent flowerpot ever contains an actual flower. Another example is the relation of *being a successor of* holding, for instance, between Lyndon Johnson and John Kennedy. Although the time frame of presidential succession does not require that both men continue to exist simultaneously, only a person who once existed could be succeeded as president, and only an existent person could take over as successor.

There is another kind of relation, however, that is essentially characterized by the absence of any requirement that all its terms exist. As we shall see in due course, this kind of relation is of primary importance for our understanding of cognitive attitudes generally. But there are mundane examples that are not cognitive in character. A very simple example is the relation of *being adjusted to*. A crescent wrench might be adjusted to a nut of some nonstandard dimension, even though no nuts of that size had ever been fashioned. A somewhat more contrived example is the relation of *being tuned to,* in which a radio receiver might stand to transmissions of a given frequency. Although most radio frequencies have been assigned (by some authority or another) to specific commercial or other dedicated uses, there probably are narrowly confined frequencies to which no operating transmitters have ever been (steadily) tuned. A radio receiver might be tuned to transmissions on one of these frequencies even though no such transmissions have ever existed.[13] Yet another sort of example, not technological in nature, is the relation of *approximating* or *tending to-*

ward. The complex system of atmospheric pressures over the surface of the earth is always tending toward a state of equilibrium, which it never reaches because of other factors (incident solar radiation, evaporation from ocean surfaces, etc.) that keep the system out of balance. The fact that such an equilibrium never actually exists does not keep the earth's weather system from tending toward it.

We may refer to relations like these as *virtual* relations.[14] By way of definition, let us say that a virtual relation is a relation between two or more terms, not all of which need exist at any time for the relation to hold between them. Some relations of this sort, like those noted above, have no direct involvement in our cognitive attitudes. But there is an important subgroup of virtual relations that play a central role in our cognitive activities generally. As we shall see in chapter 9, to be sure, these relations are the basis of cognitive intentionality.

These relations are akin to relations like picturing, which itself is obviously a virtual relation. Think of Monet's painting of a grainstack on the outskirts of Giverny (chapter 3), embellished to include the depiction of certain furnishings in the foreground identifying it as a painting of a view through a window of a certain cottage in that vicinity. The painting is related to the grainstack by the relation of picturing, and it would remain so related whether or not the grainstack (which, if it existed, may have served Monet as a model) had ever actually existed. Or consider a photographic copy of Monet's painting, perhaps intended for inclusion in a book of art history. Whereas the photographic copy is concretely related to the painting itself—since something must exist in order to be photographed—it is related virtually to the object that Monet painted, inasmuch as it also depicts a grainstack that may never have existed.

Pictures such as paintings and photographs are germane to our cognitive lives in the obvious sense that all paintings—and most photographs—are produced intentionally. But such pictures usually are not constituents of specific acts of cognition. Photographs and paintings, that is to say, are the results of such acts, but they generally are not internal to cognitive activity itself. A virtual relation at the very heart of our cognitive activity, by contrast, is that involved in the representation of SOAs. Let us consider some specific examples.

The linguistic expression "snow's being white," when used as a representation of snow's being white, is virtually related to that SOA. There is no difficulty, accordingly, in understanding how the expression can serve in its role as a representation even when the SOA represented is not actually present. Even if all snow were to melt from the face of the earth—

indeed, even if no snow had ever been encountered in the first place—
"snow's being white" might still represent the SOA of snow's being
white. This is because virtual relations, by definition, do not require that
all their terms exist. Another example comes with Deirdre's belief that
the children are in the garden, where the representation in question is
some neuronal process (a matter discussed in chapter 8) picking out the
SOA of the children's being in the garden. This process stands in that representational relationship whether or not the children are actually in the
garden. Recall also the case of Monet's painting, with a label (e.g.,
"comme ça") to the effect that the scene nearby is just the way it is depicted as being within the painting. For someone addressing the labeled
picture as a propositional object, and thereupon believing that the scene
is arranged the way the picture shows it (i.e., believing that the proposition is true), the picture itself serves as a representation of the SOA
therein depicted. And it does so regardless of whether that SOA in fact is
the case. These examples are typical of cognitive representations generally,[15] which are virtually related to the SOAs they are taken to represent
and which, accordingly, can represent those SOAs whether the latter are
present or not.

Other consequences of the representational relation's being virtual in
character will come under consideration in following chapters. For the
moment, it is enough to note, by way of summary, that representations
cannot be related to what they represent in the manner that smoke is
(causally) related to fire.[16] The relation between smoke and fire is a concrete relation. An important fact about representations, on the other hand,
is that they are virtually related to the things they represent. As a second
general requirement of representation, accordingly, we have:

> (GR2)   In order for a symbol to serve as a representation, it must be vir-
> tually related to what it comes to represent.

Applied to the representations of SOAs specifically, the sense of (GR2)
is that a symbolic expression serves as a surrogate for an SOA just insofar as it can stand in for that SOA whether or not the latter is ever actual.

4.   Requirements for the Correct Use of Representations

Requirements (GR1) and (GR2) concern the nature of the relation between a representation and the thing it serves to represent. These requirements hold for representations generally (pictures, descriptions,

singular terms, etc.), regardless of the way we happen to use them. There are other requirements that pertain to their proper use and to how this use is learned by a cognitive agent. In keeping with the focus of the chapter overall, our concern in this section will be with certain requirements in particular that govern the correct use of descriptive phrases representing SOAs.

If one were a thoroughgoing conventionalist in such matters, one would look for prerequisites for the correct use of descriptive phrases in the regularities of linguistic usage maintained by cooperating members of particular groups. The reasons it is correct among speakers of English to symbolize snow's being white by the expression "snow's being white," one would be inclined to say, are akin to the reasons it is correct in England to drive on the left side of the road. If the conventions of word use were different in relevant respects, we might refer to snow's being white by the expression "snow's being green" instead. Someone who deviates from the established patterns of use, willfully or otherwise, would be in no worse position than Humpty Dumpty, who chose to mean by "glory" what other speakers mean by "a nice knock-down argument."[17] If other speakers could be induced to follow suit, then what had been deviant would become the correct use of the expression.

At the opposite extreme in matters of meaning is the essentialism endorsed by Humpty Dumpty in another mood, when he said to Alice, "my name means the shape I am" and chided her for having a name that means no shape in particular. To get the use of representations right, from this viewpoint, is to use them in a manner that reflects the character of the things they represent. As the sonorous appellation "Humpty Dumpty" suggests the configuration of its rotund bearer, so "butterfly" suggests the motion of something that "flutters by," "thunder" (read "thu-u-un-n-nder") suggests the rumbling sound of thunder, and so forth. According to this view, in its extreme version at least, the right use of representations has nothing to do with convention and everything to do with essential features of their referents. If "snow's being white" is the correct expression for snow's being white, the reason is to be sought in the nature of that SOA, rather than in the fact that English speakers customarily use "snow" for snow and "white" for the color of its typical appearance.

Now, while there are indeed some terms that enter language through arbitrary convention (e.g., "gluon" and other terms of particle physics), and others (such as "butterfly" and "thunder") that presumably are adopted to fit the character of their referents, it is scarcely credible to think of all save a minor subset as being of either sort exclusively. The reason for bringing these two inherently implausible views into the discussion is just to isolate an assumption they both incorporate that runs counter to the requirements spelled out below. The picture of language acquisition sponsored by conventionalism depicts an enterprising subgroup of a linguistic community agreeing initially on what certain terms are going to mean and then informing subsequent learners of the right way to use the terms in question. In either transaction, the matter of singling out and identifying the things to which the terms are supposed to refer is taken to be unproblematic. The person engaging in the transaction somehow fixes unambiguously on the relevant object and then pairs it up with the term that thereby comes to represent it. According to essentialism, in turn, learning to attach the right nomenclature to an object involves not only a previous ability to identify the object, but also an ability to discern its essential features. While some manner of insight may be required to accomplish the latter, picking out the relevant object for purposes of naming is something that just happens as a matter of course.

The assumption both views share, in brief, is that someone undertaking to learn the proper representation for a particular object or SOA is already prepared to identify the thing represented. On some levels of sophistication in language acquisition, perhaps, this assumption is not entirely unrealistic. Someone who has the referential resources of a given sector of language already well under control might encounter little difficulty in singling out a particular set of circumstances while discussing alternative ways of referring to it (e.g., "the aunt of one's father might be called one's grandaunt," or "given the properties of that particle, why not call it a gluon?"). This is so in the case of learning a second language particularly, where referring expressions can often be learned under the accommodating rubric of meaning-equivalence. But referential resources of this sort are not always available when expressions for unfamiliar objects or SOAs are being introduced into language initially. And they typically are unavailable as well to individuals extending their verbal competencies into unfamiliar territories of a given language, however well known these might be to other users of the same language. In such cases, one's ability to discriminate among relevant SOAs develops hand in hand with one's ability to represent them symbolically. Learning to identify the SOAs, that is to say, is part of the same process as learning how to represent them correctly.

Consider the nature of this interdependency in a few concrete illustrations. The language of the Inuits living in the northern reaches of Labrador contains over two dozen different names for snow, designating qualities of snow masses they have practical need to distinguish in coping with the weather above the sixtieth parallel. For most, there are no corresponding terms in English (Italian, Swahili, etc.); and people who do not speak a language native to such regions generally would be incapable of identifying most of the various qualities in question. Although paraphrases might be provided where specific names are missing ("*mauja,*" e.g., means roughly "soft, deep snow footsteps sink into"), someone unversed in the native language could not be expected to identify the precise circumstances in which a given paraphrase applies (e.g., the circumstances of *mauja* piling up along the seashore).[18]

How could someone whose linguistic competence is limited to non-Inuit languages learn to pick out and identify these various qualities of snow? A natural first step would be to find a native speaker with whom one could communicate (in a language other than Inuit) and to gain an initial idea of the features by which various snow types are distinguished. Next would come a process of trial and error in which misidentifications would be corrected by one's mentor and identifications close to the mark would receive corroboration. Interactions of this sort would involve reference to the snow types in question, through expressions one would learn as the process continued. By the time the transaction is over, and one has gained the perceptual skills by which the various snow conditions themselves are distinguished, one has also gained the verbal facility to represent these SOAs in a communicable manner. The two skills are acquired in tandem fashion: by learning to identify the snow conditions one encounters perceptually, one gains ability to represent them linguistically; and by learning the linguistic representations, one gains the ability to distinguish their perceptual counterparts.

The foregoing example concerns the acquisition of skills already established within a linguistic community by someone from a foreign linguistic group. Now consider how these skills might emerge within the community initially. What might account for the ability among the Inuits themselves to identify SOAs involving so many different types of snow? For one thing, there must be a persistent need to adjust the conduct of daily life to these various snow conditions. While such a need might arise occasionally on the individual level, the need in question is largely a communal matter, affecting the survival of the group itself under adverse weather conditions. Accurate forecasts must be made, precautions taken, support networks established, supplies laid in—along with many other accommodations on the community level—to see the group through the dark winter ahead. But group adaptations of this general sort require communication about the factors to be taken into account. An upshot is that the ability of individuals within the group to identify the snow conditions upon which their livelihood hinges develops concurrently with the linguistic means to discuss them communally. The ability to discriminate among relevant SOAs goes hand in hand, once again, with the ability to represent them in a communicable manner.

A further example takes up the case of an individual undertaking to gain skills that are already established elsewhere within the linguistic community. Many people find it difficult to recognize poison ivy in the wild, both because of its resemblance to similar plants and because it comes in several different varieties. Other people have no difficulty in detecting its presence and are fluent in the vocabulary by which its presence is represented. How does someone from the former group learn to identify poison ivy and thus change membership to the latter group? The answer is, in basically the same way that the nonnative in the first example above learns to identify the various snow types from the native speaker—by trial and error monitored by a cooperative teacher who already possesses the skills at issue. But interaction with a teacher involves shared linguistic competencies. And the process of learning to identify the SOA of poison ivy being present adds facility in reporting its presence to the range of competencies shared by teacher and learner. The upshot, yet again, is that skill in identifying SOAs that once were elusive comes hand in hand with an ability to represent them symbolically.

Examples of this sort could be multiplied at will, but the interdependency they illustrate should now be apparent. This interdependency can be articulated in a pair of requirements, labeled "LR" for "learning requirements." First comes:

(LR1)   For S (a cognitive subject) to learn how to identify X (an SOA) when immediately present, S must learn the correct use of some representation R by which X's presence can be communicated symbolically.

This requirement appears at first to admit obvious counterinstances, such as cases of what psychologists refer to as "operant discrimination"[19] that occur without transactions in public language. Like other organisms with comparable visual systems, human beings are prone to various kinds of conditioning that encourage selective responses to certain features of their perceptual environment. Could not an artist become sensitive to a new shade of blue without talking it over with other persons to whom the shade is familiar? Could not a musician become aware of a new tonal quality without help from conversation with knowledgeable colleagues? The answer in either case, of course, is "Yes." The point to be made in response, however, is that our present concern is not the development of perceptual acuity as such, which is an episode privy to the individual perceiver having to do with the discrimination of preexisting perceptual circumstances. Our concern is the identification of SOAs, which have no identity apart from how we come to represent them. And the manner in which we come to represent them involves the use of a shared symbol-system.[20]

To repeat, SOAs are not entities with identities that are fixed before we encounter them, like many of the objects we encounter in our natural environment. Thus lacking an independent identity of its own, an SOA relies for its identifying features upon distinctions brought to bear in the use of the symbols representing it. This was the main lesson of section 2 above. The primary lesson of the present section, in turn, is that learning to identify SOAs for what they are is a matter of learning the features that distinguish them for purposes of representation. But learning the features by which they are distinguished when we come to represent them is tantamount to learning the proper use of the representations involved. Hence (LR1).

The learning transaction cited in (LR1), in effect, is the opposite of what Wittgenstein called "ostensive teaching."[21] Instead of teaching terms by uttering them while pointing at their proper objects, the procedure behind (LR1) is a matter of teaching the nature of what a term represents by demonstrating the proper use of the representing term. The learning involved in either case, of course, is the receptive pole of the teaching relation.

There is a corollary of (LR1) that should be noted before we pass on the second learning requirement, namely:

(C1)   All identifiable SOAs have corresponding representations sanctioned within a linguistic community.

Read in one way, this corollary appears tautologous. Given that SOAs generally receive identity from the way they are represented, no SOAs have identity that lack representation. And needless to say, there are no SOAs with distinct identity that we can mention specifically without means to represent them (another angle that makes the corollary appear tautologous). But read another way, (C1) reaffirms the conclusion of section 2 above: that SOAs have no identity in and by themselves. And this conclusion did not appear tautologous in advance of its arguments. The purpose of restating this conclusion in the form of (C1) will become clear in the section below when it is combined with corollary (C2) of the next requirement.

In keeping with the limitations noted at the beginning of this section, the next requirement pertains to the representation of SOAs in particular. It resembles a more general principle that approaches truism; namely, that in order to learn the correct use of a symbol, one must learn what the symbol stands for. Where the following requirement departs from truism is in its specification of what this latter amounts to. To learn what a representation (R) of an SOA (X) stands for is to learn how to identify that SOA when it is immediately present to the subject (S) concerned. Hence:

(LR2)   For S to learn the correct use of R as a representation of X, S must learn how to identify X when immediately present.

As a corollary (subject to the limitations above), we have:

(C2)   All representations with communally sanctioned use have identifiable SOAs to which they correspond.

The sense of "communally sanctioned use" in (C2), as in (C1) above, is equivalent to that of "correct use" in the (LR) requirements. More will be said about this sense in the paragraphs below.

The rationale for requirement (LR2) comes from section 3 above, with its distinction between two ways an SOA might engage the attention of a cognitive subject. One way is for the SOA to "present itself" to the subject, in which case it is present without mediation (i.e., immediately present). The other is for it to be represented by a symbolic surrogate, in which case it is made present through the means of a representation (hence, mediately present). The sense of (LR2) is that the availability of a representation R for use in the latter capacity depends upon one's ability to identify the relevant SOA when present in the former manner and that, accordingly, a subject's gaining the ability in question is a condition for using the representation in that capacity. Put more directly, the sense is that S's acquiring competence in the use of R as a surrogate for X is conditional upon S's being able to identify X when encountering it directly. If one cannot identify X for what it is when X is in one's immediate presence, then any pretense of invoking

X through the medium of representation is an empty use of the symbols involved.[22]

What is this ability to identify X when it "presents itself" to the subject immediately? The approximate answer indicated by the (LR) requirements is that S's ability to identify X when immediately present amounts to a particular competence in the use of symbolic surrogates for X. But what competence in particular? To make this precise, it will be helpful to introduce some "technical" terminology.

5.   The Designative Use of Representations

Let us say that an SOA is *actually current* when it is an aspect or feature of the world as it is (in the sense discussed in section 1 above). And let us refer to the mode of use in which an expression serves as a representation of an SOA that is actually current as the *designative use* of that expression. A representation serves as a designation,[23] accordingly, when it is being used to represent an SOA that is actually current simultaneously with the circumstances of its use. The expression "the sky's being cloudy," for instance, is used as a designation under circumstances concurrent with those constituting the sky's actually being cloudy.

In this definition of being actually current, it will be noted, there is no mention of a particular cognitive subject to whom the SOA "presents itself." Indeed, an SOA might be actually current under circumstances in which no subject happens to be currently involved. To be actually current is for an SOA to be an aspect of the actual world, whether this status is revealed to a subject or not. The special sense given the term "designation" above, accordingly, does not require that S's use of R as a designation be confined to cases in which X is immediately present to S. In order to work this sense of designation into an explication of the ability to identify an SOA that is immediately present, one further bit of technical terminology is needed.

The lesson of the previous section, appropriately rephrased, is that a language user gains competence in the designative use of a representation as part of the same process by which he or she learns to identify the SOA represented. Insofar as the representation is part of a public symbol-system, becoming competent in its designative use is a matter of learning the conditions under which it is correctly used in that capacity as a regular part of public discourse. Let us refer to these conditions as the *conditions for the correct designative use* of a representation.

To repeat, the conditions for the correct designative use of a representation are the circumstances in which the SOA it represents is actually current. The conditions for the correct designative use of the expression "snow's being white," for instance, amount to little more than the circumstances of snow's actually appearing white, to persons of normal vision, under normal viewing conditions.[24] In the case of "Deirdre's having a unique set of fingerprints," or "Lake Superior's being the largest body of water on the continent," the conditions are more complicated. In order to pin down the relevant criteria for the latter (to continue the example from section 2), we would have to discuss both the techniques available for measuring large boundaries and the application of these techniques to the water areas in question. The actual occurrence of circumstances of this sort, more fully spelled out, constitute the conditions for the correct use of the concerned representation in a designative capacity.

An example of a different sort is the case of the representation "my feeling hungry," where the conditions for its correct use as a designation are the circumstances of my experiencing pangs of hunger, recognizably distinct from other varieties of stomach discomfort. What this example illustrates is that satisfaction of the relevant conditions need not be evident in just *the same manner* to different individuals who share use of the same representing expression.[25] In the case of SOAs like D's having a unique set of fingerprints, which are "objective" in the sense explained in section 2 above, satisfaction of the conditions will be evident in basically the same manner to all individuals concerned. In the case of "subjective" SOAs like D's being hungry, on the other hand, the satisfaction of the relevant conditions will be evident in one manner to D herself (involving reference to her personal hunger pangs), and will be evident in another manner to other persons not directly aware of her personal experiences (typically, in a manner involving reference to her hunger-related behavior).

By way of summary, the *designative use* of a representing expression is its use as a representation of an SOA that is actually current, and the *conditions for the correct designative use* of the expression in question are the circumstances that constitute the currency of that SOA in the actual world. These definitions were introduced for their help in responding to the question of what it is to be able to identify an SOA when that SOA is immediately present to a subject. The approximate answer given at the end of the previous section is that one's ability to identify an SOA when immediately present consists in a particular competence in the use of symbols by which that SOA is represented. We are now prepared to specify the competence in question.

A subject S is able to identify an SOA X that is immediately present just in case S knows the conditions for the correct designative use of some available representation of X and can tell that those conditions are satisfied upon encountering X directly (i.e., without mediation). Since being able to tell whether the relevant conditions are satisfied requires knowing what those conditions are, moreover, we can say more simply that learning how to identify X when immediately present is learning how to tell, without mediation, whether the conditions are satisfied for the designative use of its representations.

There is another manner of putting this result that some readers might find more intuitive. As should be already apparent, (LR1) has the form "P only if Q," where P is "S learns how to identify X when immediately present" and Q is "S learns the correct use of R as representation of X." The form of (LR2), in turn, is "Q only if P." The conjunction of these two requirements, accordingly, is:

(LR1,2)   S learns how to identify X when immediately present *iff* S learns the correct use of R as a representation of X.

As we have just seen, however, learning how to identify X when immediately present is tantamount to learning how to tell whether the conditions for the correct designative use of R are satisfied. This gives us the biconditional:

(BC)   S learns the correct use of R as a representation of X *iff* S learns how to tell whether the conditions for the correct designative use of R are satisfied.

What (BC) says, in upshot, is that learning the correct use of R as a representation is a matter of learning to recognize immediately the occurrence of the particular circumstances that constitute the SOA correctly represented by that symbolic expression.

There is nothing surprising about the result when expressed in this fashion. Indeed, one might wonder whether the somewhat tortuous exercise pursued above is really necessary to achieve such obvious results. The response to this uneasiness is that the exercise in question has provided precise points of departure for further explorations in the chapters that follow, some of which lead to results that are much less intuitive. Before embarking on these further explorations, however, let us consolidate the various findings of the chapter thus far.

6. Representations and States of Affairs

The argument of section 2 above culminates in the observation that SOAs depend for their identity upon the symbol-systems we employ in representing them. The culminating point of the previous section is that one learns the use of the symbolic expressions by which SOAs are represented by learning the conditions for the correct designative use of those expressions. A consequence of the two results together is that these conditions play a key role in linking symbolic expressions with the SOAs they are taken to represent. Viewed from one side, these conditions are seen to establish the identity of the SOAs those expressions come to symbolize. Viewed from the other, they establish requirements for the correct use of the symbols by which these SOAs are represented. The SOAs, on the one hand, and the symbolic expressions, on the other, are inseparable partners in the representational relationship.

This consequence is little more than a restatement of the joint upshot of (C1) and (C2) above. (C1) is of the form "Every P corresponds to a Q," where P is "identifiable SOA" and Q is "communally sanctioned representation." And (C2) has the form "Every Q corresponds to a P." Taken in combination, the two corollaries therefore yield:

(C1,2)   There are no identifiable SOAs without sanctioned representations and no sanctioned representations without corresponding SOAs.

Bearing in mind that the discussion generating these corollaries was concerned with representations of SOAs specifically (in contrast with the more general concern of section 3), we see in (C1,2) a statement of a kind of isomorphism between SOAs and their communally sanctioned representations. Because of the identity-conditions for SOAs on the one hand, and the sanctioned use requirements for representations on the other, there is an invariable correspondence between the two types of entity.[26]

The matter might be viewed from yet another, more fanciful, perspective. On one hand is (A) the world as it actually is, presenting (B) various aspects for cognitive subjects to fix upon in their efforts to understand it. On the other hand are (C) symbolic representations that marshal these aspects in a communicable way, enabling (D) cognitive subjects to cooperate in their efforts of understanding. The aspects (B) are what we have been referring to as actual SOAs. In addition to SOAs actually current in the world as it is, there are others the world might conceivably make current, which subjects (D) have learned to identify in absentia, as it were. Among the representations (C) that symbolize these various SOAs, in like fashion, some are currently available for use as designations—that is, some are representations of SOAs that are actually current—while the remainder enable us to ponder "how things might be otherwise" and retain potential for use as designations in other than present circumstances. Whether currently employable in a designative capacity or not, however, any representation of proper standing must be capable of designative use. And only subjects capable of using a representation correctly in this capacity are capable of using it properly under any circumstances at all.

In the early days of the human race before symbolism was invented, the world (A) was there for subjects (D) to confront directly. And in those days, that was the only way in which the world could be confronted (i.e., directly), since neither SOAs (B) nor the symbolism (C) to represent them had yet appeared on the scene. Although the world had its full complement of objects-with-properties, and of various processes and events duly distributed through time, the world had not yet been apportioned into discernible aspects that could be standardized for representation by a standard set of symbols. When standardization occurred, it took the form of more or less firmly established conditions for the identification of certain circumstances with which distinct symbols could be associated. And it was by means of these conditions that (B) and (C) were joined in association—that is, that SOAs and symbols were brought together into what we have been calling the "representational relationship."

Before (B) and (C) were interposed between (A) and (D), human beings were incapable of communicating symbolically. Communication would have been limited to physical promptings and to the groans and cries that serve as "natural signs" of a person's inner feelings.[27] At this stage, there were no SOAs to be known and no propositions (incorporating representations) for the persons involved to believe. And needless to say, there would have been nothing like the propositional attributes of truth and falsehood, nor any means of mounting inquiry into the deeper nature of things. But after the interpolation of (B) and (C), all these things became available. There were aspects of the world that were capable of being known, and there were representations of the status of these aspects in the actual world that admitted belief. And there was truth to be gained by disciplined inquiry, inasmuch as the world had become segmented into aspects deliberately tailored to move inquiry in fruitful directions. The ways of cognition now were open to the human person, who became what Aristotle would one day call a "rational animal."[28]

The relevant burden of these remarks, fancy aside, is to suggest that the world becomes "cut up" into knowable bits, as it were, by the imposition of symbol-systems incorporating standardized conditions of applicability. Although the analogy of the "cookie cutter" comes to mind in this connection, this analogy might well prove more misleading than helpful. When one thinks of the dough to which a cookie cutter is applied, one is likely to think of a largely amorphous material that admits almost any shape the cook sees fit to impose upon it. The dough, so to speak, has very little to say about the shapes that will emerge when the cutter is applied. But the world is far from being an amorphous mass, ready to admit any form we choose to fix upon it. The patterns of language, in any case, do not *alter* the world as such; instead, they bring together features that the world already possesses in forms sufficiently regular to permit symbolic representation. There are, of course, new features the world takes on when people learn to use language — like that of including creatures in its midst that communicate by using symbols. But the interposition of (B) and (C) between individual subjects (D) and the world (A) at large brings about changes in (D) far more extensive than changes in (A), the most extensive being those associated with symbol use itself.

Among more substantial changes of this sort are the emergent capacities of belief and knowledge. Belief is concerned with the use of symbols in that it takes propositions as its proper object, propositions being representations of SOAs associated with ascriptions of status to the SOAs represented. And according to the analysis of chapter 3, at least, the statuses of note are being and not being the case. Knowledge is concerned with the use of symbols, in turn, insofar as SOAs receive identity from the way they are symbolized and knowledge is directed toward actual SOAs. An actual SOA is one that in fact is the case, from which it follows that knowledge is a way of relating to what is the case. Both belief and knowledge, in their respective ways, are concerned with the status occupied by SOAs.

But what is it for an SOA to be the case? And when we think of an SOA as not being the case, what is the status we conceive it to occupy? These questions are pursued in the following chapter.

Notes

1. The most thoroughly worked out account of SOAs currently available is found in the early sections of Ludwig Wittgenstein's *Tractatus Logico-*

Philosophicus (*Annalen der Naturphilosophie,* 1921). While the present treatment is indebted to this account in many respects, there are basic differences regarding the ontological status of SOAs that appear in the course of the discussion below. Another robust discussion of SOAs to which the present account is more closely related is that of C. I. Lewis in *An Analysis of Knowledge and Valuation* (La Salle, Ill.: Open Court Publishing, 1946), esp. chap. 3. Since there nonetheless are many differences of detail that make it unhelpful to cite this discussion on more than an occasional basis, it is appropriate to acknowledge a general indebtedness to Lewis's careful, and in many ways groundbreaking, work. Yet another influential work in which the terminology of SOAs figures prominently is R. M. Chisholm's *Theory of Knowledge,* 1st ed. (Englewood Cliffs, N.J.: Prentice-Hall, 1966). Particularly useful is Chisholm's comparison of his terminology in this regard (72n2) with that of other philosophers, including Whitehead and Von Wright as well as Lewis. Also to be noted in this regard is D. M. Armstrong's *A World of States of Affairs* (Cambridge: Cambridge University Press, 1997), which appeared too recently to have influenced the present discussion.

2. This, I take it, constitutes a basic difference between SOAs as presently conceived and the "situations" of situation-semantics, for which see, for example, Jon Barwise and John Perry's "Situations and Attitudes," *Journal of Philosophy* 68 (1981): 668–691.

3. In order to be consistent with the use of an unabbreviated "state of affairs" in quotations from the *Tractatus,* I maintain the practice of not abbreviating the expression in my discussion of this work. Locations of passages quoted from the *Tractatus* are given in the numbering system peculiar to that work (rather than page numbers).

4. The distinction between the world (2.04) and reality (2.06), I take it, is that reality consists of certain states of affairs *being* the case and certain others *not being* the case (i.e., reality is the occupation by states of affairs of those statuses), whereas the world is constituted by all states of affairs that happen to be the case.

5. See 4.51–4.52 and 5.101. While the conception of an elementary proposition defined in chapter 4 above differs from Wittgenstein's in basic respects, the present account of how other propositions are compounded out of elementary propositions is in essential agreement with his account.

6. The conception that complex states of affairs are compounded out of atomic facts in a manner paralleling the compounding of complex out of elementary propositions (rather than by some sort of causal connection; see 5.136 in this regard) is a key part of what is often referred to as the "logical atomism" of the *Tractatus.*

7. Perhaps the Aristotelian is right in maintaining the view that the world is made up of substances with properties. In this case, there will be aspects that the world might present consisting of certain substances possessing certain properties. Or possibly the Whiteheadian is right in viewing the world as composed of simple monads that are capable of becoming. Then there will be

SOAs consisting of simple monads being in the process of becoming. A more likely alternative, perhaps, is that contemporary physics is on the right track in working with conceptions of basic entities characterized by mathematical functions. If so, then the world will present SOAs consisting of entities being characterized by mathematical structures. As far as the present conception of SOAs is concerned, one alternative is as acceptable as another. Indeed, this is the point of the considerations above showing why SOAs are neither processes, nor events, nor objects-with-properties. SOAs are not constituent parts of the world, which precludes their being identical with entities of any particular sort that might qualify for inclusion among the world's basic components. Whereas the *Tractatus* lays stress upon propositions being depictions of the world's basic constituents, the present account should be understood as equally pointed in its denial that SOAs, which propositions represent, are constituents of anything at all. Instead, they are aspects the world might present, without presupposing anything about the nature of what stands behind these presentings.

8. Ludwig Wittgenstein, *Philosophical Investigations*, G. E. M. Anscombe, trans. (New York: Macmillan, 1953): sec. 94.

9. This illustration relies upon the assumption that these early inhabitants lacked techniques of linear measurement accurate enough to distinguish unambiguously between the sizes of Lake Superior and Lake Michigan, for example, and also that no given group of people were aware of all the lakes on the continent in a manner enabling a comprehensive judgment of their relative sizes.

10. In the current literature of cognitive science it seems to be accepted practice to mount long discussions of the roles representations are supposed to play in our cognitive activity while saying little or nothing about the nature of these representations themselves. A notable example is Jerry Fodor's *Representations* (Brighton, Sussex: Harvester Press, 1981) which, apart from a remark in the introduction that mental representations are "often called 'Ideas' in the older literature" (26), leaves the reader to guess what the term providing its title is supposed to stand for. For this and other reasons that will appear in due course, the use to which the term is put in the present study should be kept distinct from the often casual associations upon which the current literature of cognitive science is prone to trade.

11. For a case in which the two functions share dominance, imagine the term "mat" inscribed in either red or green ink (the other terms being in black) in order to indicate the color of the mat to a knowledgeable reader.

12. What counts as concrete may well vary from context to context. The reason we feel comfortable describing a relation between fictional fire and fictional smoke in a novel as causal, for example, is that in this context both terms of the relation would count as concrete.

13. A radio receiver clearly might *remain* tuned to transmissions of a given frequency when the station previously emitting these transmissions goes off the air. The relation between tuner and no-longer-existing transmission, pre-

sumably, is no different from that between tuner and a transmission that never existed.

14. The term "virtual" comes from optics, with no intended connection with the fashionable nomenclature of "virtual reality" in contemporary consumer-oriented electronics technology. The virtual focus of an optical surface is the place from which an image apparently emanates, whether or not the object represented by the image in fact occupies that place. We may say, accordingly, that the viewer of such an image is virtually related to whatever the image represents.

15. As noted above, pictures generally are of cognitive significance in a manner pertaining to the intentions of the artist or to the viewer's understanding of those intentions. In the last example, the picture also is part of a proposition (the picture-cum-label) that is an integral part of a cognitive subject's belief.

16. Actual smoke, of course, is a sign of fire. A picture of smoke, however, might be taken to represent fire, although it might be taken to represent various other things as well. But in the sense of representation under discussion, actual smoke under normal circumstances is not a representation of the fire that produced it. (A possible counterinstance is coded smoke signals representing the fire by which they are produced.)

17. From Lewis Carroll's *Through the Looking Glass* (made public in 1871), chap. 6.

18. The example comes from a list of Inuit terms featured in a recent newspaper account, where verbatim accuracy is not of the essence.

19. For this terminology, see B. F. Skinner's *Science and Human Behavior* (New York: Macmillan, 1953), chap. 7.

20. A cognitively relevant form of representation that does not employ symbols of a public language is the internal representation responsible (as argued in chapter 9) for the intentional character of cognitive attitudes generally. Since internal representations of this sort are not symbols we *use,* in any proper sense, and accordingly are not symbols we *learn* to use, they are not germane to the present discussion. The nature of such internal representations is the topic of chapter 8.

21. Wittgenstein, *Philosophical Investigations,* secs. 6, 9. Another difference is that Wittgenstein's ostensive teaching in the first instance (section 6) is concerned with entities like blocks and slabs that, unlike SOAs, have features of their own independent of the way we learn to identify them. The numeral series of section 9 may be closer to SOAs in this regard.

22. To help marshal one's intuitions in this regard, one may consider the following chain of inferences. If (i) S is unable to identify circumstances in which SOA X is actually present, then (ii) S will be unable to identify X upon actually encountering it. Further, if (ii) S is unable to identify the particular X expression R is supposed to represent upon actually encountering that SOA, then (iii) S does not know *what* R represents (in the sense that one does not know what "light bulb" represents if, in plain view of a light bulb, one cannot

recognize it as an instance of what is represented). Moreover, if (iii) S does not know what a given symbolic expression represents, then (iv) perforce S is unable to use that expression correctly as a representation. It follows, by a series of straightforward inferences, that if (i) a person is unable to identify the circumstances in which an SOA purportedly represented by a given symbolic expression is actually present, then (iv) that person is unable to use the expression coherently as a representation. The person's purported use of the expression under such conditions, in brief, is incoherent.

23. With this definition, the term "designation" is being withdrawn from its general use as an approximate synonym for "description" or "name," and is reserved for a more restricted use during the remainder of this discussion. Commonplace examples of designations abound in current linguistic practice. Think of a manufacturer's name attached to a product. A token-equivalent of the symbol "FORD" applied to the body of a motor vehicle designates the SOA of this vehicle's having been produced by the company of that name and (if the token is correctly applied) attests that this SOA is in fact the case. Consider also a gender symbol (e.g., "MEN") on the door of a washroom, or an "EXIT" sign marking the way to an exit. Or consider the symbol of a diagonal line across the outline of a burning cigarette, which not only represents the SOA of smoking being prohibited, but also designates the circumstances of this prohibition being locally in effect.

24. There is no appeal here to "the opinion of the majority," suggesting that snow is white just in case "most people say so." The point is merely that snow's appearing white when viewed under normal viewing conditions, *whatever* that might amount to, constitutes the identity of the SOA of snow's being white. This is just one of the "many examples of conditionals having the form if P and causally relevant conditions are normal then Q," to which Richard Fumerton refers in *Metaphysical and Epistemological Problems of Perception* (Lincoln: University of Nebraska Press, 1985), that "we understand and justifiably believe without having the slightest idea which conditions are normal" (152).

25. Satisfaction of the relevant conditions is a matter of their being realized—that is, for the circumstances in which the concerned SOA is actually current to hold within the world as it is.

26. If we take the correspondence to involve representation-types in the manner of chapter 3 and make explicit the assumption that a correctly used representation picks out an SOA uniquely, the relation between representation and SOA is seen to be that of one-to-one correspondence. However, nothing essential to the argument rests upon this provision.

27. This remark, needless to say, is a gross oversimplification. A somewhat fuller account of the transition from "natural signs" to an articulate symbol-system is proposed in chapter 11 of my *Cybernetics and the Philosophy of Mind* (London: Routledge & Kegan Paul, 1976).

28. In, for example, *De Anima* 415a8.

Chapter 7

STATES OF AFFAIRS
AND BEING THE CASE

1.   Ascriptions of Status to States of Affairs

It has been taken for granted in preceding chapters that SOAs either are
the case or are not the case, with no consideration of other possible statuses. The main purpose of the present chapter is to attempt an elucidation of what it *means* to say of an SOA that it is or, alternatively, *is not*
the case. This topic is more complex than may appear at first glance,
and in the course of the following discussion will provide occasion for
reflection on being (and not being) the case in the several domains of
empirical SOAs (section 3), SOAs of logic and mathematics (section
4), and SOAs involving necessity and contingency (section 5). The
topic is continued in the final section with a consideration of the truth-
conditions of counterfactual conditionals. But first in order is the question of whether there are status-ascriptions other than being the case
and not being the case that call for recognition, or whether our purposes
are better served with these basic two alone. This question is the concern of the present section.

   One way of becoming convinced that there is a problem here is to
think of various ways in which propositions might be temporally indexed. Consider the proposition that Socrates died by taking hemlock,
for instance. According to the received account of that event, which we
have no reason to doubt, Socrates died by taking hemlock sometime
during the year 399 B.C. It is a fact that Socrates died by taking hemlock, and the proposition to that effect is a true proposition. But how are
we to conceive the structure of the proposition in question?

   In our previous examination (in chapter 3) of simple declarative sentences like "snow is white" as expressions of propositions, we found it

necessary to distinguish between the role of the verb as part of the predicate ("is white") and its role as part of an implied status-ascription ("is
the case"). Pulling these two roles of the verb apart, we arrived at the
more explicit "snow's being white is the case" as a propositional rendition of the simple sentence "snow is white." A similar duality of verbal role is involved in the propositional use of the sentence "Socrates
died by taking hemlock." But in this case, the separation of the predicative and status-ascriptive uses of the verb is not entirely routine. One
way to parse the sentence in its propositional employment is "Socrates'
dying by taking hemlock was the case." In this rendition, the tensed
component of the verb is removed from the description of the SOA
(leaving the tenseless "Socrates' dying by taking hemlock") and retained in the status-ascription ("was the case"). Another parsing is
"Socrates' having died by taking hemlock is the case," where the status-ascription is the temporally noncommittal "is the case" and the past
tense is applied within the description of the SOA itself. The question
to be faced is whether, in separating an implied status-ascription from
the predicate of the sentence, the original tense should go with the predicate or with the status-ascription. For purposes of ordinary communication, to be sure, it might make little difference. But our concern at this
point is not just with communication, but with arriving at a coherent
general account of what it is for an SOA *to be* the case. And it would
complicate the matter considerably if we had to come up with a similar
account for SOAs *having been* the case as well.

Moreover, if we adopt the practice of indicating tense in the status-
ascriptions of propositions (as in "Socrates' taking hemlock was the
case"), then there are more tenses to be accommodated than just the
simple past. Consider the proposition that the sun will shine on Harvard's next commencement, or the proposition that the Tories are about
to be wiped out of office. Do we want to sanction status-ascriptions like
"will be the case" or "is about to be the case"? Along with these and
other tenses we might be called upon to deal with in ascribing status to
(accordingly untensed) SOAs, moreover, there are temporally indexed
adverbial expressions of one sort or another that might be central to the
sense of a proposition. In the case of the proposition that Socrates died
by hemlock in 399 B.C., for example, do we want to have available a
status-ascription like "was the case in 399 B.C."? And what about "is often the case" or "is probably the case"? Although locutions like these
often show up in ordinary discourse—consider "as is often the case in
such matters, things turn out other than expected" and "it's probably the
case that he will never know the difference"—it is not clear that we

should welcome the complications such locutions would bring to a general account of propositional status-ascriptions.

While complication itself is not a deciding factor, before making a decision on the matter we should at least be aware of how extensive the complications are. In chapter 3, we worked through an account of truth and falsehood applying to propositions incorporating one of the two basic status-ascriptions. The gist of this account is that, for any SOA X, "X is the case" is true just if X is the case, and false if X is not the case, whereas "X is not the case" is true just if X is not the case, and false if X is the case instead. As any reader who worked through this account will recall, there were difficulties enough to handle with only two status-ascriptions involved. Imagine how these difficulties would be compounded if we factored in ascriptions involving tenses ("will be the case") and modalities ("might be the case") as well.

Another complication concerns propositional attitudes. Chapter 2 contains an account of propositional belief and discusses the relation between the truth-value of a given belief and that attaching to its propositional object. But if inflections of tense are incorporated in various statuses ascribed to SOAs in the formulation of propositions, then keeping current with the truth, as it were, would often require *changing* status-ascriptions as time progresses. To see how this might work, imagine the case of Phaedo (the character in the namesake dialogue) who truly believed that Socrates died by taking hemlock and who believed this not only on the day of the event, but also on the occasion of recounting the event afterward (e.g., to Echechrates and Terpsion). Let us characterize Phaedo's belief in accord with the option of removing all temporal indicators from the descriptive component of the proposition and introducing them into the status-ascription instead. Thus conceived, the SOA is simply Socrates' dying by taking hemlock. What Phaedo believed on the evening of the event, accordingly, is the proposition representing that SOA as being the case—that is, the proposition that Socrates' dying by taking hemlock *is* the case. In the days and months following the event, however, what Phaedo believed regarding this SOA, as long as his belief remained true, would be the distinctly different proposition that Socrates' dying by hemlock *was* the case. And since one's belief itself changes with a change in its propositional object (see chapter 9), it follows that Phaedo had a different belief regarding Socrates' dying on the days after the event than he had on the day of the event itself. This consequence, at best, seems counterintuitive, and not one we should wish to deal with if we could justifiably avoid it.

There are similar disadvantages to be encountered in the treatment of topics following if status-ascriptions were subject to qualifications of the sort being considered. The deciding point against this option, however, is not just the extent of the difficulties it would introduce into the account, but the further fact that no advantages of note would follow its adoption. Although coming to terms with the concept of SOAs has proven difficult enough in its own right, the task would have been no easier if tenses were banned from the representations that figured in the account of the chapter above. The SOA of Socrates' *having died* by taking hemlock, for instance, and that of his *dying in 399 B.C.* (both of which *are* the case) are not inherently more difficult to account for than the "tenseless" SOA (which "*was* the case") merely of Socrates' *dying* by taking hemlock. And although dealing with nonempirical SOAs like husbands necessarily being married introduces complications of its own, as soon to be seen, these complications are no more formidable than those of accounting for a status-ascription like "is necessarily the case." If nothing is gained by introducing qualifications of this sort into status-ascriptions, however, then the difficulties it brings with it make this option undesirable.

What the findings of this brief excursion into the realm of modified status-ascriptions indicate, accordingly, is that this realm for our purposes needs no further exploration. For the remainder of this work, as in the parts preceding, SOAs will be thought of as admitting only two statuses—that of being the case and that of not being the case. Let us now attempt to explicate what those statuses amount to.

2. Being (Not Being) the Case Defined

A number of specifically defined terms were introduced in the previous chapter (section 4) for their help in clarifying the nature of the competence required for a cognitive subject to identify an SOA that is immediately present to the subject. To repeat the key definitions, an SOA is *actually current* when it is an aspect or feature of the world as it is — that is, of the actual world. A representing expression R serves as a *designation* when it is used as a representation of an SOA that is actually current. The *conditions for the correct designative use* of a representation are the conditions under which it is correctly used in that capacity. These conditions are satisfied, in turn, by the circumstances that constitute the actual currency of the SOA represented. In the case of the illustrative expression "snow's being white," the circumstances in

question are those of snow's appearing white to persons of normal vision under normal viewing conditions (appropriately fleshed out as
needed for one or another purpose). The SOA of snow's being white is
immediately present to a subject who is aware of those circumstances
without the intervention of symbolic surrogates (e.g., those involved in
inference). According to (LR1,2) and (BC) of that chapter, learning
how to identify this SOA when immediately present requires learning
the conditions for the correct designative use of its representations.

These terms may be put to further use in a general definition of being (and not being) the case:

(DG)   An SOA X is (is not) the case *iff* the world is such that the circum-
       stances in which X is actually current are (are not) present within it.

Once the definition is at hand, it may appear superfluous. For in the case
of empirical SOAs, like snow's being white, there are other ways of expressing it that would do just as well. Since the circumstances that constitute the actual currency of X satisfy the conditions for the correct
designative use of its representations, X is (is not) the case if and only
if those conditions are (are not) satisfied (i.e., those circumstances are
present). And since the presence of the circumstances constituting the
actual currency of X is tantamount to X's actually being current, X is
(is not) the case if and only if X is (is not) actually current. Moreover,
since X is actually current when X is an aspect of the world as it is, X
is (is not) the case if and only if X is (is not) an aspect of the world as
it is.

There are several features of (DG), however, that make it preferable
to these other formulations as a definition of being (and not being) the
case. One is that it applies to empirical and nonempirical SOAs alike
(the point of its being general), whereas the concepts of actual currency
and, derivatively, of correct designation seem out of place with nonempirical SOAs. We return to such matters in section 3 below, where
more is said about the nature of nonempirical SOAs.

Another advantage of (DG) is that it defines both *being the case* and
not being the case in terms explicitly of how the world *is*. An SOA is
the case just when the world is such that the circumstances in which it
is actually current are present; and an SOA is not the case just when the
world is such that these circumstances are not present within it. This
eliminates the need for "negative facts" of any sort to serve as an ontological underpinning for what is not the case.[1]

Yet another point in favor of the definition (DG) is that it forestalls any temptation to invoke an ontology of "possible worlds" by way of providing a home for SOAs that are not currently actual.[2] An essential tenet of the present view is that there is only one world, but that this world presents different aspects from moment to moment. An aspect presented at a given moment counts at that moment as an actual SOA. And an actual SOA unavoidably is possible as well. There are other aspects the world might present under other circumstances but does not present at a given moment. But even these SOAs at least are possible. All aspects of the world as it *is* or *might be* count among possible SOAs, including those that are actual at a given moment. In brief, all SOAs perforce are possible,[3] and at any given moment there are some that are actual as well. As far as SOAs are concerned, the only distinction between actual and possible is that between SOAs that are the case and those that are not. As far as the world itself is concerned, in turn, the distinction between actual and possible does not even apply.[4] Although the actual world obviously changes from moment to moment, this changing world is the only world there is. And by the provisions of (DG), this world serves as ground to SOAs both actual and merely possible; for merely possible SOAs are those that are not the case, and the latter are defined with reference to the world as it is.

3.   How the Definition Applies in Empirical Contexts

In the opening pages of his *Critique of Pure Reason,*[5] Kant distinguished between *a priori* and *a posteriori* judgments. A judgment is *a priori,* in Kant's sense, if its truth could be determined prior to any empirical application (as with the judgment that $5 + 7 = 12$) and *a posteriori* if the course of experience is relevant to its truth-determination (as with the judgment that snow is white). A judgment is analytic by Kant's definition, in turn, if its truth depends upon the relation between its subject and predicate concepts (as with the judgment that all husbands are married), and a judgment is synthetic if it is not analytic. In Kant's view, analytic judgments are all *a priori,* and *a posteriori* judgments are all synthetic, but there are certain judgments nonetheless that are both synthetic and *a priori.* His primary examples of the latter were taken from mathematics, most prominently the judgments that $5 + 7 = 12$ and that a straight line is the shortest distance between two points. A major task of the aforementioned *Critique* was to account for the possibility of synthetic *a priori* judgments.

Although Kant's solution to this problem has few contemporary adherents, and although the very terms in which he posed it have been widely criticized,[6] it is a fair guess to say that most philosophers thinking about such matters today are not prepared to dismiss Kant's distinctions out of hand.[7] There seems to be something importantly different, with respect to truth-conditions, between the judgment that snow is white and the mathematical judgment that $5 + 7 = 12$, and again between judgments of both these sorts and the judgment that all husbands are married persons. The breakdown of topics between this and the following section corresponds roughly to Kant's distinction between the *a posteriori* and the *a priori,* save that we shall be talking about the empirical and the nonempirical instead. The present section continues the discussion already under way of how definition (DG) applies to empirical SOAs.

In the context of this discussion, an SOA counts as empirical if the circumstances in which it is actually current involve contingencies of an observable sort. Put otherwise, an empirical SOA is one for which the difference between being and not being the case is primarily a difference in observable circumstances. Familiar examples are the SOAs of the sky's being cloudy, of Deirdre's gate's being shut, and of snow's being white. Even within this limited set of examples, however, there is a further distinction to be made, often expressed by the terms "particular" and "general." The SOA of Deirdre's gate's being shut involves a particular set of circumstances, occurring (or not occurring) in a particular locale at a particular time. The SOA of snow's being white, by contrast, has constitutive circumstances of a more general character, not limited to particular times and places. What is white in this case, that is to say, is not a particular expanse of snow, but all snow masses wherever and whenever they are found.[8]

For a more precise expression of this distinction, we may take advantage of terminology already familiar from the preceding discussion. A symbolic expression is used as a *designation* when it serves to represent an SOA that is actually current; and the *conditions for the correct designative use* of a symbol are the circumstances that, when they occur, constitute the actual currency of the SOA represented. Let us say that an SOA is *spatiotemporally particular* if the conditions for the correct *designative* use of its symbolic representations are such that their satisfaction involves circumstances that are spatiotemporally specific. And let us say that an SOA is *spatiotemporally general* if the satisfaction of its respective conditions involves circumstances without spatial or temporal restrictions. A typical example of the first, as noted above, is the SOA of a given gate's being shut; and of the second, the SOA of snow's being white. The distinction is worth making for several reasons. One is to support the observation that not all empirical generalizations take the form "all S is P." Some seem appropriately cast in this form (e.g., all creatures with hearts have livers), but others become false when stated so baldly (e.g., all swans are white). The generalization that all snow is white is of the latter sort, inasmuch as various atmospheric conditions (e.g., soot in the air) can affect the color of snow. Snow's being white is an SOA that is spatiotemporally general, but its generality accommodates the influence of local weather conditions.

Another merit of the distinction is that it helps us make a useful comparison between empirical generalizations of the form "all S is P" and certain nonempirical statements that take the same form. An example of the latter is the statement that all husbands are married. Despite its formal similarity with "all creatures with hearts have livers," the SOA engaged by the statement "all husbands are married" is constituted by circumstances that are nonempirical in important respects. This is evident in the fact that someone undertaking to check whether this SOA is actually present would be ill advised to check the marital status of a representative sample of husbands. The constituting conditions of SOAs like all husbands' being married is the topic of section 5 below.

With an empirical SOA, on the other hand, whether general or particular, the circumstances constituting its actual currency are of the sort normally encountered in sensory observation. And whether an empirical SOA is particular or general, our ability to deal with it through the medium of symbolic representation requires our being able to identify these circumstances. This condition is articulated in (LR2) of the preceding chapter, which applies without regard to the type of SOA involved: learning how to employ an expression correctly as a representation requires learning how to identify the thing it represents when that thing is immediately present.

What is it for a *general* SOA to be immediately present? For an SOA to be immediately present is for it to "present itself" without mediation by representation.[9] But the domain in which its presence is manifested need not be restricted to specific locales. When an SOA like Deirdre's gate being shut is immediately present, its presence is manifested in a particular spatiotemporal location: the place where the gate is, at the time when it is shut. But when a general SOA is immediately present, there is no privileged place or time at which that presence is manifested. It might be immediately present to any cognitive subject who has learned the empirical circumstances by which that SOA is constituted. When such an SOA is immediately present, it is present to any subject who has learned those circumstances and knows that they prevail within the actual world.[10]

The sense in which a general SOA might be immediately present to an observer is not wholly unlike that in which a particular SOA might be currently in the world and yet not be observed by any particular observer. Consider the SOA of the temperature at the North Pole being $-40°$, the presence of which is designated by an appropriate expression R. By (LR1) of chapter 6, it suffices for the correct use of R as a representation of this SOA that one has the ability to identify circumstances under which the SOA would be actually present, with no additional requirement that one encounter the SOA personally. Put another way, what is required to sanction the use of R as a representation of X is that there be a conditional statement "(a) only if (b)" specifying in its consequent (b) the occurrence of circumstances in which X would be the case, and in its antecedent (a) the conditions under which the occurrence of those circumstances might be detected. In order for the expression "its being $-40°$ at the North Pole" to be available for sanctioned use as a representation, it suffices that some suitably specific conditional statement can be formulated to the effect that, if appropriate measuring instruments were situated on the scene (etc.), then a local temperature of $-40°$ would be recorded.

What is required for the SOA in question to be the case, moreover, is the presence within the world of the circumstances constituting its actual currency. Since these circumstances are specified in the relevant conditional, the SOA in fact is the case just when the conditional in fact is true. Thus the expression "its being $-40°$ at the North Pole" represents an actual SOA just in case it is true that $-40°$ would be recorded in that vicinity by properly calibrated measuring instruments, *if* such instruments were in place on the scene.[11]

Return now to the general SOA of snow's being white and the question of what counts as its immediate presence. For that SOA to be the case is tantamount to the following conditional statement's being true: wherever snow is found under normal atmospheric conditions, if observed by normal observers in natural light, and so forth, the snow will appear to be white in color. Since being the case is equivalent to being actually current, to know that the SOA is actually current is to know that the conditional statement (or some equivalent) is true. This latter is something one *might* come to know through the medium of symbolic representation, as when informed of the fact by another person's saying so. Alternatively, one might come to know the fact immediately—without relying on this medium—as when one knows enough about optics to realize why it is a fact. A general SOA X is immediately present to a cognitive subject N if N knows immediately that its associated conditional is true—that is, knows immediately the conditions under which the SOA's status of being current would make itself evident.

There are similarities between this view and verificationism, which in its most general form is the doctrine that the meaning of an empirical statement is tied to conditions under which it would be shown to be true. Most notably, the considerations summed up in (C2) of the previous chapter make the proper use of representations conditional upon there being identifiable SOAs for them to represent. Since SOAs are identifiable only by someone able to specify the circumstances in which they would be the case, and since the occurrence of such circumstances establishes the truth of propositions affirming them to be the case, the effect is much the same as verificationism's characteristic tenet that only statements that can be verified are empirically meaningful.[12]

Let us review how this works from the present perspective. It has been noted a number of times already that learning how to employ a particular representing expression as a designation requires learning how to identify the SOA that expression is supposed to designate. But the dependence of our ability to use representations properly upon an ability to identify what they might be used to designate goes deeper than that. Unless we are able to identify the circumstances that would establish an SOA as actually current, we are unable (by [LR2] of chapter 6) to represent that SOA in a coherent fashion under any circumstances whatever. Put positively, the requirement comes to this: in order for a person to avoid incoherence in the use of any expression as a putative representation of an SOA, it is required that the person be able to identify the circumstances under which that SOA would be current in the actual world.

The type of incoherence in question is illustrated by the mundane case of a child who has learned to mouth expressions like "snow is white," which its parents understand as representations of snow's being white, but who has not yet learned to pick out the SOA such expressions are normally taken to represent. Not being able to tell what snow's being white actually amounts to, the child will not be able to participate coherently in normal conversations involving that particular SOA; the child will not see the point of the simile "white as snow," for example, and will be unable to answer questions about the color difference between snow and coal. The child's incoherence in this regard lies in its inability to grasp the sense of these expressions when it hears them used by other people.

Less mundane illustrations are provided by expressions like "an irresistible force meeting an immovable object" and "there being exactly nine million and two fish in Lake Michigan." The problem with the first is that there simply are no conceivable circumstances that could be taken as constituting an SOA in which an irresistible force encounters an immovable object, and hence no circumstances under which the putative SOA might be actually current that might be identified by an avowed user of such an expression. Just as there is no conceivable SOA as a rectangle's being circular, so there is no conceivable aspect the world might present that would count either as an object resisting an irresistible force or as a force imparting motion to an immovable object. The trouble with the second expression, on the other hand, is not logical incoherence, but rather the lack of counting procedures that could distinguish that exact number of fish from nine million fish "give or take several." Not only is the actual number of fish in the lake continually changing from moment to moment—due to some fish dying off, some being hatched, and others jumping in and out of the water—but moreover there is no effective way of tallying individual fish with that degree of accuracy over such a large area at a given time. A similar difficulty affects any measurement of the distance between the earth and the moon that purports to be exact down to a fraction of a centimeter. Even if measuring techniques (based on radar or laser, e.g.) capable of such a degree of accuracy were available, it would remain arbitrary whether the relevant measurement should be conceived as between mountains or valleys, for example, and at what point in the moon's orbit the measurement should be taken. The upshot is that there is no identifiable set of circumstances that would constitute the actual currency of such putative SOAs, and thus there are no symbolic expressions by which they could be coherently represented. The expression "an irresistible force meeting an immovable object" does not represent an SOA that might conceivably be present, and neither does "there being exactly nine million and two fish in Lake Michigan."[13]

Similar results might be reached from a verificationist perspective. But the difference between the views in question appear to be no less substantial than the similarities. For one, the present account has little to say about either meaning or verification. Instead of meaning, we have been talking about representation; and while there certainly are overlaps between the two topics (e.g., meaninglessness is a form of representational failure), no distinctive "theory of meaning" as such emerges from the present discussion. As far as verification itself is concerned, while the actual presence of an SOA obviously provides verification for a proposition affirming that it is the case, the present account has nothing specific to say about how verification might be secured. Given the exclusion of justification from our immediate concerns, such details remain beyond the scope of the present discussion.

Another difference is that the present account breaks the link maintained by verificationism between verification and knowledge. According to verificationism of the traditional stripe, our empirical knowledge is limited to propositions that are capable of being verified. But if knowledge is a mode of access to SOAs, as argued in chapter 5, and not propositional belief that is adequately justified, then the verifiability of a proposition is only incidental to our knowing the SOA that the proposition represents. If the argument above is to be trusted, indeed, it is conceivable that one might come to know a given SOA without entertaining—and, hence, without verifying—any propositional attitudes whatever in its regard.

A further difference may be equally revealing. Verificationism is a doctrine about empirical meaning, with no direct implications regarding the meaning of nonempirical statements. But the account applied above with regard to empirical SOAs extends to SOAs that are not empirical as well. Let us set verificationism aside as an extraneous distraction, and take up the topic of nonempirical SOAs.

4. How the Definition Applies in Nonempirical Contexts

We turn now to SOAs in nonempirical contexts, corresponding roughly to the Kantian *a priori*. Kant divided *a priori* judgments into analytic and synthetic, relying primarily on mathematics for examples of the latter. We will begin with SOAs in mathematical contexts, saving the (Kantian) analytic for the following section. The sequence of topics in the present section is: (i) SOAs of arithmetic, (ii) SOAs of geometry, (iii) SOAs involving directional measurement, and (iv) SOAs involving logical entailment. The concern here is not to come to terms with alternative views of these topics (too large a task by far), but merely to explain how the above definition (DG) of being the case applies in contexts that are not empirical in character.

(i) Recall the characterization of SOAs with which we worked in chapter 6—namely, SOAs as aspects or features of the world as it is, or as it might be should other conditions prevail. This characterization might appear ill suited from the outset to circumstances of mathematical character. If mathematical truth could not be otherwise, as Kant was convinced, what is the point of even mentioning the world as it *might* be? And as far as the *actual* world is concerned, does it possess any *aspects* we should want to designate by the expression "5 + 7 = 12"? If the fact that 5 + 7 = 12 is an aspect of anything at all, it would seem to be an aspect (or feature) of a system of serially arranged integers in which 5 increments and 7 increments make 12 altogether. In order to get past initial misgivings like these, we need to consider carefully what might count as an SOA in arithmetic.

If 5 + 7 equaling 12 is an aspect of the world, as would seem to be required for it to count as an SOA, then it is so only by being "piggy-backed" on another SOA. This other is the SOA of the relevant number system being the prevalent system in actual use for counting, calculating, and similar operations. What comes first is the SOA of this system prevailing; then comes the fact that this prevalent system specifies 12 as the sum of 5 and 7. If we want to call this latter fact an SOA, we need to remain aware of its difference from the SOA that supports it. Let us refer to the fact in question as a *second-tier* SOA, in contrast with the *first-tier* SOA that determines its status. Strictly speaking, it is the first-tier SOA that is a feature of the world, whereas the second-tier SOA (that represented by "5 + 7 = 12") is a feature of the number system on the tier below.

The second-tier SOA concerns the world in a derivative manner only, being entirely dependent upon the provisions of its supporting number system. And a full expression of its identity should make this dependency explicit. The full expression of the SOA of 5 plus 7 equaling 12 is not the perfunctory "5 + 7 = 12" or an equivalent,[14] but something along the lines of "a number system prevailing in which 5 + 7 = 12." The form of this full expression is:

a ... system prevailing in which _____,

which signifies a second-tier SOA (a representation of which goes into the blank ___) nested within a first-tier SOA (the representation of which is then completed by filling in the ellipsis with an identification of the relevant system).

Being nested in this manner within its first-tier host, the formula "5 + 7 = 12" is buffered from affairs in the world and is thus immune from empirical disconfirmation. It is because of this immunity that its truth is *a priori*. But if understood in the sense of its full expression, the formula is divested of its *a priori* status. For while the world indeed is *actually* such that a number system prevails in which 5 + 7 = 12, the world *might* be such that some other system prevailed, one providing no sanction for the formula in question.[15] It might even be such that *no* number system whatever prevailed within it, in which case there would be no truths involving relations among numbers.[16]

If the formula "5 + 7 = 12" is understood in the sense of its full expression, accordingly, the truth that it expresses is *a posteriori* instead. This may be seen by bringing (DG) to bear, in combination with the definition of truth in chapter 4. A proposition representing SOA X as being the case is true if and only if X is the case. Let X be the first-tier SOA of a number system prevailing in which 5 + 7 = 12. By (DG), X is the case if and only if the world is such that the circumstances in which X is actually current are present within it. Since the world might be such that these circumstances are not present, X in fact might not be the case. And if X were not the case, then a proposition representing it as being the case would be false. But the formula "5 + 7 = 12," when understood in the sense of its full expression (with positive status-ascription implied) is such a proposition. Thus the truth of this formula depends upon how things are in the world, which means that it is *a posteriori* and not *a priori* as Kant maintained.[17]

What circumstances constitute the prevalence of a given number system in the world? For our purposes, the details are unimportant. But included among such circumstances, clearly enough, would be the system's being available for use, as well as its having been adopted in most societies where people count and calculate. Its having been adopted, in turn, includes people within these societies teaching the system to novices and trusting one another to use it properly in interpersonal dealings. Among things not included are that *all* societies use it (a society that tallies on fingers and toes exclusively might be said not to have a number system) and that all users agree upon the *extent* of its proper use (whether it is applicable, for instance, in a "hedonic calculus").

In short, if "5 + 7 = 12" is understood as an elliptical expression for the first-tier SOA more fully expressed by "a counting system prevailing in which 5 + 7 = 12," then the SOA it expresses is or is not the case under conditions given by definition (DG). Taken in its second-tier sense alone, on the other hand, strictly speaking it does not express an SOA at all. For the sum of 5 + 7 being 12 is not an aspect of the world, but is a feature rather of our prevailing number system. In the second-tier sense, what it expresses is established nonempirically (insofar as inferences within formal systems count as nonempirical) and is not contingent on matters of experience.[18] But what it expresses in its fuller sense is ultimately empirical and is or is not the case depending on how things stand in the world.

(ii) Kant's favorite example of *a priori* truth in geometry is the judgment that a straight line is the shortest distance between two points. While this holds within the Euclidean system, which is the only system Kant thought possible, other geometries were discovered soon after the *Critique* was published in which this truth is not available.[19] Since some of these "alternative" geometries have found empirical applications, the question arises about the manner and the extent of geometry's *a priori* character and about whether in some sense it might be empirical after all. While questions like these would require further discussion before their import becomes entirely apparent,[20] the brief remarks below indicate the direction such a discussion might take.

The distinction between first- and second-tier SOAs introduced above with regard to arithmetic applies (perhaps more obviously) in connection with geometry as well. It is a feature of Euclidean geometry that a straight line is the shortest distance between two points in (Euclidean) space. This feature is a second-tier SOA, with no status relative to the world at large save that conveyed by the geometry that provides its basis. Whatever relation it may bear to the world at large is established by a first-tier SOA, that of a geometrical system prevailing that has this feature—that is, the feature of a straight line being the shortest distance between two points. This first-tier SOA is empirical in character, inasmuch as its being the case or not being the case depends upon how things stand in the world.

What makes geometry more complicated than arithmetic in this respect is that the circumstances that constitute the prevalence of a given system are domain-specific in a way that seems peculiar to geometry. For purposes of measurement on or near the surface of the earth, or within the solar system generally, Euclidean geometry provides highly accurate results, enough so for us to say that this system prevails for purposes of spatial mensuration within that domain. Measurement of interstellar spatial relations, however, seems best served by the provisions of a non-Euclidean geometry.[21] This pair of circumstances warrants positive status-ascriptions to the first-tier SOAs *both* of a geometrical system prevailing for mundane (earth-related) use, in which a straight line is the shortest distance between two points, *and* of another system prevailing for interstellar use, in which the shortest distance between two points is not a (Euclidean) straight line. Although these SOAs appear in conflict when expressed elliptically (as second-tier SOAs solely), in their fuller expressions no conflict appears.

(iii) There are other kinds of measurement applying to the earth's surface that have not inspired formulation in well-defined systems. But they are supported nonetheless by systems of sorts, which yield *a priori* truths (in the Kantian sense) similar to those of geometry. One such is the system of measurements along and at right angles to a fixed standard meridian (measurements of latitude and longitude, respectively). Another is the system of radial directions around a "floating" center (north, east, south, and west, 90° apart in that order, with northeast, southwest, etc., as angular "splits" in between). One *a priori* truth within this latter system—the system of the portable compass—is that, for any A and B, if A is north of B, then B is south of A.

But the fact of B's being south of A if A is north of B is a second-tier truth, which is embedded in a first-tier SOA of the relevant (compass) system prevailing for purposes of directional measurement. And this first-tier SOA is empirical and contingent. The world might be such that some alternative system prevailed, such as one with radial directions around a fixed center. Imagine the center fixed at the geographic North Pole (from which all directions are south in the currently prevalent system). In this system, each point of the compass would be identified with one particular longitude (extending in a half-circle to the geographic South Pole), and A would be situated north of B only if both were located on exactly the same longitude. Within this system, it would count as an *a priori* truth that if A is +5° (i.e., 5° of latitude in one direction) north of B then B is −5° north of A. But it would not be true that if A is (some degree) north of B, then B is south of A, since for B to be south of A would require both to be on a longitude (i.e., south) that is situated opposite from north.

Although a system of this sort undoubtedly would serve less well than our familiar system for most practical purposes, it is one nonetheless that *might* prevail in the world. Within the context of the system that currently prevails, it indeed can be determined *a priori* that if A is north of B, then B is south of A. But there is nothing *a priori* about the first-tier truth that the system providing this consequence actually prevails. For this first-tier SOA to be the case, according to (DG), is for the circumstances by which it is constituted to be present within the actual world. If the world were such, on the other hand, that these circumstances were not present, then the SOA would not be the case. And if this first-tier SOA were not the case, then it would no longer count as an *a priori* truth that if A is north of B, then B is south of A. Indeed, this latter might no longer count as true at all.

(iv) Whereas logic for Kant dealt with "rules of the understanding in general" (*Critique of Pure Reason,* A52), we tend to think of logic today as concerned primarily with axiomatic systems. Be this as it may, truths of logic submit to basically the same analysis as the truths of mathematics and of directional measurement treated above. The example used below is from modal logic, but the point to be made applies to other branches of logic as well.

Systems of modal logic typically are discussed in relation to the systems S1 through S5 originally distinguished by C. I. Lewis.[22] It is a truth of S2 (and hence of S3 through S5) that if a conjunction of propositions is possibly true, then each proposition within the conjunction is possibly true as well. Intuitive as this implication may seem, however, it is not available within S1. Thus if it is the case that S2 (through S5) prevails as the relevant system(s) of modal inference, then this implication holds, but not if S1 alone prevails instead. In terms of tiered SOAs, the SOA of the implication's holding is a second-tier SOA nested within the first-tier SOA of S2 being (among) the prevailing system(s) of inference. But since that first-tier SOA might not be the case (S1 exclusively, e.g., might prevail instead), whether it is true that the possibility of a conjunction entails the possibility of its conjuncts is a matter of contingency, dependent upon whether a certain first-tier SOA in fact is the case.

The main difference between this and the cases considered previously is that, while mathematical systems prevail over large segments of civilized society, systems of modal logic are used mostly by small groups of specialists. So what a given system's prevailing comes down to in the case of modal logic is its being adopted for some particular theoretical use.[23] Other systems of logic (e.g., the syllogism and the propositional calculus) are in use more widely. But inasmuch as no specific system of logic holds sway by necessity, there are no logical truths whose status in application to empirical subject matter is not contingent upon how things happen to stand in the world.

5. Implication among States of Affairs

Returning to the Kantian distinctions once again, we recall that *a priori* judgments are divided into analytic and synthetic. We have been looking at the rough equivalent of Kant's synthetic *a priori* in the preceding section. We turn now to judgments (propositions) that Kant would have considered analytic,[24] the truth of which he supposed to be knowable in advance since it was based on the predicate's being "included" in the subject. An explicit (and uninteresting) example would be the judgment that all red apples are red. A somewhat more nuanced judgment of this sort would be one affirming that all husbands are married, relying implicitly on a definition of husbands as married males. An understanding of the *a priori* character of statements of this sort is available through the present conception of SOAs and of what it is for them to be the case, without relying on the notion of implicit definitions. The key to this understanding is the conception, introduced in chapter 6, of the criteria for the correct designative use of a representation.

In the terminology of that chapter, by way of a brief review, a symbolic expression used to represent an SOA under circumstances in which it is actually current is referred to as a "designation" of that SOA. These circumstances are what we have been calling the "conditions for the correct designative use" of that representation. According to the biconditional (BC) of chapter 6 (section 4), we learn these conditions as part of learning the use of that expression as a representation of the SOA in question. Another thesis defended in chapter 6 is that SOAs are not *pre*formed constituents of the world at large, but that the identity of a given SOA is actually determined by the conditions for the correct designative use of its representations. Another way of putting the effect of (BC), accordingly, is that we learn how to identify SOAs as part of the very process by which we learn to represent them symbolically. What an SOA is, one might say, is what we learn to count as the circumstances the presence of which constitutes the conditions for the correct use of its representations in a designative capacity; and the conception that holds the two members of this equation together is that of the conditions for the correct designative use of a representation.

Let us now consider what happens when the conditions for the correct designative use of two expressions overlap, in such a fashion that one falls entirely within the scope of the other. Suppose that the conditions for the correct designative use of a representation of SOA X are constituted by the conjoined presence of circumstances A, B, and C. This means that X is identified by those particular circumstances, and that the conjoined presence of those circumstances counts as X actually being current as well. Suppose further that the corresponding conditions for SOA Y are constituted by a subset of the foregoing circumstances—say, circumstances A and B together. A consequence is that the conditions for the correct designative use of a representation of Y are satisfied *as a matter of course* whenever the respective conditions are satisfied for SOA X. From this it follows, in turn, that whenever SOA X is actually current in the world, then Y *invariably* is current as well. As a result of the circumstances identifying Y being a subset of the corresponding circumstances for X, the fact of X's being current entails the currency of Y as a necessary concomitant.

When the conditions for the correct designative use of representations of Y are bound up with the corresponding conditions for X in this fashion, let us say that SOA Y is *implicated* in SOA X and, in turn, that X *implicates* Y. For an example that will by now be familiar, take the SOA of N's being married (Y) and the SOA of N's being a husband (X). Among the conditions for correctly designating N as married are that N be of a certain age, that N has been party to certain legally binding agreements with another person, and so on. The same conditions apply also to designations of N as a husband, along with the additional criterion that N be male. Since the conditions for N's being a husband include those for N's being married, satisfaction of the former assures satisfaction of the latter as well. In this manner, the SOA of N's being a husband implicates the SOA of N's being married. N's being married is literally included in N's being a husband. And tracing this inclusion relation back to conditions for the correct designative use of representations as we have done provides an explanation of how the implication in question comes about.[25]

One thing to note about the relation of implication between X and Y is that it is not a relation between propositions. Hence it is not the same as the logical relation of entailment.[26] Nor is it a version of what some contemporary metaphysicians label '*de re* necessity'.[27] There is nothing necessary about one set of conditions being incorporated in another (it could be otherwise);[28] indeed, no modal terms have been employed in the definition. In point of fact, all that is required for X to implicate Y, by definition of the implication relation, is that the list of conditions that authorize use of representations of X in a designative capacity *include* the corresponding conditions for the designation of Y.[29] And there is nothing necessary about the manner of inclusion involved.

The point can be put another way. For SOA X to implicate SOA Y, it is enough that the conditions for correct designation applying to X—for example, A, B, and C being jointly present—*as a matter of fact* include the corresponding conditions for Y (e.g., the joint presence of A and B). There is no requirement that one set of conditions include the other "necessarily" (whatever that might mean). The relation of inclusion involved is entirely extensional.[30] If the conditions pertaining to the SOA of N's being married, to return to our example, *in point of fact* are included among those pertaining to N's being a husband, then N's being a husband is implicated in N's being married. No modal terms are involved in this characterization. And the relation of inclusion on which the characterization is based is no less extensional than the mention of potatoes among required items on a weekly shopping list.

Despite the brute extensionality of the inclusion relation on which it is based, however, the implication of N's being married in N's being a husband guarantees (where the implication holds) that a husband *invariably* is married. For the implication in question sets up a conditional relation between being a husband and being married that holds without regard for how the world might be otherwise (otherwise, in this case, than the designation-conditions being so related). This provides a basis, in turn, for a conditional relation among empirical propositions unrelated by logical structure that is considerably stronger than the standard material conditional.[31] The conditional proposition that N is a husband only if N is married, for example, holds true invariably; and it does so without regard to the truth-value of its antecedent proposition. The basis for its invariable truth is the *de facto* implication of being married in being a husband.

In general, when SOA X implicates SOA Y, the conditional [[X/yes] only if [Y/yes]/yes] is invariably true. The conditional is invariably true in the sense that its truth does not depend upon the truth-value of either of its components. Another way of putting the point is that it invariably is the case that the truth of [X/yes] is accompanied by the truth of [Y/yes], regardless of how things stand in other respects. To say this, however, is tantamount to saying that it necessarily is the case that if [X/yes] is true, then [Y/yes] is true also.[32]

We turn in the final section to a characterization of dispositional properties in terms of this conditionality based on implication among SOAs.

6.   Localized Implications and Their Enabling Conditions

If SOA Y is implicated in SOA X, then when X is the case Y necessarily is the case as well. But for any empirical X and Y, whether X implicates Y is a contingent matter. When X implicates Y, that is to say, Y necessarily accompanies X. But as stressed above, there is no necessity that X implicate Y. Whether X in fact implicates Y depends upon the presence of circumstances that make the designation-conditions of X completely overlap those of Y. What makes the implication of Y by X contingent is that, for any empirical X and Y,[33] these circumstances might not be present in the actual world.

Let us call the circumstances responsible for this overlap of designation-conditions the *enabling conditions* of Y's being implicated in X. By way of illustration, we may return to the implications of being married in being a husband. Although in contexts where the implication holds someone who is a husband necessarily is married as well, there are other conditions under which the implication in fact might not hold. There are conceivable circumstances, as already noted, in which a man with whom a woman cohabits might be known as her husband even though they have not been married in an officially sanctioned ceremony.[34] Given a context in which the implication holds, however, the reason it holds is the presence of one or another social system in which marriage has a legally defined status and in which the designation "husband" is limited to males that are legally married. The presence of such a system is the enabling condition of the implication in question. When the world is such that legal provisions of this sort are present in a given social context, then the implication holds within that context. Under other circumstances, the implication fails to hold, and there is no necessity that a husband is a married person.[35]

Let us distinguish again the various SOAs involved in this enabling relation. First, there are the SOAs of someone's being a husband and of that person's also being married. Second, there is the (composite) SOA of being a husband *implicating* being married. And third, there is the SOA of a certain legal system's providing the basis for that second SOA. This latter is the same as the SOA of that legal system's serving as the enabling condition of the implication of the SOA of being married in the SOA of being a husband.

The enabling condition of the implication of being married in being a husband, one might say, is the presence of certain legal provisions, or customs with legal status, that hold without specification of particular persons or places within the social context in question. There are cases of another sort, however, in which implications among empirical SOAs are supported by enabling conditions of a more highly localized character. Consider the example of an object's being soluble in water, a typical case of what is known as a "dispositional property."

By commonly accepted definition, a substance x is water-soluble just in case it dissolves when immersed in water. To develop the example, let us reformulate the definition as follows:

(A)   x is water-soluble *iff* when (Bi) x is immersed in water then (Bii) x
dissolves.

The sense of the conditional "when . . . then ___" in the right-hand
member of the biconditional cannot be that of the standard 'only if' of
truth-functional logic; for a conditional involving the latter is rendered
true by the falsehood of its antecedent, and we do not consider a substance to be water-soluble by reason of its never being immersed in water. Nor can the connective in the right-hand member be the strict
implication of standard modal logic, since there is no inconsistency in
something's being immersed but not dissolving. The sense, one may
propose, is rather that of SOA (Bii) being implicated in SOA (Bi).

Before unpacking this proposal more fully, we should also consider
the effect of the main connective '*iff*'. Once again, the effect is not that
of the standard biconditional of truth-functional logic, for our accepted
use of the term "water-soluble" is not such that "x is water-soluble" just
happens to share its truth-value with "x dissolves when immersed in
water." The effect of '*iff*' in this context clearly is to mark a termino-
logical equivalence.[36] The sense of the definition overall is that a
thing's being water-soluble *just is* being so disposed that its dissolving
is implicated in its being immersed in water. Two key questions now
need to be addressed. First, in what manner is there an implication of
(Bii) in (Bi)? And second, what conditions enable this implication?

A substance is water-soluble, the definition informs us, just in case
its dissolution inevitably accompanies its immersion in water—accompanies immersion not just time and again, but invariably accompanies
it without intelligible exception. An important proviso, of course, is that
circumstances of immersion must permit the disposition to be effective;
a lump of sugar coated with wax will not dissolve in water, nor will a
superchilled lump dissolve (readily) in hard ice. Circumstances of immersion permitting, however, water-solubility amounts to dissolution
invariably attending immersion. And the sense of the present proposal
is that what this amounts to in turn is the SOA of the substance's being
immersed implicating the SOA of its subsequently dissolving. Thus,
for any substance x appropriately designated water-soluble, the conditions identifying the SOA of x's being immersed in water include those
identifying the SOA of x's dissolving. For example, a lump of sugar is
properly designated as being immersed in water (as distinct, say, from
being dipped under water while coated with wax) only when shortly
thereafter it begins to dissolve. If dissolution does not occur on sched-

ule, then either the substance was not properly immersed or else it was not soluble in water initially.

If the substance in question was not water-soluble initially, however, this means that the circumstances enabling an implication of this sort themselves were missing. What are the circumstances enabling the implication of something's dissolving in its being immersed in water? What is the enabling condition, in other words, of that implication? The answer, obviously enough, is "the property of being water-soluble." But that expression has two distinct senses, only one of which applies in the answer just given. In the nonapplicable sense, the property of being water-soluble is nothing other than the dispositional property (as defined above) of a thing's dissolving being implicated in its being immersed in water. And a dispositional property of this sort cannot serve as its own enabling condition. In the other sense, however, the property of being water-soluble is that of possessing a certain physical structure that causes the molecules of a substance to go into solution when water is present. What exactly the structure might be is a question belonging to physical chemistry. But once that structure has been identified, the property of being water-soluble has been identified as well. And this is the property of water-solubility that serves as the enabling condition whereby being dissolved is implicated in being immersed in water on the part of the substance possessing the property.

The point may be put more succinctly as follows: There is a *definitional* identity between a thing's being water-soluble in the *first* sense and the implication of its dissolving by its being immersed in water; and there is a *contingent* identity[37] between a thing's being water-soluble in the *second* sense and its having a physical structure that liquefies upon immersion in water. The answer to the question above is that the enabling condition of a thing's water-solubility in the first sense is just its being water-soluble in the second sense, the sense pertaining to physical makeup.

Returning now to the definition (A) of x's being water-soluble as a matter of x's dissolving (Bii) when immersed in water (Bi), we may note how the foregoing analysis accounts for the fact that the conditional "when (Bi) then (Bii)" remains true even when the antecedent is false—that is, even when the conditional itself is counterfactual. The implication of (Bii) in (Bi) holds whenever its enabling condition is met. Since being water-soluble in the sense of physical structure is its enabling condition, this means that the implication holds for any water-soluble substance even when that substance is not immersed in water.

But for (Bii) to be implicated in (Bi) is for it invariably to be the case that the substance in question dissolves when immersed in water. Hence the conditional "when (Bi) then (Bii)" is true even when counterfactual.

Exactly parallel accounts can be given of counterfactuals based on other dispositions.[38] The counterfactual "if that piece of butter had been heated to 150°F, it would have melted" (Nelson Goodman's example)[39] is true just because butter has a physical structure that enables the implication of its melting in its being heated to such a high temperature. And the counterfactual "if Robbins had slipped and fallen at Thanksgiving Ledge, he would have been killed" (Alvin Plantinga's example)[40] is true just because Robbins is a thing of such physical structure that his falling 2,500 feet to the valley floor implicates his being killed.

Counterfactuals involving the use of instruments call for a somewhat more complicated analysis. An example comes with a point developed in section 3 above, to the effect that an SOA of its being −40° at the North Pole is actually current just in case a reading of −40° would be recorded if suitably calibrated instruments were installed on the site. In order for this SOA to be actually current, it clearly is not required that instruments of the appropriate sort be actually present on the scene. What is required is that the conditional "if suitably calibrated instruments were present, then −40° would be recorded" be true even when its antecedent is contrary to fact. Maintaining the same general approach to counterfactuals as in the case of dispositions above, we want to pin down a sense in which a −40° reading would be implicated by the presence of suitably calibrated measuring instruments on the scene. How might that work?

What happens in cases involving the use of instruments in this fashion seems to involve two distinct stages. First, an instrument (the polar thermometer) is designed and calibrated to assure a reading (−40°), when set in place, that corresponds accurately to the ambient temperature of the site. When this stage is satisfactorily completed, then an instrument is at hand so constructed and calibrated that its presence assures an accurate indication of the ambient temperature. The second stage involves adopting the instrument's reading as a criterion of ambient temperature. At this stage, a −40° temperature at the North Pole (to continue the example) is treated as identical to the temperature indicated by the properly installed instrument. This means that the presence of the instrument implicates a −40° reading *just in case* this is the ambient temperature where the instrument is located. An ambient temperature of −40° thus comes to serve as the enabling condition for the implication of an equivalent reading being indicated by the SOA of the instrument being properly located to measure that temperature.

In brief, the first stage is to engineer a set of circumstances (the instrument and its appropriate use) for the specific purpose of implicating a correct instrument reading ($-40°$) just when the enabling condition ($-40°$ ambient temperature) is present.[41] And the second stage is to adopt the instrument reading, taken under the right circumstances, as a criterion for establishing the ambient temperature. Once the instrument reading has come to serve as a criterion of ambient temperature, accordingly—which means that the ambient temperature is treated as identical to the temperature indicated by the instrument reading—then the conditional "if the instrument is in place, it will read $-40°$" is true just in case it is true that the ambient temperature is $-40°$. Under these circumstances, the truth-value of the antecedent is irrelevant. Even when counterfactual, the conditional is true, provided only that the ambient temperature is actually $-40°$. The ambient temperature, in effect, thus serves the counterfactual as the basis for its truth, inasmuch as it serves as the enabling condition for the implication reported in counterfactual form.

A final point to note is what might happen to falsify the conditional. One possibility is that the enabling conditions of the implication are not present, which means merely that the ambient temperature is other than $-40°$. The other is that, although the enabling conditions are present (the ambient temperature is actually $-40°$), the instrument needs recalibrating or perhaps redesigning. Given a properly designed and calibrated instrument, however, it can be relied upon to produce a reading identical (contingently identical, we now see) to the ambient temperature. Thus, given an ambient temperature of $-40°$. it is true that a reading of $-40°$ would be registered if the instrument is properly put in place. And this conditional retains its truth-value even when no instrument is actually located on the scene.

Notes

1. "Negative facts" are invoked most notoriously in Wittgenstein's *Tractatus Logico-Philosophicus* (*Annalen der Naturphilosophie,* 1921), 2.06, 2.201, 2.221, 4.0641, 4.1, to provide sense for negative propositions. As part of our brief survey in the previous chapter of the *Tractatus'* account of states of affairs, we noted that the meaning or sense (*Sinn*) of an elementary proposition is the atomic state of affairs that it represents (2.221) (i.e., that it pictures by way of the structural isomorphism on which Wittgenstein's "picture theory of meaning" is based). Given that the period at the end of this sentence is black, for instance (adapted from 4.063), there is a true proposition that the point is black and a true proposition as well that the point is not white. What gives the former proposition

sense is the "positive fact" that the point is black, while the sense of the latter proposition in turn is the "negative fact" that the point is not white. Inasmuch as "positive" and "negative facts," respectively, as Wittgenstein defines them (2.06), are the existence and nonexistence of states of affairs, this means that the account given of what a proposition represents is different for affirmative and for negative propositions.

In the present account, by contrast, whether a proposition is affirmative or negative has no bearing on what it represents. What it represents is an SOA that is ontologically neutral (chapter 6, section 1), with its quality (affirmative or negative) hinging on difference of status ascribed. With (DG) now at hand, we see that *not being the case* can be defined in the same manner as *being the case,* without recourse to the notion of nonexistence—that is, without invoking negative facts. Both statuses are defined with reference to how the world is and to whether certain circumstances are or are not present within it. Snow's being white is the case just when the world is such that the criteria are satisfied for its correct designation, and it is not the case just when those criteria are unsatisfied. While the discussion of such matters inevitably involves some terminology of negation ("is *not* the case," "*un*satisfied," etc.), the nonsatisfaction of criteria is no more a negative fact than is a thing's being what it is and *not* another thing.

Other prominent treatments of negative facts (or their equivalents) for similar purposes are in Plato's *Sophist* (with its account of not-being) and in Russell's lectures (reprinted in *The Philosophy of Logical Atomism,* David Pears, ed. [LaSalle, Ill.: Open Court Publishing, 1985], see 78).

2. For an example of this use, see Alvin Plantinga's "World and Essence," in *Universals and Particulars: Readings in Ontology,* M. Loux, ed. (Notre Dame, Ind.: University of Notre Dame Press, 1976). This, of course, is not the only use to which the notion of "possible worlds" has been put.

3. Several points need to be made to keep this remark in perspective. One is to draw attention to (BC) and (C1,2) of chapter 6, (sections 4 and 5, respectively), which limit identifiable SOAs to those for which there are representations with communally sanctioned designative use. Another is that the manner of speaking according to which all SOAs are possible does not introduce what Fumerton (*Metaphysical and Epistemological Problems of Perception* [Lincoln: University of Nebraska Press, 1985], 56) calls an "ontology of possibilia." I agree with Fumerton in denying existence to SOAs that are merely possible. (For a disappreciation of nonexistent states of affairs as objects of false propositions, beliefs, etc., see Richard Fumerton, *Metaepistemology and Skepticism* [Lanham, Md.: Rowman & Littlefield, 1995], 74.) Yet another is to note that this conception of possibility does not apply to the sequencing or conjunction of SOAs themselves. There is another sense of possibility, to which we return below, in which it is impossible that the SOA of the gate's being open, for instance, should be the case simultaneously with that of the (same) gate's being shut.

4. There is no suggestion here that someone so minded might not define a conception of possible worlds to serve this or that theoretical purpose. The

point is that such a conception, and the difficulties that come with it, are not germane to the present study.

5. Immanuel Kant, *Critique of Pure Reason,* N. K. Smith, trans. (New York: St. Martin's Press, 1965), introduction, sec. 1.

6. For notable examples, see W. V. O. Quine's "Two Dogmas of Empiricism" and Morton White's "The Analytic and the Synthetic: An Untenable Dualism" in, respectively, Quine's *From a Logical Point of View* (Cambridge, Mass.: Harvard University Press, 1953) and *Semantics and the Philosophy of Language,* Leonard Linsky, ed.(Urbana: University of Illinois Press, 1952).

7. An indication of the continuing importance of his views on such matters is the frequency with which Kant is cited by the contributors to *A Priori Knowledge,* Paul Moser, ed. (Oxford: Oxford University Press, 1987).

8. The expression "snow's being white," of course, might be used in a more restricted sense to represent the color appearance of snow in a particular locale, or within the experience of a particular observer. Thus Beatrice might know that snow is white in the sense of being able to identify the color of the snow outside her window (white, not yellow, etc.). But she also might know that snow is white in the sense of understanding enough about the physical makeup of snow to know that (uncontaminated) snow, wherever encountered, will present a white appearance to normal observers. It is this more general sense of the expression that is being contrasted here with the particular SOA of Deirdre's gate being shut.

9. A more familiar sense of "immediately present" (explained, e.g., in Fumerton's *Metaphysical and Epistemological Problems of Perception,* 57) is that of being accessible without inference. Since inference involves representation, this sense is accommodated by the understanding of immediate presence specified above.

10. There is a distinction to be made between the immediate presence to an individual subject of the general SOA of snow's being white and the presence to that individual of the (second-order) SOA of its being the case that *generally* snow is white. The immediate presence of the former does not require that the latter be immediately present as well. Insofar as the subject's access to the latter depends upon induction, hence upon symbolic representation, this access could not be immediate. One way in which access to the former might be immediate is for the subject to have a direct (nonsymbolic) grasp of laws of optics that show why snow presents a white appearance to normal observers under normal circumstances of viewing. This possibility receives further discussion below. In either case, the SOA of snow's being white itself counts as empirical. What makes an SOA empirical, by the present account, is not that its presence is always *established* empirically (which it may be or not), but that the circumstances in which it is actually current are empirically evident when they occur.

11. For the SOA to be the case is for the conditional statement to be true in the sense that the truth of its consequent is a result of the truth of its antecedent. Truth in this sense obviously is not truth of the *material* conditional, which

might be true merely as a result of the antecedent's being false. It obviously is not the case that the temperature at the North Pole stands at −40° whenever no instruments are there to measure it. An explication of the requirements for truth of counterfactuals like this is proposed in the final section of this chapter.

12. A recent discussion of verificationism that is generally appreciative may be found in Fumerton's *Metaphysical and Epistemological Problems of Perceptions,* 32–34; see also 169.

13. The problem with these expressions as putative representations is that there are no identifiable circumstances in which what they purport to represent would actually be the case. It should be pointed out that the mere linguistic act of articulating the expression does not have the effect of identifying the missing circumstances. There are, for example, no identifiable circumstances in which "the mome raths outgrabe" would represent an actual SOA, and thus there is no coherent representational use of that expression. Needless to say, merely enunciating the expression (in speech or writing, e.g.) would not have the effect of identifying such a set of circumstances. If the expression has no coherent use in the first place, it cannot be coherently used to provide a use for itself.

A related point is that our undoubted ability to count exactly nine million and two items in some certain regard (e.g., total miles on the odometers of a large fleet of automobiles) does not guarantee that a tally of that degree of accuracy makes sense in other circumstances where precise counting procedures are not available. Certain groups of objects admit precise counts and others do not. The present point is not blunted by perfunctory invocations of what is often called the "law of the excluded middle," the proper applicability of which in this case ("either there are exactly nine million and two fish in Lake Michigan or there are not") would require intelligible use of the expression in question.

14. This is not to say there is something defective about "5 + 7 = 12" as a formula of arithmetic, which would be absurd, but rather to point out that this expression by itself does not represent a first-tier SOA—that is, does not represent an aspect of the world itself (actual or otherwise).

15. This may be intuitively hard to see, perhaps in part due to the firm hold of the sums-tables drilled into us as children and the counting system we share with almost everyone we meet. But it is not unthinkable that other rules of counting prevail. Explorations of various other possibilities and of what they amount to may be found in D. Gasking, "Mathematics and the World," *Australasian Journal of Philosophy* 18, no. 2 (September 1940), 97–116; H.N. Castaneda, "Mathematics and Reality," *Australasian Journal of Philosophy* 37, no. 2 (August 1959), 92–107; and K.M. Sayre, "Gasking on Arithmetical Incorrigibility," *Mind* 71, no. 283 (July 1962), 372–376.

16. Not to beg the question against the Platonist, we should say that at least there would be no SOAs involving truths (true propositions) concerning numbers. By (C1) of the preceding chapter, there are no SOAs that cannot be com-

munally expressed, and communal expression of SOAs involving propositions about numbers requires a common system of enumeration. There was a stage in the development of human society, presumably, in which no such system was available.

17. Kant's confidence that truths of arithmetic are *a priori* reflected a series of problematic assumptions, including (1) that the serial order of the prevalent number system is based on the serial order of successive moments in time, (2) that only the prevalent number system is compatible with temporal seriality, and (3) that the experience of all rational persons is temporally structured. Assumption (1) is the only one for which Kant argued; but (3) is certainly dubious, and (2) seems most likely false.

18. According to the definition of proposition-type in chapter 3, different token propositions belong to the same type if they are the same in quality, on the same level, and true under the same circumstances as other members of that class. Arithmetical propositions like "5 + 7 = 12" might appear to pose a problem in that regard, inasmuch as the first-tier SOA rendering "5 + 7 = 12" true does the same for "3 + 7 = 10," "5 + 9 = 14," and others, which clearly are not members of the same proposition-type. The resolution of this apparent difficulty comes with the observation that the truth-conditions of "5 + 7 = 12" are not merely the empirical circumstances that constitute the prevalence of its supporting number system, but also the systematic circumstances of this latter's generating "5 + 7 = 12" as a true formula. Whereas the empirical component of these truth-making circumstances is shared by "3 + 7 = 10," "5 + 9 = 14," and any number of other arithmetical formulae, the systemic component is not. The systematic circumstances whereby "5 + 7 = 12" is generated as a true formula (12 being the 7th successor of 5) are different from those generating "3 + 7 = 10," and so on, as formulae with the same status.

19. Although the shortest distance between two points might still be defined as a "straight line" in such a system, the line in question would not be a Euclidean straight line.

20. Key philosophic literature on these questions includes A. Einstein, "Geometry and Experience," reprinted in *Readings in the Philosophy of Science,* H. Feigl and M. Brodbeck, eds. (New York: Appleton-Century-Crofts, 1953), 189–194; H. Reichenbach, "The Philosophical Significance of the Theory of Relativity," reprinted in *Readings,* Feigl and Brodbeck, eds., 195–211; and C. Hempel, "Geometrical and Empirical Science," reprinted in *Readings in Philosophical Analysis,* H. Feigl and W. Sellars, eds. (New York: Appleton-Century-Crofts, 1949), 238–249.

21. While measurements on and near the earth's surface typically involve both measuring rods (or equivalent) and optical instruments, and have no explicit theoretical component, interstellar measurements are almost exclusively optical and engage the special theory of relativity as interpretive context. For the contribution of non-Euclidean geometry to the general theory of relativity, see Einstein, "Geometry and Experience," 192, and Reichenbach, "The Philo-

sophical Significance of the Theory of Relativity," 204, both in *Readings in the Philosophy of Science*, Feigl and Brodbeck, eds.

22. In C. I. Lewis and C. H. Langford's *Symbolic Logic* (New York: Dover Publications, 1932); appendix II, in which S1 through S5 were first so designated, was written by Lewis. By way of brief description, S1 begins with a set of primitive symbols (including the operators ' − ', '∧', and 'M', for negation, conjunction, and possibility, respectively); a few intuitively plausible formation rules and transformation rules; definitions of Disjunction, Strict Implication, Strict Equivalence, and Necessity; and a few axioms with direct parallels in the propositional calculus. S2 is generated from S1 by the addition of an axiom providing that if the conjunction of p and q is possible, then p is possible itself. It is from this axiom, of course, that the implication discussed in the text above derives. S3 is generated from S1 with the addition of an axiom to the effect that if p entails q, then necessarily the impossibility of q entails the impossibility of p. S4 is generated from S1 with the addition of the axiom that if p is necessary, then necessarily it is necessary that p is necessary. And S5 comes from S1, finally, by adding the axiom that the possibility of p entails that necessarily p is possible. Although defined independently, S4 is included in S5 (in the sense that all theorems of the former are theorems of the latter), S3 is included in S4, S2 is included in S3, and S1 is included in S2.

23. For discussions of the suitability of various systems of modal logic for various theoretical uses, see E. J. Lemmon, "Is There Only One Correct System of Modal Logic?" *Proceedings of the Aristotelian Society*, supplementary vol. 33 (1959), 23–39; and Susan Haack, *Philosophy of Logics* (Cambridge: Cambridge University Press, 1978), 197–203.

24. Many philosophers eschew the concept of analyticity today on the grounds that it is too much bound up with a murky analytic/synthetic distinction. No stand on this or related issues is implied by the use of Kantian terminology as a matter of convenience in the present context.

25. The relation among SOAs that I term "implication" is similar to what Chisholm calls "inclusion" in his *Theory of Knowledge*, 1st ed. (Englewood Cliffs, N.J.: Prentice-Hall, 1966), 72. Chisholm, in this work, does not explore the *source* of such a relation, which in the present context is located in conditions for the correct designative use of representations of the SOAs involved.

26. To put it another way, X's implicating Y is not the same kind of implication as that of a proposition about X implying a proposition about Y.

27. The expression '*de re* necessity', strictly speaking, means necessity in things, in contrast with '*de dicto* necessity' as necessity in sayings or words. In contemporary metaphysical discussions, however, the expression is often used more specifically to indicate a view some call "essentialism." See, for example, Alvin Plantinga, *The Nature of Necessity* (Oxford: Clarendon Press, 1974), 14.

28. The masculine member of an unmarried, cohabiting couple *might* be recognized as a husband, for example, as might someone with spousal obligations to a woman under some form of "common law."

29. The manner of inclusion need not be explicit, as in the case of X and Y above. Suppose that SOA T is identified by conditions S, C, and D, that S is equivalent to A and B, and that SOA U is identified by B and C. Then T implicates U even though T's conditions do not include those of U explicitly.

30. In his "Two Dogmas of Empiricism," Quine observes that Kant's characterization of analyticity appeals to a "notion of containment" of predicate in subject terms that is "left at a metaphysical level" (21), and goes on to argue that analyticity, although interdefinable with other notions such as meaning-equivalence and synonymy, cannot be defined in a manner that escapes this circle of intentional notions. The concept of implication among SOAs, as characterized above, is not a member of Quine's "intentional circle." Nor is the characterization left at a "metaphysical level." For what it is worth, we might take the extra step of defining analyticity as the property of implication between the subject and the predicate terms of a proposition of the form "(all) S is P." Inasmuch as implication is entirely extensional in character, this provides an entry into Quine's intentional circle that itself is "out of the loop."

31. A proposition p is materially conditional upon another proposition q (to repeat) in case p and q are not true and false, respectively, and there is no entailment linking the truth-values of p and q. This relation is generally considered "weak" in that the conditions for its presence are satisfied both by p's being false and by q's being true (individually) without regard to the truth-value of the other proposition.

32. This is a standard way of characterizing a relation of strict entailment between the propositions [X/yes] and [Y/yes] in question. Without begging any questions about the relation between this conditionality based on implication among SOAs and the strict entailment of modal logic (see note 21 above), we will adopt the familiar arrow as a symbol for the former conditionality. Thus the definition (using the notation from chapter 3 for proposition types):

$$\{*[X/yes] \rightarrow *[Y/yes\} =_{df} X \text{ implicates } Y.$$

33. The contingency of "empirical necessities" arising from implication among empirical SOAs is similar to that of the "nonempirical necessities" of logic and mathematics, according to the treatment of these latter in section 4 above. In either case, the necessity in question holds only under circumstances that might not be actual. In the case of logic and mathematics, such circumstances constitute a first-tier SOA of a certain formal system prevailing for purposes of reasoning within some relevant domain. In the case of implication among empirical SOAs, these circumstances are what are called *enabling conditions* in the text below.

34. An example would be a society recognizing "common-law husbands" (and/or wives), as it were, without dubbing their relation a "common-law marriage." The possibility of such circumstances is one reason it seems unadvisable to undertake explication of the involvement of being married in being a husband (or wife) in terms of meaning relations. It remains an open

possibility, nonetheless, that there are cases in which the enabling condition of an implication does boil down to a meaning relationship. The implication of being extended in being a physical body (Kant's example) seems to be a case in point.

35. Richard Fumerton distinguishes three kinds of subjunctive (counterfactual) conditionals (*Metaphysical and Epistemological Problems of Perception*, 140): "(1) those that assert entailment between antecedent and consequent, (2) those that assert nomological sufficiency between antecedent and consequent, and (3) those that assert that the antecedent *together with* some set of conditions that obtain is nomologically or logically sufficient for the consequent" (Fumerton's emphasis). A conditional "if x is a husband, x is a male" based on the present implication relation would be closely analogous to Fumerton's type (3).

36. From this it follows, of course, that the two sides of the biconditional strictly entail each other, but only insofar as any proposition strictly entails itself under alternative formulations.

37. The identity here is contingent in the sense that sensations are sometimes said to be contingently identical with brain processes. For an example of the latter, see J. J. C. Smart, "Sensations and Brain Processes,"*The Philosophy of Mind*, V. C. Chappell, ed. (Englewood Cliffs, N. J.: Prentice-Hall, 1962), 160–172.

38. Nelson Goodman (in "The Problem of Counterfactual Conditionals," in *Semantics and the Philosophy of Language,* Linsky, ed.) observes that "a satisfactory theory of . . . disposition terms . . . would solve a large part of the problem of counterfactuals" (231). While the highly compressed account here is too brief to count as a "satisfactory theory" of the former, the above results support Goodman's observation.

39. Goodman, "The Problem of Counterfactual Conditionals," 231.

40. Plantinga, *The Nature of Necessity,* 177. The enabling condition in this example is a bit more involved than in the other examples, including as it does not only Robbins's vulnerable skeletal structure, but such other facts as his not having been let down to the valley floor on a shaft of vigorously uprising air, not having landed on a very thick bed of rushes or in a very sturdy safety net, and so forth.

41. In terms of Fumerton's threefold distinction (cited in note 35), the first stage is to engineer a set of circumstances that are nomologically sufficient for the concerned instrument reading just when the enabling condition is present. This makes the conditional "if a properly prepared instrument is in place then a reading of $-40°$ will result" itself an example of Fumerton's type (2). If the enabling conditions were added to the antecedent, a conditional of type (3) would result.

PART III
LANDMARKS OF COGNITIVE THEORY

Chapter 8

INTERNAL REPRESENTATIONS

1. Why an Account of Internal Representations Is Needed

In one familiar sense of the term, experiences like hunger and pain are "private" to the person experiencing them, while the expressions we use to represent these experiences—"hunger," "pain," and so on—are as much part of a public language as terms like "block" and "slab" and "pillar." There are representations of another kind, however, that are "private" in a rather different sense, without regard to the character (public *or* private) of the objects they serve to represent.[1] The representations here in question are private in the sense of being internal to the mind of the person employing them and of serving that person in a representational capacity without appearing as tokens in a public language. It is the task of this chapter to provide an account of internal representations of this sort and to come to terms with some of the problems they pose for the present approach. By way of preliminaries, let us look briefly at some reasons for thinking there are representations of this sort in the first place.

These reasons have to do with the private character of certain propositional attitudes. Among the various attitudes identified in chapter 1 as attitudes of propositional stance, there are some that by nature seem almost exclusively public. One example is the attitude of testifying, as when Deirdre attests to all concerned that the gate was closed when last she checked it. Testifying is not the sort of thing one does without an audience, and hence not a thing one can do without employing propositions expressed in public language. Other attitudes typically involving publicly articulated propositions are protesting, contending, and declaring. There are some attitudes of propositional stance, on the other hand, that frequently, or even usually, are adopted and maintained without direct public disclosure of the propositions involved. A clear ex-

211

ample is the attitude of thinking. If Deirdre thinks that the children were hiding in the apple tree just to gain her attention, this is a thought she may choose not to articulate publicly. Other propositional attitudes we often "keep to ourselves," for one reason or another, are those of concluding, suspecting, and believing. What this means specifically is that the token propositions that serve as their objects are not formulated in public language. To make sense of attitudes like this that are not publicly manifested, it seems practically unavoidable to postulate propositional entities of some sort internal to the minds of the subjects concerned. Inasmuch as propositions invariably include a representational component in their structure, moreover, we must be capable of entertaining representations of comparably private character. The question that ensues is how to make sense of representations that are not articulated in a public symbol-system.

It might be helpful in addressing this question to recall the distinction drawn in chapter 3 between token propositions and their respective types. One purpose of this distinction was to accommodate the fact that people often are taken to have asserted the same proposition while employing different phrases ("snow is white," "white is the color of snow," etc.), or even while employing expressions from different languages (*"der Schnee ist weiss"*). The point of the distinction in this prior regard is that while each assertion engages its own specific token proposition, the several assertions count as assertions of the same propositions just in case each of the token propositions involved belongs to the same proposition-type. Token propositions invariably are concrete, in the sense of having physical existence in space and time. And it is this concrete character of a token proposition that enables it to serve as the proper object of an individual propositional attitude. Serving as an object of assertion, of belief, and so forth, as it were, is one use to which a token proposition might be put. While proposition-types, on the other hand, are entirely abstract, and hence cannot be put to any (concrete linguistic) use at all, the assertion of a token proposition thus counts as the assertion of its corresponding type as well. The upshot is that while different people never assert (believe, etc.) the same token proposition, it is a common matter for them to assert tokens of the same proposition-type. And this in effect is to assert (believe, etc.) the same proposition.

Pursuing the same line into the domain of propositional representations that are internal to the mind, we remain beholden to the requirement that internal propositions count as concrete tokens of abstract proposition-types. Being abstract, the types themselves are unavailable for use as objects of private beliefs, thoughts, and so forth. So there apparently must be some sense in which the propositional objects of such attitudes take the form of concrete tokens within the mind of the subject concerned. One problem to be addressed in this regard is how such representations might be conceived as concrete in the requisite sense.

The problem of concreteness would seem to be solved as a matter of course if mental representations generally were neurophysiological states. And this, of course, is just the way they are conceived by most people working in cognitive science today. As we shall see, however, this way of thinking about internal representations is subject to severe difficulties. Although the prevalent conception ultimately may prove itself at least partially correct, these difficulties must be handled before we can remain comfortable with the type of solution it provides. Let us begin the task of this chapter by reviewing what contemporary cognitive science has to say about representations in the mind of the subject.

2. Problems with Conceiving the Mind as a "Symbol Manipulation" System

Among the various accounts of mental representations as neurophysiological states found in the literature of current cognitive science, the most thoroughly worked out remains that of Jerry Fodor.[2] Fodor's treatment of cognitive attitudes has already come under criticism in chapter 1, with regard to his assumption that all such attitudes are propositional in character. As we saw to the contrary, several of the attitudes he explicitly identifies as propositional are attitudes toward SOAs instead.[3] A further problem with Fodor's account in this regard comes with his notion that a person's having a propositional attitude is a matter of that person's being in some relation to an internal representation.[4] In Fodor's view of such things, presumably, both the person and the representation are physical entities, and the only obvious relation between them would be that of whole to part. One thing that Fodor leaves unexplained in his account, however, is how the relation of a whole to its part—or any other intelligible relation between an organism and its brain states—could constitute an *attitude* toward anything at all. Yet another problem is that he apparently takes for granted that representations by themselves, unaccompanied by anything equivalent to status-ascriptions, can serve as depictions of how things stand in the world. Although Fodor certainly is not alone in taking this for granted, the result is that what he calls "propositional attitudes" are attitudes toward entities (mere representations of SOAs) that lack truth-value. The upshot of these particular problems, one might reasonably conclude, is that Fodor is operating with seriously flawed conceptions both of propositions and of propositional attitudes.

Nonetheless, Fodor could be wrong in his treatment of propositions and propositional attitudes and still be basically right in his conception of internal representations. What the argument following is intended to show is that Fodor's treatment of representations in the mind is seriously flawed as well. The basic defect of his approach in this regard, as we shall see, is its reliance upon the computational model to make sense of the notion of internal representations.

The computational model featured by contemporary cognitive theory is a way of thinking of the brain and its cognitive processes as analogous to a computer and its computational operations. Put succinctly, it is a way of thinking according to which the brain is conceived as an organic computer, operating on its own internal formulae in just the manner that a digital computer, through a series of strictly physical transactions, operates on formulae of its own computing language. This conception is at the heart of what Fodor calls "the basic idea of modern cognitive theory."[5] In a nutshell, the "basic idea" is the notion that the brain, like its technological counterpart, is characterized by a mapping relation that pairs physical states of the system with formulae in the computing language, in such a fashion as to ensure that the physical processes of computation will preserve all relevant semantic features of these internal formulae. Against the background of this basic idea, the causal interactions among brain states (e.g., perceptions influencing beliefs, which in turn influence desires and purposes) can be explained in terms of the physical processes of computation, while the semantic features of these states (such as meaning, truth, and reference) can be explained in terms of the mapping relation they share with these physical structures.

This conception of the brain as an organic computer has been examined from a variety of critical perspectives in recent years.[6] One criticism that has been raised repeatedly bears upon the tactic, inherent in Fodor's and similar approaches, of undertaking to explain the symbolic capacities of the brain's internal representations by analogy with symbolic capacities possessed by certain internal states of a digital computer. As any sober view of computation by artifacts (digital or otherwise) should make clear, to the extent that internal formulae of a computing mechanism possess symbolic capacities at all, this is only by virtue of the computer's having been programmed by a user with the symbolic applications in question specifically in mind. Despite the "trade" description of certain complex computing systems as "symbol manipulators," the semantic features of the computing states being manipulated depend entirely upon the intentions of the human users. Inasmuch as the purported symbolic capacities of digital computers can be explained only with reference to the symbol-using capacities of the humans using them, accordingly, it is of no avail to attempt to explain the latter in terms of the former.[7] Although the computational approach to cognition has attracted a well-endowed following, both academic and industrial, it lacks the conceptual resources needed to make sense of the mind's capacity for using symbols.

There is nothing new about criticism of this nature, and (as already noted) there is no lack of forceful voices to make the criticism stick. But there are other problems with computationalism, no less fundamental, that emerge from the general requirements for representation developed in chapter 6. The first general requirement (GR1) in question, we recall, is that a symbol, in order to serve as a representation, both must be present itself to a cognitive subject and must draw the subject's attention beyond itself to the thing it represents. The second requirement (GR2) is that for a symbol to serve as a representation, it must be virtually related to what it represents. As we shall see, the computational approach to representations comes into trouble on both scores. Let us consider first how it fares with (GR1).

Requirement (GR1) sets down a condition to be met by symbolic representations generally. Not all representations, needless to say, are symbolic in character. There is a sense in which smoke represents fire, in which parched soil represents drought, and in which solubility represents a certain chemical makeup. There is a sense of the term "represents," that is to say, that is roughly equivalent to "indicates" or "is a sign of" in their common meanings.[8] But there is a more specific (although no less common) sense in which a representation serves as a *symbol* for what it represents. All concrete token propositions in a public language are representations of this symbolic sort; and this is the sense of representation to which (GR1) applies. If internal representations are to play a like role, they too must qualify under the conditions of this requirement.

What (GR1) requires, to repeat, is both that the representation in question be capable of engaging a subject's awareness itself and that it be able further to direct the subject's attention beyond itself to the thing it represents. The first part of this dual requirement is a necessary condition of the second, inasmuch as a symbol cannot direct a subject's attention to something beyond itself unless it is capable of engaging a subject's awareness initially. There are no symbols, that is to say, of which a subject employing them remains unaware. And it is precisely in this regard that it makes no sense to think of neurophysiological states as serving in the role of internal representations. Granted that neuronal states as such play some role—perhaps an essential role—in our awareness of the world around us, this role cannot be one in which they function as symbolic representations. The reason is simply that a typical cognitive subject almost never is aware of his or her neuronal states as such.[9] It is conceivable, to be sure, that people other than the subject concerned might come to be aware of neuronal states serving in some such role. Just as an engineer might single out a particular electronic circuit for inspection during a computer checkup, so a skilled neurosurgeon might single out and identify a particular neuronal circuit as playing some kind of representational role. But the neurosurgeon in question would not be the subject allegedly employing the circuit as a symbolic representation. And the subject supposedly employing the circuit in that role typically will not be aware of the circuit in question.[10] From this it follows that the circuit (or brain state, etc.) will not serve to direct the subject's attention beyond itself to something else that it might be taken to represent. The result is that brain states by themselves are not qualified to serve in a symbolic role. Although such internal states are unproblematically concrete, as required of token propositions generally, they are not capable of serving as symbolic representations in the manner needed to make sense of the computational account.

The computational account of internal representations encounters difficulty as well with regard to the second general requirement (GR2). One of the merits claimed for the basic idea behind the computational account of cognition, as noted above, is that it enables a causal explanation of the brain processes in which representations allegedly are involved.[11] Not only are the semantic features of the system in question supposed to "take care of themselves"[12] by virtue of being mapped onto the features involved in actual computation; the basic idea also trades upon a supposition to the effect that the actual computation of a cognitive system (if the system is working properly) proceeds by strictly causal interactions among its parts. But if this supposition is correct, as it is for standard computing systems at least, then the basic idea seems to carry with it the assumption that the referential role of the system's internal representations can be accounted for on the basis of causal interactions exclusively. The problem with this is that reference, like all forms of representation, is a virtual relation, and it is hard to see how any virtual relation could be accounted for in terms of the concrete relations involved in strictly causal interactions.[13]

To see how the problem arises with the referential relation in particular, consider a given representation R that refers to object X specifically. Now, in order for R to refer to X specifically, there must be something about the relation between representation and object that associates R with X exclusively, as distinct from some different object Y. In the case of a cognitive subject S, this distinguishing mark would be in the intentional structure of the attitude S entertains toward X while employing R as its representation. If X is the SOA of the sky's being cloudy, for example, and S is entertaining a belief about X, then the factor that associates S's propositional representation with X is the intentional structure by which S's belief is directed toward that particular object. What exactly an intentional structure of this sort amounts to will come under detailed consideration in the following chapter. For present purposes, however, it is enough to note that intentionality cannot be invoked as part of an explanation of what might make a representation refer to one specific object rather than some other within the context of a system of strictly causal interactions. The reason is that intentionality, as we shall see shortly, depends upon the presence of a representational component within the cognitive attitude involved, and hence that it cannot be relied upon as part of an explanation of representation when the latter itself is in question. To put it another way, the reason we cannot invoke intentionality to help explain a problematic aspect of the representations alleged to be involved in a computational system is that intentionality itself involves representation; and appealing to a factor that depends upon a problematic feature will not make that feature less problematic.

In the context of the computational model of cognition, given the exclusively causal character of the interactions involved, the only explanation available of what it might be in the relation between R and X that makes R refer to X *specifically* would have to be in terms of those causal interactions themselves. But in order to achieve a causal explanation of R's relation to X, the object X itself would have to enter somehow into the causal interactions involved. Inasmuch as R's reference to X is a virtual relation, however, X itself may well be nonexistent. And since causation, by contrast, is a concrete relation, nonexistent objects cannot enter into causal interactions. Thus the strictly causal character of a properly functioning computational system, considered by most advocates of the computational model to count in its favor, actually precludes an intelligible account in computational terms of how internal states of the system might be endowed with reference.

Now, it must be admitted by advocate and critic alike that computationalism has had very little to say about how exactly *any* semantic property might be "preserved" by purely computational operations. But reference, as we have seen, poses particular problems. Lacking further details of how a computational account of reference might go, we may reasonably conclude that the computational model simply lacks the resources to make sense of representation internal to the mind. Maybe there is some sense in which neuronal circuits stand *surrogate* for objects outside the nervous system; and maybe there is some way as well in which they *present* such objects indirectly within the subject's awareness. But if so, the manner in which they do so is not just an "internal" version of the role played by token representations in a written or spoken public language.

Perhaps it is time to set computationalism aside with its many inherent difficulties and to look elsewhere for an account of internal representations.

3. Learning the Use of Symbols: Its Afferent Counterpart

The difficulty the previous section began with is that of reaching a coherent conception of token propositions internal to the mind that might serve as concrete objects of propositional attitudes that are never publicly expressed. For reasons reviewed above, it appears unpromising to rely for a resolution of this difficulty upon the computational approach that dominates most work in cognitive science today. But the problems computationalism encounters in accounting for internal representations are not peculiar to that approach alone. They affect any attempt to make sense of representations "in the mind" that treats such representations as close analogues of concrete written and spoken symbols employed in a public language. A major source of disanalogy, noted above in connection with general requirement (GR1), is that the subject is seldom (if ever) aware of any states or processes within his or her own central nervous system that might conceivably play a representational role, in the manner that we perforce are aware of the symbols we employ as representations in public language.

A corollary of this disanalogy is that we do not use our own internal states in a representational role, any more than we use hair follicles to grow hair or use our hearts to pump blood. And since there are no internal states that we use in the fashion that we use symbols in a public language for representational purposes, it follows that we do not *learn* to use any of our internal states or processes for such purposes. This being the case, the learning requirements (LR1) and (LR2) of chapter 6 (section 4) seem to have no direct application to internal representations, whatever these latter may turn out to be. At first thought, this might appear to be a substantial difficulty for *any* attempt to make sense of internal representations, computational or otherwise. For if requirements (LR1) and (LR2) do not even apply to internal representations, it seems to follow that such representations cannot meet these requirements. And if they are genuine requirements, how can any kind of purported representation that does not meet them count as genuine itself?

Although requirements (LR1) and (LR2) do not apply to internal representations in the manner that they apply to symbolic representations of a public language, however, we may nonetheless be able to employ them as "leverage points" for extracting fresh insight both into how internal representations probably function and into what they must be *like* to function in that fashion. To mine this insight, we need to shift tactics and to consider certain processes that very likely take place in the mind when we learn to use symbols in a public language. The way to look at these requirements for purposes of understanding how internal representations function, according to this new tactic, is not with regard to how such representations *meet* the requirements, but with regard to *what happens internally when* the requirements are met. Our concern in the present section is the first requirement, with (LR2) set aside for the following section. We return subsequently to the question whether there might not be a sense after all in which internal representations meet the requirements in question.

The first learning requirement (LR1) specifies a condition that must be met for a given subject S to gain the ability to identify an SOA X when X is immediately present to S. The condition is that S must learn how to communicate the presence of X to other people by an appropriate use of some symbolic representation R. In effect, what (LR1) says is that S's learning to identify X when immediately present depends upon S's also learning how to communicate the presence of X by the correct use of some representation of X made available in a public language.

A number of comments regarding this requirement are in order before we move to consider its neurological consequences. For one, since in general it is unlikely that a subject would be able to identify an SOA under any circumstances whatever if he or she is unable to identify it when immediately present, (LR1) actually is broader in scope than it might appear at first reading. Since being able to identify X under other circumstances arguably is conditional upon being able to identify it when immediately present, and since this latter in turn is conditional upon being able to communicate the presence of X in a public language, the effect of (LR1) overall is to make the identification of X under any circumstances whatever conditional upon an ability to employ the symbolic resources of a public language to communicate its presence to other people. In brief, a subject S is able to identify a given SOA X only if S has use of some representation R by which to symbolize the presence of X to other users of a shared language. Although this requirement may not be intuitively obvious in its own right, it is supported by the several considerations examined in chapter 6.

Another feature of (LR1) calling for comment is the scope of the term "some" (qualifying "representation") in its conditional clause. The point is not that there is one particular representation R of X that S must learn to use correctly if S is to learn how to identify the presence of X. The point, rather, is that S must acquire use of symbolic resources for indicating the presence of X made available by some public language. In the process of gaining use of these resources, there may be some particular representation with which S first becomes familiar; but the wording of (LR1) is not intended to draw attention to this particular R. While there must be at least one such R available to S for symbolizing X as a bare minimum, the sense of the requirement is just that S must be able to represent X symbolically in order to learn the identity of X in the first place. In a standard case, S might well have use of a considerable number of different symbolic devices for indicating the presence of X to other speakers of his or her language(s).

Yet another noteworthy feature of (LR1) is that it makes learning to identify X conditional upon the use of symbolic devices from a *public* language. While the considerations upon which this requirement is based (in chapter 6) do not overlap with Wittgenstein's well-known arguments against what he calls "private language,"[14] their effect is very much the same. Behind the publicity requirement in the present case is the predominantly public character of the criteria by which SOAs are identified.[15] The criteria in question are those for the correct use of publicly available symbols to designate the actual obtaining of what they represent. To learn the correct designative use of such symbols is tantamount to learning the identity of the SOAs they are used to designate. It is in this manner that the identity of SOAs is bound up with the symbolic resources of public language. It does not follow from these considerations alone that there are no objects to which one might refer in some kind of "private language"; but if there are, SOAs (as presently conceived) are not among them.

Let us now shift perspectives from external to internal, and make an effort to single out certain neurological factors that come into play as S learns to identify a given SOA X. When a cognitively endowed organism perceives a determinate set of circumstances in the world, or in some other way becomes aware of their presence, and then goes on to report those circumstances in terms of a public symbol-system, something physical happens in the brain of that organism. When Camille, for instance, perceives that the sun is shining, her becoming aware of that SOA is accompanied (and in part, perhaps, constituted)[16] by a set of neuronal processes in her visual cortex. As a set, moreover, these processes are physically distinct from other processes that would accompany her becoming aware of the SOA of the sky's being cloudy, for example, or those of snow's being white or the gate's being shut. If the neuronal processes involved in her perception of these SOAs were not significantly different under these various circumstances, then she would not be perceiving different SOAs.

If C is not actually *perceiving* that particular SOA, but is *thinking* that the sun is shining instead, then again there will be something happening in some part of her cortex that marks the presence of that particular thought. What is happening will be different from what happens when she thinks that the sky is cloudy, or when she thinks any number of other distinguishable thoughts. And the same holds for when she *believes* that the sun is shining, or *hopes* that SOA will turn out to be the case, and so forth. Not only will her thinking and believing that the sun is shining involve significantly different brain states or processes than her thinking and believing that the sky is cloudy, but the processes involved in her *thinking* and *believing* that the sun is shining, moreover, will share enough in common with the corresponding processes involved in her *perceiving* or *hoping* that the sun is shining to account for all of these mental activities on her part being concerned with the same SOA—that of the sun's shining, as distinct from the sky's being cloudy, or some other SOA.

There is no need for present purposes to speculate about just *how similar* the brain processes involved in her thinking and perceiving a given SOA X must be to count as being concerned with that SOA specifically, or about just *how different* these processes must be from those involved in thinking or perceiving another SOA Y for these to count, respectively, as being concerned with a different SOA. It is enough to recognize that for each distinct SOA a given subject is capable of distinguishing, whether by perception or thought or some other relevant faculty, there is a set of neuronal occurrences somewhere in that subject's cortex with features uniquely associated with that SOA. For convenience of reference, let us label this set of circumstances 'NX_a' — the set of neuronal (N) occurrences associated with the awareness (a) of SOA X.[17]

There is a restricted sense of the term "represents" in which NX_a might be said already to represent the SOA X when the presence of that SOA actually elicits its activation. The sense is that in which a yellow skin represents a ripe banana or a falling barometer represents a change in weather. A falling barometer represents a change in weather insofar as it registers particular atmospheric circumstances that themselves are part of weather changes already under way. Similarly, NX_a represents X when actually present to the subject insofar as the neuronal occurrences in question register the presence of that SOA through its impact upon the subject's central nervous system.[18] In neither case, however, does the representation yet have a *symbolic* dimension. Like the falling barometer, the events involved in NX_a under these conditions are related to what they represent by way of being causally associated with the latter. Given the requirement that a sign or symbol represents a thing or object only when it is *virtually* (not just causally, and thereby *concretely*) related to what it represents, we have not yet arrived at an understanding of how NX_a might represent SOA X in a manner that is symbolically significant.

There are important respects, however, in which the neuronal activities associated with a subject's cognitive dealings with a given SOA differ from the falling barometric pressure associated with worsening weather conditions. Return to Camille and her awareness that the sun is shining. Although the process of the sun's emitting radiation that eventually impinges upon the nervous system of a sentient organism is a causal process through and through, Camille is not prepared just as a natural matter of course to pick out the sun's shining as an SOA she would have any interest in noting or in communicating to her fellow language users. Obvious as the circumstances that constitute the SOA of the sun's shining come to be once we learn to identify them, the ability to identify them as such — as circumstances constituting that SOA in particular — is something we acquire through interaction with other people. As emphasized in chapter 6, there are skills of discrimination to be learned, as well as skills of a linguistic nature, before a subject is prepared to communicate verbally with other language users regarding any given SOA. Just as a child must learn to distinguish hunger pangs from other discomforts of the stomach in order to use language properly for reporting its hunger, so Camille must have learned to discriminate sunlight from other ambiances of her visual environment in order to share talk with other people about the SOA of the sun's shining.

Now, part of C's learning to single out the sun's shining as an SOA of particular human interest, we have been assuming, is the acquisition of a set of neuronal responses somewhere in the upper reaches of her nervous system that comes to serve as a reliable indicator of that particular SOA. This is the set of neuronal occurrences labeled 'NX$_a$' in the paragraphs above. Since there presumably are countless circumstances in C's visual environment, however, that might from time to time have an impact upon her nervous system but that are never singled out for particular notice by members of her linguistic community, there must be countless configurations of neuronal activity that never come to function as indicators of distinct SOAs. The configuration NX$_a$ that has come to signal the SOA of the sun's shining in particular must have been involved in some kind of "refining" or "conditioning" that distinguished it from these "anonymous" configurations. This process, however it actually comes about, would have the effect of consolidating NX$_a$ into a relatively stable neuronal configuration that can be activated repeatedly in connection with that particular SOA.[19] And this process would be initiated in the course of C's becoming aware of the significance attached to this SOA by other members of her linguistic community. Although NX$_a$ may well be elicited on a given occasion by a causal sequence tracing back to the presence of its associated SOA in C's visual environment, that is to say, its being singled out as a configuration playing a distinct role in C's cognitive affairs is a direct result of the fact that the SOA in question has been endowed with shared human significance. This is one respect in which NX$_a$ differs in its representational role from the yellow skin of the banana and the falling barometer.

What kind of process might be responsible for preparing NX$_a$ to play this distinct representational role? Part of the answer comes with the requirement laid down with (LR1), making the ability to identify a given SOA dependent upon the ability to designate the presence of that SOA by use of the symbolic resources of a public language. For Camille to acquire the capacity to deal symbolically with the SOA of the sun's shining, however, more is required than the formation in her upper nervous system of a stable set of neuronal occurrences regularly associated with the presence of that SOA. It requires as well the formation of another pattern of neuronal events in that part of the cortex that controls her verbal behavior. To get some sense of the other sort of pattern involved, however, we need to look carefully at the neurological counterpart of the second learning requirement (LR2). This is the task of the following section.

4. Learning the Use of Symbols: Its Efferent Counterpart

The effect of (LR2), as we have seen, is to reverse the conditionality of (LR1). For S to learn the correct use of R as a representation of X, S must learn how to identify X when immediately present. For X to be immediately present to S is for it to be present without mediation—that is, for it to be present to S without help from any medium of representation. For most SOAs of a particular (as distinct from a general) character,[20] this amounts to being present as part of S's perceptual field. The effect of (LR2), accordingly, is to make S's ability to use any symbolic expression correctly as a representation of X conditional upon the ability to identify X when S perceives it directly—that is, the ability to "tell an X when you see one."

Thus understood, (LR2) seems relatively straightforward and less in need of argument than its companion requirement (LR1). For empirical SOAs at least, being able to "tell an X when you see one" is roughly the same as knowing what an X is; and clearly, if S does not know what an X is, then S will be incompetent to use a public symbol-system reliably in order to communicate about X. Another thing to note regarding (LR2) is that the proviso it imposes is entirely general. Not only does it hold for all SOAs (empirical or otherwise); but for any given SOA X, moreover, it holds for any symbolic representation R that might be available as a stand-in for X. When we turn to the neurological counterpart of (LR2), accordingly, we should be prepared to deal with a brain state or process no less comprehensive in scope than the state or process NX_a associated with the presence of X in the subject's general field of awareness. The afferent neuronal process NX_a, on the one hand, is actively involved whenever the subject is aware of X, regardless of the mode of awareness concerned. The efferent neuronal process involved in the implementation of (LR2), on the other hand, must bear upon any mode or manner of representing X in a public symbol-system available to S—writing, speaking, sign language, Braille, and so on, in English, French, German, or any other communal language.

What this latter neuronal state or process must assure is that for any representation whatever to be available for proper use in symbolizing a given SOA, the subject must be able to identify that SOA for "what it is" upon encountering it directly. Let us refer to this neuronal state or process by the label 'NX_r'—the neuronal (N) occurrences associated with the subject's representation (r) of X. In what manner might NX_r operate in the subject's cortex to match the generality of NX_a in its respective domain?

For one thing, NX_r will not itself function as a representation. Taken by itself, there is nothing to distinguish it from one of the semantically endowed "internal formulae" with which the computational model of cognition purports to do business. Characterizing NX_r in the manner above does not identify a brain state better situated than such internal formulae to sustain semantic properties like truth and reference. In particular, there is nothing about NX_r thus far described that would enable it to enter into the subject's field of awareness; hence there is nothing to suggest how it might direct the subject's awareness beyond itself to something else it might be taken to represent. This precludes its meeting general requirement (GR1) directly, for reasons parallel to those discussed above in connection with the internal formulae of computationalism. As far as general requirement (GR2) is concerned, it is enough to note that nothing has entered into the description of NX_r to this point that would explain how it might acquire intentional content. As matters stand, NX_r is little more than a neuronal process playing a certain functional role in the subject's *use* of representations, and that role is not one in which it serves as a representation itself.[21]

In one manner of speaking, NX_r functions so as to map symbolic competence onto competence in recognizing the items symbolized. In this respect, the neurophysiological function of NX_r is not unlike the logical role assigned proposition-types in the discussion of chapter 3. The role of proposition-types is to group together token propositions that share the same truth-conditions. This role is served, to continue the manner of speaking employed above, by a mapping of token propositions onto truth-conditions;[22] and proposition-types are logical constructs tailor-made to serve this role. Analogously, competence in the use of representations for a given SOA X is mapped onto competence in identifying X whenever present. And the general role of NX_r is to provide mappings of this sort for all representations involved. As far as the analogy goes, accordingly, we are conceiving NX_r (for all SOAs X) as playing the same sort of role in the nervous system of a cognitively endowed organism as that played by proposition-types in the logical grouping of their token instances.

There are substantial differences, of course, that make the analogy approximate at best. Apart from the fact that the two mappings take place in different domains (logical and neurophysiological), proposition-types distinguish classes of token propositions, while NX_r deals with representations that are not themselves propositional. And while proposition-types serve merely in a manner of grouping their respective tokens, NX_r serves rather in a role of operational restraint. Taking these (and other) differences into account, we nonetheless may find the analogy instructive. For what it tells us is that the role of NX_r is intimately bound up with that of NX_a in the structuring of the subject's general field of awareness. Because of the tie between NX_a and NX_r as presently conceived, there are no SOAs the subject is capable of identifying that he or she is not also capable of representing symbolically, nor are there any symbolic representations of SOAs the subject is competent to employ that do not correspond to SOAs he or she is able to identify.

This interdependency on the physiological level, to be sure, corresponds directly to the combined learning requirement (LR1,2) of chapter 6. What this combined requirement articulates is the mutual dependence between learning the correct use of symbolic representations of a given SOA and learning how to identify that SOA when immediately present. And what our discussion of the neurophysiological counterpart of (LR1,2) has provided thus far is a mutual interaction between the functioning of two key faculties of the central nervous system that endow the cognitive organism with its symbol-using capacities. On the afferent side is the state or process NX_a that serves to integrate the subject's awareness of distinct SOAs. And on the efferent (verbal performance) side is the state or process NX_r that serves to regulate the subject's language use in a manner that makes it publicly intelligible. One way of conceiving the complex function served by the two conjointly, accordingly, is to think of it as the neurophysiological structure enabling the combined learning requirement (LR1,2) to be met.

In the previous section we appealed to the learning requirements of chapter 6 for help in formulating the general outlines of a viable account of internal representation. In the course of the ensuing discussion, we have defined two neuronal states or processes, NX_a and NX_r, both of which have something essential to do with the mind's symbolic activity, but neither of which seems provisioned to serve in the role of internal representation by itself. With the realization that these two states function interactively, however, we are now provided with a rationale for bringing them together as one complex brain function. Although the components of this complex function have their own functions to perform severally, these subfunctions are always executed in an interactive fashion. Let us adopt the label 'NX_{ar}' for use in referring to this complex neuronal function.

With the complex state or process NX_{ar}, we finally have a plausible candidate for the role of internal representation. The task of the following section is to develop this claim further and to consider the status of NX_{ar} in light of requirements (GR1) and (GR2).

5. The Two Functions Combined:
Internal Representations as Representings

Given a subject S capable of dealing symbolically with various and sundry SOAs $X^1, X^2, \ldots, X^n$, the neuronal structure of S's central nervous system will contain the requisite circuitry to sustain the complex functions $NX^1_{ar}, NX^2_{ar}, \ldots, NX^n_{ar}$. But these circuits will never all be active simultaneously. At a given moment in S's cognitive affairs, only one (or at most a few) will be playing an active role in S's behavior, and the rest will be lying ready for other occasions.[23]

If we refer to such a function NX_{ar} as an internal representation, following the proposal in the section immediately above, then we will have to recognize a distinction between representations that have been activated and those that have a potential for activation but are not currently active. More will need to be said about what it is for such a representation to be activated. But first let us look more carefully at the sense in which the functions of this sort might be conceived to serve as representations.

It has been noted already that of the subfunctions NX_a and NX_r, neither is a representation in the manner alleged for the "internal formulae" of computationalism. Nor is the complex function NX_{ar} itself such a representation. In whatever sense NX_{ar} might count as an internal representation, it is not an internal counterpart of publicly manifest representations like "snow's being white" and "the gate's being shut." The SOA of snow's being white, for example, may be represented by a variety of token expressions, including "snow's being white," "white being the color of snow," "*dass Schnee weiss ist,*" and so on. But the complex function NX_{ar} corresponding to snow's being white is not another token symbol by which this SOA can be represented. One reason NX_{ar} is not a member of the class of tokens including "snow's being white" and the rest, of course, is that NX_{ar}, unlike these others, is not an expression within a public symbol-system. But there is a deeper reason as well. Each of the token expressions "snow's being white," "white being the color of snow," and so on, is related to snow's being white (X) by the relation that any public symbol bears to the thing it represents. But NX_{ar} is not related to X in this manner. NX_{ar}, rather, is an internalized *correlate* of the relation in question. To put it another way, NX_{ar} is not a term of that relation, but rather a counterpart of that relation itself. How so?

Expressions like "snow's being white" are symbols used by cognitive subjects to represent the SOA of snow's being white. On a given occasion of such use, a function of the sort we are calling 'NX_{ar}' is activated in the language-processing part of the subject's cortex. The activation of NX_{ar} is therefore the internal counterpart of the subject's public act of representation. From the neurological point of view, the activation of NX_{ar} *constitutes* the subject's representation of X. In this sense, it is accurate to speak of the activation of NX_{ar} as a representation. But it is not a representation in the same sense as the symbolic expressions employed by the subject for that purpose. It is a representation, rather, in a gerundive sense—the sense of an activity (or process) of *representing*.

There is a public way of representing the SOA of snow's being white, which involves use of the symbolic provisions of a public language. On the occasion of such an event, the complex function NX_{ar} is activated within the cortex of the subject involved. But there is a "private" way of representing this SOA as well. This is the way engaged when the subject *thinks* that snow is white, or confidently *believes* that such is the case, with no communication of a public nature to indicate this thought or belief. When something like this happens, an activation of NX_{ar} occurs as well; but the activation is triggered by internal, rather than external, occurrences. And as a result of this *activity* of representing, the subject's thought or belief is directed toward that specific SOA.

The purpose of this section thus far has been to pin down a sense in which the neuronal configuration NX_{ar} can serve in the function of representing even though it is not a symbolic representation itself. This sense is now near at hand. Before proceeding further in this regard, however, it will be helpful to consider more carefully what it means to speak of this function's being activated. From a neurological perspective, of course, activation is a matter of the concerned circuits being energized—of neurons "firing" and electrochemical impulses being transmitted. But this is not the sense of activation that presently needs clarifying. What we need to understand more clearly is the cognitive upshot of this activity, as it pertains specifically to the function of representation.

For NX_{ar} to be activated in the function of representation is for its subfunctions NX_a and NX_r to exercise their characteristic roles, and to do so in the interactive manner examined above. The characteristic role of NX_a is to provide a focal point around which the subject's field of awareness can be structured. In the case of a normal subject, without competing interests and unusual distractions, when NX_a is active the subject's attention is focused on the SOA X to which NX_a pertains. The characteristic role of NX_r, on the other hand, is to single out that portion of the subject's verbal repertoire that is available for symbolizing the presence of X and to ready the subject for the employment of whatever symbolism is appropriate. The interdependency of NX_a and NX_r is such that these two functions are engaged simultaneously. But one or the other may dominate as the subject's interests vary. If a person senses a situation that might prove dangerous, for instance, his or her first concern will be to identify the threat, with a verbal report of the situation becoming relevant only later. In a context of ordinary conversation, on the other hand, concerns of word choice might dominate, without direct attention to the subject matter concerned.

For present purposes, the reason for dwelling upon the duality of function involved in the activation NX_{ar} is to stress the distinction between the different roles it incorporates—one pertaining to the structure of the subject's awareness, the other governing the subject's use of symbolic language. The reason this distinction is worth stressing is that the complex function NX_{ar} can be activated from either direction. Indeed, it can be activated in other ways as well. But let us look first at activation from its two poles respectively.

To make a start, let us consider some commonplace instances in which NX_{ar} is activated by occurrences pertaining primarily to NX_a— that is, by occurrences in the subject's object-oriented field of awareness. Suppose that Deirdre had observed that the gate was shut when the children went out to play and that she subsequently informs Duncan to this effect when he asks whether the children are still in the garden. Here, the relevant NX_{ar} (in Deirdre's cortex, with X being the SOA of the gate's being shut) was activated by D's perception of that SOA, and only subsequently did she find occasion for expressing the matter verbally. For a second example, suppose that Camille is planning a day at the beach and notes before she leaves that the sun is shining. Although she arrives at the beach before finding opportunity to share her appreciation of this fact with another person, she would have been ready to do so at any appropriate moment during the time intervening. In Camille's case, as in that of Deirdre, readiness for a certain verbal behavior was initiated by the perceptual presence of an SOA that the words in question might appropriately represent, leaving the enactment of that behavior to be determined by further circumstances.

Now consider a number of instances in which NX_{ar} is activated by verbal occurrences—that is, by occurrences pertaining primarily to the subfunction NX_r. Imagine that Duncan steps around the corner, sees that the gate is open, informs Deirdre to that effect, and sets out with her to check on the children's whereabouts. Upon hearing Duncan say, "The gate is open," Deirdre's thoughts turn immediately to what those words portend. The complex function NX_{ar} has been activated by its verbal component NX_r, and as a result, NX_a becomes active as well. Or imagine that D is entertaining the children with stories of mythical creatures, including one about unicorns, an animal they had not heard of previously. D explains that unicorns are like horses with a single horn on the forehead, whereupon the children start thinking of what it would be like to encounter one directly. Here D's words describing what it is to be a unicorn induce thoughts in the children about what those words represent. For a further example, return to Camille, who upon leaving her room finds herself absentmindedly muttering, "It probably will be cloudy when I get to the beach." When she dwells upon the words she finds herself uttering, her thoughts then turn to what these words represent. As a result of her habit of idle soliloquy, her mind becomes fixed on the prospect of gloomy weather. In each of these cases, the subject's thoughts became focused on some specific SOA, under the influence of language by which that SOA is commonly symbolized.

Commonplace as these examples may be, they serve to emphasize the point that the complex function NX_{ar} can be activated either by occurrences in the subject's field of objective awareness (as focused by NX_a) or by occurrences pertaining to his or her linguistic competence (under the control of NX_r). But there are other ways in which NX_{ar} might be activated as well. By way of illustration, imagine that Duncan has been thinking of a recent incident in which the gate had been left open and the children subsequently had been found in a neighbor's yard. Duncan *believes* that suitable precautions have been taken on the present occasion and finds himself looking for confirmation that the gate is still shut. In this case, the relevant NX_{ar} (with X the SOA of the gate's being shut) has been activated neither by language nor by direct observation, but by a train of thought leading to the concerned SOA. Or imagine that one of D's children has been musing about rare animals she would like to encounter and recalls hearing of creatures like horses with single horns on their heads. Her *thinking* about the mythical unicorn has been triggered by thoughts of other animals with kindred features. For yet another example, suppose that Camille has endured a number of cloudy weekends recently, inducing pessimism about the weather on her current outing. Without hearing words to that effect, in public or in private, she finds herself *hoping* fervently for sunny weather when she arrives at the beach.

In each of these cases, the subject has been made aware of a particular SOA and has been ready to speak of that SOA openly should an appropriate occasion arise. The neurological basis for these conditions, according to the account above, is the activation of the relevant cortical function NX_{ar}. While this function might be activated either by direct observation or by verbal promptings, as illustrated previously, these most recent examples show that it can be activated by occurrences wholly internal to the mind of the subject as well. As a result of occurrences of this sort, D *believes* that the gate is shut, the child *thinks* of unicorns as creatures with a certain distinctive feature, and C *hopes* for sunny weather when she arrives at the beach. Here is a series of internal representings accomplished without direct involvement of a public symbol-system. The point of having examples like these at hand is to prepare the way for consideration of how the representational function NX_{ar} might after all comply with the general requirements for representation (GR1) and (GR2), to which task we now turn.

6. How the General Requirements Apply to Internal Representings

The first requirement (GR1) is that a representation must be capable both of presenting itself to a cognitive subject and of drawing the subject's attention beyond itself to the thing it represents. The problem encountered in this regard by all previous candidates for the status of internal representation is that brain states or processes, under normal conditions at least, are not open to awareness on the part of the subject involved. And if a putative symbol is not an object of awareness itself, it is hard to see how it could direct the subject's awareness to something else it might be taken to represent. Such seems to be the case with representations in public symbol-systems at least. Since neither NX_{ar} nor its subfunctions NX_a and NX_r themselves are perceptible under normal conditions, this rules out their serving a representational role after the fashion of symbols in a public language.

As we recall, however, the sense in which NX_{ar} is being treated as a representation is not that of a symbol standing in for an SOA. The sense, rather, is that of the *activity* of representing—the sense of something's being done, as distinct from a symbol involved in the doing. The conjecture now being pursued is that NX_{ar} is the function typically engaged in a subject's cortex *when* that subject undertakes an act of representing involving symbols in a public language. When a subject S sets about to indicate a given SOA X by use of a symbolic representation R, that is to say, it is by activation of the function NX_{ar} that this transaction is accomplished. While S's awareness of R itself is to be accounted for as a standard instance of sense perception, the transfer of S's awareness from R to X must be due to something happening in the process of NX_{ar}'s activation.

As shown by several examples above, however, use of representations in a public symbol-system is not the only way NX_{ar} might be activated. The function it serves might be engaged as well by the subject's thinking about X or by a direct perceptual encounter of some sort with the SOA X itself. Whatever its manner of activation, the brain processes involved in this complex function are responsible for bringing X to a point of prominence within S's field of awareness. Insofar as the activation of NX_{ar} is responsible for the subject's awareness being directed to SOA X, indeed, its activation is the neurophysiological equivalent of the subject's awareness of X itself.

Given this understanding of its representational role, NX_{ar} clearly ought not be held accountable to (GR1) in the manner of symbols within a public language. If NX_{ar} is the function by which such symbols are enabled to represent, rather than itself a representation, then no impediment to its representational role results from the fact that it is not itself accessible to the subject's awareness. Activation of this function is the *means* by which requirement (GR1) is satisfied by the symbols of a public language, and there is no further stipulation in this requirement regarding the means by which it is satisfied.

If we understand NX_{ar} as providing the means by which symbolic representations are enabled to meet the conditions of (GR1), however, the question then arises of how NX_{ar} in turn is able to serve in that capacity. When a subject employs the expression "snow's being white" to represent the SOA of snow's being white, for example, what is it about the function involved that enables it to concentrate the subject's attention on that particular SOA? When Deirdre hears Duncan say, "the gate is open," what is it about the function NX_{ar} thereby activated that enables it to bring the SOA those words designate to a place of prominence in Deirdre's awareness? Or when thoughts of recent dismal weather lead Camille to focus her hopes upon the eventuality of sunny skies that afternoon at the beach, what is it about the concerned NX_{ar} that enables it to single out that particular X as a primary object of her attention? The answer in each case is the same we should give if asked what it is about a given NX_{ar} that serves to bring X to the subject's attention when that SOA is an object of external awareness. What is the answer when NX_{ar} is externally activated?

When X is directly present within S's field of perceptual awareness, the interdependency between NX_a and NX_r assures that S will be able to identify X as an SOA appropriately signaled by certain linguistic representations. When X is the SOA of the sky's being sunny, for example, then the interaction between NX_a and NX_r in Camille's cortex enables her to identify X as an SOA appropriately represented by expressions like "the sky is sunny." The linguistic competence brought to bear in this situation is provided by the subfunction NX_r. The factor that focuses her attention upon this particular SOA, however, is the subfunction NX_a, which (by definition) is a set of neuronal occurrences uniquely associated with that SOA. Due to the interactive character of the function NX_{ar}, its subfunctions are always activated together. But it is the activation of NX_a specifically that brings X to a focal point of the subject's awareness.

When SOA X is directly present within the subject's field of perceptual awareness, in other words, then NX_a itself is activated on a perceptual basis, and with it the complex function NX_{ar}. When NX_{ar} is activated on a verbal basis, on the other hand, it is NX_r instead that first becomes active. But whatever the source by which NX_{ar} is made active, both of its subfunctions are involved in the process. And no matter how this process is set into motion, it is the activation of NX_a specifically that directs the subject's awareness to the concerned SOA. When Deirdre hears Duncan say "the gate is open," it is by virtue of this subfunction that her thoughts are turned to the SOA of the gate's being open. And similarly for the other cases discussed above.

The answer to the question above of how NX_{ar} is enabled to direct a subject's awareness to a particular SOA when it is internally activated, that is to say, is that it does so by means of a subfunction adapted to that purpose specifically[24]—the subfunction we have labeled 'NX_a', the activation of which is uniquely associated with awareness of that particular SOA.

The primary task of this section has been to evaluate the complex function NX_{ar} in the role of internal representation, with regard to the general requirements (GR1) and (GR2) specifically. What we have seen thus far is that NX_{ar}, while not constrained by (GR1) itself, may be conceived as the neurophysiological underpinning of a subject's ability to employ symbolic representations in a manner that accords with this requirement. While the account of how this works is clearly provisional, and stands in need of improvement in many respects, it at least seems to rescue the concept of internal representation from the morass in which it is left by current computational theories of cognition. What is to be said with regard to the remaining requirement?

(GR2) requires that a representation must be virtually related to what it represents. Its upshot is that the relation between representation and object represented cannot depend upon the latter's existence. Given our concern with the representation of SOAs specifically, the requirement is that this representation does not depend upon the SOAs represented actually being the case. Inasmuch as NX_{ar} can be activated, among other ways, by occurrences at its verbal pole NX_r, this requirement is met automatically. It is met automatically, that is to say, insofar as we are enabled by this function to grasp the nature of SOAs that we never encounter through direct awareness. This is something we commonly do, for example, as a result of conversing with other people. A standard means is by verbal definition, as when Deirdre explained the nature of unicorns to her children, who of course had never seen such a creature. But there are other examples as well that are not conversational. If D, upon realizing that the gate is open, begins to speculate upon the worst that might happen to the children, she finds herself thinking about SOAs some (or all) of which will never be actual. Since cases like these can be multiplied indefinitely, we have adequate assurance that the representations involved do not depend upon the existence of the things represented.

By showing how neuronal activity of the sort involved in the complex function NX_{ar} can be conceived in accord with these general requirements for representation, we have removed what appear to be the major obstacles to accepting these activities for what they purport to be: internalized underpinnings of representational acts of the sort typically accomplished by the use of public language. This account of internal representation will figure prominently in the discussion of intentionality in the following chapter. The remaining task of the present chapter is to consider how these representations might be made propositional.

7. Propositional Objects of Private Cognitive Attitudes

The problem with which this chapter began is that of making sense of propositions "in the mind," such as might serve as the proper objects of private attitudes like thinking and surmising. While these are not the only propositional attitudes that typically do not involve propositions formulated in public language, the fact that we often "keep our thoughts to ourselves" is enough to show that the problem is genuine. By way of responding to the problem, our concern in the previous section has been to develop a conception of internal representation that will provide the equivalent of a descriptive component[25] for the internal propositional objects in question. What the foregoing discussion has yielded is an account of representation in the sense of *representing* that can be accomplished by processes within the cortex of the cognitive subject. While representations of this (active) sort are not accessible as part of a public symbol-system, and hence cannot serve as components of token propositions, they nonetheless provide the basis for a sort of representational activity that can play a role equivalent to that engaged with the help of propositions in a public language. When activated, the complex function NX_{ar} actively directs the subject's awareness to SOA X, and thus constitutes an internal representing of that SOA. Activation of this function, in other words, is a cortical process that has the effect of bringing X to the subject's awareness. What still needs to be provided is a sense in which an internal representation of this general sort might take on a status-ascription and thereby represent X as *being* or as *not being the case*.

Now, there are various modes in which a status-ascription might function in conjunction with an internal representation. One is that simply of distinct neuronal indications of status, corresponding to "being the case" and "not being the case" in natural language. Another is to think of a distinct location within the nervous system (something like the central processing unit of a digital computer)[26] to which the function of NX_{ar} might be "transferred" in some manner or another to indicate indirectly what is (or what is not) the case. Yet another is to think of the NX_{ar} as being actively incorporated into a system of neuronal circuits ready to guide the subject's actions in response to environmental promptings. The effect of this would be for the SOA in question to be represented as being the case just when the subject is ready to act as if in fact it were the case.

Perhaps the simplest way of proceeding in this regard, however, is to deal with status-ascription at one level removed, and to think of the internal equivalent of the proposition [X/yes (no)] (which ascribes status to the first-order SOA X) as nothing more than a representing of the *second-order* SOA of X being (not being) the case.[27] The circumstance of *X being the case* or of *X not being the case,* after all, is every bit as much an SOA as X itself. So all we need to make sense of an ascription of status to an SOA picked out by an internal representing of the relevant sort is to think of it as functionally equivalent to a higher-order representing of X being (or not being) the case. In this manner, the general account of internal representation developed above can be extended to cover internal representings that are specifically propositional. Nothing more would seem to be needed to provide objects for private attitudes of the sort we have been considering.

Notes

1. Mention of privacy in this regard may call to mind Wittgenstein's concern with "private language" in *Philosophical Investigations* (G. E. M. Anscombe, trans., [New York: Macmillan, 1953], secs. 269, 275, and associated passages), having to do with a "language" referring to experiences of which the subject concerned alone is aware. The topic discussed in the present chapter differs from Wittgenstein's "private language problem" in the following crucial respects: (1) The representations we are concerned with themselves are "private" (in a sense yet to be clarified) to the subject employing them, while (2) the objects they represent on occasion might be publicly accessible.

2. Fodor's treatment of representation is laid out mainly in *The Language of Thought* (New York: Thomas Y. Crowell, 1975) and in *Representations* (Brighton, Sussex: Harvester Press, 1981).

3. Perceiving and remembering, for example. For citations, see Fodor, *The Language of Thought,* 75–77, 77n.

4. For a statement to this effect, see Fodor, *Representations,* 187.

5. *Representations,* 240.

6. Relevant criticisms may be found in John Searle's "Minds, Brains, and Programs," *Behavioral and Brain Sciences* 3, no. 3 (September 1980), 417–424; John Heil's "Does Cognitive Psychology Rest on a Mistake?" *Mind* 90 (1981), 321–342; K. Sayre's "Intentionality and Information Processing: An Alternative Model for Cognitive Science," *Behavioral and Brain Sciences* 9, no. 1 (March 1986), 121–138; and Steven Horst's *Symbols, Computation and Intentionality: A Critique of the Computational Theory of Mind* (Berkeley: University of California Press, 1996).

7. This criticism is detailed in K. Sayre, "Cognitive Science and the Problem of Semantic Content," *Synthese* 70 (1987): 247–269.

8. There is, of course, a sense of "sign" that makes it an approximate equivalent of "symbol." This is not the sense here in question. The sense in question is that of "symptom" or "indication."

9. Of course, it might be maintained (e.g., by a so-called mind-brain-identity theorist) that twinges and pains, and so forth, of which the subject unquestionably is aware, are themselves identical to neuronal states and that, as such, they might come to be interpreted by the subject as symptoms of certain bodily malfunctions. If so, then neuronal states of this sort might conceivably function as symbolic representations in the sense to which (GR1) pertains. If this is allowed, the point to be made is that twinges and pains are not typical in this respect of internal states generally, including those that would have to function as representations of external SOAs like snow's being white if the computational account of the matter were correct.

10. Unless the subject is in possession of something like what H. Feigl called an "autocerebroscope" in "The 'Mental' and the 'Physical'," *Minnesota Studies in the Philosophy of Science,* vol. 2, H. Feigl, M. Scriven, and G. Maxwell, eds. (Minneapolis: University of Minnesota Press, 1958), 370–497, especially 456ff.

11. See, for example, Fodor's *Representations,* 241, and John Haugeland's essay "Semantic Engines," in *Mind Design,* John Haugeland, ed. (Montgomery, Vt.: Bradford Books, 1981), 24. In these discussions, what are called "formal" properties of computational systems are those governed by computational "rules," where the rules in question are applied "automatically"—that is, by causal interaction among the parts of the computing mechanism.

12. This way of putting it derives from Haugeland, "Semantic Engines."

13. For the contrast between virtual and concrete relations, see section 3 of chapter 6.

14. See note 1 above.

15. See chapter 6, sections 2 and 5 in particular.

16. While the present discussion is intended to remain neutral on the general topic of mind-brain identity, it would seem anachronistic to deny that brain processes have some role to play in perceptual awareness. For an attempt to account for the nature of that involvement in terms of information theory, the interested reader may wish to refer to K. Sayre, *Consciousness* (New York: Random House, 1969), chaps. 6, 7, and 8.

17. From this point on, the present account is parallel in certain respects to the information-theoretic account of intentionality developed in Sayre, "Intentionality and Information Processing," 134–137 specifically. What is here labeled 'X_a' corresponds approximately to the patterned set of cortical events C in that context, when this pattern is freed from direct stimulus control (for which, see 137–138).

18. Most organisms with highly developed sensory capacities (like dogs and monkeys, as well as humans) are served by distinct neuronal functions that register the presence of circumstances somehow vital to their interests. These brain events may be said to represent those circumstances in much the manner

that NX_a represents the SOA that when present elicits its activation. Representations of this sort are not symbolic and by themselves have no uniquely cognitive role. The next stage of the present enterprise, undertaken in the pages immediately following, is to sketch out an account of how these essentially noncognitive representations might be augmented to take on symbolic significance. As might be expected, this augmentation has the effect of adding skills in the use of language to basic perceptual skills.

19. A biologically based account of this process employing basic concepts of technical information theory is offered in Sayre's "Intentionality and Information Processing," 121–138.

20. For the distinction between particular and general (empirical) SOAs, see chapter 7, section 3.

21. The function served by NX_r is one of linking the subject's competence in the use of certain symbols with a competence to identify the object symbolized. The generality of this function, corresponding to the generality of (LR2) noted above, is simply that all symbolic representations of X available to the subject are subject to the restriction this linkage imposes.

22. More specifically, a given proposition-type *[X/yes] maps all token propositions that fall within it onto the truth-conditions shared by those token propositions.

23. This noted, we will drop the superscript (in 'NX^i_{ar}') and continue use of 'NX_{ar}' in a manner allowing 'X' to range over SOAs generally.

24. Efforts to account for this adaptive function in terms of technical information theory may be found in Sayre, "Intentionality and Information Processing," section 9 and postscript specifically. It should be noted that the present account is concerned only with how a subject's awareness is directed toward specific objects as part of thinking about them, or the like, not with the nature of awareness itself. For views on the latter, which I (still) am inclined to favor, an interested reader may refer to my *Consciousness,* chaps. 5–7, and *Cybernetics and the Philosophy of Mind* (London: Routledge & Kegan Paul, 1976), chap. 9.

25. The descriptive component of the proposition [X/yes] is the representation replacing the variable 'X'. For this terminology, see chapter 4, section 5.

26. Rejection of the computational theory of representations does not preclude use of computer analogies for instructive purposes.

27. The concept of ordered levels of SOAs is explained in section 5 of chapter 4.

Chapter 9

INTENTIONALITY

1. Several Senses of "Intentional"

Not many topics in philosophy are more tangled than that of intentionality. Although it would be unrealistic to expect unanimity on all aspects of the topic, there is an approach to intentionality suggested by the results of the preceding chapters that some philosophers might find attractive. The purpose of the present chapter is to spell out the basic details of this approach.

There are several reasons for the topic's general untidiness that seem relatively easy to identify. One is the variety of quite different senses in which the term "intentional" is used in philosophic discourse. There is the sense (i) of something done deliberately or on purpose, which philosophy takes over from ordinary language. Another sense, more or less restricted to philosophy, is that (ii) characterizing the directionality of a cognitive state—the sense in which one's thought of an elephant, for example, is *about* that object. Add to this its strictly philosophic use (iii) describing a propositional context in which co-referring terms cannot always be interchanged without change in truth-value (a use often taken over by "intensional" with an "s"), and we have a set of meanings that not only are problematic individually, but that seem to invite confusion among themselves.

Another source of untidiness is the perhaps unavoidable fact that different philosophers see different connections among these three kinds of intentionality. Inasmuch as things done deliberately (sense [i]) are typically done after thinking about them (sense [ii]), should we consider purposeful action and directed thought to be intrinsically related? Or, inasmuch as cognitive attitudes both are directional (sense [ii]) and establish intentional contexts of reference (sense [iii]), does it follow that problems of co-reference apply also to the direc-

239

tionality of cognitive states (e.g., to beliefs themselves as well as to sentences about beliefs)? While intentionality in any single sense is hard enough to understand itself, the difficulties multiply when these senses interact.

Yet another cause of unclarity is that there seems to be no generally shared conception of what it is about intentionality that requires philosophic attention, even when limited to a particular sense. Discussions of the directional character of thought (sense [ii]) in the analytic tradition, for example, show little overlap with continental discussions of the same phenomena.[1] And even within the analytic traditional itself, there seem to be almost as many different characterizations of referential opacity (a consequence of intentionality in sense [iii]) as there are individual philosophers writing on the matter.

This much understood, the reader should know that it is no part of the purpose of this chapter to undertake a survey of what philosophers in any particular tradition have had to say about intentionality or to ferret out inadequacies in one or another account of the topic. My primary aim is to work out a prima facie plausible treatment of the directional character of cognitive states (sense [ii]), in light of the accounts of propositions and of symbolic representation offered in earlier chapters. A subsidiary aim is to extend this treatment of the directionality of cognitive states to a provisional analysis of what it is about sentential intentionality (sense [iii]) that precludes preservation of truth-value under substitution of co-referential terms. The result here, as the reader will notice in due course, is somewhat at variance from what one would be led to expect by standard analyses (like that of Quine, for instance).[2] As far as intention in the sense (i) of purpose is concerned, finally, nothing new is suggested by the present approach.[3] Whether this counts for or against this approach is a matter left for the reader's own judgment.

Although the discussion below has little to do with treatments of intentionality in the phenomenological tradition generally, it should be noted that the current interest of English-speaking philosophers in the topic traces back in large part to the writings of Franz Brentano.[4] I shall begin my discussion of the intentional content of cognitive states with some remarks about Brentano's conception of "intentional Inexistence."

2.   The Intentional Content of Beliefs

Brentano thought he had caught the distinction between the mental and the physical in what he termed the *"intentionale Inexistenz"* of the contents of mental states.[5] *'Inexistenz'* in this expression means (roughly) "existing in" (or "in-existing," like "indwelling," "inhabiting," etc.), while *'intentionale'* means (again roughly) "directionality of awareness" (or "awareness tending-toward," in the sense of "*at*tending"). The idea was that mental phenomena have contents existing in the "directional awareness" of mental states themselves, while physical phenomena are not oriented toward "in-existing" contents.

Inasmuch as there are mental states that by their very nature are not directed toward contents, like feelings of lassitude and of general malaise, Brentano is often taken to have been mistaken in identifying the *intentionale Inexistenz* of content as the mark of mental states generally. Nonetheless, the cognitive attitudes surveyed in chapter 1 all seem to have the intentional structure to which he drew attention. When C discovers that the sky is sunny at the beach, her discovery is *about* that SOA—i.e., the SOA of the sky's being sunny. D's hope that the children are safe is *about* the SOA of the children's being safe. And when N predicts that the sky soon will cloud over, the prediction is *about* the sky's clouding over.

This is true as well of D's belief that the gate is shut. Let us return to D's belief for a more careful look at its intentional structure. Belief is an attitude with a propositional object. The object of D's belief in particular is (a relevant instance of) the proposition that the gate is shut. But her belief is not *about* the proposition. Her belief is about the same thing the proposition is about—namely, the SOA of the gate's being shut. That SOA, we shall say, is the content of the proposition and, derivatively, the content of D's state of belief.

By the *'content'* of a belief, let us understand what the belief is *about*. In believing that the gate is shut, D engages in a relation with a proposition. This proposition is *what* she believes—it is the *object,* that is, of her cognitive attitude.[6] But what she believes is not the same as what the belief is about. What the belief is *about* is the same as what its object is about—i.e., the SOA represented by the descriptive component of that proposition.[7] As part of engaging in the relation with the proposition, she also engages in another relation—a relation with what her belief is about. And the first thing to say about this further relation is that it, unlike her relation with the proposition itself, is a relation with intentional characteristics.

In order to pin down what this all amounts to, we should remain alert to the fact that "belief" (like similar cognitive terms) is commonly used in at least three distinct senses. One sense is that of the attitude itself. In believing that the gate is shut, D adopts a particular stance toward that proposition. That stance constitutes her attitude of belief. Let us refer to this attitude by the label 'belief(1)'.[8] Inasmuch as D could adopt the same attitude toward any number of different propositions, her belief(1) is independent of the proposition she happens to entertain on this particular occasion.[9]

What D happens to believe on this particular occasion is the proposition that the gate is shut. This proposition constitutes her belief in a second sense of the term—let us label it 'belief(2)'. D's belief(2), that is to say, is the object of her attitude of belief(1). This belief(2) might be shared by other persons, inasmuch as other subjects might also believe(1) that the gate is shut. A belief(2), accordingly, is independent of the person who happens to believe it. Just as D might adopt the same attitude of belief(1) toward any number of different propositional objects, so any number of personally different attitudes of belief might be adopted toward the same belief(2). One way to express this fact is to say that belief(1) and belief(2) are *externally* related.

When Deirdre adopts an attitude of belief (her belief[1]) toward the proposition that the gate is shut (her belief [2]), the overall result is an integral state of belief that we may label 'belief(3)'. D's belief(3) embodies a unique relation joining (i) D as subject, through (ii) her attitude of belief, to (iii) the propositional object of that particular attitude. If she were to enter into an attitude of belief toward another proposition— say, the proposition that the gate is open—then she would enter into a different state of belief(3). Whereas first she believed(3) that the gate is shut, she now would believe(3) that the gate is open instead. While belief(1) does not change with a change in its propositional object, as noted above, a state of belief(3) is dependent for its identity upon the particular belief(2) contained within its structure. Similarly, whereas a particular belief(2) is independent of the person or persons who happen to believe(1) it, the identity of a belief(3) depends upon the person involved. If Duncan should also come to believe(1) the proposition that the gate is shut, the result would be a different state of belief(3) than Deirdre's belief(3) with which we started. This dependency of a given belief(3) upon its constituents may be expressed by saying that a belief(3) is *internally* related to the belief(1) and the belief(2) contained within it.

It is within the context of this internal structure of her overall state of belief(3) that the further relation of D to the intentional content of her belief is to be understood. The attitude of belief(1), just by itself, has no intentional content, inasmuch as belief(1) is independent of any particular propositional object. Nor should we attribute intentional content to belief(2) itself, inasmuch as the relation between a proposition and what it is about (in abstraction from a subject) is a relation devoid of directional awareness.[10] What has intentional content is D's state of belief(3) instead. And inasmuch as this belief(3) consists of her attitude of belief toward the proposition that the gate is shut, the content of this particular belief(3) is what that proposition is about—the SOA of the gate's being shut.

Let us recapitulate the story thus far. When a subject (S) takes up an attitude of belief(1) toward a particular proposition (belief[2]), the result is a state of belief(3) comprising (i) the subject, (ii) the attitude, and (iii) the propositional object of the attitude. What the state of belief(3) is about is determined by the propositional object of its constituent attitude.[11] What the belief(3) is about is not that proposition itself, but is rather the same thing as what the proposition is about. Since what the proposition is about is the SOA picked out by its descriptive component, the proposition that the gate is shut is about the SOA of the gate's being shut. D's belief(3), accordingly, is about the same SOA. And since the content of belief(3), by definition, is what the belief is about, the SOA of the gate's being shut is the intentional content of that belief(3).

One thing this recapitulation makes clear is that the characterization above of Deirdre's belief(3) as a unique state in which D is joined to a particular proposition through an attitude of belief was incomplete. Also partaking in that relation, in addition to (i) the subject, (ii) the attitude, and (iii) the propositional object of the attitude, is (iv) the intentional content of the belief(3) overall. A more completecharacterization is that the state of belief(3) is one in which a subject is related to an intentional content, by way of an attitude of belief(1) toward a propositional object (belief[2]). The overall structure of S's state of belief(3) is laid out in figure 9.1, with (1), (2), and (3) the three senses of belief respectively, and R_i the intentional relation between subject and content.

The functional components by which the identity of S's belief(3) is fixed are S's attitude (belief[1]), the propositional object (belief[2]) of that attitude,[12] and of course the subject S itself. But since the propositional object is about the SOA X, that SOA also must be factored into the schema as the intentional content of the state of belief(3) overall.[13] The representational role of the proposition, accordingly, is spelled out explicitly to make that content part of the diagram.

It should be emphasized that the intentional content of S's belief(3) is the first-order SOA X itself, and not the second-order SOA of X being (or not being) the case.[14] In the case of Deirdre's belief(3) that the

Figure 9.1 The Components of the State of Belief

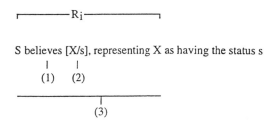

gate is shut, for example, the content is the SOA of the gate's being shut, not the higher-order SOA that constitutes the truth-condition of her belief(3)[15]—that is, the gate's being shut being the case. This is because the content of her belief(3) is what the propositional component of that belief(3) is about; and what the propositional component of that belief(3) is about is the SOA of the gate's being shut itself, without regard to the particular status the proposition ascribes to that SOA.[16] A consequence is that Deirdre and Duncan, for instance, can have conflicting beliefs about the same thing, as when their beliefs assign different statuses (being and not being the case) to the same SOA (the gate's being shut). In such a case, the two beliefs have the same intentional content, but they conflict in the stands taken regarding the status of that content. Although more will be said on this topic in the following section, this at least explains why R_i is depicted in figure 9.1 as a relation between S and X, and not between S and the second-order SOA of X having the status s.

3.   The Intentional Structure of Belief

This characterization of the intentional relation between the believing subject and the content of belief sets up an explanation of the source of intentionality that is intuitively straightforward and metaphysically uncluttered. Brentano's concept of the *intentionale Inexistenz* of the contents of mental states was intended to accommodate both the directional character of states like belief and the fact that these contents need not exist in any "ordinary" sense in order for the mental states in question to be *about* them. Paraphrased in terms more familiar to analytic philosophy, the latter point is that the truth-value of a statement saying that S engages such-and-such a mental state directed toward X is independent from the truth-value of a statement saying that X exists. To take an example from Roderick Chisholm,[17] the truth of the statement that Diogenes was *looking for* an honest man tells us nothing about the truth-value of the statement that there *are* honest men. In other words, Diogenes could have been looking for an honest man even if no honest man had ever existed. The question this suggests, of course, is how a subject could be intentionally related to a nonexistent object.

Brentano's solution was to give the content of an intentional state a kind of existence—*Inexistenz*—within the state of mind itself. This solution has struck many readers as the invocation of a "shadowy" sort of existence that is hard to reconcile with a robust sense of physical reality. Even philosophers without commitments to a physicalist metaphysics may be uncomfortable with this requirement of Brentano's solution. In fact, it would be desirable to have an account of intentional content that is acceptable without regard to metaphysical allegiances. Such an account is made available by the concept of virtual relations introduced in chapter 6.

A virtual relation, we recall, is a relation between two or more terms, not all of which must exist, or ever have existed, in order for the relation to hold between them. An example offered previously is that of a radio receiver being tuned to transmissions on a given wavelength, even though no transmissions on that wavelength may ever have occurred. The point of introducing this relation in chapter 6 was to formulate a basic requirement that any symbolic expression must meet in order to represent an SOA—the requirement, namely, that the expression be virtually related to the SOA in question. Among other examples of virtual relations cited there to illustrate this requirement is the case of Monet's painting of a particular grainstack, which represents an object that may never have existed. Yet other examples are the case of the linguistic expression "snow's being green," which represents the nonexistent SOA of snow's being green, and the case of a certain neuronal activity in Camille's brain, which represents the SOA she hopes will not prevail of the sky's being cloudy when she arrives at the beach.

Now, the relation between a representation and what it represents, despite being virtual, is not in itself an intentional relation. The reason is that intentionality, in the sense of primary concern to Brentano and to ourselves alike, is a feature of mental states, and there typically is nothing mental about the relation per se between a representation like a picture and the object or SOA it represents. Nonetheless, the representational relation shares that feature of the relation between a cognitive state and its intentional content that is illustrated by the case of Diogenes and his search for an honest man. Just as the statement that Diogenes was looking for an honest man carries no entailment regarding the existence of honest men, so the statement that Monet's painting represents a grainstack carries no entailment regarding the existence of grainstacks. If we conceive of the relation between a cognitive state and its intentional content as having a representational component, this will help explain why that relation does not depend upon the existence of its content.

Looking back now at the relation symbolized 'R_i' in figure 9.1 above, we see that one component of this relation indeed is the representational relation between the descriptive component of the proposition [X/s] and the SOA X that it represents. The remaining component, however, is the attitudinal relation between S and the object of S's cognitive attitude — in this instance, the attitude of belief. Since belief unproblematically is a mental attitude, this component contributes the mental aspect of intentionality that is missing from the representational relation alone. The relation between an attitude of belief(1) and its propositional object, it may be noted, is a form of what was called a "concrete relation" in chapter 6. The mark of a concrete relation is that both of its terms must exist within some appropriate time frame for the relation in question to hold between them; and it is no more intelligible that a subject believe a nonexistent proposition than that a proposition be believed by a nonexistent subject.

The result is that the *concrete* relation between a subject S and the proposition that S believes, together with the *virtual* relation between the proposition and the SOA represented by its descriptive component, constitute the intentional relation between the believing subject and the content of the subject's belief(3). The constituency of R_i thus conceived is diagrammed in figure 9.2, in which 'R_c' and 'R_v' stand for "concrete relation" and "virtual relation," respectively. What this diagram shows, in terms of the three senses of belief of figure 9.1, is that the intentional re-

Figure 9.2 The Intentional Structure of Belief

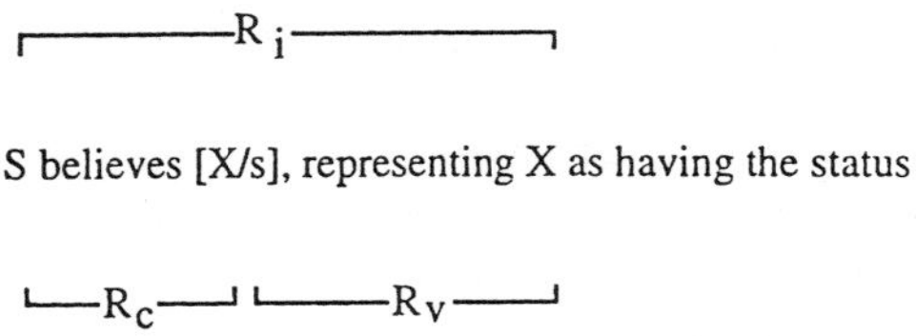

$$\vdash\!\!\!-\!\!\!-\!\!\!-\!\!\!-\!\!\!-\!\!R_i\!-\!\!\!-\!\!\!-\!\!\!-\!\!\!-\!\!\!-\!\dashv$$

S believes [X/s], representing X as having the status

$$\vdash\!\!-\!\!R_c\!-\!\!\dashv \quad \vdash\!\!-\!\!\!-\!\!R_v\!-\!\!\!-\!\!\dashv$$

lation between S and the content of S's belief(3) consists in the concrete relation of S's believing(1) the propositional object, belief(2), together with the virtual relation between belief(2) and the SOA represented by its descriptive component.

Basically the same analysis should be available for other cognitive states, including not only other states of propositional stance,[18] but also states comprising the other kinds of cognitive attitudes distinguished in chapter 1. Before turning to these further matters, however, it is germane for us to dwell briefly on one further consequence of this analysis of the intentional relation into a pair of relations, one concrete and one virtual. Among the undoubted virtues of the computational model of cognitive activity, as characterized in chapter 8, is that it offers an intelligible account of how cognitive states can participate in causal processes within the brain. The basic idea, we recall, is that causal interactions among brain states are to be explained in terms of physical processes of computation, while the (alleged) semantic or intentional features of these states are supposed to be explainable in terms of their regular correlation with these physical structures. While the computationalist approach to cognitive activity seems inadequate for a variety of reasons, some of which are noted in chapter 8, no alternative approach can be expected to do better without a credible account of how cognitive states might be capable of causal interaction. According to the approach to cognition being developed in these pages, a cognitive state has entry into the causal processes of the brain through the concrete relation that is part of its makeup. The major differences between the computational account and the present approach in this regard are, first, that there is no presumption in the present approach that these causal processes are computational in nature and, second and more importantly, that the intentional features of cognitive states are not left to "take care of themselves" by virtue of being "mapped" onto causal features of the brain states involved. The intentional features of cognitive states are "taken care of," instead, by being bound up with the virtual relation in which every configuration of neuronal activities that has representational capacities must participate.[19]

4. The Intentional Structure of Other Cognitive States

All attitudes of propositional stance, as their label indicates, are attitudes taken toward propositional objects. If Camille asserts that the sky is cloudy, then what she asserts is the proposition that the sky is cloudy. In the case of C's attitude of assertion, moreover, the same distinction can be made among three senses of "assertion" as was made in section 2 above among three senses of "belief." There is the act of asserting (assertion[1]), along with the proposition asserted (assertion[2]), and the overall state (assertion[3]) constituted by C's adopting that particular attitude toward that particular proposition. The content of this assertion(3) is the SOA of the sky's being cloudy, and the intentional relation between C and this content comprises the concrete relation of C to the proposition asserted along with the virtual relation of the proposition to the SOA it represents. Basically the same analysis is available with regard to the remaining attitudes of propositional stance identified in chapter 1. There is S's agreement(3), consisting of S's act of agreement(1) and the proposition agreed to (agreement[2]), the intentional content of which is the SOA represented by that proposition; and so on for concession, conclusion, declaration, and the like.

In regard to attitudes of cognitive access like discovering and discerning, however, a somewhat different analysis is required. An indication of this is the fact that terms of cognitive access generally do not admit use in three distinct senses in the manner that typifies terms of propositional stance. While the term "discovery" (by way of exception) might stand either for the act of discovery ("discovery[1]") or the thing discovered ("discovery[2]"), it would seem odd to apply the term "ascertainment" to the fact or SOA that a person ascertains. Equally odd would be the use of "discernment" or "recognition" to signify something discerned or something recognized. More important than this point of terminology, however, is the fact that attitudes of cognitive access are attitudes not toward propositional objects, but toward actual SOAs. An unavoidable consequence of this fact is that the intentional structure of cognitive states like discovery and discernment cannot be understood in terms of virtual relations between *propositions* and the SOA they represent.

The same situation holds with respect to attitudes of assessment, like anticipating and predicting, and attitudes of projection, like wishing and fearing. Since Deirdre, in anticipating that the gate will still be locked, is not anticipating a proposition, the intentional content of her state of anticipation overall cannot be explicated in terms of propositional representation. And likewise for her fear that the children nonetheless may have strayed or her wish that she had latched the gate more securely. Let us look at the intentional structure of attitudes like fearing before returning to such attitudes as discerning and anticipating.

As is the case with attitudes of projection generally, fear is directed toward an eventuality. The term "eventuality" was enlisted in chapter 1 as a term for SOAs, past, present, or future, the status of which is unspecified at the time the term is used.[20] In fearing that the children may have left the garden, D stands in an attitude of fear toward that eventuality. The object of her fear is not a representation of that eventuality, either propositional or otherwise. (If fearful upon sight of the sign "Vicious Dog," one fears the dog, not the sign.) The object of her fear is the SOA itself—the eventuality of the children's having left the garden. Upon initial consideration, indeed, the relation of fear between D and that eventuality may seem to have no representational component at all. There is the subject (Deirdre), the attitude (fear), and the object of the attitude (the eventuality in question), with no immediately obvious role left to be played by a representation.

But D could not fear *that* eventuality, as distinct from some other, unless that eventuality were somehow *present* to her awareness. And since the SOA in question is not present to her directly (in which case it would have determinate status and no longer be an eventuality), it must be present to her awareness in surrogate form. It must be present, that is to say, in the form of a representation. As suggested by the discussion in chapter 6, a representation is both an alternative mode of presentation (*repre*-sentation) and an alternative way of being present (re*present*ation). In some fashion or another, Deirdre's fear must be directed to the eventuality of the children's having left the garden by a representation of that SOA. But what is the nature of the representation involved, and how does it fit into the structure of her cognitive state?

For one thing, it is clear that the representation that directs Deirdre's attention toward the specific eventuality of the children's having left the garden must somehow be in her mind, as distinct from being formulated in a public system of symbols. Although we still know too little about the workings of the central nervous system to have more than a vague notion of how internal representations of this sort might actually function, a schematic account of such representations was offered in the previous chapter. One provision of this account is that configurations of neuronal events take on symbolic significance in connection with their role (there symbolized 'NX_a') of enabling the organism to discriminate among salient SOAs in its field of awareness. As the result of repeated encounters with circumstances the perceiving subject comes to recognize as the SOA of the sun's shining in its vicinity, for instance, a repeatable pattern of neuronal activities is developed in its central nervous system that serves as a reliable indicator of that particular SOA. Patterns of this sort come to serve a more extensive role as they become associated with the subject's verbal behavior;[21] but in the process, they retain their capacity to direct the attention of the organism toward specific SOAs that might be present in its cognitive environment. Neuronal patterns of this sort are plausible candidates for the role of directing D's attention toward the eventuality she fears.

Given the notation adopted for this purpose in chapter 8, the label 'NX_{ar}' is available for signifying the internal representation directing the attention of a cognitive subject upon SOA X.[22] Using the symbols 'R_i' (for "intentional relation"), 'R_c' (for "concrete relation"), and 'R_v' (for "virtual relation") as before, we can now lay out the overall intentional structure of subject S's state of fearing X (see figure 9.3). The relation between S and NX_{ar} by which S's attention is directed toward X is a concrete relation, inasmuch as the relation could not hold if either of its terms was nonexistent. This relation may well be largely causal in nature, depending upon the neural mechanisms by which the focusing is accomplished.[23] The relation between NX_{ar} and X itself, on the other hand, is that of representation to the object represented, and hence qualifies fully as a virtual relation. Together, these two relations—concrete and virtual, respectively—combine to constitute the intentional relation (R_i) between S and the content of S's state of fearing. In contrast with the case of believing discussed above, the content of S's fear overall is also the object of S's attitude of fearing. Whereas with S's belief that X is the case, that is to say, the object of belief is the proposition that X is the case, and the intentional content is the SOA X that the proposition represents, in the case of fearing and other attitudes of projection, the SOA in question serves the role of object and of intentional content alike.

Cognitive states accompanying attitudes of access, in turn, share the intentional structure of states of projection in all relevant respects, save

Figure 9.3 The Intentional Structure of the State of Fearing

┌─────────────R_i─────────────┐

S's fear is directed by NX_{ar}, representing X (which may or may not be the case)

└────────R_c────────┘└────R_v────┘

that the SOAs providing the objects toward which they are directed are required to be the case. As a typical example, suppose that Camille opens the shades on her study window and discerns that the sky is cloudy outside. As is the case with attitudes of access generally, C could not have entered into this attitude of discernment unless the SOA that stands as its object had the status in the world of actually being the case. C could not have discerned this particular SOA, moreover, unless her attention were focused upon it in something like the manner we have already considered in connection with the state of fear. Although the SOA of the sky's being cloudy, in the case we are now imaging, is directly present when Camille opens the shades, there are many other SOAs that are present to her at the same time in the same direct fashion (the grass outside being green, the shrubs being in bloom, etc.). But the only one of these that Camille discerns under the circumstances (she is still thinking of going to the beach) is the SOA of the sky's being cloudy. Accordingly, there must be some representation functioning in her upper nervous system that serves to direct her attention toward this SOA specifically. Labeling this internal representation of the SOA (X) in question 'NX$_{ar}$' as before, we can produce the schema in figure 9.4 showing the intentional structure of the state of discernment overall. S's relation with NX$_{ar}$ is a concrete relation, since it holds only between terms that actually exist. The relation between NX$_{ar}$ and X itself is a virtual relation, for reasons cited repeatedly in the foregoing discussion. And these two relations combine, as in figures 9.2 and 9.3, to constitute the intentional relation (R$_i$) between the subject and the content discerned.[24]

Let us turn finally to attitudes of assessment, conveniently exemplified as above by the attitude of predicting in particular. As far as the intentional structure of their respective cognitive states is concerned, the only difference between prediction and the state of discernment con-

Figure 9.4 The Intentional Structure of the State of Discernment

$$\underset{\text{S's discernment is directed by NX}_{ar}\text{, representing X (which is the case)}}{\overline{\qquad\qquad\qquad R_i \qquad\qquad\qquad}}$$

$$\overline{\qquad\qquad R_c \qquad\qquad}\quad\overline{\quad R_v \quad}$$

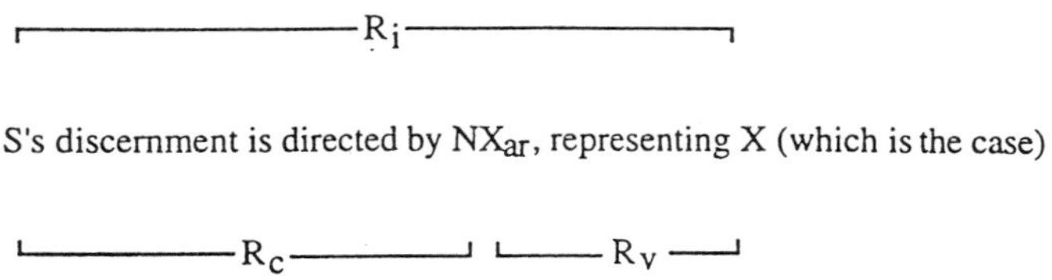

sidered above concerns the status of the SOAs that provide intentional content. Insofar as a given SOA must actually be the case in order to serve as the object of an attitude like discerning, and inasmuch as the object of such an attitude is identical with the content of its corresponding cognitive state, the intentional content of a state of discernment must be a SOA that in fact is the case. Since attitudes of assessment take objects that determinately either are or are not the case indifferently, on the other hand, the cognitive states in which such attitudes participate draw their contents from SOAs with either (determinate) status. In other respects, the intentional structure of attitudes like predicting is identical to that of the state of discernment schematized above. This provides the schema of figure 9.5.[25]

Another feature shared with attitudes of access, as indicated above, is that the intentional content of attitudes like predicting turns out to coincide with the proper object of the attitude concerned. What C discerns is the same SOA that provides content to her state of discernment; and what S predicts, likewise, is the very SOA that serves as content of S's state of prediction. This feature, we have noted, is shared by attitudes of projection as well. In their role as objects, the status allowed these SOAs to vary from type to type. But intentional contents as such are not characterized by status, which is why the relation R_i in the schemata above does not include the various status-ascriptions in question.

Among the results of this section to be emphasized by way of summary, to be sure, is the fact that cognitive attitudes of all four sorts under consideration yield cognitive states in which the subject is intentionally related to an SOA as content. It is this commonality of intentional content that provides the basis for interaction among cognitive states of different sorts (perceptions influencing beliefs, beliefs influencing desires and hopes, etc.), rather than the spurious notion so

Figure 9.5 The Intentional Structure of the State of Prediction

$$\text{┌────────────}R_i\text{────────────┐}$$

S's prediction is directed by NX_{ar}, representing X (with a given determinate status)

$$\text{└────────}R_c\text{────────┘ └────}R_v\text{────┘}$$

widely maintained in cognitive studies today that all cognitive attitudes take propositional objects.[26]

Another result to be emphasized is that the intentional relation between subject and content in all cases is constituted by a *concrete relation* between the subject and a representation, on the one hand, and by a *virtual relation* between the representation and what it represents, on the other. It is through its concrete component in particular that a cognitive state is enabled to interact causally with facets of the organism's nervous system. What is noteworthy about the virtual component, in turn, is that it provides intentional features to the cognitive state overall, on a basis that is no more challenging metaphysically than the mundane relation between a picture and the SOA it depicts. Although a committed materialist may still find something objectionable about this approach to intentionality, no reasonable objection can be based on allegations involving "mysterious" mental entities. The intentional content of cognitive states originates in representation, of a sort typified by (but not restricted to) the token symbols of a public language.

5. The Opacity of Propositions about Cognitive States

A proposition is standardly termed 'extensional' just in case its truth-value remains unchanged with the interchange of extensionally equivalent expressions—that is, of co-referential names or descriptions, or of component propositions with identical truth-values.[27] Otherwise, a proposition is termed 'intensional'.[28] A proposition is intensional, that is to say, just in case there are extensionally equivalent expressions that cannot be interchanged within its context while preserving its truth-value overall—cannot be interchanged, so to speak, *salva veritate*. Propositional contexts that are intensional in this sense are commonly characterized as 'referentially opaque'.[29] Among familiar examples of referentially opaque propositional contexts are "believes that ____," "hopes that ____," and "knows that ____," along with various other reports of cognitive attitudes in propositional form.

Consider the stock example of someone's belief that Cicero denounced Catiline.[30] Let us take the someone in this case to be Claudius, a Roman of the first century B.C. who knew Cicero only by the surname "Tully," and who was present on the occasion when the denunciation took place. Claudius thus came to believe that Tully denounced Catiline. But what exactly was the object of this belief? And what precisely its intentional content?

Since belief is an attitude of propositional stance, we know that Claudius's belief had a propositional object. In order to engage the issue of referential opacity, we must assume that its object was a proposition formulated in public language.[31] So what he believed specifically was a token of the proposition-type *[Tully having denounced Catiline/ yes].[32] The proposition he believed, moreover, was formulated in a symbol-system with which Claudius was intimate. It was not formulated in English, or in any other modern language, and it was not formulated in terms (like "Cicero") that Claudius himself would not employ under the circumstances. The answer to the question of exactly what *object* Claudius believed, accordingly, is that he believed a token proposition, expressed in Latin, to the effect precisely that Tully denounced Catiline.

The *content* of a subject's belief, on the other hand, is not the proposition that the subject believes, but rather the SOA that the proposition is about. The content of Claudius's belief on this particular occasion was the SOA represented as being the case by the propositional object of his belief. It was the SOA that Claudius *himself* would acknowledge as the set of circumstances that had occasioned his belief and that he himself would have been prepared to identify as what his belief was about. (Imagine the following conversation, in translation: Companion—"Well, what do you believe about Tully's political involvement now?"; Claudius—"I believe that Tully has just denounced Catiline.") Expressed in contemporary English, the content of Claudius's belief was the SOA represented by "the person known (by Claudius) as Tully, having denounced Catiline."

Let us now formulate a proposition *about* Claudius's belief, saying that Claudius believed that Tully denounced Catiline. But what specifically should we understand *our* proposition to be about? Suppose our proposition takes the form of the declarative sentence "Claudius believed that Tully denounced Catiline." The present question is, what SOA do we acknowledge as being represented by the descriptive component of that sentence?[33] There are two alternatives at least, with quite different upshots. Alternative (1) is the SOA of Claudius having believed a token of the proposition-type *[Tully having denounced Catiline/yes], which is the type *we* (knowing Tully also by the name "Cicero") could just as well symbolize by the label '*[Cicero having denounced Catiline/yes]'. Alternative (2) is the SOA of Claudius having believed a token proposition the *intentional content* of which is represented (in our present symbol-system) by 'the person known (by Claudius) as Tully, having denounced Catiline'. And since Claudius did not know the person in question by the name "Cicero," this content obviously could *not* be represented also by "the person known (by Claudius) as Cicero, having denounced Catiline."

We started with the propositional expression "Claudius believed that Tully denounced Catiline," and then distinguished two SOAs that proposition might be understood to represent as being the case. What is the relation between these two SOAs? To get at this question, let us sub-divide alternative (1) into the SOA(1a) of Claudius having believed a to-ken of the proposition-type *[Tully having denounced Catiline/yes] and the SOA(1b) of Claudius having believed a token of the proposition-type *[Cicero having denounced Catiline/yes]. Given the conventions for formulating labels for proposition-types specified in chapter 3, SOA(1a) and SOA(1b) are one and the same SOA. The point to note is that interchanging extensionally equivalent names ("Tully" and "Cicero") in *our* characterization of (1) does not produce characterizations of distinct SOAs. Now distinguish SOA(2a) and SOA(2b) as follows.[34] SOA(2a) is merely alternative (2) relabeled—that is, the SOA of Claudius having believed a token proposition the intentional content of which is represented by "the person known (by Claudius) as Tully, hav-ing denounced Catiline." SOA(2b), by contrast, is characterized in just the manner of SOA(2a), save that "Tully" is replaced by "Cicero"— which is its equivalent for us, but not for Claudius. SOA(2b), that is to say, is the SOA of Claudius having believed a token proposition the in-tentional content of which is represented by "the person known (by Claudius) as Cicero, having denounced Catiline." And it is obvious by inspection of these two characterizations that SOA(2a) and SOA(2b) are not identical. Since SOA(2a) is merely SOA(2) relabeled, moreover, SOA(2b) is not identical with SOA(2). The reason in either case is sim-ply that the person known by Claudius as Tully was not (we have been assuming) simultaneously known by him as Cicero.

This enables us to answer the question about the relation between alternatives (1) and (2) above. SOA(1a) is characterized as the SOA of Claudius having believed a token of the type *[Tully having de-nounced Catiline/yes]. By definition, a token of this proposition-type is a proposition the intentional content of which is the SOA of Tully (so known by Claudius) having denounced Catiline—that is, a propo-sition the intentional content of which is represented by "the person known (by Claudius) as Tully, having denounced Catiline." Hence, SOA(1a) and its equivalent SOA(1b) are identical to SOA(2a). But since SOA(2b) is different from SOA(2a), it is different also from alternative (1), in either of its two formulations. The cumulative upshot of this comparison is the following: (i) Alternatives (1) and (2) are one and the same SOA; and although (ii) interchange of co-referential expressions in a characterization of (1) does not change the SOA characterized, (iii) a comparable interchange of equivalents in the characterization of (2) ("Cicero" for "Tully") *does* result in a change in the SOAs concerned.

These results have an obvious bearing on the topic of referential opacity. One consequence in this regard is that propositional expressions of another person's beliefs may be opaque, but also may not—depending upon how the belief in question is specified. If the other person's state of belief is specified *with regard to its propositional object,* a third-person report of that belief is referentially "transparent."[35] It is only when the state of belief is specified *with regard to its intentional content* that a propositional report of that belief exhibits the opacity attributed indiscriminately to all such reports in the standard literature.

Let us view this result from another angle, continuing Claudius's belief as an illustration. If, by saying that Claudius believed that Tully denounced Catiline, we purport to enunciate a proposition the descriptive component of which is characterized in the manner of alternative (1) above, then an expression of our proposition would be [(∃y) (y being Tully ∧ Claudius believing a token of *[y having denounced Catiline/ yes])/yes].[36] Inasmuch as we (as formulators of the propositional context) know Tully by the name "Cicero" also, that name (or any other name we use for that person) could replace "Tully" in the regimented proposition without change in truth-value. The effect of this particular proposition is to identify the alleged denouncer in terms familiar to us and then to say that Claudius believed that this person denounced Catiline.

However, if by saying that Claudius believed that Tully denounced Catiline we purport to enunciate a proposition whose descriptive component is characterized in the manner of alternative (2), then the regimented proposition would be something like [Claudius having believed a token of *[the person known (to me, Claudius) as Tully, having denounced Catiline/yes]/yes]. And if this overall proposition is true, as we have been assuming, then it would be rendered false by substituting "Cicero" for "Tully" (since Claudius knew that person as Tully, but not as Cicero).

What these considerations show is that third-person belief-reports are inherently ambiguous. If a report that S believes p is understood as a report about the *propositional object* of S's belief, then there is no requirement that the proposition in question be reported in a manner that S would recognize. There is no requirement, in particular, that the proposition in question be characterized in terms of one rather than another member of a set of co-referential expressions in order to preserve its proper truth-value. To put it another way, if a person's belief is identified with respect to its propositional object, a third-person report of that belief is referentially transparent.[37]

On the other hand, if a report that S believes p is understood as a report on the *content* to which S becomes intentionally related by holding that belief (R_i of figure 9.2), then the truth-value of that report depends not only on the relevant facts of the matter, but also on the manner in which that content is present in S's cognitive awareness. Since the manner in which the SOA of Tully's denouncing of Catiline was present to Claudius might be quite different from the manner in which the same content is present to us (who might use "Cicero" rather than "Tully" in formulating the report), the truth of the report overall depends not only on the facts of the denunciation, but on the particular terms used in characterizing that content as well. When a person's belief is identified with respect to its intentional content, that is to say, a third-person report of that belief is referentially opaque.

Another way of getting at the ambiguity ties in with the distinction between the concrete component (R_c in figure 9.2) and the virtual component (R_v) of S's state of belief overall. If a report of S's belief is understood as a report of the concrete relation between S and the propositional object of S's belief (belief[2] of figure 9.1), then that report is extensional in character—that is, the report is referentially transparent. But if it is understood as a report of the intentional relation between S and the content of S's belief, then the report itself is an intensional proposition, which makes it referentially opaque. The reason is that the intentional relation between S and the content of S's belief (R_i of figure 9.2) comprises a virtual relation (R_v) between a representation and the content in question. To serve in the role of a representation *for* S, that representation in some fashion must be recognizable *by* S as a representation of that particular SOA. This means that S both must be conversant with the symbolism of that representation and must understand it as a surrogate for that SOA. In the case of Claudius and his belief that Tully denounced Catiline, it means that Claudius must be conversant with the symbolism in which his representation of Tully's denouncing Catiline is formulated—as he is with "Tully" but not with "Cicero." This shows how intensionality (with an "s") traces back to intentionality (with a "t") as its source and, more ultimately, how it depends upon the virtual relation between representations and the SOAs they represent.

Similar analyses are available for reports of cognitive attitudes of the other sorts distinguished in chapter 1. Let us look briefly at how the analysis goes in the case of realization, which (along with recognition, discernment, discovery, etc.) is typical of attitudes of cognitive access. Having married the widow of his murdered father, Oedipus realized that he had married Jocasta. In reporting Oedipus's circumstances, the reader will note that the preceding sentence has employed a proposition specifying what Oedipus realized. But what SOA should we understand this proposition as representing? One alternative is the SOA of Oedipus's realizing another SOA that *we* might indicate equally well either by "his (Oedipus's) having married Jocasta" or by "his (Oedipus's) having married his mother." If the proposition is to be understood as being about this SOA, then an appropriate articulation in regimented form would be [($\exists$y) (y being Jocasta $\land$ Oedipus realizing he had married y)/yes]. Here, "Jocasta" could be replaced by "Oedipus's mother," or any other co-referential expression, without affecting the truth-value of our proposition. The proposition, that is to say, is referentially transparent. According to Sophocles, it is also true; for Oedipus realized that he had married Jocasta, whom *we* (but not Oedipus, until later) can identify as Oedipus's mother.

As a second alternative, the proposition might be about the SOA of Oedipus's realizing another SOA identified with regard to the content of *his* state of realization. This content is the SOA represented (approximately, in English) by "his (Oedipus's) having married Jocasta," but not by "his (Oedipus's) having married his mother." The reason it cannot be represented by the latter is that the content of *his* state of realization is representable only by a symbolism that *he* is able to interpret as standing in for that SOA.[38] If our proposition about Oedipus's state of realization is to be understood in this alternative manner, then an appropriate articulation in regimented form would be [Oedipus realizing the SOA of his (Oedipus's) having married Jocasta/yes]. Here "Jocasta" cannot be interchanged *salva veritate* with "Oedipus's mother." Hence the proposition in this case is referentially opaque.

The upshot is the same as in the case of propositional reports of belief examined previously. When the SOA represented by a propositional report of another person's realization is identified with respect to the object of that attitude (the actual SOA the subject realized), then the report itself is referentially transparent. When that SOA is identified with respect to the intentional content of the state of realization overall, however, the propositional report is referentially opaque.[39] Such is the case with attitudes of cognitive access generally, including finding, discerning, recognizing, and knowing.

The same result can be expected to hold for third-person reports of the remaining cognitive attitudes as well. Suppose that Claudius expresses a hope that Tully's denunciation will not have severe political repercussions. If in reporting that event we identify Claudius's hope with respect to its *object* (i.e., the eventuality he hopes will be the case), then the denunciation in question can be attributed with equal effect to either Tully or Cicero, which means that our report is referentially transparent. If Claudius's hope is identified with respect to what it is *about* (i.e., the intentional content of the hope as Claudius entertains it), on the other hand, then the report is referentially opaque, inasmuch as "Cicero" cannot replace "Tully" without a change of truth-value. And so it goes with other attitudes of projection. Or suppose that Claudius predicts reprisals on the part of Catiline. If in reporting that event we identify Claudius's prediction with respect to its object, then the result will be a report that is referentially transparent. Otherwise, the report will turn out to be opaque, depending for its truth upon the manner in which the prediction is reported. Predicting in this respect is typical of attitudes of assessment generally.

6. Opacity in Propositions of Other Sorts

An underlying theme of the previous section is that the source of intensionality in reports of another person's cognitive attitudes is the requirement that the representations involved in those attitudes be understood in a specific fashion by the person employing them. Representation also is the key to problems of intensionality in modal contexts. Consider the often discussed case of the cardinality of the planets.

It just so happens that the solar system contains nine planets. Thus "9" and "the number of planets" are co-referential expressions. Now, as a strictly arithmetical inequality, the proposition that 9 is greater than 4 is necessarily true, which is to say that 'L(9 is greater than 4)' is a true proposition.[40] But 'L(the number of planets is greater than 4)' *apparently* is false, since there could be only three planets or perhaps none at all. Inasmuch as a propositional context is extensional just in case its truth-value remains unchanged with the interchange of referentially equivalent expressions, it follows that 'L(9 is greater than 4)' lacks extensionality.

But *is* 'L(the number of planets is greater than 4)' a false proposition? In one reading, yes, in another reading, no—depending upon what SOA we take "the number of planets being greater than 4" to represent. Suppose we wish to formulate a proposition to the effect that it is necessary that the number of planets, whatever it might be, is greater than the number 4. A regimented version of this proposition is L[(∃x) (x being the unique number that in fact is the cardinal number of the planets ∧ x being greater than 4/yes]. This proposition is clearly false, since the number of planets in fact might be four or less—that is, it is *not* necessary that this number is greater than 4.

On the other hand, suppose we intend to formulate a proposition to the effect that it is necessary that the number 9, which just happens in our era to be the number of planets, is greater than the number 4. A regimented version of this proposition is L[(x) (x being the unique number that happens in this era to be the cardinal number of the planets ⊃ x being greater than 4)/yes]. This proposition in fact is true. And its truth is not affected by replacing the expression referring to 9 (i.e., the expression "the unique number that happens in this era to be the cardinal number of the planets") by other expressions with the same reference (e.g., "the successor of 8 in the series of positive integers," or simply the numeral "9"). The number 9 is greater than the number 4, no matter how one refers to either number.

In the first case, the expression "the number of planets is greater than 4" represents the SOA of the number of planets, however numerous, being greater than the number 4. In the second case, typographically the same expression represents the SOA of the number 9, which just happens currently to be the number of planets, being greater than the number 4. The difference between these two cases comes down to the difference between (a) our understanding "the number of planets" as referring to the cardinal number of the membership of the class of planets (which might vary from era to era) and (b) our understanding it as referring to a member of the series of positive integers. But only in the latter case does "the number of planets" refer to the same thing as the numeral "9"—namely, the ninth member of the series of positive integers (which presumably does not vary from era to era).

The upshot of this brief case study is that if "9" in 'L(9 is greater than 4)' is replaced by a *genuinely* co-referential expression, then the modality of the context alone does not preclude extensionality. Whether the expressions "9" and "the number of planets" are genuinely co-referential, in turn, depends upon how we understand them as representations. Once again, the source of the intensionality of propositional contexts is seen to lie with the choice of interpretation we impose on inherently ambiguous representing expressions.

Although the literature on this topic is concerned by and large with the intensionality of cognitive and of modal contexts, there are other propositional contexts that fail extensionality because of interpretations associated with various representations within them. Suppose a notation were established for various properties of plane figures, in which each of the three angles of a triangle is symbolized by "A" plus an appropriate subscript. Given this notation, the expression "the equation $A_1 = A_2 = A_3 = 60°$ symbolizes an equiangular triangle" might count as a true proposition.[41] Yet, despite the fact that "equiangular triangle" and "equilateral triangle" are co-referential expressions, this proposition would be falsified if the latter replaced the former. For another example, suppose that a zoologist with a special interest in cardiovascular systems has marked a file cabinet with a heart cut from a valentine, which is taken whimsically as a symbol for creatures with hearts. Here "the heart-shape symbolizes animals with hearts" expresses a true proposition. Nonetheless, although "animals with livers" refers to the same creatures as "animals with hearts," it is not true to say that the heart shape symbolizes animals with livers. The source of intensionality in these cases is neither cognitive nor modal; rather, it lies in the interpretations governing the use of the representations involved.[42]

We return to considerations of intensionality in the final chapter. To conclude the present discussion it is enough to reiterate the main themes of the current chapter in capsule form. The intensionality (with an "s") of propositional contexts reporting other persons' cognitive attitudes has been traced back to the intentionality (with a "t") of those cognitive attitudes themselves, which in turn has been seen to derive from the virtual relation between representations and the SOAs represented. Given the metaphysically neutral characterization of virtual relations in chapter 6, this should make the present account amenable to philosophers of any doctrinal allegiance. Intentionality is as commonplace as the use of symbols. And intensionality, in turn, is no more mysterious than the interpretations required as part of their use.

Notes

1. Exceptions may be found in the works of Roderick Chisholm, Dagfin Föllesdahl, and Hubert Dreyfus, prominent among philosophers who have been influenced by both traditions.

2. Key texts by Quine on the topic are "Reference and Modality," chap. 8 of *From a Logical Point of View* (Cambridge, Mass.: Harvard University Press, 1953); section 44 of *Word and Object* (Cambridge, Mass.: MIT Press, 1960); and "Quantifiers and Propositional Attitudes," chap. 15 of *The Ways of Paradox* (New York: Random House, 1965).

3. For a statement of one view on this topic, an interested reader might consult my *Consciousness: A Philosophic Study of Minds and Machines* (New York: Random House, 1969), chap. 3 esp.

4. Franz Brentano, *Psychologie von Empirischen Standpunkt* (Leipzig: Duncker and Humblot, 1874); see vol. 1, bk. 2, chap. 1 specifically. Brentano's influence upon analytic philosophy was channeled by some of the early writings of Roderick Chisholm; see, for example, the chapter entitled "Intentional Inexistence" in Chisholm's *Perceiving: A Philosophical Study* (Ithaca, N.Y.: Cornell University Press, 1957).

5. Brentano, *Psychologie,* vol. 1, bk. 2, chap. 1, par. 5. I owe to Steven Horst the observation that Brentano's distinction between the mental and the physical does not neatly overlap with the corresponding distinction employed by most contemporary English-speaking philosophers. What we tend to call "mental states" include some (e.g., qualia) that Brentano classified as physical. This discrepancy does not affect the following argument.

6. Some writers on this topic use the terms "content" and "object" in senses other than these, but the present use is in no way idiosyncratic.

7. See chapter 4, section 5. The descriptive component of [the gate being shut/yes] is the expression to the left of the slash, which picks out the SOA of the gate's being shut.

8. Along with this labeling convention go the verb forms 'believe(1)', 'believed(1)', and so forth. The same for 'belief(2)' and 'belief(3)' to follow.

9. D's belief(1) is an attitude of a sort that might be instantiated in other persons as well (e.g., Duncan might also believe[1] that the gate is shut). So we might say that there is a general attitude of belief(1) that can be shared by different persons. This general attitude thus is independent not only of any particular propositional object, but of any individual person holding the attitude as well. But D's belief(1) in particular is independent only of its propositional object, not of the person D herself. Our discussion throughout this section will be of cognitive attitudes and intentional states on the personal level only.

10. For purposes of the present discussion, the relation between the proposition and what it represents does not itself comprise an intentional relation. Intentionality comes into the scene with the cognitive attitudes subjects adopt toward representations of various sorts.

11. The content of a particular attitude of belief(1) was identified above as the same as what its propositional object is about. This same content now is being identified as the content of the state of belief(3) in turn.

12. In figure 9.1 the propositional object is indicated by the format '[X/s]', adopted in chapter 3 for use in formulating concrete propositions. (The corresponding format for abstract proposition-types is '*[X/s]'.) In the case of externally expressed propositions, "X" stands for a concrete representation of an SOA and "s" stands for a status-ascription. In the case of internal propositional objects, the concrete proposition in question may be conceived as an internal representation of the second-order SOA of X being the case (for which, see section 6 in chapter 8).

13. It will be noted that the status ascribed to X by the propositional object [X/s] is not part of the state of belief(3). See the discussion below for explanation.

14. The rank-ordering of SOAs is discussed in section 5 of chapter 4.

15. The truth-condition of the proposition [X/yes] (discussed in section 4 of chapter 4) is the higher-order SOA of X being the case. Since a belief(3) shares the truth-value of its constituent proposition, it also shares that proposition's truth-condition.

16. If the proposition were about the status being ascribed to the SOA as well, then we would not be able to formulate conflicting propositions about the same thing. In general, if [X/yes (no)] were about the second-order SOA of X being (not being) the case, instead of just the first-order SOA X itself, then [X/yes] and [X/no] would not be propositions about the same thing and thus would be incapable of contradicting each other.

17. Chisholm, *Perceiving,* 169.

18. What is meant here are attitudes that take propositional objects; see chapter 1, section 3.

19. A general idea of how such configurations might be endowed with representational capacities was offered in chapter 8.

20. An eventuality is an SOA that the subject addresses as having *indefinite* (or unknown) status, not one with a determinate status *other than* being the case or not being the case.

21. As NX_a becomes interactive with NX_r, the neuronal process that supports the subject's use of symbolic representations in a public language, the functions of NX_a and NX_r become merged into the complex function NX_{ar}. According to the account of chapter 8, NX_{ar} answers to the description "internal representation" in the specific sense of a *representing* effected by the relevant neuronal circuits.

22. Although the role alluded to in figure 9.3 is played by the specific subfunction NX_a (see note 21 above), the complete notation 'NX_{ar}' will continue to be used in this regard.

23. If so, then the causation in question is of the sort involved in the homeostasis of information-processing systems, as distinct from that involved in mechanical computation. As will be noted in connection with figure 9.4, the same kind of representation NX_{ar} may be involved in attitudes of access, including knowing. Here, we have an account of a representational function that

might relate a knower to an object of knowledge without entailing the presence of propositional representation of the sort involved in belief. Paul Moser acknowledged the possibility of such an account in *Knowledge and Evidence* ([Cambridge: Cambridge University Press, 1989], 20), but found no such account in circulation at that time to sustain critical assessment.

24. There is no tension between the requirement that X must actually be the case in order to serve as the object of an attitude like discerning (perceiving, knowing, etc.) and the participation of the same X in a virtual relation that does not in turn require that it be the case. The fact that an object represented by a given R happens to exist does not prevent the relation between them from being virtual (the same relation would obtain if X happened not to exist).

25. Following the pattern of the schemata in figures 9.3 and 9.4, the assumption here is that S's attention is directed toward the intentional content by some manner of internal representation (symbolized 'NX_{ar}'). Unlike the case with 9.3 and 9.4, however, this assumption is somewhat arbitrary, inasmuch as attitudes of assessment (like those of stance) might also be focused upon their content by representations in public language. While this possibility remains open in the case of other attitudes as well, it seems much less likely to occur in connection to attitudes of projection and access.

26. See chapter 1 for criticism of this notion.

27. See "Two Dogmas of Empiricism," in Quine, *From a Logical Point of View*, 30 esp.

28. Although usage varies, "intensional" (with an "s") generally is applied as a characterization of propositional contexts, while "intentional" (with a "t") is applied to mental states and their contents. See Quine's "Reference and Modality," in *From a Logical Point of View*, esp. 156, for an example.

29. See Quine, "Reference and Modality," esp. 142.

30. The example is adapted from Quine's *Word and Object*, sec. 30.

31. Since the problem of referential opacity concerns the effect of interchanging extensionally equivalent expressions upon the truth-value of the containing context, the problem must be set up in terms of a context in which interchange of this sort makes sense. Although Claudius's belief may have been internally instantiated as well, the problem does not arise in connection with propositions employing internal representations only.

32. The expression '*[Tully having denounced Catiline/yes]' is to be understood, according to the provisions of chapter 3, as a label for the proposition-type of which [Tully having denounced Catiline/yes] is a token instance. Inasmuch as proposition-types have been defined as classes of their token instances, and insofar as classes themselves do not serve as representatives, proposition-types as such play no role in the intentional structure of belief as analyzed in the previous section. The object of Claudius's belief, accordingly, must have been a token of that type, rather than the proposition-type just by itself.

33. The descriptive component of [Claudius believing that Tully denounced Catiline/yes], once again, is the expression to the left of the slash,

with the expression to the right serving as status-ascription. For reasons examined in chapter 3, a similar distinction between descriptive and status-ascribing components must be understood as present in propositional expressions of ordinary language.

34. For reasons soon to become apparent, SOA(2a) and SOA(2b) are not subdivisions of SOA(2).

35. Quine, in *Word and Object* (144n), credits Russell and Whitehead with first using the term in this sense.

36. While the use of quantifier and variables in this expression should be perspicuous as it stands, readers who question the accessibility of the variable within the propositional expression to quantification should refer to the discussion of this matter in chapter 4.

37. This is in agreement with Quine's observation in *Word and Object,* sec. 30, that the construction "a believes that p" may be either opaque or transparent, depending on certain referential features of the sentence substituted for "p." Whereas Quine makes "substitutivity of identity" (142) without change in truth-value the mark of referential transparency, a belief is transparent by the present account when identified with respect to object rather than content. Other respects in which the present account differs from Quine's are in tracing intensionality (with an "s") back to intentionality (with a "t") and in making the distinction between opacity and transparency applicable to cognitive attitudes other than propositional.

38. The structure of Oedipus's relation to the content of his realization is depicted in figure 9.4, appropriately relabeled to pertain to realization instead of discernment.

39. With attitudes of cognitive access, it may be recalled, the object of the attitude and the intentional content of the attitudinal state overall are one and the same SOA, save that in the former case (the object), but not the latter (the content), that SOA must be actual. What makes reports of attitudes toward SOAs identified with respect to content opaque is the requirement that the subject understand the intentional content in terms of some specific set of representations.

40. In regimented form, this is the proposition L[9 being greater than 4/yes], where 'L' is read "it is necessary that." A discussion of the contingent basis of this necessity is provided in section 4 of chapter 7.

41. The proposition in question is to the effect that this equation symbolizes a triangle *as* being equiangular (saying nothing about the equality of its sides), not merely that the triangle it happens to symbolize *is* equiangular (and, as a consequence, equilateral as well).

42. Inasmuch as representation is symbolic depiction, and as cognitive agency typically is involved in the use of symbols, all representation takes place in a broadly cognitive context. The point here is that intensionality in these cases stems from the way representations are treated within them, and not from their cognitive character as such.

Chapter 10

INFERENCE AND THE GAIN
OF KNOWLEDGE

1. The Concept of an Increasing Store of Knowledge

One of the most widely debated issues in philosophy during the modern period has been that of the capacities and limitations of rational inference as a means for extending human knowledge. The fact that this issue has not received much attention in the late twentieth century should not be taken as an indication that it has been resolved or that it is not as important as it was once thought to be. Recent neglect of the issue may be due in part to a "specialization" of attention among epistemologists on questions of justification, under the assumption that an adequate account of the evidence (supposedly) needed to convert true belief into knowledge would provide a basis for answering other questions about the range of knowledge itself. But even if recent debates about justification were brought to a point of resolution, there would still be unanswered questions about how inference contributes to knowledge and about the limits of reason as a mode of access to the world.

Among the findings of the preceding discussion that bear upon these questions is the identification of knowledge as a form of cognitive access to the actual world, as distinct from an attitude toward propositional objects. A consequence is that if rational inference is to contribute to the advancement of knowledge, it must somehow be able to extend the reach of the mind beyond the propositions produced by its deductive arguments. Another result that helps show how this might happen is the distinction among an SOA X (e.g., snow's being white), the proposition representing X as being the case (e.g., [snow being white/yes]), and the higher-order SOA of that proposition's being true.

267

A relevant consideration stemming from this distinction is that, whereas a deductive inference cannot properly be said to yield knowledge of its propositional conclusion as such, it might yield knowledge of the higher-order SOA of that conclusion's being true.

The primary purpose of this final chapter is to marshal earlier findings of this sort having to do with the relations between knowledge and inference and to bring them to bear on the question of how deductive inference can contribute to an expanding body of human knowledge. While no major contribution to this very important question can be made within the scope of the discussion remaining, the prospect of even a minor contribution makes the venture worth undertaking.

To make a beginning, we may note that the concept of an expanding body of knowledge itself is not entirely perspicuous. In thinking of the body of human knowledge, one might guess, many people tend to think of a collection of oversized volumes, recording the accumulated truths[1] of human experience—the "archives," as it were, of successfully completed inquiry. But truths can be recorded only in the form of true propositions, no collection of which is equivalent to an accumulation of knowledge. It is conceivable, presumably, that some great collection of propositions might be amassed that contains *reports* of the most significant knowledge accumulated over the course of human history. But a collection of such reports would no more be a collection of human knowledge than a record of names in a phone book is a collection of (the relevant sector of) a city's adult population. In what manner *can* human knowledge be accumulated?

The sense of knowledge with which we are now concerned is that of a cognitive access to the world as it is, as distinct from the knowledge of persons and places (e.g., knowing one's barber) and the knowledge of acquired skills (e.g., knowing how to use a slide rule) with which it was contrasted in chapter 5. But the use of "knowledge" in this cognitive sense admits further subdivision, following the various uses of "belief" distinguished in chapter 9. There is the cognitive *attitude* of belief itself (belief[1] in that earlier context), the *proposition* (belief[2]) that serves as object of the attitude, and the overall *state* of belief (belief[3]) comprising a given subject's belief(1) on a particular occasion toward a given belief(2). In addition, there is belief as an attitude toward a specific proposition that can be shared by a number of different persons. If both Deirdre and Duncan believe that the gate is shut, for instance, then the two persons share the same belief. What they share in this case is not just the general attitude of belief(1) itself, and not just some (unspecified) relationship to the same propositional object. Nor is what they share the same state of belief(3), inasmuch as this state is always peculiar to a given cognitive subject. What Deirdre and Duncan share is belief(1) as a *general attitude* toward tokens of the same propositional type.[2]

In similar fashion, we may distinguish knowledge as an attitude (knowledge[1]) toward an actual SOA, the SOA (knowledge[2]) known on a certain occasion, and the overall state (knowledge[3]) of the subject's knowing a specific SOA in some specific set of circumstances. As in the case of belief, moreover, there is knowledge in yet another sense that permits the sharing of knowledge among different persons. Suppose that both Beatrice and Camille know that the sky is cloudy, having arrived at Lake Michigan for a day at the beach. They share more than the attitude of knowledge(1) in general, inasmuch as they both have knowledge of the same SOA. And they share more than a general access to that SOA, since the attitude of each is one of knowing specifically (as distinct from recognizing or discerning, etc.). What they share is knowledge(1) as a general attitude toward identically the same SOA of the sky's being cloudy. Let us refer to knowledge in this further sense as "knowledge(4)."

In which of the various senses above can we intelligibly speak of the expanding accumulation of knowledge? Inasmuch as there is no intelligible manner in which cognitive *attitudes* can be gathered together in increasing measure, as it were, knowledge(1) drops out immediately. The individual state of knowledge(3) seems equally unpromising; for although there may be some sense in which knowledge(3) might be accumulated on a personal basis, as when Deirdre's state of knowing that the children are safe is added to her previous knowledge(3) that the gate is shut, it seems clear that in talking about the accumulation of human knowledge we are not talking about a collection of individual personal states. The accumulation of human knowledge, at the very least, is knowledge that can be shared by different persons. This reduces the field of candidates to knowledge(2) and knowledge(4).

A subject's knowledge(2), in a given case of knowing, is the actual SOA that serves as the object of knowledge(1). The question with regard to knowledge(2) is whether the body of human knowledge might plausibly be conceived as an accumulation of actual SOAs that become known through the course of human cognitive experience. Consider our body of scientific knowledge as a subset of human knowledge generally. Is it plausible to think of scientific knowledge as the accumulation of actual SOAs made known in the course of scientific inquiry? The case for an affirmative answer appears to be supported if we substitute the term "truth" for "actual SOA." There is a sense of "truth," as may be recalled from chapter 4, in which a truth is an actual SOA—not a proposition with a positive truth-value, but an aspect of the world by which a proposition is rendered true.[3] In this sense of the term, a scientific *truth* is an aspect of the actual world revealed as a result of scientific inquiry. And it indeed seems plausible, at least initially, to think of scientific knowledge as a body of truths made known through the inquiry of the scientific community.

Another available manner of speaking is to say that scientific knowledge consists of all the *facts* made known through that process of inquiry. Like "truth," the term "fact" also is used in two distinct senses,[4] one of which is that of an actual SOA. So we might speak of facts accumulating within the body of knowledge, as more and more SOAs become known to the scientific community. At first blush, it seems equally plausible to think of the accumulation of facts made known in this fashion as the accumulation of scientific knowledge itself.

If we think further about this notion of knowledge as an accumulation of truths or facts, however, the question arises of the *manner* in which such SOAs might be accumulated. SOAs, actual or otherwise, obviously cannot be gathered together in some central "repository" of facts or truths, as bags of wheat can be gathered into a communal granary. The manner of accumulation cannot be a matter of relocation, with facts consigned to special storage areas as they become known. This brings back to mind the image of the "archives" of human knowledge, consisting of a propositional record of the many truths discovered in the course of human experience. It does make sense, clearly enough, to think of a collection of written (or electronically imprinted, etc.) records, gathered together in some oversized library. The initial plausibility of the notion of an accumulation of truths or facts, indeed, may result from a confusion of the two senses of "truth" or "fact" noted above as (i) a true proposition and as (ii) an actual SOA. While it does make tolerably good sense to speak of a collection of true propositions, the notion of a collection of actual SOAs seems to make no sense whatever. And this latter is the sense in which facts and truths are items of knowledge(2).

The manner in which knowledge can be accumulated is not a matter of relocation or of reassignment to a central repository. It is a matter, rather, of expanding access, as more and more SOAs become accessible within the community of knowers. A useful analogy in this respect may be the expansion of the known world during the sixteenth century, as more of the world became known to European merchants and explorers. The expansion of the known world, obviously enough, was not a matter of the world itself becoming larger or parts of it being relocated for commercial convenience. Expansion in this case, rather, was a matter of increased access, as more of the world became known as the result of discovery. Expansion in the body of human knowledge, similarly, is not an increase in the size of a collection of items. It is rather an increase in the extent of the actual world to which humankind has cognitive access.

The sense of the term in which human knowledge can be accumulated, accordingly, boils down to knowledge(4)—knowledge in the sense of specific cognitive access that can be shared by different individuals. If both Beatrice and Camille know that the sky is cloudy, to return to our example, they share a general attitude of knowledge(1) toward this specific SOA. And it is this shared relation of access to this SOA that constitutes their sharing of knowledge(4). As additional people arrive on the beach, they too can share in this relationship. And as more of the world's weather becomes accessible to human cognition— say, through weather satellites and automated sensors—the more extensive becomes our body of shared meteorological knowledge. Knowledge(4) thus can be shared by different persons and can be expanded by extension to additional SOAs. It is knowledge in this sense, surely, that we have in mind in speaking of the body of human knowledge generally, as a form of knowledge that can be accumulated and can be shared by different persons.

One consequence of this conception of human knowledge is that a body of knowledge has no identity apart from the community of individual persons to whom it is known. If a given community of knowers is composed of individuals N_1 through N_m, then the knowledge at hand within that community consists of nothing more nor less than access to the group of relevant facts known by one or more of those individuals. If N_j alone within that community knows a certain SOA X_i,[5] and N_j departs from the community, then X_i is lost from its body of knowledge. Take Fermat and his "last theorem" as an example. Assume that Fermat in fact knew an SOA consisting of some particular configuration of formulae constituting a proof of the theorem in question and that no other mathematician knew that SOA. Then before his death a grasp of that fact (such-and-such a configuration of formulae being a proof of the theorem) was part of the body of mathematical knowledge, but it no longer was so after Fermat died. This would be the case even if Fermat had left some record of how the proof goes, but the record could not be deciphered by other mathematicians.

Let us take Fermat's case to the extreme and imagine that all mathematicians have died with no ready replacements. Although they have left large numbers of mathematical documents behind them—journal articles, textbooks, personal notes, and so on—no one is able now to read these documents, because no one understands the symbolism in which they are written. Before the mass departure of the mathematicians, there was an extensive body of mathematical knowledge, consisting of their communal access to many facts regarding the provability of theorems, the properties of axiom sets, and other such matters. But since no one is left to whom these facts are accessible, the body of mathematical knowledge has shrunk to nothing. The textbooks and other documents still remain in which the knowledge of the mathematicians had been recorded; but since the formulae they contain are no longer intelligible, they no longer serve their previous role of providing access to the domain of mathematical truth. If a new generation of talented individuals someday succeeds in deciphering portions of this symbolism, then corresponding portions of what was known previously might be rediscovered, and the body of mathematical knowledge once again might become substantial. But until this happens, nothing remains of the previous body of knowledge, despite the extensive documentation still to be found in the libraries.

The point of this imaginary excursion is that the body of knowledge associated with a field of inquiry—whether mathematics, science, or geographical exploration—consists of access to the SOAs that become known to individual persons, and not of the propositions or other symbols by which these SOAs might happen to have been represented. The point can be illustrated more prosaically by the following considerations as well. Computer programs have been written that enable high-speed digital machines to produce valid proofs of logical theorems. One such program reported by Hao Wang[6] generated complete proofs of over 200 theorems from *Principia Mathematica*[7] in an average time of about one proof per second. The output of the program in any single case was an array of propositions, in logical notation, that constitutes a proof of the theorem in question. Suppose that an advanced theorem-prover of this sort has been developed that is capable of generating hundreds of proofs each day in predicate calculus and set theory, and that a sizable number of these were proofs of theorems that had not been proven previously. A staff of logicians has been assigned to sift through this output to identify new proofs of particular significance; but since they have fallen behind in this task, there are several potentially important proofs on the computer printout that have never been worked through by a flesh-and-blood logician. The question now arises whether our knowledge of logic is being expanded each day by the production of these as yet unexamined proofs. The propositions are in place that show how the proofs go, but they remain proofs unknown by any individual logician. Do the unexamined contents of the printout as they stand add to our body of logical knowledge?

If the arguments of the section up to this point are acceptable, the answer is an unqualified "no." The propositions on the printout neither constitute knowledge themselves (in *any* sense of the term) nor stand as objects of knowledge of a potentially shared cognitive attitude (in the sense of knowledge[4] above). Being as yet beyond the ken of the logicians in question, any logical truths they might happen to represent remain external to the corpus of logical knowledge. This corpus consists of logical facts that have come within the ken of individual logicians, and it is expanded only as new facts actually come to be known.

2. Inference as Means of Knowing the Truth-Values of Propositions

A mechanical theorem-prover of the sort mentioned above is able to generate logical proofs on its own because logical deduction is a strictly formal procedure. Logical deduction is formal in the sense that it proceeds by application of rules of inference that pertain only to the logical form of the symbols involved, without regard for what those symbols might be taken to represent. In the case of proof by a trained logician, the procedure begins with a set of initial propositions (axioms, postulates, definitions, etc.), moves through a series of intermediate formulae derived from these by explicit rules of formal inference, and concludes with the derivation of the theorem to be proved from earlier formulae within the series. In the case of the mechanical theorem-prover, the procedure begins with axioms or postulates expressed in digital form, moves forward according to rules of inference in the form of mechanical procedures for digitalized-symbol transformation, and terminates with the production of a formula expressing the theorem in question. In either case, logical proof is a matter of constructing a series of formulae in which later members follow from earlier members by application of appropriately formulated procedures of formal inference and which terminates with a formula expressing the proposition to be demonstrated.

One lesson already drawn from our story of the mechanical theorem-prover is that mechanically produced proofs do not add to the store of human knowledge until they come under the knowledgeable survey of human beings capable of comprehending them. But there are still questions to be answered about how the comprehending grasp of a set of propositions can be converted into knowledge of an actual SOA. For a logical proof in itself is nothing more than a configuration of logically ordered propositions; and the propositions comprising the set cannot serve as objects of knowledge themselves. In the story, we recall, a group of trained logicians was assigned the task of sorting through the mass of formulae produced by the machine in search of results that might prove logically significant, and it was allowed that the disclosure of such results might contribute to the body of logical knowledge. But what happens in the course of the logicians' activity that could convert their awareness of sets of formulae into knowledge of logical SOAs?

It should be apparent that the source of this problem has nothing to do essentially with the manner in which the formulae constituting the logical proofs in question were produced. Even in the case of proofs produced by a flesh-and-blood logician, we have the problem of understanding how the logician's dealings with the symbols on the worksheet could eventuate in knowledge of logical truths. Nor does the problem stem from the fact that the sets of formulae we have been considering up to now constitute proofs of theorems in logic, rather than proofs in other disciplines. No matter what the subject matter of the proof, the question arises how any procedures undertaken with respect to a set of propositions can contribute to our store of knowledge about the world at large. The source of the problem is that deductive proof deals exclusively with propositions, whereas what we *know* are not propositions but SOAs.

A partial response to the problem begins with the observation that among SOAs that might be present in the actual world, some are SOAs *involving* propositions. An example is the SOA of the proposition that snow is white being true. SOAs involving propositions were termed "higher-order SOAs" in chapter 4; and it is clear that there are certain higher-order SOAs of this sort that might come to be known as a consequence of a logician's dealings with a deductive proof. If the logician has been careful in constructing the deduction and has made sure that each step is authorized by an applicable rule of inference, then he or she may be said to know the higher-order SOA of that series of propositions constituting a valid proof of the final conclusion. If the logician knows that the premises of the deduction are true, moreover, then this knowledge, in conjunction with knowledge of the proof's validity, may lead to knowledge that the conclusion itself is true. There does not appear to be any immediate problem about the manner in which a logician's dealings with a deductive proof might yield knowledge of SOAs involving the propositions of which the proof is composed.

But this is a partial response at best. The primary challenge of our problem is to understand how deductive inference can produce knowledge of the world at large—not merely knowledge concerning the propositions involved in the inference, but knowledge of the SOAs these propositions represent. Let us attempt to formulate the problem more precisely. Suppose that N has constructed a sound deductive proof of the proposition that SOA X is the case. This would amount to a valid deduction from true premises of some token of the proposition *[X/yes].[8] As a consequence of coming to know that the deduction is sound, N might also come to know that this proposition is true. But doesn't the proof yield more than that? Doesn't the proof lead N to the knowledge that SOA X is the case as well? If it did not, we would have to concede that the proof reveals facts only about the propositions it involves, but nothing about the SOAs those propositions represent. The problem is to understand how this outcome can be avoided.

By way of simple illustration, consider that N has deduced the proposition that Socrates is mortal from the premises that all men are mortal and that Socrates is a man. Given that the deduction is sound, it has the effect of showing that the conclusion *[Socrates being mortal/yes] is a true proposition. But the SOA (i) of this proposition's being true is not the same as the SOA (ii) of its being the case that Socrates is mortal. Why not? Because (ii) is a first-order SOA standing as truth-condition[9] for the proposition that Socrates is mortal, while (i) is the second-order SOA of that truth-condition's being realized. It has seemed unproblematic all along that our acquaintance with a deductive proof might yield knowledge of the second-order SOA of the proof's conclusion being a true proposition. What has yet to be made clear is how any dealings N might have with the proof could provide knowledge of the first-order SOA (ii) of its being the case that Socrates is mortal.

This is the problem we have now to face. A sound deductive proof of a proposition [X/yes] might yield knowledge of the SOA of that proposition's being true. But the second-order SOA of [X/yes] being true is not the same as the first-order SOA of X being the case. What we have to understand is how the deduction might yield knowledge of the SOA of X being the case as well—that is, how deduction can yield knowledge of the world at large, as distinct from knowledge involving propositions by which its various aspects are represented.

Once the problem is stated in these terms explicitly, it may appear that the answer is next to trivial. The (apparent) answer begins with the observation that if someone knows that SOA X is the case, then that person knows as well that a proposition [X/yes] representing this fact constitutes a true proposition. By reverse token, the answer continues, if a person knows that [X/yes] is true, then he or she knows as well that X is the case. Why? Because [X/yes] being true is extensionally equivalent to X being the case, in the sense that one holds when and only when the other holds as well.[10] And if the SOA of [X/yes] being true is extensionally equivalent to the SOA of X being the case, then knowing one is tantamount to knowing the other. Hence, if someone knows (e.g., by deduction) that [X/yes] is true, then that person also knows that X is the case.

This answer has the ring of plausibility but, in fact, is unacceptable. The claim on which it is based is that N's knowing the SOA of [X/yes] being true is tantamount to N's knowing the SOA of X being the case, on the grounds that the two SOAs are extensionally equivalent. And this claim is simply erroneous. It is erroneous for the same reason that it would be erroneous to claim that Oedipus's knowing he had married Jocasta is tantamount to knowing he had married his mother, on the grounds that "Jocasta" and "Oedipus's mother" are extensionally equivalent. The source of error in both cases is referential opacity.[11] A context is referentially opaque, in the sense here relevant, if preservation of truth-value cannot be assured with the interchange of extensionally equivalent expressions. The fact that the expression "knows that ___" establishes a referentially opaque context is shown by what Oedipus knew and failed to know about his marriage. Oedipus knew that he had married Jocasta; and we know that "Jocasta" is extensionally equivalent to "Oedipus's mother" (in that both expressions refer to the same individual). But it does not follow from this pair of facts that Oedipus knew that he had married his mother. In fact, he did not, until the tragic climax of the story. Similarly, the fact that a given person N knows that [X/yes] is true, in conjunction with the fact that [X/yes] being true is extensionally equivalent to X being the case, does not assure that N also knows that X is the case. Although a given person may in fact know both SOAs on a given occasion, knowledge of the latter does not come automatically with knowledge of the former. Hence the answer proposed above falls short of the mark.[12]

In what direction ought we look for a satisfactory answer? A hint is provided by the following consideration. If Oedipus knows that he has married Jocasta, and if he knows in addition that Jocasta is the same person as his mother, then Oedipus knows that he has married his mother. Similarly, if N knows by deduction that [X/yes] is true, and in addition knows the truth-conditions of that proposition—that is, knows that [X/yes] is true if and only if X is the case (which we have presumed *ourselves* to know throughout the discussion thus far)—then N knows that X is the case as well. But knowledge of the truth-conditions of [X/yes] is not part of what N comes to know merely by deducing that proposition from a set of true premises. One thing this consideration shows is that other resources are needed if knowledge of the world at large is to be reached by means of deductive inference.

Another thing this consideration shows is that these other resources have something to do with knowing the truth-conditions of the propositions concerned. Let us examine more carefully how knowledge of truth-conditions might enable deductive inference to yield knowledge about the world at large.

3. Deductive Knowledge Extended via Knowledge of Truth-Conditions

Consider a simple example in which deductive inference quite clearly expands the scope of human knowledge. Suppose that no one knows the name of Thomas Stokes's mother, but that N (a genealogist) knows that Thomas was born in Little Fiddling in 1601 and that M (a warden of the only church ever to stand in the parish) knows (from a page of an old church register containing parents' names only) that Mary Stokes was the only woman to give birth in Little Fiddling that year. N and M then meet and pool their information, deducing at once the proposition that Mary was Thomas Stokes's mother. Whereas no one knew before that this proposition is true (the proposition *[Mary Stokes being the mother of Thomas/yes]), after the deduction this would be known by both M and N. The SOA of this being a true proposition thus would be added inferentially to the store of human knowledge.

But now let us suppose that M and N know more than this as an indirect consequence of their deductive inference. Let us suppose that they know as well the actual SOA of Mary Stokes being the mother of Thomas (SOA Y). This they know on the basis of two items of knowledge. For one, they know (by deduction, as above) that [Y/yes] is true. And second, they know the truth-conditions of that proposition—that is, they know that [Y/yes] is true if and only if Y is the case. Knowing (a) the SOA of [Y/yes] being true, and knowing (b) the SOA of [Y/yes] being true if and only if Y is the case, they know as well (c) the SOA of Y being the case. The upshot is that their knowledge of (a) is extended to knowing (c), on the basis of their additional knowledge of (b).

Contrived as it may be, the case has been portrayed as one in which a subject's knowledge is extended in a manner that is entirely straightforward but could not be achieved by deductive inference alone. M and N first inferred deductively that the proposition [Y/yes] is true. On the basis of this inference (given the truth of its premises), they arrived at knowledge of the (second-order) SOA of (a) that proposition's being true. Then, by bringing to bear their *additional* knowledge of (b) the truth-conditions of the proposition in question, they arrived at the further knowledge of the (first-order) SOA of (c) Y being the case. As the story is intended to be understood, this latter step from (a) and (b) to (c) is one they achieve by *extralogical* means. It must be acknowledged, nonetheless, that this latter step looks superficially like a further deductive argument. If this step in fact were nothing more than an additional deductive argument, then the point of the example would obviously be undercut.

The step from knowing (a) the SOA of [Y/yes] being true, and knowing (b) the SOA of [Y/yes] being true if and only if Y is the case, to knowing (c) the SOA of Y being the case looks superficially like a deductive argument because it appears (on the surface) to have the form "p. p *iff* q: therefore q." And as anyone with a smattering of logic knows, that is the form of a valid argument in the propositional calculus. The crucial point, however, is that the step from knowing (a) and (b) together to knowing (c) as a consequence is *not* a step of logical inference. The two components that provide the basis for this step of knowing are not propositions. Knowing (a), first, is not the *proposition* that [Y/yes] is true, but rather *knowledge* of the *SOA* of [Y/yes] being true. And knowing (b), similarly, is not the biconditional *proposition* that [Y/yes] is true if and only if Y is the case, but rather *knowledge* of the *SOA* of that biconditional's being true. Nor is the resulting state of knowing (c) a proposition in turn, for a state of knowing is nothing like a proposition. The upshot is that the progression of states of knowing in question—from knowing (a) and (b) together to knowing (c)—is not a progression that can be symbolized in propositional logic.[13] The step to knowing (c), in brief, is not a step of logical inference.

What the imaginary example of Thomas Stokes illustrates, accordingly, is the effect of combining *semantic* resources with resources of logic in the acquisition of knowledge. M and N arrived at knowledge of the truth of the proposition [Y/yes] by deductive inference from propositions whose truth they had known previously. The semantic resource that came into play at that point was their knowledge of the truth-conditions of the proposition in question. As a combined result, they came to know an SOA in which propositions had no involvement — namely, the (first-order) SOA consisting of Y being the case.

Consider another illustration of similar nature. Oedipus and Jocasta have just been married, and neither knows their relation through Oedipus's murdered father. Tiresias alone knows of this relation, but he does not yet know of the recent marriage. So no one knows that Oedipus has married his mother. Now Oedipus and Tiresias meet, share their privy information, and infer that Oedipus's wife is also his mother.[14] Oedipus now knows the (second-order) SOA of the proposition's being true that Jocasta is his mother. Knowing the truth-conditions of that proposition as well, Oedipus also comes to know the (first-order) SOA of its actually being the case that Jocasta is his mother. The tragic outcome of the story follows from this latter knowledge, as distinct from any knowledge regarding the truth-values of propositions. And this latter knowledge depends essentially upon semantic resources available to Oedipus — namely, upon his knowing the truth-conditions of the proposition he had inferred with Tiresias.

Other illustrations could be generated ad libitum. Suppose that Duncan deduces from equations of classical physics that a space probe launched at a given time, with a given speed along a given trajectory, will fall into orbit around the planet Jupiter. If the inference is known by D to be sound, then D comes to know the (second-order) SOA of the deduced proposition in fact being true. If D also knows the truth-conditions of that particular proposition (which he should as a result of his technical training), then he also comes to know the (first-order) SOA of its being the case that the probe will fall into orbit around Jupiter. Or if D infers by a deduction that is known to be sound that it is true that the continents float on molten rock, then, given knowledge on D's part of what makes that proposition true, D will also know the SOA of the continents' being supported in that particular manner.

In general: if N comes to know by inference the truth of a given proposition [X/yes], and if in addition N knows the truth-conditions of that proposition, then N gains knowledge of the (first-order) SOA of X being the case. This, in a nutshell, is the way N's knowledge can be extended with the help of deductive inference to knowledge of what is the case in the actual world. This extension depends essentially upon semantic resources that cannot be incorporated into the inference itself.

4. The Limitations of Deduction When
Truth-Conditions Are Unknown

The question might arise at this juncture whether we possess these semantic resources just as a matter of course, by virtue of being competent speakers of a natural language. And if we do, then the considerations above might seem to accomplish little more than belaboring the obvious. The best way to show that we do not is with reference to examples of valid deductive inferences that lead to conclusions without known truth-conditions, showing how knowledge of first-order SOAs—knowledge of how things stand in the world at large—is blocked by this semantic deficiency.

Now, there are innumerable instances of valid deductive inferences in which the person performing the inference is unacquainted with any truth-conditions attaching to the conclusions. For one, think of N reaching the conclusion of a Lewis Carroll sorites, having deduced validly that babies cannot manage crocodiles.[15] But N (let us assume) has no idea of what it would be to manage crocodiles and, hence, no idea of what counts as being unable to do this. So N fails to know the truth-conditions of the proposition deduced—that is, N fails to know what is the case in the world when babies are unable to manage crocodiles.

Since any valid sorites referring to the notion of managing crocodiles in its conclusion will also refer to that notion in one of its premises, however, then if N has no idea what it is to manage crocodiles, N presumably will be unable to determine the truth-value (if any) of that premise. This means that N presumably will be unable to determine whether the inference is sound (i.e., has true premises as well as being valid). And there is nothing noteworthy for present purposes about an unsound inference not yielding knowledge of the world at large. What we should be looking for, to settle the question above, is a deductive inference that the subject might reasonably think to be sound but that fails to produce knowledge of how things stand in the world because the truth-conditions (if any) of its conclusion remain unknown.

There is an important point to note about the Lewis Carroll sorites, however, before we move on to look for more substantial examples. In setting up the conditions of this example, we have assumed that N does not know the truth-conditions (if any) of the purported proposition that babies cannot manage crocodiles. This is not to assume anything about N's ability to produce an instance of the general biconditional '[X/yes] is true *iff* X is the case' in which 'X' is replaced by "babies being unable to manage crocodiles" or some equivalent expression. If N is moderately competent in the use of English, then the production of a particular biconditional of this description should be a relatively routine matter. But being able to spell out a biconditional of this sort for a purported propositional expression is not the same at all as knowing the truth-conditions (if any) of the expression in question. N presumably could produce a biconditional of this sort for the senseless formula "the mome raths outgrabe," or for any other pseudo-proposition employing nonsense terms. In the case of any *proper* proposition (e.g., [snow being white/yes]), a biconditional of this form (e.g., [snow being white/yes] is true *iff* it is the case that snow is white) defines what it is for that proposition to be true. In this manner, it identifies the truth-conditions of the proposition. But the biconditional identifies these truth-conditions only for someone who already understands its right-hand member—that is, for someone already prepared to tell when these truth-conditions are met.[16] The lesson here is that one does not know the truth-conditions of a purported propositional expression merely by being able to articulate (however authoritatively or self-confidently) a biconditional of this form for the expression in question.[17] In order to know the truth-conditions of a given proposition, one must *understand* the circumstances in which these truth-conditions would be satisfied.

Let us look at another valid deduction yielding a conclusion the truth-conditions of which N fails to know—this time, a deduction N has good reason to consider sound. Suppose that N has constructed the following version of the ontological argument:[18]

	(1)	Nothing more perfect than God is conceivable	(premise)
	(2)	Failure to exist is conceived for all things as a lapse from perfection	(premise)
	(3)	If God does not exist, then something more perfect than God is conceivable	(from [2])
hence	(4)	God exists	

Also suppose that—as far as N's conceptions of God and of existence are concerned—N knows that the premises (as intended) are true (i.e., suppose that N knows that he or she can conceive nothing more perfect than God, etc.). So, if the argument can be shown valid, N also knows that the conclusion (4) is true.

Now let N take advantage of the following formulation (with 'g' for "God," 'P_{yx}' for "y is conceivable as more perfect than x," and 'F_x' for "x has the perfection-making property in question") to show that the argument is valid:

$$(1') \quad -(\exists y)P_{yg} \qquad \text{(premise)}$$
$$(2') \quad (x)(-F_x \supset (\exists y)(P_{yx})) \qquad \text{(premise)}$$
$$(3') \quad -F_g \supset (\exists y)F_{yg} \qquad \text{(instantiation of [2'])}$$
$$\text{hence} \quad (4') \quad F_g \qquad \text{(from [1'] and [3'])}$$

The upshot, under these hypothetical circumstances,[19] is that N knows that the conclusion is true—that it is true that God has the perfection-making property in question (which N conceives, perhaps unadvisedly,[20] to be existence).

But suppose, finally, that N proves unable to specify what it would be for God to have this property, in the sense of being unable to identify the criteria for the correct designative use of the representation "God exists."[21] This means that N is unable to specify the circumstances under which the SOA of God's existing would be the case. But the circumstances in which this would be the case are precisely the truth-conditions of the conclusion of the argument above. The consequence is that N fails to know the truth-conditions of that conclusion and, accordingly, fails to know the SOA of its being the case that God exists. Despite having come to know by a sound deduction that the proposition that God exists is true, N does not know that God exists. The reason is that N lacks the semantic resource needed to move from knowledge of the second-order SOA of that proposition's being true to knowledge of the first-order SOA of its being the case that God exists. The semantic resource N lacks, once again, is knowledge of the truth-conditions of the proposition in question.

Other cases in which knowledge of first-order SOAs seems to be blocked at the level of truth-conditions might suggest themselves to the reader.[22] For the moment, it is enough to summarize the results of our consideration thus far. It is a commonplace of logic that deductive inference can fail to yield knowledge about the world at large as a result of either the inference being invalid or its premises being false. A third potential source of failure lies with the semantic relation between a proposition and those aspects of the world the presence of which would make it true. The aspects of the world that would make a given proposition true, of course, are the truth-conditions of that proposition. And if N does not know what those truth-conditions are, then N cannot know the aspects of the world in question merely as a result of knowing that the proposition is true. When this happens, then N's advance in knowledge is blocked at the level of propositional truth and cannot progress to the level of (nonpropositional) facts in the world at large.

5. Other Limitations of Inference as a Source of Knowledge

If a person knows the SOA of snow's being white, then perforce it is the case that snow is white, since knowledge is restricted to SOAs that are actually the case. To know the SOA of snow's being white is not the same as knowing the SOA of *its being the case* that snow is white, inasmuch as the SOAs involved are of different orders (base-order and first-order, respectively). But a person who knows a base-order SOA X (like snow's being white) is in a good position to know the first-order SOA of X being the case as well. While knowing X is not the same as knowing that X is the case,[23] nothing is lacking in the cognitive circumstances of a person N who knows SOA X to prevent N from becoming cognitively aware of the first-order SOA of X being the case. And if that happens, then N presumably[24] will know this first-order SOA in turn. Whatever the details of the transition might amount to in a given case, knowing X provides an occasion on which N might make the transition to knowing the SOA of X being the case almost as a matter of course.

If N knows the SOA of X being the case, moreover, and has occasion to formulate a proposition to that effect, then N already is in a position to know that the proposition is true. While knowing that X is the case is not sufficient for knowing that a proposition to that effect is true,[25] knowing the former provides an occasion on which the latter knowledge is easily accessible as well. In brief, just as there is a ready transition to be made from knowledge of the base-order SOA X itself to knowledge of the first-order SOA of X being the case, so there is an equally smooth transition to be made from knowledge of that first-order SOA to knowledge of the second-order SOA of the proposition that X is the case being true.

But transition in the other direction is more severely constrained. In order to progress from knowing the truth of a proposition [X/yes] to knowing the first-order SOA of X being the case, as we have seen, one must be able to identify the latter as the circumstances under which the proposition is true. One must be able, that is to say, to identify the circumstances of X being the case as the truth-conditions of the proposition in question. In short, one must be able to identify the truth-conditions of that proposition. (This ability, to reiterate, is more than the perfunctory matter of being capable of substituting an expression representing the SOA [e.g., "snow's being white"] for 'X' in the biconditional '[X/yes] is true *iff* X is the case'. As already emphasized, the ability in question, rather, is the distinctly nonroutine matter of being able to identify those features of the world at large that must be present if the proposition is to count as true.) The previous section was concerned primarily with knowing truth-conditions as a necessary requirement for passage from knowledge of the truth of a deductively inferred proposition to knowledge of some nonpropositional aspect of the world at large. But the same requirement obviously holds for knowledge of propositional truth arrived at by other means as well. No matter how N arrives at knowledge of the truth of a given proposition, N must know the truth-conditions of that proposition in order to know the first-order SOA that the proposition represents.

The question now arises whether there are comparable provisions enabling one to move from knowing the first-order SOA of X *being the case* to a state of knowing the base order SOA X itself. Take an example from the relatively recent flight from earth to the moon. Let X' be the base-order SOA of the moon's having a solid surface, and [X'/yes] the proposition representing this SOA as being the case. Before the Apollo flight, it was known by inference (from facts of astronomy, physics, etc.) that the proposition [X'/yes] is true. And since the truth-conditions of that proposition were well known within the scientific community, it was known as well that X' is the case. Before the Apollo flight, however, no one from earth had gained access to the SOA X' itself. Some among us knew the first-order SOA of X' being the case, but none of us knew the base-order SOA itself of there being a solid surface on the moon. The question is whether there were any resources available by which we might have come to know this latter SOA before the Apollo flight landed upon that surface. Barring the questionable matter of photographic access,[26] the answer surely is that there were not.

Knowing is an attitude of cognitive access, in the manner of finding, noticing, perceiving, and so on. For a subject N to know SOA X' is for N to be cognitively in the presence of X'—to be situated so that X' is manifest in N's cognitive awareness.[27] When the astronauts landed on the surface of the moon, they had clear access to the SOA of that surface's being solid. Before the landing, however, there were no cognitive resources, either formal or semantic, by which anyone could have come to know that SOA. We knew the first-order SOA of its being the case that the surface of the moon is solid, but no means were available for an epistemic transition to knowledge of the base-order SOA itself—that is, to knowledge of the actual SOA of the moon's having a solid surface.

In particular, there were no *inferential* means by which anyone, prior to the landing, could have come to know this base-order SOA. Al-

though scientists in the space program obviously were guided by inference in their successful efforts to place an observer on the moon, no
amount of inference just by itself could move an observer into a position of cognitive access to its surface. And so it is with empirical SOAs
generally.[28] Although inference may yield large accumulations of
knowledge about what *is the case* in the world, inference by itself is
powerless to provide cognitive access to base-order aspects of the
world themselves. One never comes to know a *base-order SOA* merely
by arranging propositions in consequential order. And there are no additional provisions (e.g., of semantics) by which knowledge arrived at
by inference can be converted into knowledge of such SOAs. In the
case of empirical knowledge at least, all knowledge of base-order
SOAs is achieved by means of access in which inference based on
propositions plays no direct role.

This is not to deny that inference might play an important *ancillary*
role as part of the process by which a given base-order SOA becomes
accessible to knowledge. In the case of the Apollo moon landing, for instance, NASA scientists were guided by an enormously complex web
of inferences in constructing the mechanisms and in charting the tra-
jectories by which human observers could be placed on the moon. This
web of inferences, as it were, constituted a kind of conceptual itinerary
leading from a position of knowing higher-order SOAs regarding the
composition of the moon to a position of knowing the base-order SOA
itself of its surface being solid. But the actual progression from stage to
stage along that itinerary required changes in the cognitive circumstances of the potential knowers themselves, and could not be accomplished by any means relying upon the devices of propositional
inference alone. This is one distinct limitation on the powers of rational
inference as a means of gaining knowledge about how things stand in
the world. Rational inference is strictly incapable of providing cognitive access to what throughout this study we have been calling "base-
order SOAs."

A further limitation pertains to higher-order SOAs of the sort we
come to know by logical inference and to those we come to know, in
turn, by knowing the truth-conditions of propositions. For reasons
examined in section 2 above, it may be recalled, logical inference by itself produces knowledge only regarding the truth-values of propositions. In the standard circumstance of our knowing the truth-conditions
of the propositions thus inferred, moreover, our range of knowledge
can be extended to include the SOAs responsible for those truth-values
as well—as our knowledge of the *truth* of the proposition that the moon

has a solid surface, for example, can be extended to knowledge that it *is the case* that this surface is solid. In either case, however, what we come to know is keyed to the representational function of propositions. When we come by inference to know that the proposition [X/yes] is true, on the one hand, what we come to know, in effect, is the success of that proposition as a representation of how things stand in the world. When we bring to bear our knowledge of the truth-conditions of the proposition, on the other hand, we come to know that the SOA X it represents actually is the case given the world as it is. Routine as these reminders may appear at this point in the discussion, what they show is that all knowledge we reach by means of rational inference depends upon our ability to formulate representations of how things stand in the world.

The further limitation mentioned above is that rational inference provides access *only* to SOAs that we have learned to represent symbolically. And this is a limitation that applies to base-order and to higher-order SOAs indifferently. The upshot is that *any* access we might have to the world as it stands relies on resources beyond those provided by rational inference alone. Rational inference, that is to say, is not by itself a mode of access to the actual world.

Moreover, inasmuch as learning to represent an SOA symbolically is inextricably bound up with learning how to identify the circumstances in which that SOA is actually present (requirement [LR2] of chapter 6), it follows that rational inference can contribute to the access of *only* those SOAs we have learned to identify independently of the reasoning process itself. To put it more directly, the processes of inference alone cannot enable us to detect the presence of SOAs that we are unprepared to identify apart from those processes. This result is explored further in the final section below.

6. Concluding Remarks on Scientific Realism

The central issue in the debate on scientific realism, as I understand it, is whether the proven success of a scientific theory incorporating reference to a postulated entity might provide definitive evidence that the entity exists, despite its remaining inaccessible to observation. In terms of the present approach, which focuses on SOAs (which may or may not be the case) instead of entities-with-properties (which may or may not exist), the issue boils down to this: whether the proven success of a theory containing a propositional representation of a purported SOA's being the case might conclusively establish that SOA as actually being the case, despite its remaining inaccessible to means of access other than that provided by the theory itself. Among SOAs in question are those of protons being among the constituents of an atom, of quasars existing in the far reaches of space, and of the microstates of a closed system tending toward equiprobability (the Second Law of Thermodynamics). The position of the scientific realist is that the proven success of a theory (atomic physics, astrophysics, thermodynamics, etc.) postulating SOAs like these is definitive evidence that such SOAs in fact are the case. The conclusion of the section above, to the effect that rational inference by itself cannot enable us to detect the presence of SOAs that we are not prepared to identify independently, seems clearly to have adverse implications for this position. The purpose of this final section is (not to undertake a full critique of scientific realism, but only) to sketch out the character of these implications.

There is a way of thinking about scientific truth that lends itself conveniently to an apologia for scientific realism. According to this way of thinking, a scientific theory (e.g., thermodynamics) is successful to the extent that it is able to account for a broad range of empirical phenomena, where "accounting for" covers explaining, predicting, and describing in detail, as well as bringing the phenomena under some kind of experimental control. The theory is complete when, by consensus of the relevant scientific community (e.g., professionally competent thermodynamicists), it accounts satisfactorily for representative samples of the phenomena to which it pertains. At this point, the theory is "ready for the archives" and may be said to constitute a true account of the field of phenomena in question.

If the theory as a whole has been established as true, however, then the individual propositions that go into its formulation must all be true as well.[29] Suppose that one of these propositions represents the SOA of the microstates of a closed system tending toward equiprobability with advancing time; let us call this SOA "Z." Since this proposition is a key component of the theory overall, the truth of the theory depends upon the truth of this component proposition. On the basis of knowledge of the truth of the theory, accordingly, we can infer that this proposition regarding unobservable aspects of a system's microstructure is true as well. Assuming we have knowledge of the truth of the theory concerned, that is to say, we also have knowledge that this particular proposition is true.

Moreover, the case for realism continues, scientists competent in thermodynamics know the truth-conditions of their theoretical propositions. In the case of the proposition representing SOA Z as being the case, the truth-conditions are these: [Z/yes] is true if and only if Z is the case (where Z, as noted above, is the SOA of the microstates of a closed system tending toward equiprobability). On the basis of this knowledge, in combination with knowledge that the proposition is true, the informed scientist can come to know that Z is the case. And knowing that Z is the case, of course, is knowledge regarding unobservable microstates that approach equiprobability as time advances. The upshot is that science has gained knowledge of unobservable entities on the basis of inference from the truth of a successful scientific theory. The claim that knowledge of such entities can be obtained by inferences of this sort, the case concludes, is the central thesis of scientific realism.

There are several things about this conception of scientific truth that call for critical comment. Let us begin with a component that is clearly correct. Although a scientific theory might be formulated in terms of individual propositions (some expressed mathematically, others in the vernacular, etc.), these propositions do not receive their truth-values on an individual basis. In this respect, the propositions of a scientific theory differ from the common run of propositions in everyday discourse.[30] The proposition that snow is white (formulated in terms we understand to have relatively stable use within their proper linguistic context) is true or false depending upon criteria we learn to apply on a case-by-case basis in learning the use of our color vocabulary. With the propositions comprising a scientific theory, on the other hand, the roles these propositions play within the theory are so tightly interwoven that they tend to receive truth-values on a "package-deal" basis. This is especially true of propositions at the heart of the theory (as distinct from what Quine calls the "sensory periphery"),[31] which posit what purport to be unobservable entities or SOAs. The proposition stating the Second Law of Thermodynamics, for example, is generally assigned a positive truth-value. But the reason it is accorded this value is not that it has been found to provide an accurate representation *on its own* of what is the case in the world—the SOA, as it were, of entropy (degree of equiprobability of microstates) tending to increase with time in a thermodynamically closed system.[32] The reason it counts as true, rather, is that it plays a key role in a theory that has been found *as a whole* to provide a generally successful account of the range of phenomena to which the theory applies.

This much, presumably, is more or less in accord with the view of scientific truth attributed to the realist in the brief sketch above and should be acceptable as such. From the presumably acceptable fact that theoretical propositions receive their truth-values on a "package-deal" basis, however, it follows that the conditions under which these propositions count as true must take into account their roles within the theory overall and that they cannot be specified for individual propositions in isolation. And this consequence leads to conflict with the view of scientific truth sketched above in the realist's behalf. The conflict should be apparent from the following considerations.

By definition, the conditions under which the proposition [Z/yes] (stating the Second Law of Thermodynamics) is true are the circumstances informed people have learned to identify as those in which the microstates of a closed system tend toward equiprobability with increasing time. When appropriate members of the scientific community assign a positive truth-value to [Z/yes], accordingly, they do so—if acting responsibly—on the basis of having found that these truth-conditions are satisfied. In agreement with the scientific realist, we have assumed that the circumstances under which the Second Law is assigned a positive truth-value are those of its playing a central role in a generally successful scientific theory. Within the context of the theory, however, these circumstances are not adequately described in the perfunctory manner of "its being the case that microstates of a closed system tend toward equiprobability with advancing time." The reason a (putative) SOA thus described cannot constitute the working truth-conditions of the proposition in question is that there is no conceivable way we could ever identify this SOA as such *apart* from the way we deal with it theoretically. Apart from its role as a construct of thermodynamic theory, no individual SOA having to do with the probability of microstates has any status whatever in the empirical world. At the very least, no such (putative) SOA has status in a domain to which human reason provides cognitive access.[33]

The point bears restating. The (putative) SOA of its being the case that the microstates of a closed system tend toward equiprobability with time cannot itself be the basis on which truth is assigned to the Second Law of Thermodynamics by the working scientific community. If we try to think of this (putative) SOA as a feature the world might possess *apart* from the way we deal with it theoretically, then we find there is no conceivable way in which such an SOA could be identified (apart from the theory). This disqualifies it from constituting the *working* truth-condition of the proposition in question. Insofar as theoretical propositions purporting to represent SOAs involving microstates have any truth-value at all, their truth-conditions must consist of circumstances that properly situated investigators are capable of encountering in the course of their inquiries. In short, the truth-conditions of [Z/yes], and of similar propositions involving theoretical constructs, must be circumstances detectable by persons in a position to assess their truth-values. They must be circumstances, moreover, that qualified investigators commonly understand as actually providing warrant for positive truth-assignment. In either respect, this boils down to their being circumstances having to do with the success of thermodynamic theory overall and with the role of the Second Law within this theory. And in either respect, it precludes their being (putative) states of the world conceived independently of the relevant theory.

This conclusion may strike some readers as counterintuitive. How could the truth-condition of the proposition that snow is white be adequately characterized in the manner of "the SOA of its being the case that snow is white," it might be asked, and the truth-condition of the Second Law of Thermodynamics *not* be adequately characterizable by "the SOA of its being the case that the microstates of a thermodynamically closed system tend toward equiprobability with advancing time"? Both characterizations appear at first glance to result from routine substitutions in the general biconditional '[X/yes] is true *iff* X is the case', which served as the basis of the definition of the concept of truth-conditions in chapter 4. If this biconditional provides the pattern for an apt characterization of the truth-conditions of ordinary propositions like [snow being white/yes], why should it not do the same for propositions involving theoretical constructs like [entropy increasing with time in a thermodynamically closed system/yes] (an equivalent propositional expression of the Second Law)?[34] The answer, as I see it, comes in two parts.

The first thing to be noted in this regard has to do with the manner in which instances of the general biconditional '[X/yes] is true *iff* X is the case' are formulated in the two different cases. The intent behind the biconditional is that the expression entered to the right of '*iff*' in any given case should represent the circumstances under which the proposition indicated at the left merits assignment of the value "true." For most propositions formulated in terms of ordinary language, and representing SOAs of the sort we encounter in day-by-day experience, the same expression that serves in the formulation of the proposition will also serve adequately as a representation of the first-order SOA that constitutes its truth-condition. Thus we have "the proposition that *snow is white* is true *iff* it is the case that *snow is white*" (in regimented form, '[snow being white/yes] is true *iff* snow being white is the case'). The expression "snow is white" serves equally well on either side of the biconditional sign, in accord with the fact that both proposition and truth-condition are normally formulated in terms of nontechnical language.

The anomaly to be explained arises in the case of propositions of theoretical science that, in the interest of general intelligibility, we often choose to formulate in nontechnical terms. Thus we have the Second Law of Thermodynamics, which we formulated in ordinary terms as the proposition that entropy of a closed thermodynamic system tends to increase with time. But when we come to consider the conditions under which this proposition warrants a positive truth-evaluation, we find it puzzling that these truth-conditions cannot be expressed in the same nontechnical terms. In the example above, for instance, we set about to characterize the circumstances under which a proposition stating the Second Law actually received a positive truth-value from scientists competent to make the evaluation, and we found it necessary to say something about the role of the proposition in thermodynamic theory and about the success of the theory overall. It then appeared anomalous that we should need *different* formulations for the proposition and for its truth-conditions, when the general biconditional '[X/yes] is true *iff* X is the case' seems to call for identical replacements for 'X' on both sides of the biconditional sign.

We should be forewarned about the likelihood of anomaly of this sort by the fact that the general biconditional in question is not a template, as it were, for the mechanical production of truth-conditions. As noted more than once above, knowing the truth-conditions of a proposition is not a matter merely of being able to formulate an instance of the biconditional by entering the proposition on the left, and then reproducing its descriptive component in the position of 'X' on the right. Being able to produce '[the mome raths outgrabe/yes] is true *iff* the mome raths outgrabe' as an apparent instance of the biconditional does not amount to knowing the truth-conditions of that spurious proposition. In fact, [the mome raths outgrabe/yes] has no truth-conditions, which is the reason it is not a genuine proposition. A propositional expression of the Second Law of Thermodynamics, on the other hand, should be presumed to qualify as a genuine proposition. But it is not provided truth-conditions merely by our making replacements for 'X' on either side of the general biconditional. Its truth-conditions, rather, are dictated by the practices of competent scientists in assessing the success of thermodynamic theory overall. And there is no reason to expect that the criteria they actually employ in making this assessment could be captured by a nontechnical locution like "it is the case that entropy tends to increase with time."

The second thing to note in this connection is that if a proposition stating the Second Law of Thermodynamics in appropriate *technical* terms were entered to the left in the biconditional '[X/yes] is true *iff* X is the case', then a correct expression of its truth-conditions could be formulated by completing the right side in much the same terms. But then the question would arise, at least for the nonspecialist unfamiliar with those terms, of what SOA this proposition was meant to represent. This question would properly be answered with reference to the circumstances well-informed scientists accept as constituting the truth-conditions of the proposition. The SOA represented by the proposition could then be understood as that of those circumstances being the case. If the technical expression of these truth-conditions is glossed in nontechnical terms, they will be characterized with reference both to the role the Second Law plays in thermodynamic theory and to the overall success of this theory as an account of relevant data. For purposes of general intelligibility, however, the proposition itself will still be glossed in the familiar manner of "its being the case that entropy tends to increase in a thermodynamically closed system." We get one gloss when focusing on the truth-conditions and a rather different one when focusing on the nontechnical import of the proposition itself. This, it seems to me, is the primary source of the anomaly above. Traced back to their technical origins, however, the two glosses should be understood merely as different ways of expressing the same first-order SOA—namely, the SOA ordinarily described as its being the case both (a) that the Second Law plays such-and-such a role in thermodynamic theory and (b) that the theory overall has proven successful.

The consequences for scientific realism are directly forthcoming. The central thesis of scientific realism, briefly restated, is that we are able to gain knowledge of unobservable entities on the basis of inference from scientific theories that have been established as true. We begin with knowledge of the truth of the theories, proceed to knowledge of the truth of constituent propositions, and then apply our knowledge of relevant truth-conditions to arrive at knowledge of the circumstances by which these truth-conditions are satisfied. In the case of constituent propositions purportedly referring to unobservable entities or SOAs, the truth-conditions involve the actual presence of these entities or SOAs in domains of reality that can never be known directly. In this way, we gain access, by rational inference, to aspects of the world that remain closed to observation. This, in a nutshell, is scientific realism.

The unavoidable flaw in this way of thinking is that the truth-conditions of individual propositions within a scientific theory have nothing to do with unobservable entities or SOAs. If their truth-conditions *were* bound up with the actual presence of such things in the world, then the propositions in question could never be verified by empirical investigation. What these truth-conditions are bound up with, instead, are the *observable* circumstances by which the theory containing the propositions is established as a successful account of relevant data. The upshot is that knowledge of these truth-conditions, in combination with knowledge that the propositions are true, does nothing to push the frontiers of knowledge *beyond* the boundaries of observation. If the argument pursued throughout this chapter is correct in basic outline, there is no resource—scientific or otherwise—by which reason can reach beyond these boundaries.

Although I am aware of affinities between this result and the view known as "instrumentalism" in the interpretation of scientific theory, it is not part of my present purpose to defend instrumentalism as an alternative to scientific realism.[35] In point of fact, I think that instrumentalism tends to undervalue the contributions successful science can make to our understanding of the world at large. The fact that certain theories succeed, while others fail definitively, certainly tells us something about how the world is structured. But what that something might amount to is another question.

I am aware also of parallels between this result and the view of empirical knowledge that Kant is usually understood as developing in his *Critique of Pure Reason*.[36] While it undoubtedly would be interesting to develop these parallels in detail, this too is a project for another undertaking. The conclusion that rational inference cannot extend the range of human knowledge beyond the bounds of the potentially observable, for present purposes at least, must be left to stand or fall with the defenses provided above. Lest the reader feel that this conclusion relegates human understanding to confines that are oppressively narrow, however, we should bear in mind that much of what is potentially observable cannot always be observed as a matter of unaided perception. Among the monumental achievements of reason within the last century or so has been the piecing together of the complex "conceptual maps" that have enabled cognitive access to such empirical SOAs as protons being among the constituents of the atom, as quasars existing in the far reaches of space, and (for that matter) as the moon's surface supporting a human footfall. The upshot of this final phase of our investigation is only that such SOAs are not accessible by reason alone. But with reason in tandem with well-disciplined observation, the range of human knowledge, for all we know, may increase indefinitely.

Notes

1. One sense of the term "truth" distinguished in chapter 4 is that of a true proposition (as in "We hold these truths to be self-evident"). A contrasting sense is that of an actual SOA (as in "He finally discovered the truth of the matter"). These senses, respectively, were the second and the third discussed in the final section of that chapter.

2. The attitude of belief(1) *in general* was distinguished from individual instances of this attitude in note 9 of chapter 9. Inasmuch as individual instances of belief(1) are entertained with respect to concrete token propositions, as distinct from proposition-types (see chapter 3 for this distinction), the sense in which different subjects might believe the same proposition must amount to believing tokens of the same proposition-type. This sense of belief was not discussed in chapter 9 because belief(1) *in general* (as distinct from belief entertained by individual persons) has no intentional characteristics.

3. Truth in the sense of actual SOAs is the third sense of that concept discussed in chapter 4; see note 1 above.

4. See chapter 4, section 7. The two senses in question are fact(p) as in "stating the facts" (i.e., stating true propositions) and fact(s) as in "facing the facts" (i.e., acknowledging the relevant SOAs).

5. Knowledge(4) is such that it *can* be shared by different individuals but under certain circumstances might belong to one person only.

6. Hao Wang, "Toward Mechanical Mathematics," in *The Modelling of Mind,* K. M. Sayre and F. J. Crosson, eds. (Notre Dame, Ind.: University of Notre Dame Press, 1963), 91–120.

7. B. Russell and A. N. Whitehead, *Principia Mathematica* (Cambridge: Cambridge University Press, 1910).

8. The expression '*[X/yes]' serves as a name for the proposition-type to the effect that X is the case. See chapter 3 for an explanation of this symbolism.

9. See chapter 4, section 4, for this use of the expression "truth-condition."

10. Someone who accepts the account of truth offered in chapter 2, and who moreover views (T2) in that account as a *definition* of truth, might hold that the relation between these two SOAs is stronger than mere extensional equivalence but will agree, nonetheless, that one is the case when and only when the other is the case as well. The point here under discussion is unaffected by whether or not (T2) is viewed as a definition.

11. See the discussion of referential opacity in section 5 of chapter 9, with reference to the case of Oedipus specifically. Strictly speaking, of course, what is opaque is the propositional context reporting Oedipus's state of knowledge, rather than the state of knowledge as such. The report that Oedipus knew he had married Jocasta is opaque in that, despite the referential equivalence of "Jocasta" and "Oedipus's mother," it does not fol-

low that Oedipus knew he had married his mother. Inasmuch as the propo-sition that Oedipus knew he had married Jocasta is true, however, and the proposition that he knew he had married his mother is true just in case he knew he had married his mother, the opacity of the report in question as-sures that Oedipus's knowing he had married Jocasta is not tantamount to his knowing he had married his mother.

12. An attempt might be made to reinstate this line of response by return-ing to a key point of the discussion of referential opacity in chapter 9—the point that a referential context established by use of a verb of cognitive access ("realize," "discover," "know," etc.) might be either opaque or transparent. The context will be transparent if the cognitive state reported by use of the verb is identified with respect to the *object* of its constituent cognitive attitude, and it will be opaque if that cognitive state is identified with respect to its *content* instead. If our attribution to N of the state of knowing that [X/yes] is true were transparent, instead of opaque as assumed above (the attempt continues), then we might be authorized after all in treating knowing that [X/yes] is true as tan-tamount to N's knowing that X is the case.

How can we tell whether this attribution is opaque or transparent? The at-tribution in question would be transparent if we identify the SOA known by N in view of its status as the object N knows (i.e., from an object-oriented view-point) and it would be opaque if we identify that SOA in view of its status as content of the subject's state of knowing (i.e., from a subject-oriented view-point). (This latter is what Paul Moser calls an "individual or agent-relative" perspective, in "Physicalism and Intentional Attitudes," *Behavior and Philos-ophy* 18, no. 2 [Fall/Winter 1990], 33–41.) Which is the relevant interpretation of the attribution in question? In deciding, we must bear in mind that the issue is whether N's knowing that a given proposition is true carries with it N's knowing the SOA that renders the proposition true. The issue, that is to say, concerns what *N* knows, which is quite distinct from what *we* might know (and N might not) *about* the SOA known by N. And the possibility that poses the problem under discussion is that N might know the SOA of [X/yes] being a true proposition *without* knowing what we happen to know about the truth-conditions of that proposition. The attribution of this state of knowing to N thus proceeds from a subject-oriented viewpoint—a viewpoint focused on what *N* knows—in which the state of knowing in question is identified with re-spect to its content. Although there is another viewpoint oriented with respect to the object of N's state of knowing, this alternative viewpoint provides no au-thorization for the claim that *for N* knowing that [X/yes] is true is tantamount to knowing that X is the case.

13. The question naturally arises whether this progression could be sym-bolized in some sort of "epistemic logic" instead. The answer comes with the general observation that *any* logic that can be explicitly formalized is a logic dealing with relations between propositions only, and not with SOAs them-selves or knowledge of SOAs. The fact that the propositional components in

an epistemic logic might be *interpreted* as somehow or another standing for "knowing," or "items of knowledge," et cetera, does not change the fact that this logic deals with relations among propositional representations only. Any resources that would enable an extension of knowledge *beyond* these propositional relations must rely upon semantic, rather than purely formal, considerations. And there is no formal logic dealing directly with semantic relations.

14. The inference would be easy, even before the logical theory of Aristotle.

15. This conclusion completes the well-known sorites with the premises (1) babies are illogical, (2) nobody is despised who can manage crocodiles, and (3) illogical persons are despised.

16. In one sense of "meaning," we know the meaning of a representation of an SOA X when we know what the world would be like if the proposition [X/yes] were true. But the biconditional '[X/yes] is true *iff* X is the case' does not by itself establish this meaning. Only if we *already* know the meaning of "snow is white," for example, will '[snow being white/yes] is true *iff* it is the case that snow is white' identify the truth-conditions of the proposition to the left. If an expression has no intelligible use in the first place, it cannot be used to provide an intelligible use for itself. Meaning, that is to say, cannot be established de novo without meaningful use of the language involved. (Whether this basic requirement compromises a truth-conditional theory of meaning like that of Davidson is not immediately clear. For the kernel of Davidson's account, see Donald Davidson, "Truth and Meaning," *Synthese* 17 [1967], 304–323.)

17. Imagine someone saying in high seriousness, "The proposition that the mome raths outgrabe is true if and only if the mome raths outgrabe." Saying this surely does not exhibit knowledge of the truth-conditions of the quasi proposition in question.

18. By "the ontological argument" I mean any argument of a kind purporting to prove the existence of God on the basis of premises treating existence as a perfection-making property and engaging a conception of God as the most perfect entity conceivable.

19. This version of the ontological argument has been constructed solely for use in the present hypothetical discussion. There is no presumption that advocates of the ontological argument in other forms would be content with this formulation.

20. N's conception in this regard would be considered ill advised by someone who accepts Kant's argument in the *Critique of Pure Reason* (chap. 3, sec. 4, of the Transcendental Dialectic) that if existence were a property a thing might have in *addition* to other properties we might think of it as having, then a thing that exists cannot be the *same* as a thing we think of as not existing. In Kant's example, the "property content" of a concept of 100 real Thalers is no different from that of 100 Thalers that do not exist. N might attempt to evade this criticism, however, by making a case for treating existence as a property

(e.g., like sitting) that does not affect the *identity* of the thing that has or fails to have it.

21. The concept of the correct designative use of a representation and the criteria thereof are explained in section 5 of chapter 6. It should be noted (as a by-now-familiar point) that N does not know the truth-conditions of "God exists" as a proposition merely by being able to articulate the biconditional "the proposition that God exists is true *iff* God exists," for reasons applicable in the case of any proposition whose truth-conditions cannot be identified independently of the biconditional (see note 16 above).

22. Similar shortfalls with respect to truth-conditions seem to be a common hazard in "proposition-based" metaphysics generally, not just in philosophy of religion. Regarding the familiar definition of necessary truth as a proposition true in all possible worlds, for another case, there are no identifiable circumstances in which "a proposition's being true in all possible worlds" would represent an actual SOA—an SOA present in the actual world—and, hence, there is no intelligible representational use of that expression. A consequence is that any proposition purporting to be about such a proposition (one true in all possible worlds) lacks truth-conditions and is incapable of contributing to a coherent logical argument. Other examples of a similar nature are discussed in section 6 below.

23. The following is an instance in which N might know X without knowing that X is the case. On the basis of a casual glance in the direction of the garden, Deirdre knows that the gate is shut. But she does not pause to reflect upon the fact (perspicuous as it is) that she knows that SOA or upon requirements for something's being known (specifically, that only what is the case can be known). So under the circumstances, she might not be cognitively aware of the first-order SOA of the gate's being shut actually being the case. However, if she were to reflect on these matters, this first-order SOA would immediately become evident to her as well, and she would also know that it is the case that the gate is shut.

24. According to the analysis of chapter 5, section 1, most modes of cognitive access other than knowing serve as preludes to knowing. Exceptions are various modes by which prior knowledge is retained (e.g., remembering).

25. One might know that X is the case without concerning oneself in any way about a propositional representation of this first-order SOA.

26. Apart from the general question of whether photographic access is ever reliable enough to serve as a channel of knowledge, there is the further fact that solidity is not a direct (noninferred) visual feature of objects—that is, it is not a feature of the sort that could be displayed photographically.

27. Knowing is not a matter of having access, in the manner that a Fellow has access to the Fellows' Garden (i.e., not a matter of accessibility), but rather a matter of having *gained* access (like someone's having actually entered the garden). When one has left the presence of an actual SOA, one no longer knows that SOA itself but may well know the first-order SOA of that (base-

order) SOA being the case. To be in the presence of a first-order SOA is to be cognitively aware, in turn, of the status attaching to the corresponding base-order SOA.

28. There may be SOAs of a nonempirical nature such that circumstances in which N could know the first-order SOA of X being the case are ipso facto circumstances in which N could know the base-order SOA itself. An apparent instance comes with the base-order SOA of Lewis's S2 being derivable from S1 by addition of the Consistency Postulate. One way of coming to know the first-order SOA of this being the case is to trace through Lewis's own derivation in *Symbolic Logic* (C. I. Lewis and C. H. Langford, *Symbolic Logic* [New York: Dover Publications, 1932]). But anyone following this derivation would probably come to know the base-order SOA itself. It should be noted that this is an instance of someone's becoming situated to know a base-order SOA by undertaking a procedure yielding knowledge of the corresponding first-order SOA, and not a counterinstance to the general thesis that knowing that X is the case cannot be converted to knowing X itself by processes of deductive inference alone.

29. The idea is that a scientific theory, in relevant respects, is like a conjunction of propositions and cannot be true overall if any of its component propositions are false.

30. Quine is known for the view that the totality of our knowledge comprises a system that is adapted to accommodate experience by adjusting the truth-values of key statements within it. This is part of his view that the truth-value of any statement (even in logic) can be altered on occasion if compensating adjustments are made elsewhere in the system. (See "Two Dogmas of Empiricism," reprinted in W. V. O. Quine, *From a Logical Point of View* [Cambridge, Mass.: Harvard University Press, 1953].) Although adjustments of this sort may perhaps occur from time to time in the discourse of everyday experience, it seems entirely commonsensical to distinguish theoretical discourse from the discourse of everyday experience on the basis of such changes being common in the former and unusual in the latter. The truth-conditions of the proposition that snow is white, for example, are tied almost exclusively to the circumstances in which ordinary people ordinarily observe the color of snow and scarcely at all to "cultural posits" of the sort Quine talks about (physical objects, the gods of Homer, etc.), which we decide to accept or not to accept on a systemwide basis.

31. Quine, "Two Dogmas," 43.

32. There may in fact be no thermodynamically closed systems—no systems, that is to say, without external sources of energy. Lack of such systems, however, would not render the proposition in question (the Second Law of Thermodynamics) false or inapplicable. The probable lack of such systems, rather, indicates that the role of the Second Law within the theory is not one exclusively of representing an *empirical* SOA.

33. Among results of chapter 6 are that learning the use of any representation of a given SOA depends upon learning how to tell when the criteria for the

correct designative use of such representations are satisfied (section 5) and that the identity of a given SOA is established by those criteria (section 6). An upshot is that no identifiable SOA lacks representations criteria for the correct designative use of which are applicable by potential users under accessible circumstances. The reason there can be no SOAs that are "in principle" beyond access is that representations of such putative SOAs would have no applicable criteria of correct designative use, and that there would be no basis, accordingly, on which the concerned SOAs could be identified.

34. One theoretical construct in this proposition is the concept of a thermodynamically closed system which, like a frictionless surface, probably will never be found exemplified in the universe at large.

35. A case for scientific realism is often made on the basis of what might be called an "argument from success." One version attempts to lay a trap for the instrumentalist, who (in one stereotype at least) maintains that the sole epistemic goal of a scientific theory is to provide an effective instrument for the anticipation and control of natural events. Only by assuming that a theory provides an accurate description of the world as it is, the realist argues, can we *explain* its ability to serve successfully in this instrumental role. But the view that the theory is accurate, down to the details of its postulated entities, is just the view of scientific realism itself. Hence the very credibility of the instrumentalist's characterization of science, says the realist, rests upon acceptance of the realistic view. (Scientific theory must *be* what the realist claims it is in order for it to *do* what the instrumentalist says it does.) But this argument is just confused. What *explains* the success of science is its meeting the standards by which success is defined—that is, exhibiting the features by which acceptance by the scientific community is warranted. The independent existence of its postulated entities is not among these features. (How could it be, inasmuch as the existence of such entities cannot be corroborated *independently* of the theory?) By involving the putative existence of these entities, the realist becomes involved in a "metascientific" level of explanation that draws no credibility from the scientific facts themselves. (Consider the "queerness," moreover, of postulating an entity a *second* time in order to explain the success of its first postulation.)

36. Kant's *Critique of Pure Reason* was first published in 1781.

WORKS CITED

Adams, R. M. "Theories of Actuality." *Nous* 8 (1974): 211–231. Reprinted in *The Possible and the Actual,* Michael J. Loux, ed. Ithaca, N.Y.: Cornell University Press, 1979.

Armstrong, D. M. *Perception and the Physical World.* London: Routledge & Kegan Paul, 1961.

———. *A Materialist Theory of the Mind.* London: Routledge & Kegan Paul, 1968.

———. *The Nature of Mind and Other Essays.* Ithaca, N.Y.: Cornell University Press, 1981.

———. *A World of States of Affairs.* Cambridge: Cambridge University Press, 1997.

Audi, R. *Belief, Justification, and Knowledge.* Belmont, Calif.: Wadsworth, 1988.

Austin, J. L. "Other Minds." In *Philosophical Papers,* J. O. Urmson and G. J. Warnock, eds. Oxford: Oxford University Press, 1961.

———. "A Plea for Excuses." In *Philosophical Papers.*

Ayer, A. J. "Phenomenalism." *Proceedings of the Aristotelian Society* 47 (1946–1947): 163–196.

———. *The Problem of Knowledge.* London: Macmillan, 1956.

Barwise, J., and J. Perry. "Situations and Attitudes." *Journal of Philosophy* 68 (1981): 668–691.

Braithwaite, R. B. "The Nature of Believing." *Proceedings of the Aristotelian Society* 33 (1932–1933): 129–146.

Brentano, F. *Psychologie von Empirischen Standpunkt.* Leipzig: Duncker and Humblot, 1874.

Castaneda, H. N. "Mathematics and Reality." *Australasian Journal of Philosophy* 37, no. 2 (August 1959): 92–107.

Chisholm, R. M. *Perceiving: A Philosophical Study.* Ithaca, N.Y.: Cornell University Press, 1957.

———. *Theory of Knowledge.* 1st ed. Englewood Cliffs, N.J.: Prentice-Hall, 1966; 3rd ed., 1989.

Davidson, D. "Truth and Meaning." *Synthese* 17 (1967): 304–323.

———. "On Saying That." *Synthese* 19 (1968–1969): 130–146.

Davis, W. "Knowledge, Acceptance, and Belief." *Southern Journal of Philosophy* 26 (1988): 169–178.

Dennett, D. C. *Content and Consciousness.* New York: Humanities Press, 1969.

Dretske, F. I. *Knowledge and the Flow of Information.* Cambridge, Mass.: MIT Press, 1981.

Dummet, M. "The Significance of Quine's Indeterminacy Thesis." In *Truth and Other Enigmas.* Cambridge, Mass.: Harvard University Press, 1978.

Einstein, A. "Geometry and Experience." Reprinted in *Readings in the Philosophy of Science,* H. Feigl and M. Brodbeck, eds. New York: Appleton-Century-Crofts, 1953.

Feigl, H. "The 'Mental' and the 'Physical'." In *Minnesota Studies in the Philosophy of Science,* vol. 2, H. Feigl, M. Scriven, and G. Maxwell, eds. Minneapolis: University of Minnesota Press, 1958.

Fodor, J. *The Language of Thought.* New York: Thomas Y. Crowell, 1975.

———. *Representations: Philosophical Essays on the Foundations of Cognitive Science.* Brighton, Sussex: Harvester Press, 1981.

Frege, G. "The Thought: A Logical Inquiry." A. M. Quinton and M. Quinton, trans. *Mind* 65 (1956): 289–311.

Fumerton, R. *Metaphysical and Epistemological Problems of Perception.* Lincoln: University of Nebraska Press, 1985.

———. *Metaepistemology and Skepticism.* Lanham, Md.: Rowman & Littlefield, 1995.

Gasking, D. "Mathematics and the World." *Australasian Journal of Philosophy* 18, no. 2 (September 1940): 97–116.

Gettier, E. "Is Justified True Belief Knowledge?" *Analysis* 23 (1963): 121–123.

Goldman, A. "What Is Justified Belief?" In *Empirical Knowledge,* Moser, ed.

Goodman, N. "The Problem of Counterfactual Conditionals." In *Semantics and the Philosophy of Language,* Linsky, ed.

Grayling, A. C. *An Introduction to Philosophical Logic.* Brighton, Sussex: Harvester Press, 1982.

Haack, S. *Philosophy of Logics.* Cambridge: Cambridge University Press, 1978.

Haugeland, J. *Mind Design.* Cambridge, Mass.: MIT Press, 1981.

———. "Semantic Engines." In *Mind Design,* Haugeland, ed. Montgomery, Vt.: Bradford Books, 1981.

Heil, J. "Does Cognitive Psychology Rest on a Mistake?" *Mind* 90 (1981): 321–346.

Hempel, C. "Geometrical and Empirical Science." Reprinted in *Readings in Philosophical Analysis,* H. Feigl and W. Sellars, eds. New York: Appleton-Century-Crofts, 1949.

Horst, S. *Symbols, Computation, and Intentionality: A Critique of the Computational Theory of Mind.* Berkeley: University of California Press, 1996.

Kant, I. *Critique of Pure Reason,* N. K. Smith, trans. New York: St. Martin's Press, 1965.

Lehrer, K. "Belief, Acceptance, and Cognition." In *On Believing: Epistemological and Semiotic Approaches,* Parret, ed.

Lemmon, E. J. "Is There Only One Correct System of Modal Logic?" *Proceedings of the Aristotelian Society,* supplementary vol. 33 (1959): 23–39.

Lewis, C.I. *An Analysis of Knowledge and Valuation.* La Salle, Ill.: Open Court, 1946

Lewis, C. I., and C. H. Langford. *Symbolic Logic.* New York: Dover Publications, 1932.

Linsky, L., ed. *Semantics and the Philosophy of Language.* Urbana: University of Illinois Press, 1952.

Loux, M. "Ontology." In *The Synoptic Vision: Essays in the Philosophy of Wilfred Sellars,* C. F. Delaney, M. Loux, G. Gutting, and W. D. Solomon, eds. Notre Dame, Ind.: University of Notre Dame Press, 1977.

Mackie, J. L. "Simple Truth." *Philosophical Quarterly* 20 (1970): 321–333.

Moser, P. "Types, Tokens, and Propositions: Quine's Alternative to Propositions." *Philosophy and Phenomenological Research* 44, no. 3 (March 1984): 361–375.

———. *Knowledge and Evidence.* Cambridge: Cambridge University Press, 1989.

———. "Physicalism and Intentional Attitudes." *Behavior and Philosophy* 18, no. 2 (Fall/Winter 1990): 33–41.

———, ed. *Empirical Knowledge: Readings in Contemporary Epistemology.* Lanham, Md.: Rowman & Littlefield, 1986.

———, ed. *A Priori Knowledge.* Oxford: Oxford University Press, 1987.

Parret, H., ed. *On Believing: Epistemological and Semiotic Approaches.* Berlin: Walter de Gruyter, 1983.

Plantinga, A. *The Nature of Necessity.* Oxford: Clarendon Press, 1974.

———. "World and Essence." In *Universals and Particulars: Readings in Ontology,* M. Loux, ed. Notre Dame, Ind.: University of Notre Dame Press, 1976.

Pollock, J. *Contemporary Theories of Knowledge.* Lanham, Md.: Rowman & Littlefield, 1986.

Price, H. H. "Some Considerations about Belief." *Proceedings of the Aristotelian Society* 35 (1934–1935): 229–252.

Prior, A. N. *Objects of Thought,* P. T. Geach and A. J. P. Kenny, eds. Oxford: Clarendon Press, 1971.

Pritchard, H. A. *Knowledge and Perception.* Oxford: Clarendon Press, 1950.

Pylyshyn, Z. *Computation and Cognition: Toward a Foundation for Cognitive Science.* Cambridge. Mass.: MIT Press, 1986.

Quine, W. V. O. *From a Logical Point of View.* Cambridge, Mass.: Harvard University Press, 1953.

———. "Reference and Modality." In *From a Logical Point of View.*

————. "Two Dogmas of Empiricism." In *From a Logical Point of View.*

————. *Methods of Logic.* Rev. ed. New York: Henry Holt & Co., 1960.

————. *Word and Object.* Cambridge, Mass.: MIT Press, 1960.

————. "Quantifiers and Propositional Attitudes." In *The Ways of Paradox.* New York: Random House, 1965.

————. *Ontological Relativity and Other Essays.* New York: Columbia University Press, 1969.

Ramsey, F. P. "Facts and Propositions." *Proceedings of the Aristotelian Society,* supplementary vol. 7 (1927): 153–170. Excerpted in *Truth,* George Pitcher, ed. Englewood Cliffs, N.J.: Prentice-Hall, 1964.

Reichenbach, H. "The Philosophical Significance of the Theory of Relativity." Reprinted in *Readings in the Philosophy of Science,* H. Feigl and M. Brodbeck, eds. New York: Appleton-Century-Crofts, 1953.

Ring, M. "Knowledge: The Cessation of Belief." *American Philosophical Quarterly* 14, no. 1 (January 1977): 51–59.

Russell, B. "The Relation of Sense-Data to Physics." In *Mysticism and Logic.* London: George Allen & Unwin, 1910.

————. *The Philosophy of Logical Atomism,* D. Pears, ed. La Salle, Ill.: Open Court, 1985; first published in 1913.

————. *The Problems of Philosophy.* London: Oxford University Press, 1913.

————. *An Inquiry into Meaning and Truth.* London: George Allen & Unwin, 1940.

Russell, B., and A. N. Whitehead. *Principia Mathematica.* Cambridge: Cambridge University Press, 1910.

Ryle, G. *The Concept of Mind.* New York: Barnes & Noble, 1949.

Sayre, K. "Gasking on Arithmetical Incorrigibility." *Mind* 71, no. 283 (July 1962): 372–376.

————. *Consciousness: A Philosophic Study of Minds and Machines.* New York: Random House, 1969.

————. *Cybernetics and the Philosophy of Mind.* London: Routledge & Kegan Paul, 1976.

————. "Intentionality and Information Processing: An Alternative Model for Cognitive Science." *Behavioral and Brain Sciences* 9, no. 1 (March 1986): 121–138.

————. "Cognitive Science and the Problem of Semantic Content." *Synthese* 70 (1987): 247–269.

Searle, J. "Minds, Brains, and Programs." *Behavioral and Brain Sciences* 3, no. 3 (September 1980): 417–424.

Skinner, B. F. *Science and Human Behavior.* New York: Macmillan, 1953.

Smart, J. J. C. "Sensations and Brain Processes." In *The Philosophy of Mind,* V. C. Chappell, ed. Englewood Cliffs, N.J.: Prentice-Hall, 1962.

Sosa, E. "The Raft and the Pyramid: Coherence versus Foundations in the Theory of Knowledge." In *Empirical Knowledge,* Moser, ed. (1986)

Stich, S. *From Folk Psychology to Cognitive Science: The Case Against Belief.* Cambridge, Mass.: MIT Press, 1983.

Strawson, P. *Introduction to Logical Theory*. London: Methuen, 1952.

Tarski, A. "The Concept of Truth in Formalized Language." In *Logic, Semantics, Metamathematics*, J. H. Woodger, trans. Oxford: Oxford University Press, 1956.

Vendler, Z. *Res Cogitans: An Essay in Rational Psychology*. Ithaca, N.Y.: Cornell University Press, 1972.

Vlastos, G. "The Unity of Virtues in the *Protagoras*." *Review of Metaphysics* 25 (1972): 415–458.

Wang, H. "Toward Mechanical Mathematics." In *The Modelling of Mind*, K. M. Sayre and F. J. Crosson, eds. Notre Dame, Ind.: University of Notre Dame Press, 1963.

White, M. "The Analytic and the Synthetic: An Untenable Dualism." In *Semantics and the Philosophy of Language*, Linsky, ed.

Williams, D. C. "Of Essence and Existence and Santayana." In *Animal Faith and Spiritual Life*. Lachs, ed. New York: Appleton-Century-Crofts, 1967.

Wittgenstein, L. *Tractatus Logico-Philosophicus* (*Annalen der Naturphilosophie*, 1921).

———. *Philosophical Investigations*, G. E. M. Anscombe, trans. New York: Macmillan, 1953.

Wolterstorff, N. *On Universals*. Chicago: University of Chicago Press, 1970.

Index

ABOUT THE AUTHOR

Kenneth M. Sayre received his A.B. (Mathematics, 1952) from Grinnell College and his M.A. and Ph.D. (Philosophy, 1954, 1958) from Harvard University. From 1953 to 1956 he was assistant dean of the Graduate School of Arts and Sciences, Harvard University, and from 1956 to 1958 systems analyst with Massachusetts Institute of Technology. Since 1958 he has taught at the University of Notre Dame, where presently he is professor of philosophy. He has held visiting appointments at Princeton University (1966–67), Bowling Green State University (1981), Merton College, Oxford (1985), and St. Edmund's College, Cambridge (1996).

He is author or editor of fifteen previous books, the most recent of which are *Plato's Literary Garden: How to Read a Platonic Dialogue* (1995) and *Parmenides' Lesson: Translation and Explication of Plato's* Parmenides (1996).